19
33
129
170
269
253

THE AMERICAN URBAN SYSTEM

A
GEOGRAPHICAL PERSPECTIVE

THE
AMERICAN
URBAN SYSTEM

A
GEOGRAPHICAL PERSPECTIVE

R. J. Johnston
University of Sheffield

Longman
LONDON

Longman Group Limited
Longman House
Burnt Mill, Harlow, Essex, UK

*Published in the United States of America and Canada
by St. Martin's Press, Inc.*
© 1982 by St. Martin's Press, Inc.

First published 1982
British Library Cataloguing in Publication Data

Johnston, R.J.
   The American urban system.
   1. Cities and towns—United States
   I. Title
   306.7′6′0973   HT123

ISBN 0-582-30101-7

Manufactured in the United States of America

To Joan with many thanks

PREFACE

THIS BOOK PROVIDES a new perspective for teaching American urban geography. It is intended as an introductory text, one which can be used as basic background reading for an undergraduate course on urban geography. As such, it makes no assumptions of prior knowledge or technical skill; the arguments are self-contained.

Publishers' lists show many books on urban geography. Why write another? Most current urban geography texts are crowded with facts, detailed case studies, and techniques. The "quantitative revolution" that swept through American geography in the 1950s and 1960s stimulated a great volume of empirical research, much of it in urban geography. This research provided a wealth of descriptive material on the American urban system. It was unable, however, to advance understanding of urban phenomena very far because of its methodology. During the 1970s, a growing number of geographers argued that explanation and understanding, as opposed to description and prediction, require a greater appreciation of social, economic, and political contexts than had been typical of geographical work. These geographers have been concerned to develop theories of evolving spatial patterns, with especial reference to the impact of trends in capitalism on the urban scene. To some extent, these two approaches have become antagonistic, the one emphasizing detailed empirical studies of particular spatial patterns and the other focusing on general theories. A bridge between the two is needed. In a general context, this was attempted in my *City and Society* (Penguin Books, 1980). Every country has many unique features, however, so a separate bridge is needed to link general theories of urban development and morphology to the particular national circumstances. This is what is attempted here for the United States.

What is most original in this book is its governing idea that the geography of America's urban places is determined by America's political economy. This perspective is introduced in Part One of the book, which outlines the subject of urban geography and sets out the framework of the American political and economic environment. Part Two (chapters three, four, and five) treats the urban system as a whole, analyzing such topics as urban sizes, locations, and functions. I emphasize the urban system as a product of historical and economic circumstances, however, and so the three chapters have a strong historical basis, presenting a chronology of the developing urban pattern. Part Three (chapters six, seven, and eight) turns to the internal structure of urban areas and the spatial patterns within the individual places. Again, I stress the relationships between economic trends and their spatial realizations, as well as certain basic features of a capitalist society, such as class conflict. The three chapters deal, in turn, with the social, economic, and political geography of American urban areas. Finally, Part Four (chapters nine and ten) turns to a topic of considerable contemporary interest—the urban crisis. American cities suffer, in varying degrees, from a range of economic and social ills. These problems are outlined and set in the context of the book's perspective. Attempts to cure these urban troubles, and their potential for success, is the final topic of the book.

This, then, is not a conventional text. It outlines a broad introductory framework into which the details of American urban geography may be set and understood. As essay more than textbook, this volume does not follow academic conventions of footnotes and references, which I believe interrupt the flow of an argument. All the sources of specific materials are cited and acknowledged, of course. Each of the four parts has a "Further Reading" section at the end. Since a particular work may be relevant to several chapters, such an organization was considered superior to providing a bibliography at the end of each chapter. The literature on urban geography is very large, of course; only a small, introductory selection is provided here.

In producing this book I have been helped by a great many people, and I thank them for their advice and encouragement. Risa Palm first stimulated me to write it; Michael Dover, Iain Stevenson, and Peter Hall encouraged me to keep going. Sheila Ottewell drew many of the diagrams; Peter Morley, John Owen, and David Maddison did all the photographic work. And for the tenth time in six years, Joan Dunn has produced an excellent manuscript from a handwriting that only she can decipher accurately; for this and much other help I am deeply grateful.

R. J. Johnston

CONTENTS

THE
AMERICAN
URBAN SYSTEM

A
GEOGRAPHICAL PERSPECTIVE

PART ONE

The STUDY
of
URBAN GEOGRAPHY

THE CASE FOR study of urban areas is very strong; such places dominate the organization of virtually all societies, and in a large number, including the United States, they contain a majority of the population. As foci of economic, social, and political life, therefore, it is not surprising that they receive considerable attention from social scientists. Each social science has its own perspective on the urban place: geography's concerns are twofold, focusing on the spatial elements, which pay special attention to such questions as "what is where?" and "why move from one place to another?" and the environmental, relating to man's interrelationships with nature. This perspective is outlined in Chapter 1, which provides a brief overview of the subject matter of urban geography.

Urban geographers have been criticized mainly for paying insufficient attention, in their attempts to explain the patterns they identify and describe, to the economic, social, and political forces that shape decision making on locational issues. Along with other geographers, they have tended to isolate their explanations from those provided by other social scientists and have elevated the spatial element in society to a dominant, independent position that is hard to justify. The basic aim of this book is to avoid taking that position and to study the urban patterns of the United States within their societal context. Understanding that context is a major task, that requires the combined effort of all social scientists. Only a brief introductory outline is possible here, emphasizing the salient points, and this is provided in Chapter 2.

The dominant theme in American society is the operation of capitalist forces. The country's urban patterns can be explained only if that elementary fact is recognized and if urban geographers set their investigations in the proper context. This book reflects the need for such an approach and the first two chapters indicate the basic structure that is to be applied in the later parts.

1

URBAN GEOGRAPHY AND THE STUDY OF URBAN PATTERNS

THE UNITED STATES is an urban nation. Although its metropolitan areas cover only about 1.5 percent of the country's land surface, they house about three-fourths of its people. Most of this urban population is concentrated in large urban areas. In 1976 the Bureau of the Census identified 277 Standard Metropolitan Statistical Areas (SMSAs) that together housed 157 million people, out of a national total of 214 million; nearly one quarter of these metropolitan residents lived in places with 3 million or more residents, and a further 30 percent lived in places with populations of 1 to 3 million. Only about one quarter of Americans live in statistically defined rural areas, and most of these people are not directly engaged in agriculture. Indeed, of a workforce of some 87 million, only 3.4 million were employed in agriculture, forestry, and fisheries in 1976; the majority of rural residents (about 80 percent of them) are classified by the Bureau of the Census as "rural nonfarm" and are urban workers living outside the contiguous built-up areas.

As the main centers of population, therefore, urban areas must be a dominant concern of any study of American society. This concern does not result from the weight of numbers alone. Whereas the fields, farms and mines in the rural areas may be the foundation of American prosperity, it is in the urban areas that most of the crucial decisions about that prosperity are made. The towns and cities, especially the largest ones, are the focal points of the American economy, where corporations and government bureaucracies are involved in the decision making that runs the United States and where the bulk of goods and services are produced, retailed, and consumed by Americans. In addition, the coun-

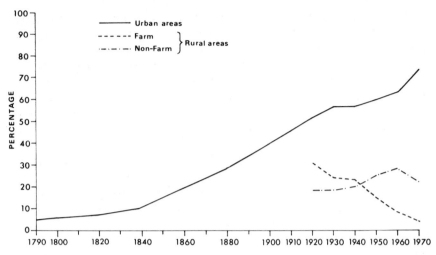

Figure 1.1. The urbanization of the American population. Data dividing the rural population into rural farm and nonfarm components are available only for the period since 1920. Source: data taken from A.H. Hawley, "Urbanization as Process," in D. C. Street (editor), *Handbook of Contemporary Urban Life.* San Francisco, Jossey-Bass, 1978, p. 6.

try's social life centers on the urban areas; most social changes are intro- duced in the largest cities and towns, from whence they diffuse, with in- creasing speed in recent decades, to the smaller settlements and the rural areas. Finally, and perhaps most important of all, it is in the towns and cities—again especially the largest—that the problems of American society are most apparent. Though unemployment, crime, poverty, and personal crises are typical of all areas, in the densely populated metrop- olises they are most visible, as a measure of the volume of social and economic change that is essential to create a healthy and prosperous na- tion.

THE RISE OF URBAN GEOGRAPHY

The United States has had large cities for a long time, but metro- politan dominance in terms of population numbers is a relatively recent phenomenon. It was the 1920 population count that produced the Bureau of the Census report that for the first time more than half the country's residents were living in designated urban areas (Figure 1.1). Before that time, despite the large rural farm sector, the towns and cit- ies had been the focal points of American economy and society, yet they received relatively little study by academics, including geographers. In- deed, before 1950 very few geographers specialized in the study of ur- ban areas; since then, the situation has changed rapidly, and by the

1960s the study of urban phenomena dominated the substantive concerns of human geographers. In making this change, geographers lagged behind their contemporaries in other social sciences—Chicago was a laboratory for much sociological work in the 1920s, for example.

It is not altogether clear why geographers avoided investigating urban areas before World War II; nor is it particularly relevant to this book. The causes of the reorientation since are more readily identified. The rapidly expanding cities and towns became an increasing focus of public attention. The depression of the 1930s had highlighted their many problems and, as a consequence of the New Deal, there developed a strong commitment to planned economic and social change, which included planning the environments in which most Americans worked and lived. Academics developed a keen interest in contributing to this planning, both in its implementation and in conducting the preliminary research so that the many aspects of the urban phenomenon might be understood. A new generation of geographers took up the challenge of the urban area, attacking such questions as "why is it there?", "why does it take that particular form and pattern?", "how is it organized?", and "how is it changing?"

The new generation of geographers in the 1950s had been trained in a discipline whose traditions had been formulated before the Second World War. The dominant ethos was empirical; geographers were people who, after careful observation in the field, described the variability of the earth's surface with the aid of maps and diagrams and with the ultimate aim of dividing the area being studied into a set of "regions," or districts with unique characteristics. Such a descriptive enterprise was deemed insufficient by the new generation, however, for the methods used were mostly imprecise and subjective. A more scientific approach that emphasized not only exact description but explanation was called for. The methods of the physical sciences were adopted for this task, and geographers, along with other social scientists, sought to develop laws and other generalizations about urban phenomena.

The particular emphasis that geographers brought to the study of urban areas was a concern with the spatial element; this concern highlighted not only the observed patterns (or "regions," in the words of the earlier generation of scholars) but also the role of spatial variables, notably distance, in influencing human behavior in urban areas. Geography, in the 1950s and 1960s, became a discipline in distance. To move from one place to another involves costs (including time) and it was argued that location decisions are made so as to minimize these costs. In economic terms, then, distance is a barrier to efficiency, and minimizing the costs involved produces optimal organization strategies. Location decisions are made so as to produce the best spatial patterns, which are those that minimize transportation costs. In social terms distance is also a barrier and it is used as such in, for example, the separation of social groups within a city. Geographers took it as their particular role within the social sciences to emphasize the significance of distance in economic and social affairs.

This study of the effect of distance on the economic and social organization of urban areas involved statistical analysis, both to describe the complex patterns resulting from the imputed cost-minimizing behavior and to test hypotheses concerning the effect of distance. Urban geography rapidly became a very technical subject, especially when compared with the earlier study of geography. But this approach was criticized on a number of grounds. Some claimed that the focus on cost-minimizing via distance-minimizing was a poor one, since the patterns it suggested were not very close to those that actually occur. Decision makers, it was claimed, are imperfect. Their information is incomplete and their ability to use it is limited; the constraints of information and human ability limit the relevance of arguments based on perfect decision making. And so the focus of urban geography shifted somewhat to studying how people actually make decisions. But the study of decision making alone ignores the constraints within which it must occur, limits that are set by economic forces and by society as a whole. Urban areas reflect the nature of an economy and a society, their goals and accepted procedures. Thus, it is now argued that to study and explain the urban phenomenon, one must set it in its context.

At present, then, urban geography is very much in a state of flux. The early, very technical approaches to description and explanation are viewed as naïve, especially in their assumptions about how people behave in a capitalist or any other society. The patterns that they have described must be set in a wider context if they are to be understood, for the urban phenomenon is not an independent entity. This argument is accepted in the present book. Although there is no deviation here from the classical aims of urban geography—the description and explanation of urban patterns and changes—the technical work of the last few decades is not presented. It is ignored not because it is irrelevant but because it provides only description, whereas the focus here is on explanation, on the derivation of theories that can account for what we observe and describe. Examples are used here, but the technical detail is not presented. The aim is to concentrate on general explanation, in an attempt to say why the American urban phenomenon has assumed its present form.

THE CONTENT
OF URBAN GEOGRAPHY

Now that the approach to be taken in this book has been defined in general terms, it is necessary to take a slightly more detailed look at the subject matter involved. What do urban geographers study? Most of their work is concerned with both small- and large-scale studies of urban places. The focus of large-scale study is the urban component of the country's settlement pattern. Towns, cities, and metropolitan areas are treated very much as points on a map, as locations for economic and social activity. On a finer spatial scale, geographers also study patterns within individual urban areas, details of the location of those economic and social activities. Both are concerned with "what is where?" but the division between them is marked. The present book is organized around that division.

THE URBAN PATTERN

The larger-scale aspect of urban geography generally includes several topics. The first is the rate of urbanization, or the process of "becoming urban." The changes that this has involved in terms of population redistribution have already been outlined. But what economic and social changes have produced such a major transformation in a little more than two centuries? Clearly, the key lies in the agricultural and industrial revolutions that have transformed the creative processes for the production of commodities and wealth; the task is to link these revolutions to the patterns on the ground.

Questions concerning the morphology of urban settlement patterns stem from this consideration of urbanization processes. Why have certain places attracted jobs and people while others have not, at least not to the same extent? A study of the pattern of urban sizes suggests a regularity that, if not peculiar to the United States, is well developed there. Basically, this regularity can be expressed as "the larger the fewer." Thus today there is only one New York, one SMSA with a population exceeding 9 million (the metropolitan complex centered on New York—the Census Bureau's Standard Consolidated Statistical Area— has some 17 million people); but there are two with about 7 million each, Chicago and Los Angeles (whose two metropolitan complexes—or SCSAs—contain 10 and 7.5 million people, respectively), and three more with about 4 million each (Detroit, Philadelphia, and San Francisco). Farther down the size continuum in 1975 there were twenty-eight metropolitan areas with populations between 1 and 3 million, thirty-seven with between 500,000 and 1 million residents, sixty-nine with 250,000 to 500,000, and 106 with 100,000 to 250,000 residents. The seven largest (population exceeding 3 million) housed one quarter of the metropolitan population.

This regularity has been observed for many decades, despite the large increases in both the number of metropolitan areas and their populations. Geographers and others have noted that this regularity indicates a consistent relationship between the rank order of a place (the largest is ranked one) and its population. In brief, this rank-size rule

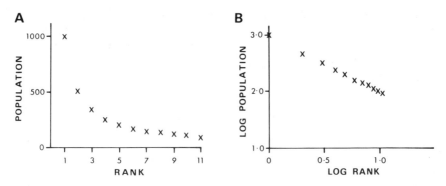

Figure 1.2. The rank-size rule. (A) depicts the inverted-J relationship between population size and rank order and (B) the transformation of this plot into a straight line by means of logarithms.

states that the population of any metropolitan area in the rank-ordering can be estimated by dividing its rank position into the population of the largest metropolitan area. Thus, if the largest metropolitan area has a population of 16 million, the fourth largest should have four million. When this relationship is graphed (Figure 1.2A), it takes an inverted-J shape. When the data are transformed into logarithms, the inverted J becomes a straight line, as shown in Figure 1.2B. *

A distribution of metropolitan areas of different sizes approximating this rank-size rule has been characteristic of the United States for more than a century (Figure 1.3), despite marked changes in the ranking of some centers, such as Los Angeles. (The horizontal axis of Figure 1.3 shows the cumulative number of cities above any particular size. Thus in 1790 there was one city with a population a little under 100,000; five with populations of 10,000 or more, and so on.) Why should this be? Why does this regularity occur in the United States, when other countries, such as Uruguay and France, are dominated by a single city? One of the aims of the next section of this book is to provide a plausible explanation of the process of urbanization that answers such questions.

Figure 1.3 shows that, despite the overall consistency of the rank-size relationship, the relative positions of some American metropolitan areas have changed considerably. Some areas have expanded more rapidly than others, and a few have actually declined. Such variations

---

*The straight line is the result of applying one of the basic laws of logarithms, that x/y = $\log x - \log y$. The equation for the inverted J of Figure 1.2A is $P_r = P_1/r$, where P is population of a place, r its rank-order position, and 1 the largest place; this equation is J-shaped, as are all relationships involving a division with a common numerator. When transformed it becomes $\log P_r = \log P_1 - \log r$, which is a straight line.

are probably as marked now as they have ever been; indeed, during the 1970s many observers noted a marked shift in the process of urbanization. Basically, the country has been divided into two general areas, the so-called Frost Belt and Sun Belt. (See Figure 1.4; note that the boundaries of these two belts are rarely defined precisely. In Figure 1.4 the Sun Belt is defined as the Southeast, Southwest, and Far West Census Regions, comprising twenty of the forty-eight contiguous states.) The former contains most of the country's largest and oldest metropolitan areas, whose continued growth was based on their manufacturing industries and financial institutions. But their supremacy is now rapidly being challenged. Between 1970 and 1975 fifteen metropolitan areas grew in population by more than 20 percent, whereas twenty-four experienced absolute declines in population. All of the former are in the Sun Belt; the vast majority of the latter are in the Frost Belt (Figure 1.4). People and jobs are moving to new areas, in very large numbers. Why?

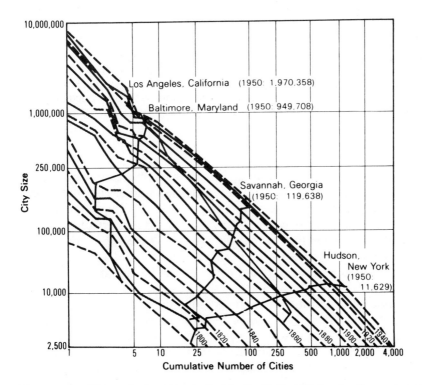

Figure. 1.3. The rank-size rule applied to the United States for the period 1790 to 1950; the changing position of certain places is indicated. Reprinted from *Economic Development and Cultural Change* by C. H. Madden, Volume 4, 1956, p. 239, by permission of The University of Chicago Press. Copyright 1956 by The University of Chicago Press.

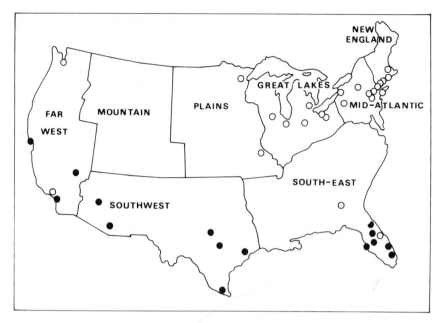

Figure 1.4. The Frost Belt/Sun Belt division and population change in metropolitan areas, 1970 to 1975. Black circles indicate metropolitan areas which grew by more than 20 percent between 1970 and 1975. White circles indicate metropolitan areas which experienced an absolute decline in population between 1970 and 1975. Population change data are from the *Statistical Abstract of the United States, 1977,* pp. 19–21.

An answer to this question about the contemporary geographical patterns of urbanization demands an understanding of current changes in the operation of the American economy. Metropolitan areas are the centers of economic activity. Most have specialized in particular forms of economic activity: Detroit, for example, has long been the center of the automobile industry; Seattle has been a major center of aircraft production for several decades; Hartford contains the headquarters of several major insurance companies; and so on. Thus one can classify places by their major roles within the American economy, according to their specializations. As these roles change in importance—as some industries boom and others decline—so the prosperity of the specialized areas is affected. To understand the current changes, therefore, we must understand the macroeconomic forces at work in American society.

The specialization of functions by metropolitan areas means that no urban area, regardless of its size, is independent; the continued prosperity of each depends on the sale of products elsewhere in the country (and overseas), the proceeds of which allow the import of goods and services not locally produced. This interdependence is the reason that the urban pattern is often characterized as an urban system. A system comprises three elements: the component parts, the links between the components, and the surrounding environment that activates the links. (An automobile engine is a good example of a simple system. Fuel from the environment is fed into a component, and via the links between components, is used to drive the engine. The exhaust is then returned to the environment as waste.) In an urban system, the components are the factories, offices, and homes; the links are the transport and communications networks that join the components and allow the movement of people, goods, ideas, and capital; and the environment is the economy and society in which the demand for certain products arises, in turn giving rise to particular components and links. Understanding how the system works and the changing importance of components and links requires one to understand the environment that drives it.

An aspect of the organization of urban systems of special interest to geographers is spatial form, since this introduces the element of locational decision making with regard to transportation costs. How are settlements of different sizes distributed across the national territory? Which settlements are linked to which others, and what are the dominant patterns of intersettlement movements? It was in tackling such questions that the "new" urban geography of the 1950s made some of its major theoretical and technical advances.

The seminal work for the "new geographers" was a thesis published in 1933 by a German, Walter Christaller, who was concerned with the size and distribution of settlements that acted as central places, or foci for the movement of goods to consumers. Each central place has a hinterland, the area served by its shops and other retail establishments. Some geographers and others (notably rural sociologists) had undertaken empirical research aimed at identifying the extent of such hinterlands; Christaller's contribution was a theory based on minimization of transportation costs, which showed that on a flat surface with a uniform population density and no barriers to movement the ideal settlement distribution would be a nested hierarchy of centers with hexagonal hinterlands. The larger the hinterland, the larger the central place serving it and the wider the range of establishments there. Figure 1.5 illustrates such an ideal distribution; the smallest settlements (at the lowest level of the hierarchy) provide frequently purchased commodities for the local areas; the next largest perform this function for an area of the same size, but also provide less frequently purchased items over a somewhat larger area; and so on. (Chapter 4 illustrates the theory in an American context.)

Christaller provided several versions of his ideal settlement pattern, and another German scholar, August Losch, produced an alternative model based on slightly different assumptions. Several American and British geographers were working along similar lines, and together their ideas formed a very fertile set of propositions for further investigation. No area of any size has a uniform plane surface and population density with free movement in all directions from every point, of course, so it was not expected that the ideal patterns would exist in the "real world." Instead, the models provided working hypotheses of what the spatial organization of an urban system should be, norms against which observed systems could be compared.

One major disadvantage of these models—which usually are grouped under the collective term of central place theory—is that they deal with only one aspect of urban functions. As well as being centers of distribution—of wholesaling and retailing—urban areas are also centers of production. It could be, of course that the distribution of factories is similar to that of shops, so that the larger the factory and its hinterland, the larger the center it is in. For such a case, central place theory would apply to production as well as to distribution. But since most factories are linked to others, and to supplies of material resources and particular markets, decisions on their locations are different from those for central place establishments. Thus an urban system consists of a production as well as a distributional component, and the locations of different types

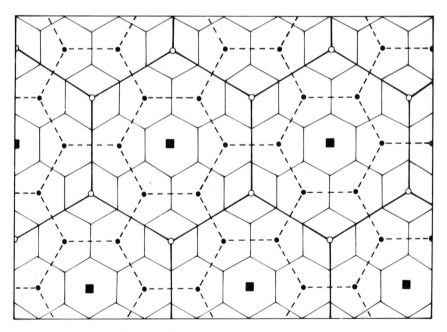

Figure 1.5. The distribution of a hierarchy of central places according to Christaller, showing three levels of center: the squares show centers at the highest level in the hierarchy, and the closed dots centers at the lowest level. Note: of the three models proposed by Christaller, this is the one referred to most often.

of factories serve to distinguish types of towns and to generate towns and cities of different sizes. In addition, there is a third component to the urban system, the organizational. This comprises the large sector of what are known as *quaternary occupations,* conducted in offices, which are necessary for fueling and maintaining the production and distribution systems; these occupations include banking and a wide range of professional as well as government services.

The distribution of population in an urban system, and the associated spatial pattern of settlements of differing sizes and types, reflects the interrelated location decisions made in these three components. The simple questions that are asked in a study of the outcome is "what is done where, and why?" These questions raise many others, and the answers provide the explanation of the changing nature of America's urban system. Chapters 3, 4, and 5 of this book attempt such an explanation.

INSIDE THE URBAN AREA

Just as the American urban system is a complex pattern to be unravelled and explained, so too is each individual American urban area. A metropolitan area such as New York is itself a major spatial system, comprising millions of households and dwellings and hundreds of thousands of places of production, distribution, and organization. The number of contacts among all these elements involves many millions of trips and messages every day. People commute to work, travel to shops and schools, visit friends and places of recreation and entertainment; businessmen contact each other; commodities flow from factories to other factories, then to warehouses and to shops, and so on. The potential for chaos in such a fluid system is immense; but on most days the metropolitan area organization survives and goals are attained. Whether they are attained in the most efficient manner is questionable, but New York has not yet atrophied. Nor have any other urban areas that, although smaller, have the same densities of trips within their restricted areas.

That the metropolitan area works—that most people reach their destinations when they want to, that goods are produced and shipped to buyers, and so on—reflects its spatial organization. Decisions to locate the units of the system's components—the households, factories, offices, transit routes, and so on—are made so as to ensure that goals can be attained. Some people have more choice than others, but the end result is a spatial organization—an intra-urban spatial system—that works. One of the keys to the system's functioning is a spatial separation that involves two related forces; the congregation of like uses and users and the segregation of unlike uses and users. Thus the major types of land use tend to be separated; shops, offices, warehouses, factories, and residences are rarely found on the same block. (Where they are, this usually reflects either a desire for such mixing in particular cases or a transition from one dominant land use on the block to another.) And within each major land use category, separation is usual. Within residential areas, for example, races are usually separated, as are rich from poor, and the young from the old; within industrial districts, clothing factories occupy separate areas from oil refineries.

The usual argument presented to explain these intra-urban patterns is that they represent an efficient way of structuring a complex organism. Thus a city's shopping centers will be structured so that the largest, which offer the widest range of goods and services—including those that are highly specialized and used by the average resident only rarely—is the most accessible, located downtown. The smallest, which cater to the frequent needs of a few people—usually for foodstuffs and other convenience goods—will be many and widely dispersed, each serving a small segment of the urban area and its population. The analogy with central place theory is obvious and has been postulated in many studies of shopping centers.

In most urban areas the major use of land is for residences. The study of the pattern of residential areas—of the social geography of the city—involves describing and explaining why different population groups live apart from one another. The degree of separation can be measured quite simply from population data that refer to subdivisions of the urban area. Table 1.1 gives a hypothetical example of a city divided into ten districts, for each of which the number of black and white residents is known (columns 1 and 2). From perusal of these two columns it is clear that there is very little mixing of blacks and whites;

Table 1.1
RESIDENTIAL SEGREGATION IN A HYPOTHETICAL CITY

District	(1) Whites	(2) Blacks	(3) Percent of Whites	(4) Percent of Blacks	(5) (3) − (4)
1	700	10	13.46	0.37	13.09
2	600	10	11.54	0.37	11.17
3	800	0	15.38	0.00	15.38
4	300	400	5.77	14.81	− 9.04
5	800	20	15.38	0.74	14.64
6	50	750	0.96	27.78	− 26.82
7	30	650	0.58	24.07	− 23.49
8	0	800	0.00	29.63	− 29.63
9	1,020	40	19.62	1.48	18.14
10	900	20	17.31	0.74	16.57
Total	5,200	2,700	100.00	99.99	88.99

only in district 4 is there a substantial number from each group. The districts differ in their populations, however, so to ease the comparison the number for each race in each district is expressed as a percentage of the city's total for that race (columns 3 and 4); an index of the residential separation of the two races is then obtained by calculating the differences between columns 3 and 4 (column 5) and adding the positive values. (The same total is achieved by adding the negative values.) This index can vary between 0 and 100; the higher the value, the more separate are the two groups. For this example, the index of nearly 89 indicates almost complete separation. In other words, 89 percent of one group would have to move to another district for the two distributions (in percentages) to be the same.

Most of the many studies of black-white separation in American urban areas produce indices of at least 75, and many exceed 90. The usual explanation for the clearcut separation between the two racial groups is that the whites congregate into certain areas and the blacks are confined (segregated) to the remainder. Other minority groups are similarly separated, both from the native white population and from each other. The more recently arrived the group, the greater its separation, so that currently the Spanish Americans, Puerto Ricans, and Filipinos are among the most separated groups, the southern Europeans who arrived more than half a century ago are less so, and the Irish and northern Europeans who preceded them even less; in most cities, however, blacks and whites are more separated than any other pair of groups, past and present.

The separation of ethnic groups—people of different racial, cultural and national backgrounds—in part reflects another major aspect of American urban areas: separation according to socioeconomic status. The main factor in this separation is income, reflected in the price paid for housing, but it is frequently indexed by occupational or educational attainment. Thus, professional and manual workers are usually not so greatly separated as are ethnic groups, and most residential areas contain some mixture of socioeconomic categories. Nevertheless, the degree to which the members of separate groups congregate together is considerable. In general, the greater the difference between the incomes of two households the less likely they are to be found in the same residential area; the index of separation between the highest and the lowest groups is usually between 50 and 70.

Finally, research has shown that residential areas can be characterized by aspects of their populations and dwellings other than socioeconomic and ethnic status. Many of these are categorized as life style or family status differences. Homes that are rented tend to be separated from those that are owned (or financed on a mortgage); apartments and single-family dwelling units are rarely found in the same district; young families live in different districts from senior citizens and from households without children; single-person and communal households tend

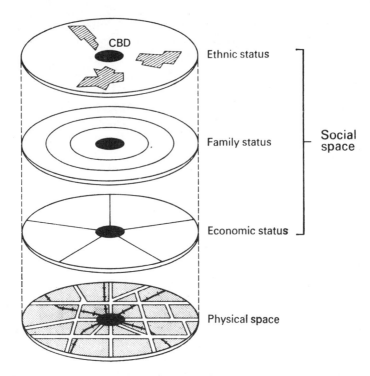

Figure 1.6.   Models of the morphology of the residential mosaic in a typical American urban area. Source: R. A. Murdie, *Factorial Ecology of Metropolitan Toronto, 1951–1961.* Department of Geography, University of Chicago, Discussion paper 116, p. 8.

to be separated from the traditional family areas; and women who participate in the workforce tend to live apart from those who are full-time homemakers. For life style or family status differences the degree of separation is usually less than for other dimensions—typically the index for the very young and the old is only about 20—but there is nevertheless this extra dimension to congregation and segregation.

Much work has been done by geographers and others to chart the degree of spatial separation between different groups in residential areas, using simple indices, such as those employed here, as well as sophisticated statistical procedures (collectively known as social area analysis and factorial ecology). All of these efforts have provided a wealth of descriptive material that prompts the questions ''why?'' and ''how?''

It is not only the degree of separation in residential areas that has been of interest to urban geographers but also the spatial mosaic and its typical form. Simple mapping shows that the black ghetto in most urban areas occupies inner-city districts, whereas most of the richest members of the white population live in certain sections of suburbia. This information leads to general models of the morphology of the residential mosaic, one for each status dimension, as illustrated in Figure 1.6. (Ethnic groups are clustered, family status groups are arranged in a series of zones, and economic status groups are distributed sectorally.) Again, these descriptions provoke questions; they demand explanations, not only of why a particular general pattern is typical of the American metropolis but how and why this pattern is maintained in a highly mobile society. (Just over half of all Americans lived in the same dwelling in 1975 that they occupied in 1970.)

Most American metropolitan areas are still experiencing population increases, many at fast rates; of those that are stagnating or declining, many are still expanding their built-up areas. The basic features of this growth and expansion are decentralization, suburbanization, and sprawl. The American town or city is spreading rapidly, with new homes, factories, and shopping centers being established at very low densities, involving much construction work so that public utilities, most obviously roads and freeways, can be provided. The relatively compact nineteenth-century city or town was built up around a single center, in which most shopping, employment, recreational and other facilities were clustered, whereas the modern urban area is a sprawling, multifocused, low-density mass linked together by highways. The prosperous areas are mainly in the suburbs. The inner city, on the other hand, is in rapid decline, as jobs, shops, and people move out; increasingly it is the repository of those who are unable to move out, the main social and economic problems of American society. Here again is a pattern demanding explanation.

CONCLUSION

A brief review of a subject with as large a literature as American urban geography can do it scant justice. This introduction has attempted merely to outline the topics that are of interest to urban geographers in the United States, concerns that form the substantive material for this book. By far the most important conclusion to be drawn from this material is that the American urban scene is a mosaic of patterns, many of which are repeated from place to place and that therefore suggest the operation of general processes. Urban geographers have been adept at describing those patterns but have as yet not moved as far in providing convincing explanations for them. The aim of this book is to strike a balance between description and explanation by concentrating on the latter.

The basic thesis of this book is that an explanation of spatial patterns is impossible from a study of the patterns themselves. The patterns are brought about by processes that are part of the operation of the

American economy and society; indeed, they reflect and help to maintain these processes. It is not possible in an introductory text of this type to present a full analysis of economy and society before proceeding to a consideration of the impact of social and economic processes on spatial form. All that can be undertaken is a sketch of the salient features, and this task is taken up in the next chapter. Following that come the two major parts of the book, the first dealing with the urban system and the second with the individual urban place. Both take a largely historical approach to the sought-for explanations, offering general theories that will serve as an outline for further research in American urban geography. The last part of the book looks at American urban problems in their spatial settings, at the geography of social and economic failure, and at the attempted solutions.

2

AMERICAN ECONOMY
AND SOCIETY

THE UNITED STATES is a capitalist country. Indeed, on most of the indices used in analyses of well-being it is one of the most successful capitalist countries. In a little more than 200 years of political independence the United States has developed a highly sophisticated, technologically advanced industrial system that pervades virtually every component of economic and social life. The consequent wealth and its associated attributes are very apparent, and the average standard of living for Americans is very high. But American society also illustrates one of the basic features of capitalism—its foundation in inequalities. In the midst of great wealth there is severe deprivation and abject poverty; although on an international scale most of the American poor are very rich, in their own nation many are underprivileged and a small minority are poor in absolute terms.

A major characteristic of capitalist economies and societies, especially the more advanced among them, is the large city. Urbanization is a *sine qua non* of capitalist development, reflecting and facilitating the operation of capitalism; hence the American city is an integral part of American capitalism. It follows, then, that the inequalities on which capitalism is based are present in the cities. Furthermore, to understand the nature of those cities they must be set in the relevant context of the capitalist system. The city is an essential element of the political economy, so before undertaking a study of it an outline of how the economy and society work is required. Such an outline is provided in the present chapter. The outline is brief, and highlights only the salient features.

CAPITALISM, ECONOMY,
AND SOCIETY

Capitalist societies in different parts of the world have evolved in various ways, depending on the antecedent conditions. Study of many of these has little or no relevance to the United States, where the evolutionary process can be encapsulated in three main stages.

The first stage is *mercantile capitalism* whose characteristic organizing feature is trade. Such an economy relies on the efforts of the merchant capitalists, who encourage economic intercourse, facilitate it, and benefit from it. Trade comes about because of two factors: the inability of any individual, household, or small group to produce all that it desires (assuming an existence that is more than bare subsistence); and the spatial variability in the ability to produce various commodities that reflects spatial variability in natural resources. The task of the merchant is to realize these two factors, both of which are only latent. He must appreciate that certain commodities are available only in certain places and convince people elsewhere that they want those commodities and that they can pay for them by producing and selling more of other commodities. The merchant's self-interest lies in his buying from one group and selling to another. The price paid to the former is as low as possible, while that charged to the latter is as high as possible, so that his costs of buying, storing, transporting, and selling are covered and a surplus remains. From that surplus the merchant pays himself a wage to support his household and uses the profits as capital to finance further mercantile activities.

Mercantile activity takes place at several different levels or spatial scales. Small-scale activity involves local trading, for example, between a buyer who purchases commodities from the farmers in a district and sells the produce to a merchant elsewhere, and a seller (a retailer) who buys from other merchants to sell to local farmers. At a larger scale are the merchants who finance the movement of goods over longer distances, from areas of surplus to those of demand. At each level the merchants are in competition. The more trade they handle—in particular, the greater the surplus that they obtain—the higher the wage they can pay themselves and the larger the profits they have to invest in more trade. Thus the more successful become more affluent. The less successful merchants will find their standard of living declining relative to that of their competitors, and perhaps absolutely, too; the volume of trade they handle may decline, their profits dwindle, and their businesses fail.

Because mercantile capitalism is based on trade, it depends on independent producers being prepared to sell goods and to buy others in return; part of the merchant's task is to convince producers of the desirability of these goods. Mercantile profits and success are based on the volume of trade handled and on the size of the surplus that accrues—that is, the difference between the buying and the selling prices. In competing to increase their surplus, merchants manipulate those prices. If they can manipulate the selling price—perhaps through a monopoly or an oligopoly—then profits may be ensured, but if many merchants are competing in the one market, this is difficult. A more effective strategy is to reduce the buying price, and of the several ways of doing this the most common has been to encourage the producer to be more efficient, to produce more at lower unit costs. Greater efficiency in production may be achieved through harder and/or better organized work, but the limits of this are soon reached in most cases. Continual increases in efficiency, as the bases for continual increases in profits, usually can be achieved only by the provision of tools that make work easier and faster. Most producers have some such tools, manufactured either by themselves or by specialized craftsmen (who must be paid out of the price received by the producers), but better tools still must be made by different processes.

Mercantile capitalism, then, involves a relatively small group of people—the merchant class—using their capital and enterprise to encourage trade and generate profits. The majority of the working population are independent producers who sell the results of their labor to the merchants. Most of these producers are in primary industries (that is, producing foodstuffs and other basic raw materials); some are craftsmen who create tools for the primary producers and for the merchants, (for example, in providing transportation facilities). Under *industrial capitalism*, the merchants are not replaced but many of the independent producers are.

Industrial capitalism involves the interaction of the three basic factors of production: land, labor, and capital. Labor is the ability to work that is possessed by all able-bodied persons. Land comprises the raw materials with which people work, the products of farming the earth and mining for its inanimate resources. The ownership of land is restricted in capitalist societies to a relatively small group. In some societies, members of this group obtained their control of this factor of production in precapitalist situations, with land ownership being vested in certain people only. In other societies ownership is achieved in the marketplace, by using the profits of mercantile activity to obtain control. In the United States, the ''opening-up'' of the frontier allowed many individuals to become land owners, at least on a small scale. This was very different from the situation in Europe. A relatively large pool of potential capitalists was created who encouraged the pursuit of individualistic, profit-oriented goals, and undoubtedly stimulated American economic growth. Finally, capital comprises assets that have financial value. Thus land is a capital asset for its owner, just as labor (including its skill, etc.) is for its owner. Capital also includes the means of production, such as factories and machines, and the money assets held by capitalists that are employed to put land and labor to work in order to produce profits as a return on capital invested. Some portion of the profits is retained for consumption by the capitalist and his dependents; the remainder is invested as capital in land and labor. Of the three factors of production, labor is the only one owned by all. In a capitalist economy it must be sold to an individual, firm, or government that controls the land and capital factors, or else the owner of labor cannot earn and survive.

Industrial capitalists use the resources at their disposal to generate profits, which provide the next generation of capital. Initially, the commodities produced were those required to increase the efficiency of farming and other primary production, but the tools so produced needed raw materials to be transformed (iron ore into iron, for example) and machinery for the transformation. Thus a whole range of industrial processes was established, and when the market for the products was saturated, other markets for other products were "created" by convincing people that they needed an ever-widening range of goods.

The main characteristic that distinguishes mercantile and industrial capitalism is the organization of labor. Most mercantile production is carried out by independent individuals who own the needed land resources and employ relatively little labor, whereas most industrial production is done by dependent individuals who must sell their labor to the capitalist in return for a wage that is spent on the means of subsistence and the various products marketed as "desirable" commodities. Because land is a fixed resource whose ownership is restricted (increasingly so as profits are used to buy up individual owners), an increasing proportion of the population must sell its labor in order to survive.

Industrial capitalists, like mercantile capitalists, compete for markets and profits. The most successful are those who reap the largest surplus, the greatest difference between cost of production and selling price. Success is achieved either by gaining control of the selling price or, more often, by keeping costs as low as possible. The latter can be achieved in part by paying low wages for much work, but there are limits to this strategy; the workers' efficiency declines because they are poorly fed, perhaps, or because their wages are so low that the industrialists' goods remain unsold. Low costs are best achieved by increasing the efficiency of labor, that is, by increasing output per unit cost. This usually involves both increasing the efficiency of the workplace and providing workers with better tools (machinery), enabling them to produce more goods in the same time. The demand for better tools creates work in other industries, so that the industrial system fuels its own expansion.

There are limits to the productivity increases that can be achieved, however, as well as to the demand that can be generated for any given commodity. As these limits are approached, the industrialists' profits tend to decline. To counter such a tendency, three strategies are available. The first is to increase the market, if possible, by expanding the number of buyers and/or the frequency of purchases; again, this has definite limits. The second is to capture a larger share of the existing market, by driving out competitors; usually it is the industrialists whose production is most efficient and returns the largest profits who succeed at this strategy. The third strategy is to diversify, to invest in other products and sectors of the economy; again, the industrial capitalists who earn the largest profits are best able to do this.

The second and third strategies just described are known respectively as concentration and centralization. Concentration involves individual sectors falling into the hands of a few owners, and centralization involves several sectors being similarly treated. These processes characterize *late capitalism,* in which a small number of large firms dominate the economy. (An alternative term is *monopoly capitalism,* which reflects the concentration.) Note that the term ''firm'' is used here for the first time. Most of the large industrial enterprises of late capitalism are owned not by individual industrial capitalists but by public companies, which are owned by large numbers of shareholders; because many of these companies are corporations, late capitalism is sometimes called *corporate capitalism.* The company replaces the individual because the latter is unable to raise the large amounts of capital needed to finance concentration and centralization. Only public companies, which borrow money from large numbers of people (savings from their wages or returns on previous investments) can provide the needed capital, and the lenders—through the shareholders' meetings—demand some say in the management of the company. Thus late capitalism is characterized by the concentration of production into a few companies and the diffusion of ownership.

Another feature of late capitalism is a change in the use of labor. As mercantile evolved into late capitalism, manufacturing replaced agriculture as the dominant activity. In late capitalism employment in manufacturing has declined, both relatively and absolutely, and has been replaced by employment in services. This has occurred for four main reasons. First, as productivity in manufacturing increases, fewer people are required to produce the needed volume of goods. Second, as concentration and centralization proceed, more people are needed to coordinate and finance production. Third, as specialization in production increases, more trade is generated, requiring more labor. And finally, as the markets for commodities become saturated, people spend a greater proportion of their incomes consuming services, the provision of which is in general still labor-intensive.

FROM COLONIAL OUTPOST
TO LATE CAPITALIST GIANT

The preceding description of the evolution of a capitalist society, from the mercantile stage through industrial to late capitalism, is a very brief and simple account of a highly complex and complicated process. It is sufficient, however, to provide the background for a presentation of the major features of the American economy and society, as a prelude to a study of its cities.

The earliest societies occupying the land area now forming the United States were precapitalist in their organization and did not develop an urban-based structure. American Indian communities were in that condition when they were invaded by European merchant capitalists in search of primary products. Rather than become integrated with the alien economic, social and cultural system, they were gradually dispossessed of their lands and decimated by both armed conflict and disease; before long the invading societies had assumed complete hegemony of the nascent United States.

The European settlement of North America was part of the colonial expansion of mercantile capitalism. Some of the immigrants were refugees, and many intended to become permanent settlers; a few established self-sufficiency, at least for a short time. But throughout the period of exploration and initial settlement the colonies maintained strong trading links with the European maritime powers, and the settlement process itself was a commercial enterprise that produced returns for European investors. Ownership of American land was vested in European monarchies, and was traded by them (permanently in some cases, on long leases in others) to capitalist individuals and companies.

As was the case throughout the Americas, the hope of finding gold stimulated many early expeditions, but other, less glamorous, commodities formed the staples for successful colonization. The continental fauna attracted hunters and trappers but it was the vast agricultural potential of the land that attracted the bulk of the investment. In 1783, when the United States achieved independence from Britain, the land area totaled 889,000 square miles, or about one quarter of its current size. The area was almost doubled in 1803 by the Louisiana Purchase, which embodied Jefferson's ideal of an expanding land-based society of farmers. In the 1840s the addition of Texas, Oregon, and the territories acquired from Mexico in 1846 extended the area of the United States to nearly 3 million square miles. The only later major expansion occurred when Alaska was acquired in 1867.

Some of this vast land area could not immediately be used for agricultural and pastoral purposes, and some still cannot. But as investment was channeled into further settlement, the farm area increased; during the second half of the nineteenth century it more than doubled, to occupy about 36 percent of the total area. This expansion continued well into the twentieth century (Figure 2.1), so that by 1950 farms covered almost half the country's land surface. The number of farms increased correspondingly, from 1.5 million in 1850, to 5.75 mlllion in 1900, and reached a peak of nearly 7 million in 1935; the population classified by the Bureau of the Census as "rural farm" peaked at 32 million in 1935. Today the farm population is only one quarter of that peak total, and the number of farms is less than half the number in 1935, reflecting increasing farm size rather than a decline in the acreage farmed.

Detailed statistics on agricultural land use before 1850 are not available. Of 294 million acres farmed then, 38 percent was under crops. Fifty years later the farmed acreage was 839 million, 38 percent of which was under crops, 23 percent farm woodland, and 33 percent under grassland pasture; an additional 768 million acres not officially owned in farms were used for grazing. At present about 1 billion acres are being farmed, 36 percent for crops, 51 percent for pasture, and 11 percent for farm woodland (over half of which is used for grazing); 288 million additional acres are used for grazing and 475 million for forestry.

The major purpose of agricultural expansion in the nineteenth century was to provide products for European consumption. In 1840 the plantation economies of the southern states exported 744 million pounds of cotton and 119 million pounds of tobacco leaf. Sixty years later 3.1 billion pounds of cotton and 335 million pounds of tobacco were exported, along with 102 million sixty-pound bushels of wheat. Exports of wheat increased in volume throughout the twentieth century, to a high of 1.2 billion bushels in 1973. Cotton exports are now only one-half their 1900 volume and less than one-third the 1912 peak; the volume of tobacco exports has remained fairly constant over the past eighty years, whereas meat exports have increased threefold in the last three decades.

During most of the nineteenth and early twentieth centuries, the United States participated in the world economy as a productive farming outpost serving urban Europe. Its export trade was crucial. Exports provided more than a quarter of all farm income in the 1920s, and primary products composed between one quarter and one-third of all exports. Today home consumption provides more than half of farm income, and "foods, feeds, and beverages" contribute only 16 percent of export earnings. Thus, although the total volume of agricultural exports has increased, it has decreased as a proportion of total production for most commodities. For example, cotton exports accounted for 51 percent of total production (by value) in 1910; in 1960, only 20 percent of production was exported, although more than twice this amount has been sold abroad in occasional years since. This trend toward greater local consumption reflects a major change in the structure of the American economy, and parallels the rise of industrial capitalism.

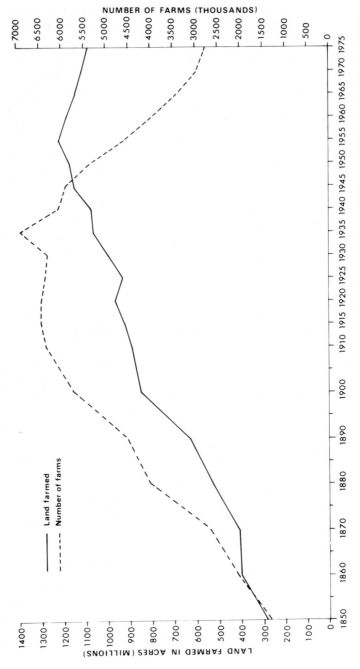

Figure 2.1. Land under farms and number of farms, 1850 to 1975. Data are from 1850 to 1910 plotted at ten-year intervals, and at five-year intervals thereafter. Source: Data from *Historical Statistics of the United States*, Part 1, 1975, Series K, pp. 17–18. Updated from the *Statistical Abstract of the United States, 1977*, p. 674.

The shift to industrial capitalism was made possible by capital accumulation resulting from private ownership of American land. Even in the colonial era there was some manufacturing, because it was impossible to import everything that society needed. Brickworks, breweries, tanneries, bakeries, printing presses, and blacksmith shops were among the many small enterprises that were fundamental to the day-to-day life of prosperous mercantile settlements, and they were the foundation of the later industrial economy. But by 1879 fixed capital investment in manufacturing was only $4.821 billion (in 1929 dollars), or less than $100 per resident. In 1957 fixed capital in manufacturing (again in 1929 dollars) was $110.45 billion, or $650 per person. By 1976 the figure had more than doubled.

With industrialization, the United States has become much more of a "closed" economy. The value of exports as a percentage of gross national product has fallen by almost half during this century, for example. Imports have declined in importance too, until the recent impact of increased world prices for such raw materials as oil and timber, which the country obtains overseas.

INDUSTRIALIZATION AND BEYOND

The outline just provided describes the economic evolution of a country from an agricultural outpost into a major industrial and largely self-sufficient nation. Its initial development was generated by overseas capital, and many of the profits were repatriated to Europe. Since the end of the eighteenth century, however, political independence and private land ownership have made possible the accumulation of local capital to finance the development process. A fertile stock of land rich in minerals was the source of the capital used for investment in frontier expansion, to exploit mineral and fossil fuel resources, and to build manufacturing industries and a transportation network. Since 1776 foreign investment has steadily declined and American economic development has very largely been financed by American capital.

As already noted in the discussion of fixed capital invested in manufacturing, the shift from mercantile to industrial capitalism is a relatively recent phenomenon for the country as a whole. (There have been industrial centers for more than a century, of course.) This shift is reflected in the changing composition of the labor force, for which detailed statistics are available only since 1900 (Figure 2.2). At that time, 37.5 percent of the employed population were engaged in agriculture; today slightly more than 3 percent of all workers are employed on the farm.

The move from agriculture to industry represented only a temporary phase in the changing occupational and employment structure, however. In 1900 farm employment plus manual labor in industry ac-

% DISTRIBUTION OF THE LABOR FORCE

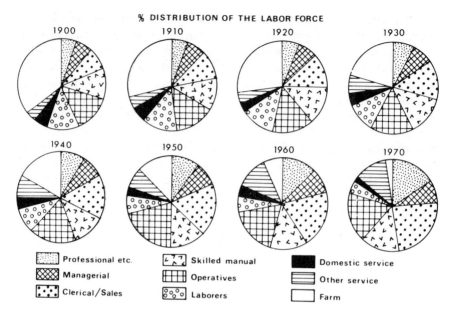

Figure 2.2.   The changing composition of the labor force since 1900. Source: Data from *Historical Statistics of the United States,* Part 1, 1975, Series D, pp. 182–232.

counted for 73 percent of the workforce; in 1977, the two together comprised 36 percent of the employed, with just over half holding white-collar jobs and the remainder in service occupations. The tertiary sector (white-collar plus service employment) has been the major source of jobs for Americans since 1940; today clerical workers alone account for almost one-fifth of all employees.

This changed occupational structure illustrates the success of American industrial capitalism in its drive to make labor productive and create a surplus for investors. So many fewer agricultural employees are needed now, not because production is less but because the tools available allow each farmer and his employees to produce so much more and to care for larger areas of land. In 1900 the implements and machinery available to American farmers were worth $740 million at current prices, or $69 per farm worker; seventy years later, the respective valuations were $34 billion and $15,444. (Adjusting for changes in the value of the dollar, investment per worker has increased by 4,700 percent.) Today there are nearly 5 million tractors—two for every farm worker—and nearly 1 million grain combines and pickup balers. Some 40 million tons of fertilizer and lime are applied to the land annually, a fifteenfold increase since 1900. As a result, about 6.5 billion man-hours are worked annually on farms, compared to 22.5 billion in 1900, when the average farm worker supplied food for only seven nonfarm workers, compared to forty-seven now. Agricultural productivity has increased at least sevenfold in the twentieth century.

These changes in American agriculture were made possible by changes in the American manufacturing industry, in which the aim has been to increase both productivity and profits. That these goals have been attained is illustrated by data on "value added" in production, which is the difference between the cost of a factory's inputs and the price received for its outputs; value added represents the extra value of commodities resulting from the work performed on them. In 1904 the average value added in manufacturing was $1,061 per employee (of which $527 was returned in wages); in 1970 it was $16,689 (of which $7,891 was returned). Adjusting for changes in the value of the dollar, workers in American industry were more than twice as productive in 1970 as they were in 1904.

The tertiary sector of the labor force serves to organize this increased scale of production; to ensure the movement of materials from producer to factory, from factory to factory, and from factory to consumer; to arrange the financing, which enables all these movements to take place; to provide the services the population demands; and to perform administrative and governmental functions so as to oversee it all. Such workers comprised 7.8 million out of 15.2 million nonfarm agricultural employees in 1900; in 1970 they were 47.3 million, or 67 percent of the total nonfarm workforce, including 3.8 million in wholesale trade, 11.1 million in retailing, 3.7 million in finance, insurance, and real estate, 12.5 million in government, and 11.6 million in services. In a late capitalist, highly productive society, it is organization, not production, that employs the most people.

LATE CAPITALISM AND CONCENTRATION

A major means of increasing the productivity of labor is to create larger organizations within which each employee performs a limited, specialized task; the greater the specialization, in general, the greater the overall efficiency, as long as the overall production process is properly organized and operated. Consequently, larger organizations earn the larger profits and, by eliminating competitors, come to dominate the economy.

The trend toward concentration has been marked in all three sectors of the American economy: the primary, secondary, and tertiary. Thus, as the number of farms declined from 6.8 million in 1935 to 2.3 million in 1974, the average acreage increased from 155 to 440. Similarly, in 1899 the 204,754 enumerated factories averaged 24 employees each and a value added per employee of $958; in 1972 the 321,000 enumerated factories averaged 59 employees each and a value added per production employee of $26,200. Three years later the average value added was $35,100. (See Figure 2.3.)

In the tertiary sector, concentration began to be a major process a little later than in manufacturing, but it has gathered pace rapidly. For example, in 1850 there were 824 banks with average assets of $650,000. By 1900 there were 14,000 (with average assets of $930,000); in 1920, 31,000 ($1.72 million), and in 1970, 14,000 again (average assets, $43.1 million.) In 1976 there were 14,672 banks (plus 33,484 branches) with average assets of $70.9 million. In the retail trade, 482,000 establishments employed 1.2 million people who each sold on average $9,230 worth of goods in 1929; forty years later, there were only 294,000 establishments with 1.7 million employees, and sales averaged $40,772. Firms with four or more separate stores sold 32 percent of all foodstuffs in 1929: in 1954 firms with eleven or more stores sold 36 percent; in 1969, 46 percent; and in 1976, 53 percent.

Farm, bank, manufacturing, and retail businesses have grown on average much larger in recent decades, as competition under industrial capitalism has concentrated ownership in relatively few firms. This is especially so with manufacturing (which, as will be shown in later chapters, is spatially more concentrated than the others). By means of aggressive tactics, competition and mergers have caused most productive sectors to become dominated by relatively few firms, although outright monopolies are prohibited by law. By 1972 the fifty largest manufacturing companies (out of a total of 321,000) were responsible for 25 percent of the total value added (Figure 2.3); the largest 200 were responsible for 43 percent of the value added and 57 percent of all assets. (In 1947 these three figures were 17, 30, and 48, respectively.) The extent of large-firm dominance varies by sector. Tobacco manufacture has been dominated by a few companies throughout the present century, for example, with the four largest producing 50 percent of all value added in the industry in 1901 and 78 percent in 1947; in contrast, for machinery manufacture the percentages were 41 in 1901 and 19 in 1947.

Thus, in recent decades American industrial capitalism has been transformed into late capitalism with the economy dominated by a few large firms. There are still many small enterprises, of course, but many of these are very dependent on the large corporations for contracts, for setting prices, and for gaining access to certain markets.

THE STATE IN AMERICAN SOCIETY AND ECONOMY

The emergence of late capitalism in the United States has been paralleled by the growth of government as employer, handler of money, and regulator of economic and social affairs. Much government activity is aimed at ensuring continued capitalist development, so as to provide

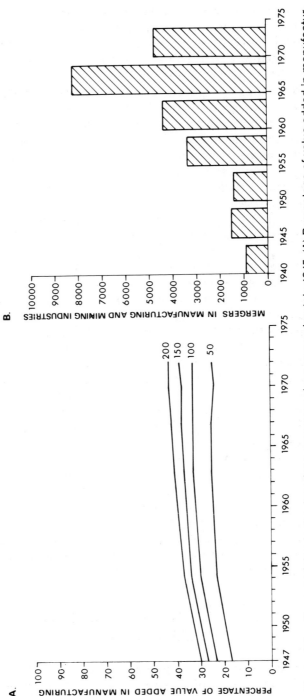

Figure 2.3. Concentration in the American economy since approximately 1945. (A) Percentage of value added in manufacturing produced by the 50, 100, 150, and 200 largest companies. Source: Data from *Statistical Abstract of the United States, 1977,* p. 810. (B) Number of mergers in manufacturing and mining industries. Source: *Ibid.,* p. 569.

31

an environment for earning profits that is stable—not challenged to any major extent by working-class militancy.

During the era of mercantile capitalism government was not called upon to play a very active role in encouraging development. It was a relatively passive ally, playing the role of a protective state. Its functions included creating and maintaining a system of law and order (one that respected private property and thereby encouraged capitalist accumulation) and providing the military protection that ensured a stable environment for business success. Initially, the vote was a restricted franchise granted to property owners only, which accounts for both the government's passive role and its nature.

The small size of the operation needed to play this passive role is indicated by the size of the government payroll in 1816—4,837 persons; the budget receipts in that year were $47 million, or $5.50 per person. There was one government employee for every 1,790 residents. Fifty years later there was one for every 917, but budget receipts were only $2.80 per capita. In 1900 there was one government employee for every 324 residents; in 1930 one for every 204; and in 1976 one for every 69. (These figures are for civilian employment only and exclude the armed forces.) Budgetary receipts also changed rapidly too, rising from $7.57 per capita in 1900 to $25.09 in 1930 to $2,404.65 in 1976.

During the era of mercantile capitalism the main government expenditures were for defense and repayment of the national debt (much of which was incurred to finance defense spending); 88 percent went for these items in 1816, and 82 percent in 1848. Much of the revenue came from land sales (33 million acres were sold in 1835–1836, for example); one of the state's major contributions to mercantile capitalism and the agricultural industry on which it was based was the sale of land in the public domains east of the Rocky Mountains. The other major source of revenue was the import tariff, designed to protect the local capitalist class.

As industrial capitalism expanded, so did the state's role. One of its major functions—also linked with mercantile expansion and the extension of the agricultural and pastoral frontiers—was ensuring the infrastructure needed for development. Thus public lands were given as grants to aid the construction of railroad routes; 41 million acres were granted in 1865 alone and 130 million between 1851 and 1871. By 1871, 38 percent of the federal budget was spent on nondefense items, and in 1901 the percentage was 55. Defense spending has increased during wartime in the twentieth century, but is now only about 25 percent of the total.

During the industrial and late capitalist periods government has come to play a much more active and productive role in the maintenance of a healthy capitalist system. For this a healthy, well-trained labor force is required and is provided by the public education system. Of every dollar currently spent by state and local governments, 34 cents goes to education. Direct expenditure on health services is relatively recent and small. Of the 7,156 hospitals in the country in 1975, 382 were operated by the federal government and 2,306 by state and local governments; together these supplied 47 percent of all the hospital beds in the country, far less than the 71 percent supplied twenty-five years earlier. Federal expenditure on two health programs—Medicare and Medicaid—began in the 1960s and by 1970 was only $9.9 billion or 5 percent of federal outlays; in 1977 these programs cost $32.2 billion or 7.8 percent of the budget. Hospitals cost only 5.4 percent of state and local government budgets in 1975. The main expenditure on health care is by individuals through insurance plans; the total spent in 1975 on subscriptions and premiums was $35.6 billion, covering 75 percent of the population for regular medical expenses and 83 percent for hospitalization. Thus governments in the United States have been much more involved in the provision of educational services than of health services, which have been left largely to the private sector. The main beneficiaries of publicly delivered health care are war veterans and the indigent (the aged and the social security beneficiaries covered by Medicaid and Medicare).

Other welfare programs, designed to protect the poor from the vicissitudes of economic circumstance largely outside their control, were instituted by the Social Security Act of 1935 and extended by legislation in the 1960s. Welfare policy can serve four functions: (1) relief of dependency, especially poverty; (2) public provision of social services, income surrogates, and market regulations; (3) mitigation of insecurity and risk; and (4) redistribution of income in favor of the poor. United States welfare policy has seldom been directed at the fourth and some analysts argue that the benefits of the other three functions are few and have been won as the result of prolonged protest only. Nevertheless, payments to individuals now comprise almost half the federal budget, with social security payments alone making up 25 percent; the Department of Health, Education and Welfare is now (in the late 1970s) by far the biggest spender of all the federal agencies, averaging about 36 percent of the total federal budget.

Welfare services and market regulation policies are far more important as part of the infrastructure needed for healthy capitalist operations than as direct payments to individuals. Thus the government is responsible for the provision of water, for industry and domestic consumption; sewage and garbage disposal and pollution control; fire and crime protection; loans to aid home building and purchase; the construction of highways; public education; agriculture price supports; the conservation of natural resources; and the planning of the environment. Furthermore, government is a major purchaser of industrial products, particularly defense goods and many high-technology products that keep many Americans fully employed.

At this stage of late capitalism, therefore, government has become a major force in the American political economy, handling a sizable proportion of the gross national product (Figure 2.4). Increasingly, and often unwillingly, governments have become involved in protecting both business firms and individual citizens from the potential and actual hazards of economic vicissitudes; the survival of capitalism is thus ensured, as profitability is guaranteed, and potential conflict between capitalist concentration and accumulation on the one hand and employee exploitation on the other is defused as much as possible.

American government has grown despite the fact that the nation remains dedicated to a free-market economy, strongly believes in individual freedom (also known as privatism) and distrusts large, strong government. The distrust of big government is reflected in the structure of American government. The federal government is restricted in its area of operations by the Constitution, which reserves many functions for the states, so that for many policies Washington can only cajole, not require. Similarly, within the states much autonomy is given to local governments; there is also a tradition of creating *ad hoc* government bodies

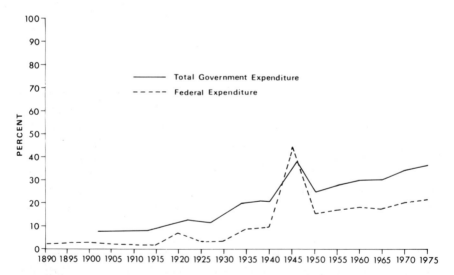

Figure 2.4.   Government expenditures as a percentage of the United States gross national product: data are plotted every five years only; as only federal expenditure data are available for 1945, total expenditures are shown for 1946. Source: Data are from *Historical Statistics of the United States,* Part 1, 1975, Series F1–5, Part 2, 1975, Series Y, pp. 335–342, Y533–566. Data for 1975 are from the *Statistical Abstract of the United States, 1977.*

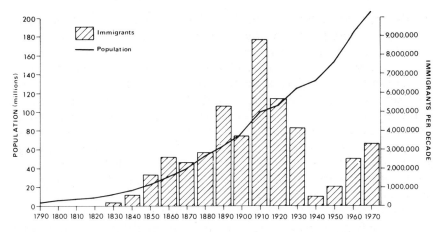

Figure 2.5. Population and immigration. Source: Data are from *Historical Statistics of the United States,* Part 1, 1975, Series A6–8, and *Statistical Abstract of the United States, 1977,* p. 81.

(special districts) to undertake specific tasks rather than allocating all functions to a single body. Thus in 1972 there was one government unit for every 2,700 Americans and one elected government official for every 420 residents.

POPULATION, ECONOMY, AND SOCIETY

The rapid growth of the American economy during the last two centuries has required a major resource not available *in situ*—people. These were needed both to provide labor and to consume the goods and services produced. The resultant population growth (Figure 2.5) has been very rapid, from 3.9 million in 1790 to 216.0 million in 1977.

Population growth in a country involves two processes; natural increase and immigration. Initially, immigration was the dominant source, with the first settlement consisting of "free" colonists from Europe. But these people were an insufficient source of cheap labor, especially for the southern plantations, and so black slaves were brought from the west coast of Africa in large numbers (140,000 between 1730 and 1760, for example) to meet the labor shortage. The slaves were freed after the Civil War of the 1860s, but they are still far from integrated into white society and remain largely at the bottom of the occupational ladder, where they are subject to much prejudice and discrimination.

The slaves provided cheap agricultural labor for the southern plantation economies, but they were not employed on the agricultural frontier that expanded north of the Ohio and west of the Mississippi rivers. This expansion was largely undertaken by immigrants from Europe, who also filled the increasing number of industrial jobs and whose descendants came to dominate the American society and economy. Since 1840 more than a million immigrants have flocked to the United States each decade, and in some of the early years of the twentieth century there were a million immigrants annually. Many were forced from their European homes when new agricultural practices eliminated the need for labor. Some fled from physical deprivation; others from religious and political persecution. Most hoped for a better life in the United States; many prospered beyond their wildest dreams, although many more endured deprivation in either rural hardship or urban slum.

Europe provided the bulk of the immigrants, at least until about 1920; a total of about 36 million made the trans-Atlantic crossing. (An exception was the influx of Chinese to the west coast during the gold rushes of the 1840s and 1850s.) Ireland was the dominant source in the early nineteenth century, following the great famines there; it provided almost half of all the immigrants in the 1840s, and a total of 2.35 million (35 percent) between 1820 and 1869. During the middle and later decades of that century, Germany and the Scandinavian countries were important sources (40 percent in the 1880s), followed by a wave of eastern and southern Europeans. (Many of the former were Jews; Italians dominated among the latter.)

The pace of immigration slowed in the 1920s as the demand for labor slackened with the depression and social tensions increased. Quotas set the maximum numbers of immigrants from each hemisphere and country; the Eastern hemisphere received the largest quota, and it now provides twice as many immigrants as Europe, mainly from the Philippines and Korea. (There is also much movement from Puerto Rico and Mexico; much of the latter is illegal.) National quotas were removed in 1965, but there is still a limit on the total annual number of immigrants.

These various waves of migration have served capitalist purposes well, providing the needed labor and also many groups prepared to accept the American ethos of hard work as the means to social and economic advancement. Because their reproduction rate has been great, the immigrants have contributed to the growth of the market and have provided a cultural pluralism that is reflected in many aspects of American life, including the urban scene. Many of the early generations suffered much deprivation as they sought to establish themselves and counter the prejudice that is often directed toward aliens. Of those long-established in the country, only the black slaves and their descendants have not overcome this prejudice and its associated discrimination, such as occurs in the job and housing markets. Identifiable racial groups have long suffered such handicaps—and not only in the United

States. Today, not only the blacks but also the Asians, Puerto Ricans, and Mexicans are targets of the xenophobia of the white majority.

Although American population growth was sparked by immigration, which continued to drive that growth substantially for more than a century, it was reproduction, by immigrants and native-born alike, that was the source of most of the new Americans. Estimates of the birth rate in the nineteenth century are difficult because of the problem of under-registration, especially among the black population, so the data in Figure 2.6 are for the white population only. (In general, the birth rate for blacks is now about 50 percent higher than that for whites but before about 1960 the differential was not so great.) Thus in the first half of the nineteenth century the birth rate was very high (equivalent to more than 250 children per year for every 1,000 women aged 15 to 44, or one child a year for every four women of child-bearing age). From 1850 to 1925 the rate dropped by half, and by 1940 it was only one-third the 1800 peak. It increased somewhat immediately after the Second World War but has fallen rapidly since; in 1975 it was only 60 percent of the 1954 postwar peak.

A major consequence of the changing birth rate has been a drop in the size of the average American family. For example, more than half of all women born between 1835 and 1839 had borne five or more chil-

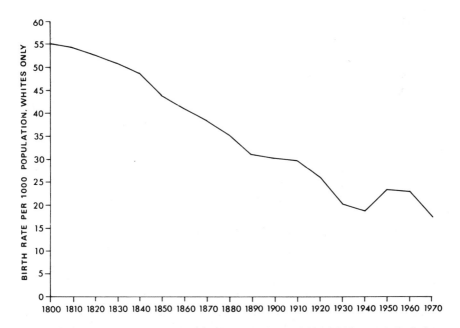

Figure 2.6. The birth rate (total live births registered per 1,000 population), for the white population only, since 1800. Source: Data are from *Historical Statistics of the United States,* Part 1, 1975, Series B, pp. 1–10.

dren according to 1910 census, and the average was 5.4 births for every woman who had reached 44. For women born between 1870 and 1874, only 33 percent had five or more children (an average of 3.7); for those born between 1895 and 1899, 19 percent (an average of 2.7); and for those born between 1920 and 1924, 17 percent (2.7 each still). However, for more than a century the modal number of children has been one or two.

Not only are families much smaller now than they were a century ago, but also, in part because of their smaller size, families are being completed much earlier in the parents' life cycle. Given that the median age at marriage is now only just over twenty for females, many mothers have completed child-bearing and their children are at school by the time the women are thirty. Furthermore, by the time the parents are about forty-five years old, it is very likely that their children have left home, in many cases to get married themselves.

The changes in family size are the result of numerous interrelated factors, some of which are associated with the increasing affluence of American society and the desire of parents to have smaller families and enjoy the material benefits available to them. The potential labor force has also been greatly expanded. Married women are no longer tied to their homes until well into their fifties by child-bearing and the rearing of young children. Many are returning to their premarital careers, while others are starting new careers and still others are leaving work only temporarily to have children. This major social change has created many tensions in a formerly male-dominated society, especially with regard to work patterns. In 1890, 3.7 out of a total of 19 million women were in the employed labor force; of those 3.7 million, 68 percent were single and 18 percent widowed or divorced. In 1970, 30.8 out of a total of 71.2 million women were in the labor force; of those 30.8 million, 62 percent were married, and 57 percent lived in the same household as their husband. The major change has come since the Second World War. In 1948, 23.8 percent of women living with their husbands were in the labor force; for those with no children under eighteen the percentage was 30.3, whereas for those with at least one child under six it was 11.9. Twenty-eight years later, the three percentages were 45, 43.8, and 37.4, respectively.

Thus there has been a major alteration in the distribution of economic roles within the family associated with the changes in family size; this alteration has presumably been paralleled in many cases by changes in the distribution of domestic roles. There has also been an overall change in attitudes about the family, as reflected in divorce rates, although, at least during the twentieth century, the shift has not been as great as many people have supposed. In the 1920s about eight married females per 1,000 were divorced; in the 1960s; the figure was ten to twelve, although by 1975 it had risen to twenty per 1,000. Many divorced people remarry, and other married couples separate without divorcing. When these two factors are considered, more than 10 percent of all white families now lack one of the parents; for blacks, the figure is 34 percent, and represents a condition associated with poverty.

In addition to the changes associated with the birth rate, family size, and participation of married women in the labor force, changes in the death rate and life expectancy are features of contemporary American society. A white male born in 1900 could expect to live 47 years and a female 49 years (for blacks, the figures were 33 and 34 only); by 1933 life expectancy for white males was 63 years and 65 for females (for blacks, 54 and 56). In 1970 life expectancy for males was 68 (white) and 61 (black) years, and 76 (69) for females. This change reflects the drop in the infant mortality rate, which fell from 99 per 1,000 for whites in 1915 to 18 in 1970 and from 181 to 31 for blacks, as a consequence of improved diet and health care.

The changes in mortality and fertility patterns have in turn affected the country's age structure. A single statistic, the median age, shows that during the past century and a half the age of the average American has increased by some 68 percent, rising from 16.7 years in 1820 to 28.1 years in 1970. (In 1950 median age was 30.2 years, reflecting the low birth rates of the 1930s.) The change has been greater for females (16.8 to 29.3; 30.5 in 1950) than for males (16.6 to 26.8; 29.9 in 1950); and much greater for whites (16.6 to 28.9; 30.8 in 1950) than for blacks (17.2 to 22.4; 26.1 in 1950). This statistic conceals much detail, however. A greater amount of detail is provided in Figure 2.7, in which the population at the end of each decade is classified into five age groups. The main feature of this diagram is the changing constitution of the "dependent population," or those persons not gainfully employed— usually children (those under fifteen, but increasingly those under twenty, due to the expansion of higher education) and the aged (those sixty-five and over). The size of the latter group more than tripled over the period shown (and continues to increase); the former declined by one-third or more, and after a brief increase in the 1950s and 1960s appears to be falling again. This change implies a major alteration in the demand for services by the dependent population; in relative terms, the demand for education is falling, while services used by the aged (many more of which must be provided institutionally because of either the absence or the unsuitability of home support) are increasing.

Finally in this section it should be noted that over the past few decades American society has witnessed an acceptance of numerous "alternative life styles," many of which are associated with the growth of the so-called permissive society, as reflected, for example, by such changing sexual mores as greater public acceptance of homosexual life styles and

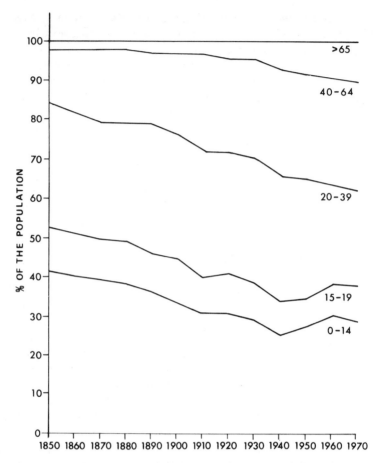

Figure 2.7. The generalized age distribution of the American population, in percentages, 1850 to 1970. Source: Data are from *Historical Statistics of the United States,* Part 1, 1975, Series A, pp. 119–134.

communal living. In much of the United States these changes have as yet had little impact, but in two or three more decades, their influence on social behavior, and thus on spatial patterns, may be considerable.

SOCIAL STRUCTURE AND SOCIAL WELL-BEING

As indicated at the outset of this chapter, the United States is, by money measures, one of the great success stories of capitalism. Americans are on the average among the richest people in the world, in health as well as in wealth, for their life expectancy is well above that of most other countries. They can rely on a vast, sophisticated technology to support them, in all aspects of their daily lives, and their democratic system is widely recognized and praised. But they also live in a society with very high crime rates. During the 1970s there were an average of 20,000 homicides, 50,000 forcible rapes, 450,000 aggravated assaults, 3 million burglaries, and 5 million larcenies and thefts reported annually; the 1974 homicide rate of 10.2 per 100,000 population in the United States was ten times that of the United Kingdom, more than twenty times that of Spain, and fifteen times that of Denmark, Greece, and Norway. The American suicide rate of 12.1 per 100,000 is also high (compared with 7.9 in the United Kingdom, 3.4 in Greece, and 4.0 in Spain), although many other advanced capitalist societies have higher rates.

The benefits of capitalist development in America are not shared equally, as is illustrated by the great increase in expenditures on social welfare programs in recent decades. This phenomenon reflects how a capitalist economy operates: by the exploitation of the majority of the population—the working class, whose only available resource is labor—by a small minority—the capitalist class, who own the means of production and employ labor so as to earn profits. Each of these two major classes, and especially the working class, is divided into many subclasses—groups usually based on occupation whose members are often in conflict with the members of other subclasses, usually over work and wages. These subclasses differ in status, in the skills required for their occupations, and in the rewards that members receive for their services to the capitalist cause. The lowest status and rewards go to the least skilled, whose labor power is poorly developed and whose bargaining position with employers is relatively weak; because they have relatively little to offer in the labor market, except their ability to do menial, boring, and sometimes hard work, these workers are usually poorly paid. (Many of these workers, notably the most recent immigrants and the descendants of the slaves, are often kept in the lowest sub-classes by overt discrimination in labor markets and in the educational system that prepares them for the labor market.) Furthermore, those with the fewest skills are likely to suffer first from any recession in the economy, and become unemployed.

Within the working class there are considerable differences in income and what follows from that. At the upper end of the scale are those in professional and skilled nonmanual occupations (often known as the middle class), whose services to and support for the capitalist system are well rewarded. Lower down are the skilled and the semiskilled manual workers, plus those in the less skilled nonmanual occupations, such as sales clerks and retail assistants. At the bottom are the unskilled manual workers and the employees in service occupations, such as domestic servants and office cleaners.

The most readily available, though far from perfect, indicator of these inequalities is provided by data on incomes. In 1976 there were about 57 million separate households in the United States; nearly one-third received annual incomes exceeding $30,000 and another one-tenth received less than $5,000. The 5 percent of households with the highest incomes received 15.6 percent of all wage and salary payments; the lowest-paid 20 percent received only 5.4 percent of all the monies disbursed. These differentials have changed only slightly since 1950, when the bottom 40 percent of households received 16.5 percent of all payments, compared to 17.2 percent in 1976.

These household income differences reflect the various wage and salary levels for the separate occupational categories. In 1976 the median weekly earnings (according to the Bureau of Labor Statistics and reported in the annual *Statistical Abstract of the United States*) were as follows:

Professional and technical	$256	Transport operatives	$214
Managerial	$289	Unskilled laborers	$161
Salesworkers	$198	Domestic workers	$60
Clerical	$158	Other service workers	$134
Craft workers	$239	Farm workers	$120
Semiskilled operatives	$162		

These differences translate into inequalities, with certain groups in the labor force receiving less than others because of their competitive situation in the job market. The median income of males was $234, for example, as compared to $145 for females, reflecting the concentration of women in certain low-paying occupations, notably clerical and domestic work. And whereas the median income of white males was $239, for black males it was $187.

Differences in competitive ability, coupled with discriminatory practices in education and hiring, mean that some groups are living in relative poverty (and some members live in absolute poverty). Blacks are strongly concentrated in the underprivileged strata of society; in 1970 they formed about 10 percent of all households, but 20 percent of those in the bottom fifth of the income scale and only 5 percent of those in the top 20 percent. Households without a resident male head also suffered more poverty, on average: they were 11 percent of the total in 1970 but formed 20 percent of those in the bottom fifth of the income distribution scale. In contrast, professional workers' families made up 31 percent of all households but 55 percent of those in the top fifth of the income scale and 76 percent of those in the top 5 percent.

Money income provides a title to wealth, a means to consumption, and the ability to provide for one's security through savings and investments. In general, the lower the income of a household, the greater the percentage that must be spent on immediate consumption. For higher income groups, some proportion can be invested as capital in the search for greater income and wealth; the returns on these investments mean that total income differences become cumulatively larger. Some 25 million Americans are now shareholders, 17 million of whom in 1975 came from households with annual incomes exceeding $15,000.

For most families and households, the largest single expenditure is on housing, so that income differentials are strongly reflected in the quality and type of housing occupied. The first major difference is in tenure. In 1975, the United States had some 72.5 million separate housing units. Nearly two-thirds of these units were owner-occupied, by people who were able to invest in a home, and build up some equity capital in it; most of the remaining third were tenants, paying rent and acquiring no wealth as a result. Only 44 percent of black households were owner-occupiers, compared to 67 percent of white households. Of all the owner-occupied units, 4.5 percent lacked complete plumbing and 1.5 percent were dilapidated; for black owner-occupiers, the respective percentages were 15.0 and 4.3. Of all the rental units, 8.3 percent lacked complete plumbing and 3.9 percent were dilapidated; for black renters, the respective percentages were 18.2 and 7.6. In addition, occupiers differ in their consumption patterns; three-fourths of all homes were wired for electricity in 1976 (that is, one quarter of all households lacked this basic utility), and of these, 40 percent had room air conditioning, 33 percent had freezers, 54 percent had electric clothes washers, and 31 percent electric water heaters.

The few inequalities listed here indicate considerable variations in social well-being within American society, differences that reflect the distribution of the rewards of the capitalist system. (Undoubtedly, these inequalities strongly influence the fact that homicide rates, at about 100 per 100,000 in the 1970s, are ten times higher for black than for white males.) From these inequalities can be inferred two basic features of American society: first, that most of the time the majority of Americans accept the social stratification into classes and subclasses; and second, they accept that as capitalism changes, so does the demand for different occupations. The more advanced the industrial technology, for example, the greater the demand for skilled workers and professional engineers; and the larger and more complex the firms operating the economy (including government), the greater the demand for managers and administrators. Expanding capitalism needs more people in the higher social strata; therefore because of the almost continuous rapid growth of the American economy over the past two centuries, many persons have been able to attain positions, both for themselves and for their children, in higher strata than they once occupied. This movement from subclass to subclass is known as social mobility, and the accepted means of achieving such mobility is via educational success, which demonstrates one's ability to perform the needed functions. (Acquired wealth can also afford social mobility—for successful entrepreneurs, for example—but is not as important as education.)

Access to opportunities for social mobility has arisen out of the changing occupational structure, which has featured a decline in farming and an increase in white-collar jobs. Many Americans have clearly availed themselves of these opportunities and have changed their social status—as defined by their occupation—quite considerably. (To do so, many have been spatially mobile, too.) But the major determinant of one's occupational category and class (that is, white- or blue-collar and middle or working) remains the class into which one was born and the category of one's first employment. Marked class differences are still passed down from one generation to the next. Tables 2.1 and 2.2 illustrate the process of social mobility, by means of data from a large sample of adult males obtained in the early 1960s.

In Table 2.1 the respondents' occupations are compared with their fathers'. Here considerable social change was expected since, for example, the final column shows that 28 percent of fathers were farmers, whereas according to the final row only 6 percent of their sons were; the greatest mobility was in the white-collar occupations (categories 1–3), which grew from 23 to 40 percent of the total. Yet close inspection of the rows shows that in many occupational categories, sons were more likely to be in the same subclass as their fathers than in any other; the main exceptions were the sons of sales and clerical workers, service workers, and laborers—all of whom have moved up the social class hierarchy—as well as the sons of those in farming. Excluding those in farming, white- and blue-collar workers remain segregated, though far from completely; of the sons of white-collar fathers (categories 1–3) 70 percent were in white collar occupations, and of the sons of blue-collar workers (4–7) 63 percent held blue-collar jobs. (These data refer to the population as a whole. For some groups, such as immigrants, the levels of social mobility vary considerably from the average.)

In a similar presentation Table 2.2 compares the 1962 respondents' first occupation with their present occupation. Again, many of those who started in farming are now no longer there, and many who started in the lower categories eventually achieved a white-collar occupation. Similarly, the barrier between white- and blue-collar occupations is apparent: 76 percent of those who started in a white-collar occupation were still in one, and 67 percent of those beginning in a blue-collar job remained there.

Although the process of social mobility just described—that greater rewards must be earned—is highly valued in American society, there is by no means a full consensus that such a system is both just and desirable. In particular, many consequences of technological change are highly problematic. Whereas greater skills are required of the engineers

Table 2.1
INTERGENERATIONAL SOCIETAL MOBILITY FOR MALES AGED 25 TO 64, 1962*

Father's Occupation	Son's Occupation									Total
	1	2	3	4	5	6	7	8	9	
1. Professional	669(41)	286(18)	260(16)	142(9)	168(10)	50(3)	32(2)	20(1)	6(0)	1,633(5)
2. Manager/Proprietor	866(23)	1,050(18)	646(18)	556(15)	341(9)	10(3)	76(2)	39(1)	13(0)	3,688(11)
3. Sales/Clerical	589(23)	614(24)	490(19)	358(14)	248(10)	118(5)	63(3)	39(2)	2(0)	2,521(7)
4. Craftsman	815(12)	1,035(16)	784(12)	1,943(30)	1,298(20)	323(5)	282(4)	50(1)	23(0)	6,553(19)
5. Operative	612(12)	640(12)	578(11)	1,270(24)	1,358(26)	311(6)	375(7)	49(1)	49(1)	5,242(15)
6. Service	164(10)	231(14)	247(15)	341(21)	340(21)	180(11)	102(6)	7(6)	4(6)	1,616(5)
7. Laborer	130(6)	177(8)	257(12)	498(23)	582(26)	201(9)	313(14)	27(1)	25(1)	2,210(7)
8. Farmer	483(5)	1,098(12)	682(7)	1,869(20)	1,946(20)	499(5)	808(9)	1,696(18)	405(4)	9,486(28)
9. Farm Laborer	22(2)	72(7)	56(6)	197(20)	250(26)	78(8)	129(13)	60(6)	98(10)	962(3)
Total	4,350(13)	5,203(15)	4,000(12)	7,174(21)	6,531(19)	1,861(5)	2,180(6)	1,987(6)	625(2)	33,911

*Numbers in parentheses in the body of the table are percentages of the row totals; those in the final row and column are percentages of the grand total.

Source: Adapted from Table J2.1 of P.M. Blau and O.D. Duncan, *The American Occupational Structure.* New York: Wiley, 1967, p. 496.

Table 2.2
INTRAGENERATIONAL SOCIAL MOBILITY FOR MALES AGED 25 TO 64, 1962*

First Occupation	Present Occupation									Total
	1	2	3	4	5	6	7	8	9	
1. Professional	1,990(64)	511(16)	349(11)	122(4)	73(2)	28(1)	2(0)	15(1)	28(1)	3,118(9)
2. Manager/Proprietor	123(13)	414(44)	261(28)	55(6)	37(4)	13(1)	5(1)	11(1)	12(1)	931(3)
3. Sales/Clerical	896(14)	1,577(25)	1,752(28)	813(13)	719(11)	260(4)	175(3)	71(1)	10(0)	6,273(17)
4. Craftsman	315(3)	640(7)	280(3)	1,415(15)	433(4)	123(1)	144(1)	65(1)	17(0)	3,432(9)
5. Operative	631(7)	1,385(14)	959(10)	2,580(27)	2,663(27)	545(6)	643(7)	203(2)	79(1)	9,689(27)
6. Service	125(9)	169(12)	116(8)	244(17)	319(23)	302(21)	126(9)	6(0)	7(1)	1,414(4)
7. Laborer	301(6)	528(11)	433(10)	1,122(23)	1,226(25)	348(7)	740(15)	102(2)	65(1)	4,865(13)
8. Farmer	32(3)	79(7)	76(6)	194(16)	167(14)	58(5)	63(5)	449(38)	63(5)	1,181(3)
9. Farm Laborer	111(2)	493(8)	259(5)	977(19)	1,124(21)	328(6)	452(10)	1,101(21)	398(8)	5,243(15)
Total	4,524(13)	5,706(16)	4,485(12)	6,822(19)	6,761(19)	2,005(6)	2,440(7)	2,023(6)	679(2)	36,146

*Numbers in parentheses in the body of the table are percentages of row totals; those in the final row and column are percentages of the grand total.

Source: Adapted from Table J2.3 of P.M. Blau and O.D. Duncan, *The American Occupational Structure*. New York: Wiley, 1967, p. 498.

and other professionals who produce the improved designs and of the administrators who manage the large firms, there is usually a decline in the demand for skilled labor. Just as in the first stages of industrial capitalism craftsmen were replaced by machines needing skilled operatives, so in the later stages those skilled operatives are being replaced by semi- and unskilled workers, and even by machines. Thus the labor force is becoming more polarized, increasing the differentials between the "haves" and the "have-nots" and diminishing the chances for social mobility of those in the lower strata.

This polarization by skills is exacerbating the underlying conflict in American capitalist society, a conflict that surfaces occasionally in various forms. Some of this conflict is focused on the workplace, as the working class—especially the manual laborers—seek to increase their wages at the expense of the profits accruing to the capitalists and the salaries paid to the middle class. The labor union movement is at the center of much of this conflict.

In addition to the conflict between labor unions and employers in the workplace there is the conflict between the privileged and underprivileged groups in the major areas of consumption. Usually this conflict is contained but occasionally it becomes a major issue within society. In recent decades, the most obvious example of this conflict has been the civil rights movement, which has focused on the prejudice and discrimination against certain minorities, notably the blacks. Much of the protest has been peaceful, yet forceful, but occasionally it has generated violence, as in the race riots of the late 1960s. Occasionally, too, more general protests surface, such as those of the poor that have led to extensions of the social welfare system in recent years. And there is much localized conflict, often born of frustration among the underprivileged and often—because they are readily available targets—directed at others very similar to themselves.

Thus the consensus view of American capitalist society—that social rewards can be earned simply by hard work and dedication, that anyone can go from the farmhouse to the White House or from the slum to the office of chairman of General Motors—is always being challenged, while most people accept their position and the agreed-upon way of moving up. Though consensus and conflict coexist, consensus almost always prevails, backed by a government which ensures that it does, if necessary by "buying off" some of the protest.

The recent changes involved in the transition from industrial to late capitalism have altered some aspects of the conflict. Under industrial capitalism it was relatively easy to identify a separate capitalist class, composed of families who owned the means of production. The majority of firms were owned by a single family; the employer was a clearly known person, and his firm was the major element in the inheritance of his eldest child. Today this is not the case for most businesses. Although there are still many small enterprises, owned and operated by one person, these are a declining percentage of the total, especially in terms of volume of turnover and employment.

In 1939, the United States had 1.8 million separate business enterprises, with total receipts of $172 billion. Of these, 59 percent were owned and operated by individual proprietors, who received 14 percent of the total receipts. There were also 470,000 corporations which earned 77 percent of the receipts. By 1970 the number of individual proprietorships had increased ninefold, to form 78 percent of all firms, but their receipts were only 11 percent of the total; the 1,665,000 corporations obtained 84 percent of the receipts. The major differentiating characteristic of the corporation is the divorce of ownership from management. Ownership is in the hands of the shareholders, of whom there are two types: individuals and institutions (the latter often being the holders of individuals' investments). Consequently, although it is possible to achieve great financial success through individual entrepreneurship, the risks are great compared to investing in corporate stock. Most individual proprietorships (75 percent) had receipts of less than $25,000 in 1974, compared to only 24 percent of corporations. Of the 2 million active corporations then, 2,000 had assets exceeding $250 million; of the $3.3 trillion in total receipts to all enterprises, 81 percent went to 242,000 corporations, which also achieved 69 percent of all profits that year. In addition, the small firms are those that are the most likely to fail: 80 percent of those that failed in 1970 had liabilities of less than $100,000. Thus for those with money to invest, the large corporations are probably the safest repositories, especially for small savers with no real chance of setting up a business on their own.

Corporate expansion under late capitalism has enabled large numbers of people to hold a small stake in the success of businesses. Some do this through direct investment via stocks and shares. Most do it indirectly, perhaps unknowingly, through banks, insurance companies, and pension funds. The net result is that the conflict between capitalist and working class has abated. In its place is conflict between investors and noninvestors, between those with large and those with small investments, and between investors in different types of business. (One byproduct is the increased volume of work for the investment intermediaries.) An increasing proportion of the population has a direct interest in the continued success of American enterprise.

This move into late capitalism and the incorporation of the population into ownership does not mean that inequalities are reduced. If anything, they have been accentuated, since those with large investments are likely to benefit most. But the shift has altered the conflict over access to the higher strata of the occupational structure. With the relative decline of the capitalist class as owners has come the rise of the managerial class, which receives the largest rewards on average. Entry into this must, very largely, be earned on merit, through educational success plus having the right connections. And so families are in conflict over educational resources, which are increasingly perceived as the major means of ensuring success in the competition for the top jobs, most of which are no longer inherited. Thus conflict, and its relationship to the ownership of wealth, is reflected in the operation of the class system in housing markets.

AMERICAN CAPITALISM
AND AMERICAN URBANIZATION

This chapter has presented only a very brief sketch of the salient elements of the development of American economy and society as they relate to the study of urban patterns, processes, problems, and policies. This outline provides the background for the remainder of the book, and is the framework for the discussion of American urbanization that follows.

The basic themes developed in this chapter relate to the nature and historical development of American capitalism. The three stages identified—mercantile, industrial, and late—are the foundations for the development of the urban system, which is the subject of the next part of the book. The class system produced by capitalism is the basis for the residential pattern of American cities—their social geography—which is the major focus of Part Three. And finally, the inequalities and conflicts central to capitalism as it continually restructures itself are fundamental to American urban problems; these are the concerns of Part Four.

SUGGESTIONS FOR FURTHER READING—PART ONE

An historical perspective on the study of urban geography is to be found in:
JOHNSTON, R. J. *Geography and Geographers*. New York: Halsted Press, 1980.

and more detailed discussions of the subdiscipline in:
HERBERT, D. T., and R. J. JOHNSTON. "Geography and the urban environment," in D. T. Herbert and R. J. Johnston (editors), *Geography and the Urban Environment*, Volume 1. New York: Wiley, 1978, pp. 1–34.

and in:
BERRY, B. J. L., and J. D. KASARDA. *Contemporary Urban Ecology*. New York: Macmillan, 1977.

There are many general texts on urban geography, including:
YEATES, M. H., and B. J. GARNER. *The North American City* (third edition). New York: Harper & Row, 1980.
HARTSHORN, T. A. *Interpreting the City*. New York: Wiley, 1980.

NORTHAM, R. M. *Urban Geography* (second edition). New York: Wiley, 1978.

KING, L. J., and R. G. GOLLEDGE. *City, Space and Behavior*. Englewood Cliffs, N.J.: Prentice-Hall, 1978.

PALM, R. I. *Geography of American Cities*. New York: Oxford University Press, 1981.

CARTER, H. *The Study of Urban Geography* (third edition). New York: St. Martin's Press, 1980.

MURPHY, R. *The American City*. New York: McGraw-Hill, 1966.

The more recent, 'radical' approaches are represented by:

CASTELLS, M. *The Urban Question*. London: Edward Arnold, 1976.

JOHNSTON, R. J. *City and Society*, Harmondsworth: Penguin Books, 1980.

For a wider perspective than that of the geographer alone, an early important volume was:

HAUSER, P. M. and L. F. SCHNORE, editors. *The Study of Urbanization*. New York: John Wiley, 1965.

More recent volumes include:

HAWLEY, A. H. and V. P. ROCK, editors. *Metropolitan America*. New York: Halsted Press, 1975.

SWEET, D. C. editor. *Handbook of Contemporary Urban Life*. San Francisco: Jossey-Bass, 1978.

The rank-size distribution of cities is also treated in:

RICHARDSON, H. W. (1974) *The Economics of Urban Size*. Lexington, Mass.: D.C. Heath, 1974.

Systems analysis in geography is covered in:

BENNETT, R. J. and R. J. CHORLEY. *Environmental Systems*. New York: Methuen, 1978.

and all of the terminology of modern geography is defined in:

JOHNSTON, R. J. et al. *A Dictionary of Human Geography*. New York: The Free Press, 1981.

Detailed references for the material covered in Chapter 1 are given later in the book.

The framework for Chapter 2 is provided by the theoretical discussion of urbanization given in:

JOHNSTON, R. J. *City and Society*. Harmondsworth: Penguin Books, 1980.

Most of the information used is drawn from the excellent compilations given in the U.S. Department of Commerce's annual *Statistical Abstract of the United States* and their two-volume *Historical Statistics of the United States* (1976).

General Surveys of the development of capitalism can be found in:

MANDEL, E. *Late Capitalism*. London: New Left Books, 1975.

BARAN, P. and P. M. SWEEZY. *Monopoly Capital*. New York: Monthly Review Press, 1968.

For a social history see:

CARROLL, P. N. and D. W. NOBLE. *The Free and the Unfree*. New York: Penguin Books, 1977.

HARRINGTON, M. *The Other America*. New York: Penguin Books, 1973.

On the state see:

JOHNSTON, R. J. *Political, Electoral and Spatial Systems*. New York: Oxford University Press, 1979.

JOHNSTON, R. J. *Geography and the State*. London: Macmillan, 1982.

BENNETT, R. J. *The Geography of Public Finance*. New York: Methuen, 1981.

3

AMERICAN URBANIZATION
UNDER
MERCANTILE CAPITALISM

MERCANTILE CAPITALISM INVOLVES the accumulation of wealth through the organization of trade. By buying goods at one price in one place and selling them for a higher price somewhere else, entrepreneurs make profits, which are used in two ways. First, profits form the basis for the purchase of goods—both consumable and capital—and services, and the level of profits enables the merchant class to consume much more than other classes (except the landlord class, which developed during the pre-capitalist era, but which, through structural changes in agriculture needed to increase rents, becomes increasingly capitalist oriented). Second, part of the profit—what remains after consumption needs have been met—is reinvested in the search for more profit, in various trade ventures that will make the merchant class even richer. The greater the proportion of profits reinvested, the greater the wealth-creating potential of mercantile capitalism.

Towns are integral to this process of merchant capitalism, for both the expenditure on consumption and the search for trading opportunities. The capital expenditure component of consumption—on housing and business premises, for example—creates urban phenomena, or permanent settlements that house not only the merchant class but those who provide services for them and are paid a portion of the surplus. And as the most efficient way of amassing surpluses, the search for trade is conducted through towns. Some towns play both roles, serving as centers of consumption and trade, and many play only the second. This chapter demonstrates how they developed these functions in the United States.

TRADE AND TOWNS

Mercantile capitalism is characterized by, among other things, many small firms engaged in various aspects of production, exchange, distribution, and consumption. The producers of commodities—a majority of them farmers, the others craftsmen—operate small, independent firms, with at most a few paid employees but perhaps several family members paid room and board rather than money. These independent concerns also comprise many of the consumers of small portions of the produce.

Trade involves the movement of commodities among these individuals and groups. It represents a stage of development beyond a bartering economy. Instead of producers and consumers coming together to bargain their products for those of others, thereby satisfying their demands, merchants buy the commodities from the producers and sell them to the consumers, who usually live some distance away.

The expansion of mercantile capitalism requires long-distance trade, since local consumption of a product can only be expanded so far. Thus transport systems are needed to move commodities from areas of production to areas of consumption, which involves workers both in the actual movement and in the manufacture of transportation media; these craftsmen and service workers must be paid out of the surplus. Furthermore, this long-distance movement takes time, so the merchant must find some means of support during the period between when he pays for the goods and when he sells them; increasingly, this involves financiers who lend money to cover the interim period and who receive an interest payment—another portion of the surplus—for the service.

Mercantile capitalism involves a division of labor, therefore, with a variety of providers of services participating in the transfer of goods from producers to consumers. This division of labor has to be articulated in both time and space, and the urban place provides the focal point. In some systems, both at the bartering stage and in the early development of mercantilism, the urban place was not a settlement, but rather an agreed meeting place where producers and traders gathered on fixed dates. Traders would move in a circuit of these periodic marketplaces, collecting produce and selling other goods (increasingly, these two functions were conducted separately); in North America, the main example of this involved the collection of furs and skins from the trappers who worked in the interior, often a considerable distance from their market point. The central collection points developed as permanent settlements, many into important river or coastal ports.

For a dispersed settlement pattern, the most efficient form of trade for the farmers (as sellers) might be for the merchants to visit them individually and remove the commodities bought. But this procedure would make it difficult for producers to bargain with merchants and to compare prices. In addition, for the merchants this would be an expensive method in terms of time and effort and thus of cost; merchants find it far less demanding if people bring whatever they have to sell to a predetermined place at a set time, thereby bearing the costs of transport themselves. And since it is the merchants who fix the terms of the trade—without them, the goods could not reach the distant markets—it is their wishes that prevail. Similarly, with those selling commodities to the agricultural producers, it would be to the producers' advantage to get personal visits from a "traveling shop"—except that they would find it difficult to compare the price and quality of goods offered by traders calling at different times, and none may call at all when certain commodities are needed. It is to the merchants' general advantage for customers to come to them. Some traveling shops still visit potential customers, particularly in areas of low settlement and density, either directly or indirectly (for example, via mail order), but in general the customer visits the seller and bears the costs of transport.

Trade is a focusing process. Merchants do not necessarily wait until they have a confirmed seller for a farmer's produce before buying from him. Instead, they buy as much as they think they will want, either at his harvest time or, in increasing quantities in recent years, before he sows his crops, and then store the produce until they can sell it. Part of mercantile capitalism, then, involves amassing produce into bulk lots. And at the other end of the process, storekeepers do not wait until a customer expresses a desire for a commodity before they obtain it; to get business, they order a supply of the commodity in advance, so that they can meet a demand when it is made. Thus risks are being taken, because traders are uncertain about future supply, demand, and price.

The town is a spatial ramification of this bulking process. It is the point to which agricultural produce is brought for storage in warehouses—there may be a spatial hierarchy, with small warehouses in small towns serving large warehouses in large towns, and so forth. The goods are then moved to the points of distribution (again, there is likely to be a hierarchy of such warehouses) in large consignments, and consumers come to one shop for the small consignments of the commodities they require for their livelihood. At the town, then, consignments of goods are organized and reorganized. A range of occupations is involved in this process. There are the merchants who buy the produce brought to the town and the storekeepers who sell the commodities taken back to the farms. There are the transport workers who carry the various consignments back and forth, and the craftsmen who maintain and build the transportation media. There are the communications specialists, who transmit information, of relevance and value to traders and others, and the financiers, who provide money for investment in the development of production and services—money that in large part they have borrowed from others or whose value is based on what is lent to them by others. And to provide various services, both for the urban inhabitants and also for rural residents who come to the town to obtain them, there are the service workers: builders, priests, doctors, teachers, and a wide range of others, employed by those with a portion of the surplus to spend on themselves.

Some mercantile capitalism develops in situ. The surplus extracted from an area is reaped by local capitalists, who both invest it in more development there and spend locally on consumption. But much mercantilism is colonialism; the surplus extracted from one area is used for consumption elsewhere and may be invested in still another area, where the projected profits are even greater. Where this colonialism occurs, two types of town develop: centers of consumption, and centers of trade. Few towns have the characteristics of only one type—if they were not at one time centers of trade, most centers of consumption would not have developed—but most are predominantly one or the other, with centers of trade the most common.

This brief introductory outline has shown how mercantile capitalism involves urbanization. The remainder of the chapter looks at the impact of this form of urbanization on the American landscape and illustrates the characteristic structure of the urban patterns produced.

INITIAL URBANIZATION:
THE GATEWAY PORTS

Urbanization in North America to some degree predates the establishment of mercantile capitalism, because the original settlement occurred in a series of colonial ventures. The parent cultures of the colonists were urban, and a first step in the settlement, even before the determination of a staple as the basis of trade, was the proclamation of a town. Such places were necessary for the administration of the new territories by the companies holding the British royal warrant and therefore allowed to engage in trade, as well as for the life style of the inhabitants. Nevertheless, the aim of most of the companies was profit, and the free settlers needed a staple commodity they could trade for European—mainly British—goods, and very soon the typical patterns of mercantile capitalism took over.

Some of the first settlements by European capitalists were concerned with winning local resources, but not with developing them: both fishing and trapping were truly exploitative activities that relied very little on permanent settlements. But most of the colonization was involved with agriculture of some kind, almost invariably the raising of crops, because techniques to preserve and transport animal products—except hides and wool—over long distances were not developed until the late nineteenth century. Agriculture required permanent farm settlements and urban places to serve them. The urban places were the hinges of the continent's development, the links between the American producers and the European consumers. Each settlement was a port, a place where commodities were transferred from one transportation medium to another, and the port was a point of articulation on the hinge.

Initially the coastline was settled through a series of independent ports. Each had its maritime links with its foreland in Europe—the source of the capital to be invested and the manufactured goods to be sold to the settlers, the center of demand for agricultural produce, and the place where profits were repatriated—and its overland links, usually waterborne in the first instance, with an interior hinterland. There were few lateral connections between ports, so that each part of America had more contact with parts of Europe than with other parts of America. Figure 3.1 suggests one possible idealized pattern of development along a coastline.

As colonization proceeded and more settlements were established, more ports were created as gateways to new hinterlands, and the average distance between neighboring ports decreased. Some became more developed than others; they could support a larger population because they handled more trade, having a more prosperous hinterland, either

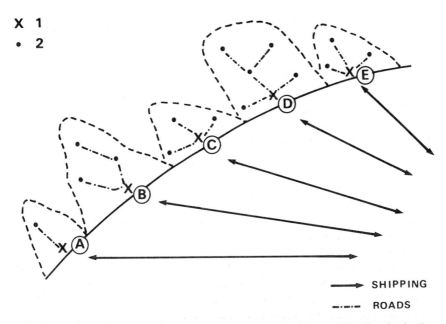

Figure 3.1.   An idealized set of colonial ports marked by an X (at level 1 in the hierarchy), arranged along a coastline with links to the European base but no lateral interconnections. Travel to the interior is by road, linking the ports to small settlements (at level 2 in the hierarchy), marked by dots.

in intensity—the amount of production per square mile—or in extent. Thus at a very early stage towns became differentiated, in terms of size and range of functions. Some became the gateways to several separate colonies: for reasons of economy, some colonies were served from an adjacent port so that, for example, when West Jersey was subdivided into ten subcolonies in 1676, only four ports were established.

Over time, adjacent ports became less independent, and lateral connections developed, largely to the benefit of the merchant capitalists. Since it was inefficient to have separate vessels linking each port with Europe, as few hinterlands produced enough to fill a ship very often, vessels would visit several American ports before collecting sufficient cargo to justify the trans-Atlantic voyage, spending time and effort that was extremely costly to the capitalists. And so a system developed whereby ocean-crossing vessels visited a few ports only, such as Boston and Charleston. The cargoes they were to take back to Europe were brought to those places by coastal vessels, which took back to the minor ports—those without trans-Atlantic connections—the imports from Europe.

Thus there developed a hierarchy of gateways to the North American continent, whose major points of contact were those ports with European connections. High status in this hierarchy was achieved on the basis of one or more factors. Many of the more important ports had environmental advantages, such as excellent deep water harbors and berthage facilities, plus large, fertile hinterlands producing considerable volumes of trades. (The latter were important to the local merchants organizing the coastal trade, since the greater the proportion of a port's trade that was locally generated, the lower the cost of bulking an oceanic cargo.) Others benefited from human endowments. The longest-settled ports had initial advantages in the growth process, and as the larger settlements they were more attractive as places for the merchants and their staffs to live: they were already major centers of consumption, for that portion of the surplus spent locally by the merchants (or by the local managers for overseas merchants) rather than sent back to their sponsors in Europe. Further, many were centers of administration, and were proclaimed overseas ports because they needed regular contacts with the colonial power; they had the resident officers who handled the various methods of taxing imports and exports, and they were defended by the colonial navies.

Thus the first stage of the urban settlement of the North American continent involved the establishment of a series of ports strung along the coast like a string of beads of unequal size. These ports were the gateways to the new continent, and served several functions as links— between American agriculture and European consumers, between European manufacturers and American consumers, and in some cases between African slave sources too, all of these links being organized by the representatives of European merchant capitalists and their associated European governments.

OPENING THE HINTERLANDS

Initial agricultural settlement was usually confined to the coastal fringe and the shores of the many deep estuaries. Inland from several of these were large, potentially fertile tracts of land that beckoned to the pioneer, and once the area was relatively safe from the wrath of the ousted Indians, the agricultural hinterlands were extended. This produced more exports and greater demand for imports, increases that were reflected in the volume of trade passing through the gateway ports.

Extending and servicing the hinterlands required an extensive and increasingly expensive economic infrastructure. The productivity of the new areas had to be sufficient to justify the investments of the merchant capitalists of the colonial companies, and, increasingly important, to encourage American residents to invest their capital in mercantile ventures, whose profits would remain in the colony to be reinvested there (less the portion spent on the conspicuous consumption of imported goods). The movement of commodities frequently required overland routes, along with wagons to effect the transfer, and where water transport was possible, boats were needed, and men to operate them. In both cases, if the new areas were more than a day's travel from the port, intermediate stopping places were needed, complete with inns, blacksmiths, and other relevant services.

As the density of agricultural settlement increased, some of the intermediate stopping places developed other functions. The local population might be sufficient to make a general store a profitable business, with residents making some of their purchases locally instead of at the port. An enterprising individual would open such a business, buying his supplies in the port and transporting them to the settlement in bulk for sale to local customers. In this way, the new settlement became a minor gateway, a subsidiary of the main port. And if production in the hinterland were large enough, the merchants buying from the farmers might also establish an agency in the new settlement, to serve as an intermediate bulking point in the movement of agricultural produce from farm to port. Warehouses would accompany the stores as the foci of local economic life.

Figure 3.2 shows how these new gateways developed. The colony port (D) serves the original hinterland. As the colony extends inland to the west, however, a resting place is needed and a new settlement is established at F. This point eventually becomes an intermediate gateway, linking the extension of the hinterland to the port, and the wagon road joining the two settlements becomes the most heavily traveled in the colony.

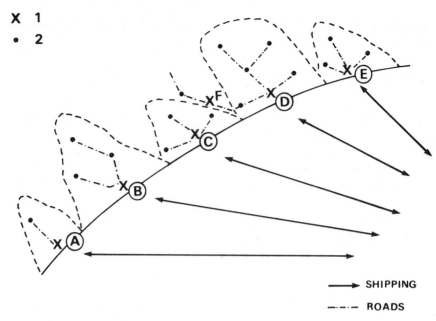

Figure 3.2. The development of an "inland gateway" opening up a new hinterland area between that served by ports C and D in Figure 3.1. Places marked by an X are at level 1 in the hierarchy.

Should the frontier expand away from the original colony in several directions, then a series of these inland gateway centers might develop. Their role is subsidiary to that of the main port. In effect they are inland ports where merchants' agents collect the produce of the hinterland rim; storekeepers serve the local population, and innkeepers and a range of other occupations service the passing transport workers. The frontier may expand at different rates along its length, however, and segments of the new land may vary in their productivity. As a consequence, the inland gateways will vary somewhat in their size, in the same way the main ports do. If the farmers they serve are prosperous, local profits might be invested in further commercial ventures in the area.

SETTLEMENT HIERARCHIES

With the extension of the hinterland, business takes on a more complex hierarchical organization, a step that is reflected in the settlement pattern. The upper level of most businesses is in the colonial homeland; their main offices are in the colony's ports, and agents—some permanent and full time, others part time—are employed in the smaller inland gateways. Local firms are encouraged by the greater volume of business, actual and potential, and entrepreneurs set up trading businesses of various kinds plus service establishments and craft industries in whatever settlements will support their operations.

Expansion of the hinterland is reflected in the main port in a variety of ways. More goods flow through it, in both directions, creating work for local labor; it becomes an attractive place of settlement for immigrants, and its hinterland attracts family settlement. As the population expands, more opportunities for businesses are created. For each type of establishment there is a typical *threshold* of viability. In detailed terms this can be measured as the volume of business needed to make such an establishment viable: below the threshold business is insufficient for the entrepreneur to make a living; above it the returns ensure a comfortable existence and perhaps small sums that can be invested, either directly or indirectly, in further ventures.

As the population and prosperity of a hinterland grow, two processes take place in the commercial sector of its organizing settlement. The first is the duplication of facilities. A settlement of 200 persons may support a single tavern; one of 400 persons should therefore be able to support two, if someone has the capital to invest in establishing a rival tavern. Second, there is the introduction of new types of business. These may be entirely new, in that until the settlement reaches a certain size the goods or services it provides are unavailable to the local residents; they must either go without or patronize establishments in larger centers some distance from their homes. Alternatively, it may be a special service formerly provided as part of a general store or smaller establishment. A settlement of less than 400 persons may be too small to support a gunsmith specialist, for example, and the local general store will be the only source of firearms, obtained from a specialist seller in a larger place (perhaps via his traveling salesmen). Once the population exceeds 400, however, an entrepreneur may be able to establish a gunsmith's store, with enough business to give him a return on his investment. In return he can offer a wider range of goods and better service than the general store operated by a nonspecialist.

These two processes are stimulated by the growth of purchasing power in the settlement and its hinterland, which in most cases is reflected in population growth. In a settled agricultural area, growing prosperity among the farming population may create sufficient demand for certain goods and services to be provided in settlements other than the original one. In almost every case, these new settlements are smaller than those that were founded first. They fill in the gaps in the settlement pattern, providing frequently required goods and services to small hinterlands. Under ideal conditions, they would produce settlement hierarchies like that illustrated in Figure 1.5 (see page 12). Such conditions never exist, of course, but settlement hierarchies can be clearly identified in many agricultural areas, and these hierarchies have been used as such by the rural population; frequently demanded goods are bought at the local center, less frequently demanded goods at a larger center some distance away, and so on.

Some farmers invest in their properties so as to make them more productive and to earn more profits. These investments involve the purchase of commodities—fencing, seeds, livestock, buildings, machinery, and so on—in the urban settlements, and any other monies neither invested in the farm nor spent on personal consumption are likely to be deposited in a bank or similar establishment in the town. (The opening of banks was a significant opportunity for mercantile ventures and involves the attraction of local capital.) Thus much of the local prosperity flows through the town, generating business and earning profits for local merchants and perhaps stimulating expansion there. As such, urban growth becomes to some extent a self-perpetuating process. But in the early settlement of the inland United States no places reached the size necessary to ensure rapid and self-perpetuating growth, in part because of the channeling of the surplus back to the ports and in part because of the low levels of prosperity of most farms. A hierarchy of small settlements did develop in some areas, but the main focus was on the ports and the inland gateways.

Settlement hierarchies developed in each separate colony. The pattern in each was peculiar to its size, shape, and route orientation of transport network, plus, in particular, the density of the population it supported. Figure 3.3 illustrates such a settlement pattern in the southern states in 1790, and it is clear that there was much less hierarchical development in the Deep South. The main difference along the coast at that time was between the wheat- and tobacco-farming areas, with the latter generating much less inland settlement. This came about because wheat is a much bulkier commodity to transport, requiring more careful handling and storage than tobacco. Thus in the hinterland of Chestertown, Maryland, during the 1770s, 1,300 family farms produced about 7.8 million tons of wheat, which required 3,165 wagon trips to convey to the port. If those same farms had produced tobacco, the crop would have weighed about 1.3 million pounds, which could have been moved downriver in flat-bottomed boats to Chestertown in only 108 trips. Clearly, wheat farming offered businessmen—in particular, those with wagons—many more opportunities at inland gateways than did tobacco farming. And at the Chestertown docks, the wheat tonnage required ten times the shipping and probably twenty to thirty times more vessels calling than would the predicted crop of tobacco, again offering greater business opportunities for ship repairers and chandlers and more work for dock labor.

Inland gateway towns were much more common in the more densely populated, productive (in tons per square mile, at least) wheat-farming areas, thereby fostering the growth of the regional port, Baltimore, so that it came to rival Philadelphia, New York, and Boston as a major center on the Atlantic coastal plain. The towns inland from Baltimore contained many inns and blacksmiths, saddlers, and wheelwrights. By contrast, further south the tobacco ports flourished, but there was little demand for settlement facilities in their hinterlands. The plantations there were much more self-contained, and generated little in the way of urban growth.

GENERAL URBAN PATTERNS

The settlements of the coastal hinterlands—the links between the American producers and the European consumers and capitalists—display two characteristic urban patterns that have been identified in many parts of the world. (See Chapter 1.) The first of these is a preeminent *primate city,* or one that dominates all the other settlements in its tributary region, as did Charleston in the southern part of the area of Figure 3.3. The primate city is a dominant colonial form and it appears not only as the port gateway linking a colonial country to its territory but in other situations ("internal colonialism") in which an area's development is being financed by outside capital that repatriates its profits. There will be low-order settlements in many of the hinterlands of the primate cities, but the latter are the foci of transportation, for both maritime and overland connections, and are preeminent in population size and the range of functions provided.

As settlement proceeds, inland gateways will develop, but their growth largely benefits the traders of the primate cities whose preeminence within their hinterlands is unchallenged. The settlement of the American coast—initially that of the Atlantic, but later of the Gulf of Mexico and the Pacific—comprises a series of these primate-city-dominated regions. Initially there were many of them, but the logic of concentrating shipping services at certain places (in terms of traders' profits) and the relative power of the merchants led to a series of coastal hierarchies, with some centers that were initially primate in their own regions becoming subsidiary to another center farther along the coast.

The second characteristic pattern is that of a *hierarchy of central places* in each separate hinterland. Each of these formed the intermediate buying and selling points. The smallest centers, which were more numerous, were the focus of daily and weekly trading for goods and services purchased widely and often by the population. The larger centers, which were fewer and more widely spaced, provided goods and services purchased less frequently for which people were occasionally prepared to travel relatively long distances. They were also intermediate bulking points for the collection of the local agricultural produce, and in some cases for its initial processing, before transport to the ports and shipment overseas.

Figure 3.3. Southern towns and cities having about fifty or more dwellings, around 1790. Source: C. Earle and R. Hoffmann, "Urban Development in the Eighteenth Century South," *Perspectives in American History*, 10 (1976): 10.

ARTICULATION OF THE SYSTEM

So far each primate-city region has been treated as if it were independent of all others, when clearly there were contacts, particularly between neighbors. These links developed between the regions during the mercantile period for two main reasons. First, the separate colonies federated into a single nation at the end of the eighteenth century, and links were forged as part of the unification process and the development of a federal administration. Second, and more important, the development of the United States came increasingly to be financed by American capital, by the profits made by indigenous merchants, financiers, and others who sought greater returns on their investments.

The growth of American investment saw merchant capitalists search beyond the hinterlands of their home towns for the most profitable areas of development. In order for such activity to flourish, information was needed about the alternative opportunities available to the merchants, and about sources of capital for those trying to float new developments. Before the introduction of telecommunications, such information had to be transmitted from person to person, either orally or in writing. The communications systems that developed not surprisingly focused on the main cities, where there were the most money-seeking investment opportunities and where those seeking capital for hinterland development gathered. As communications links grew, and the flow of capital increased, so the whole urban system became articulated into a single entity, based on the major regional centers with the largest initial hinterlands, among which Boston, Philadelphia, Baltimore, and especially New York stood out.

As these major cities grew in their dominance over the colonial and early postcolonial economy two processes were set in motion. First, more and more businesses opened, providing the local mercantile class with money to spend on consumables and to invest in capitalist ventures. So long as profits were made in the hinterlands, this growth process fueled itself, elevating the regional primate centers to even greater importance within the new country's settlement pattern. Second, the local merchant capitalists sought investments in, and extensions of, their city hinterlands, as means of using the profits to generate more. Such expansionist policies needed transport systems and, after a short period of canal building (which was much to New York's advantage, as it allowed relatively cheap movement through the Hudson-Mohawk gap), the railroad became the means of extending the trading area. Railroads were expensive to construct and required large volumes of capital.

In general, it was the financiers in the largest ports who could raise the capital needed for major transport investments and enhance the trading position of their merchants. Figure 3.4 shows this in the idealized coastline of Figures 3.1 and 3.2. Cities B and D have become the largest centers, because they serve the most extensive and prosperous hinterlands. Their merchants have financed railroads that reach not only into their own hinterlands and that of the "inland gateway" center (F) but also into the hinterlands of adjacent centers (A, C, and E). The latter then become subsidiary to the major centers, which dominate the two main regions of the evolving urban system. Of the two, D is now the gateway primate city for the largest region and, given no major differences in land productivity, should grow considerably larger than B. Cities A, C, and E are now the equivalents of inland gateway cities, their earlier independent status having been removed by trade capture from the larger places with the profits to invest in railroads.

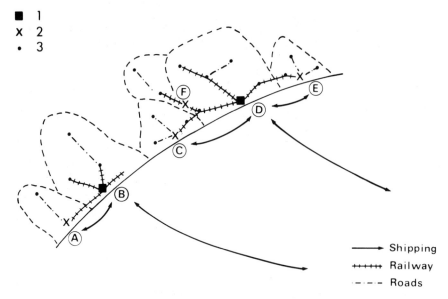

Figure 3.4. The development of an inland rail communications network in the hypothetical area of Figure 3.1, showing centers B and D as dominant, and the development of the three-level hierarchy of central places.

GATEWAYS AND THE FRONTIER

The nineteenth century was the era of the frontier and the opening-up of the interior of the United States. Like the early development of the coastal areas, the basis of frontier development was agricultural and the majority of the population lived in rural areas. Nevertheless, the focus of the development was urban, and the thesis here is that the urban pattern of the continental interior can be understood using the same gateway model as applied to the Atlantic seaboard, as many of the gateway settlements were based on original fort settlements involved in the pacification of the native Indians.

The opening of the American frontier began from a series of urban gateways, transport route foci for large regions that were settled from the new urban centers. The process was similar to the way the coastal plains were settled from the Atlantic ports, differing mainly in scale. The coastal hinterlands were mainly small. Those of the interior were extensive and much more sparsely populated, with lower densities and larger farms. As settlement progressed, new gateway towns were established to serve as subsidiaries to the ports in the original regions, and central place hierarchies developed to articulate local flow patterns and to meet local demands.

What is being suggested, then, is a general process of colonial urban development that applies to both coastal and inland locations. All gateways are ports, serving as hinges between forelands and hinterlands, but not all ports are seaports. There is one difference between the interior gateways and their predecessors on the coast, however; the latter were never independent in the American context. Much of the capital that financed the initial coastal settlement was European; the profits and the produce flowed back across the Atlantic. For the inland centers, on the other hand, the capital came initially from the coastal metropoli, and although much of the produce moved on to Europe, most of the profits remained on the coast, to be reinvested in further development or spent in conspicuous consumption on an increasingly large scale. So, just as the coastal cities were initially intermediate centers of accumulation for the European heartland, so the inland gateways served the same function for the coastal merchants. Eventually, many of the inland cities grew to a large size, rivaling some of the coastal centers, and became major capital-generating cities themselves, but this was after the initial surge of development. (Locally generated capital financed some pioneer inland urban settlements—with the establishment of trading posts, for example—but outside capital was the source for most initial large-scale urbanization.)

TRANSPORT INVESTMENT AND MERCANTILE EXPANSION

The push into the interior was a source of great competition between the coastal mercantile centers, since successful colonization brought with it not only the profits from agricultural produce but also much more trade passing through the coastal ports. The prime need was for an efficient transport network to move the produce eastward. Initially the investment was in canals, to tap the waterways of the Great Lakes and the Ohio and Mississippi river systems. By far the most successful network of canals was developed in New York; its financiers raised the capital to invest in the system that penetrated the Hudson-Mohawk gap, leading first to the Great Lakes and then to the Mississippi River (via Cleveland, Toledo, and Chicago). The initial dominance that New York gained in this way has never been seriously challenged since, though other ports have risen to greater relative status. Later, it was the railroad that forged the lasting link into trans-Appalachia; by 1850, all four main seaboard cities had built lines into the interior, with New York and Boston having the most developed networks, enabling their mercantile entrepreneurs to capitalize on their early investment successes.

Most of the major gateways to the west of the Appalachians—including Cincinnati, Indianapolis, Chicago, and St. Louis—were on the waterway system. Cincinnati, for example, was the gateway for the settlement of the Middle Ohio. Within each of the hinterlands, central place systems developed in the same way as on the coastal plain, except that the areas served were larger and the resulting hierarchies contained some relatively large centers, especially in the densely settled areas. Really large-scale growth of the urban systems only came with the development of the railroads from the 1840s on, however. Entrepreneurs in the various cities competed for local and outside capital to invest in networks that would channel produce through their stores and warehouses and bring prosperity and growth to the new urban foundations. Chicago and St. Louis entrepreneurs fought a protracted battle for the trade of the area west of the Mississippi, for example; Chicago merchants won, on the basis of an extensive railroad system that was the foundation of the city's present position in the national urban structure.

Whereas on the Atlantic seaboard hinterland development and urban and transport growth were largely coincident, inland the towns and the routes preceded agriculture. Without this development, farming to serve outside markets was impossible, except for extensive ranching that often moved its products hundreds of miles on the hoof in search of buyers. The frontier was an urban frontier. The West would not have been won without the business organization of an urban system that provided markets and supplies; without transport systems linking farms with the local gateways, with the eastern ports, and with the European markets; nor, increasingly, without a banking system that redistributed capital nationally and invested in the necessary urban and transport infrastructure. As it is, some economic historians believe that the capital invested in the westward movement, particularly in the railroads, could have been used as profitably to develop agriculture in the already settled areas. The urban pattern of merchant capitalism in the American interior reflects a particular perception of investment possibilities: extending the frontier offered more potential to investors than intensification of land use in the areas already settled.

As the density of agricultural settlement increased in their hinterlands, the primacy of many of the original gateway cities was challenged. The prosperity of the areas was such that some of the subsidiary gateways within the primate regions not only grew to be large central places but also were able to develop separate gateway functions. Independent merchants serving the local agricultural community were able to establish businesses, and local financial communities, based on profits to local capital—often earned from small starts in stores, taverns, and transport services—created an independence from the gateway in many functions. Instead of being local central places, subsidiary to the gateways, these new frontier cities became gatewyas in their own right, with their own transport networks. The original gateway cities remained primate in their local areas, as the centers for the highest-order functions, but the outer parts of their regions were lopped off, captured by local merchants.

The case of St. Louis, discussed in Burghardt's paper on gateway cities, illustrates the relative decline of the larger regional primate city. In 1850 St. Louis was preeminent in the area to the west of the Mississippi. By 1880 Kansas City had developed 250 miles farther west within St. Louis's hinterland and had a population of 17 percent of St. Louis's 350,000; still farther west both Denver and Dallas/Fort Worth were growing as major subregional central places. Twenty years later St. Louis's population had increased to 575,000, but Kansas City's was by then 40 percent of the primate's size. (By 1960 Kansas City had two-thirds of St. Louis's population of 2 million, Dallas/Fort Worth had 80 percent, and Denver nearly half.) Thus while St. Louis has grown rapidly into a major regional city, its dominance (in terms of population size) over its hinterland has declined, as competitors have emerged to the west. In a similar fashion Cincinnati lost virtually all its primacy in the Middle Ohio Valley. Its population in 1850 was 115,000; the closest of any of its six subsidiary gateways was Louisville, with 32,000. By 1960, however, although Cincinnati remained the largest city with just over one million inhabitants, Indianapolis, Dayton, Columbus, and Louisville all had between 600,000 and 700,000.

These two examples suggest that the primacy of a gateway city is a transitory stage in the development of an urban system, and that eventually a pattern more akin to that of central place theory emerges. There are two caveats to this generalization, however. The first concerns the nature of the gateway city's hinterland. The discussion of the Atlantic seaboard showed how different types of agriculture produced different types of settlement pattern, the determining influence being the density of demand for services. The same occurred in the interior, though at a different scale. The hinterlands of St. Louis and Cincinnati were densely settled and subsidiary metropoli could be supported by segments of the initial regions. But in the Upper Midwest the population was much less dense, because agriculture was far more extensive. Too few thresholds were crossed for local cities to threaten the hegemony of the merchants in the primate center of Minneapolis/St. Paul. The population of that metropolitan area now exceeds two million, but not one of its subsidiary gateways approaches even one-tenth that size.

The second caveat concerns the rise of some of the gateway cities to national status, based on the great prosperity of their hinterlands that was capitalized on by their merchants. The obvious example of this is Chicago, which, although it does not rival New York, is clearly second to it as a financial center. This is shown in the development of the American banking system, particularly the pattern of correspondent accounts by which banks in one town had accounts in the banks of another so as to facilitate the flow of capital around the country. The more correspondent links between two places, the more capital that flows between them; the more links a place has in total, the more important it is as a source of capital in the financial system.

The original gateway centers were the main banking centers in 1850, with the greatest volume of money passing through New York and Boston, Philadelphia, New Orleans, and Baltimore, Charleston, and Providence: New York handled about $30 million of business, $10 million more than Boston. Thirty-one years later, New York's financial hegemony was clear; it handled $50 billion, compared to Boston's $4 billion. By 1910 Chicago was in second place, handling $12 billion to New York's $100 billion and Boston's $8 billion. In 1876, 96 percent of all banks in the twenty-four largest cities had correspondent accounts in New York, whereas Chicago's percentage was negligible; five years later, Chicago had accounts with 60 percent of the banks and lacked any link at all with only one large city, Providence. In 1910 New York's links were 83 percent of the possible total and Chicago's were 64 percent, far more than the 16 and 11 percent for Boston and Philadelphia, respectively. A national financial system had emerged with twin, although unequal, foci, below which there was a regional organization focused on former gateways, such as St. Louis, Kansas City, Cincinnati, and New Orleans. The regional primates retained their dominance in this high-level function within the overarching national financial market centered on New York and Chicago, and later on the west coast metropolises, Los Angeles and San Francisco. This national role stimulated much growth, ensuring the predominance of New York and Chicago in their respective local hinterlands.

THE DEVELOPMENT OF A SYSTEM
OF GATEWAY CITIES

The thesis of the preceding section is that the urban pattern of the United States developed as a series of gateway cities, each primate (initially at least) over a region and responsible for the articulation of trade in that part of the national territory. As the volume of trade grew, the profits made by the local merchants and farmers increased—relative to those that were channeled back to the seaboard gateways and to European sources of capital. Some of these profits were spent locally on consumption, and many of the goods consumed had to be imported; some were invested in further development of the regional economy. In both cases this benefited the primate city, stimulating trade there and generating population and economic expansion. The initial advantage of gateway status was translated into the basis for urban growth and mercantile success.

The development of such an urban system is outlined in schematic form in Figure 3.5. Although clearly based on the United States, this outline is meant as a general representation rather than a faithful portrayal of a particular pattern; it is a model only. Thus original settlement was along the eastern and western seaboards, where a series of port primate cities developed, each dominating an independent hinterland (A). Some of these hinterlands were larger than others, reflecting productivity differentials and their capitalization by local merchants in financing the railroads that tapped the resources of the interior. Thus the second center from the northern boundary on the eastern seaboard was serving the largest territory and had grown to the largest size.

At the second stage (B) the frontier of settlement had been extended inland, and was focused on a new series of major urban centers (each marked by an X) that formed the first tier of inland gateways. Of the six that were established, two were connected by railroad, and thus were subsidiary, to the largest center on the eastern seaboard (which by now had also achieved railroad connections to its seaboard neighbors). These two inland gateways served larger hinterlands than any of the other four, benefiting both local growth and the mercantile community of the seaboard port with which they were connected and which financed the development of their hinterlands.

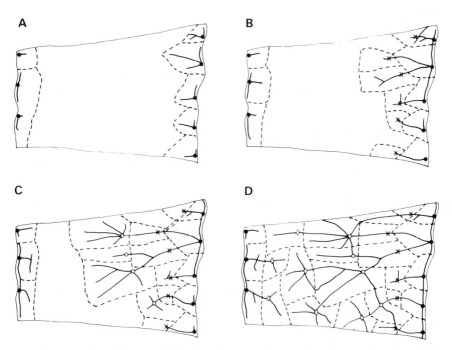

Figure 3.5.   A model of the development of an urban system in an area of continental size settled from its seaboards. The settlements identified are the gateway cities; the routes linking them are railroads; and the dashed lines mark the boundaries of the gateway hinterlands.

Westward extension of the frontier continued in the third stage (C), and railroads were built into the new territory to stimulate agricultural development. A new tier of inland gateways was established, comprising four centers (marked by open circles); three of these were linked to the major eastern seaboard city and contributed to its prosperity (and in part to that of the first-tier inland gateways through which the links passed). A large proportion of the interior territory was part of the hinterland of that port city, which meant that, through the initial advantage of its early development and the ability of its mercantile community to finance railroad construction (needed to stimulate agriculture and the export of its products), it far outstripped its coastal rivals in prosperity and growth. Meanwhile, development on the western seaboard proceeded very slowly.

By the final stage shown on the figure (D) the entire country had been incorporated into the mercantile economy and each port was within the hinterland of a major city. The final tier of inland gateways (marked by a diamond) comprised six settlements; three were linked to the dominant eastern seaboard port, two to the now expanding western centers, and one to the southeastern port. The railroad construction maintained the focus on the major port, and thus continued to channel much of the export trade through its docks. Lateral connections between inland gateways were also being built; a final stage (not shown) would clearly involve linking the eastern and western seaboards.

As stressed at the outset, Figure 3.5 is only a model that identifies the salient elements of a process of settlement. It illustrates the way in which the United States was settled, through the extension of the frontier focused on gateway cities—both seaboard and inland—which were the major centers of an expanding transport network. These gateway cities were the major centers of mercantile activity. The volume of trade and other business conducted there stimulated population growth (which in turn generated even more growth). Thus these gateways were the main centers of population in the mercantile era, a basis for continued prosperity during and after the transformation to industrial capitalism.

FILLING IN THE SETTLEMENT PATTERN

The settlement sequence of Figure 3.5 suggests that during the mercantile era the United States was spatially organized (especially in its interior) as a series of large agricultural regions, each tributary to an inland gateway city. Within each region agricultural development demanded an infrastructure of smaller settlements and transport networks that would articulate the flows of goods and services. Such infrastructures developed as local central place hierarchies.

Figure 3.6 shows the development (taken from Berry's work) of one such central place hierarchy in the area of southwestern Iowa to the east

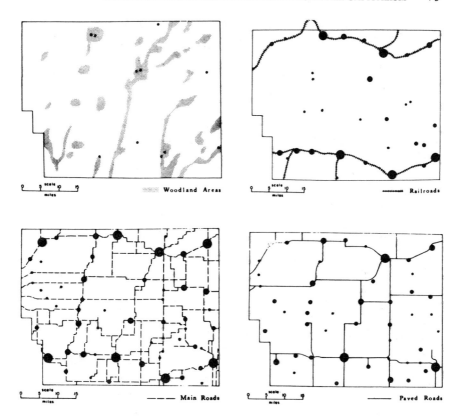

Figure 3.6. The development of the central place pattern in southwestern Iowa, from 1868 to 1956, showing settlements according to their importance in terms of the number of different services provided: patterns are shown for 1868 (top left), 1879 (top right), 1904 (bottom left), and 1956 (bottom right). Source: Brian J. L. Berry, *Geography of Market Centers and Retail Distribution,* © 1967, pp. 6–9. Reprinted by permission of Prentice-Hall, Inc., Englewood Cliffs, N.J.

of Omaha/Council Bluffs, part of the region tributary to the inland gateway of Chicago. The initial settlement (top left) was by a series of small centers, most of them within the woodland area and comprising one or two stores only. Major development only occurred in 1868–1869, when two railroads that met at Council Bluffs were constructed through the area. The stations on these railroads were the collecting points for the farmers' produce that was to be shipped to the markets farther east and were the places that attracted most of the business development to serve the farming community. Centers away from the railroad were ignored by the farmers, and the main growth, as indicated on the map showing settlement size in 1879 (top right), was in settlements with an all-important railroad station.

A network of roads was then constructed through the area to facilitate movements of farm produce to the stations and rural population to the business centers. These movements were focused on those original settlements that had the initial advantage of being on the railroad, so that the relative size of the various central places in 1904 (bottom left) reflects the path of the railroad and the settlement pattern established twenty-five years earlier (top right). Some were more important than others, offering a wider range of services and housing larger populations. Over time, as movement became easier (with the paving of roads, for example, the need for many very small centers declined), people could travel further in the same time and so, for example, many small rural post offices were closed. Thus by 1956 (bottom right) there were fewer centers, with all the larger ones at the main nodes on the paved road network; the two main east-west roads followed the railroad alignment, thus accentuating the local primacy of those settlements with the collecting facilities for farmers' produce at the railroad stations.

The pattern of central places shown in Figure 3.6 is not as regular as the ideal pattern of Figure 1.5, in part because of the linear effect induced by the railroads. But a definite hierarchy of central places is evident, involving a relatively dense pattern of local centers (most with only one or two general stores plus a few other services, such as a filling station), a smaller number of intermediate-sized centers, and a few (three in 1956) large centers offering a wider range of goods and services (including local government; the larger centers won the contests to be the county seats). And this hierarchy was put to such use by the local residents. Figure 3.7 shows the results of a survey conducted in 1934 of farmers' families (in an area larger than, but including that of Figure 3.6) who were asked where they normally went for certain goods and services. (In Figure 3.7, the large urban settlement in the Far West is Omaha/Council Bluffs; the size of the symbols for the other centers is proportional to the number of services available there.) Thus most went to the nearest church (top left) and grocery store (top right), each of which was probably in a nearby small settlement; to visit a lawyer they again tended to use the nearest ones available, most of whom were in the intermediate-sized centers (bottom left); and for women's clothing the majority made their purchases in the largest centers (bottom right), especially Omaha/Council Bluffs, which presumably offered the greatest choice.

Each primate city region within the United States was articulated through a central place system such as that illustrated in Figures 3.6 and 3.7. It was to these small centers that farmers brought their produce, in some cases for sale to a merchant or at auction, in others for direct shipment to an agreed purchaser. Here they also bought their machinery, seeds, and other capital requirements, deposited their profits, raised their loans, transacted other business, obtained local government serv-

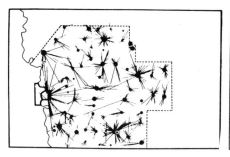 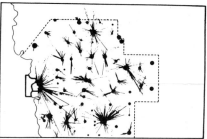

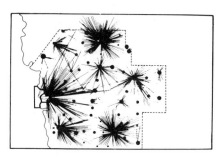 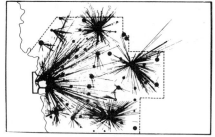

Figure 3.7.   Habitual consumer behavior of farmers' families in southwestern Iowa, 1934, showing the settlements usually visited for church services (top left), grocery shopping (top right), legal services (bottom left), and women's clothing (bottom right). Source: Brian J. L. Berry, *Geography of Market Centers and Retail Distribution,* ©1967, pp. 10–12. Reprinted by permission of Prentice-Hall, Inc., Englewood Cliffs, N.J.

ices, bought the foodstuffs not produced on the farms, and purchased the ever-expanding range of consumer goods they were convinced they needed and could afford. The nearest local center may have provided all the establishments essential to the commercial aspects of the farmer's life. Unless the center was relatively large, however, this prospect was unlikely, and he would have to visit a more distant center for certain transactions. Again, he was likely to choose the nearest.

The distance that a farmer and his family had to travel was dependent on the density of settlements; the closer together the central places, the shorter the average journey. The density of the central place system in turn reflected the nature of the farming system—in particular, the size and the prosperity of each farm. Thus in the 1950s on the rangelands of South Dakota an area of 100 square miles might contain less than 1,000 persons, whereas in the wheatlands farther south such an area may contain 1,000 to 2,000 persons and in the Corn Belt as many as 4,000 to 5,000. Clearly, the more people in an area, the greater the potential volume of business and the more establishments in the local central place. Thus relative to the residents of the Corn Belt, the farmers and their families in the rangelands were served by a lower density of small central places, had access to fewer local establishments, and had to make a longer average journey for any type of shopping. (Note that in suburban Chicago, an area of 100 square miles contained on average about 100,000 people, whereas in the city itself the number was even larger.) So each area had its central place hierarchy, but the details of the composition of the hierarchy varied from area to area according to the density of settlement (perhaps 10 persons per square mile on the rangelands, for example, and 100 per square mile in the Corn Belt).

The gateway thus links an inland frontier zone with a metropolis, located either closer to or at the seaboard. Within the frontier zone a central place hierarchy develops. In some cases, the settlements in this hierarchy are all smaller than the gateway center, which retains its position as a primate center dominating its tributary area. In other cases, the largest centers in the hierarchy grow to considerable size, becoming dominant in their own segment of the area, providing all the goods and services needed by the local populace and reducing substantially, if not removing entirely, their dependence on the original primate center. And of course there are intermediate cases in which the initial primacy of the gateway city is substantially diminished but it retains its major status. Two characteristics of the hinterland appear to influence which pattern develops: its areal extent and the density of the rural population. The more dense the population, the greater the purchasing power in any one portion of the hinterland, and thus the greater the potential for local centers to develop a wide range of service establishments. The larger the hinterland, the greater the distance many of the people are from the primate city, and the greater the potential for large central places to develop at some distance from the original dominant. Thus within the United States, the farther west that settlement spread, the more likely the gateway city was to retain its primacy.

MERCANTILISM, GATEWAYS, AND HIERARCHIES: A SYNTHESIS

Chapter 1 noted that urban geographers have identified three typical urban-size distributions: the law of the primate city, a hierarchy of central places, and the rank-size rule. Figure 1.3 showed that the last of these has provided a close fit to the American city-size distribution throughout the country's history. And yet the present chapter has used the other two models—the law of the primate city and the central place hierarchy—to describe the process of settlement evolution under mercantilism. The paradox is more apparent than real, however.

The thesis developed in this chapter is that mercantile capitalism's spatial components are founded on primate cities. These form the organizing nodes for the exploitation of a newly settled area; the economic and social system requires dominant gateway centers. With each of the hinterlands served by these gateways, a hierarchy of central places evolves to articulate the flows of goods, services, and money at the local level. As indicated in the previous section, in some areas this development of a central place pattern reduces the relative size and importance of the gateway city. Thus in some regions a primate distribution of city sizes emerges; in others there is something akin to a central place hierarchy that may fit the rank-size model fairly closely; this comes about because the variability in the productivity of parts of the region may cause centers at the same hierarchical level to have slightly different sizes. (In a densely populated area, for example, intermediate-level centers would be larger than comparable centers in thinly populated areas.)

The settlement of the United States has involved a mixture of these two types of regions. The eastern seaboard was dominated by a set of port gateway cities, each of which was a primate center, initially for a small coastal region and later for a series of inland regions as well. The immediate trans-Appalachian area was also initially organized around a set of gateway primate cities, themselves linked to the ports. But the density of settlement there meant that this primacy was gradually reduced. Farther west, however, the primacy of the inland gateways was not challenged, and places like Chicago and Minneapolis/St. Paul have retained their regional dominance; the same has been true for San Francisco, Seattle, and Los Angeles on the west coast.

The national settlement pattern is a composite of these separate, though not independent, regional urban systems. Some of the regions have large primate gateways and small central places; some have small primate gateways and small central places; some have large primate gateways and large central places; and so on. In aggregate they approximate the rank-size rule.

The United States is unique in several respects with regard to the development of its urban-size distribution, but the processes that have produced the distribution are general. Much of the world, certainly nearly all of it outside Western Europe, has been settled in a similar way, via primate gateway cities, most of which are ports. Some serve only small national hinterlands—such as Montevideo in Uruguay—and have retained their dominance over an array of small central places in the interior. Some serve large hinterlands, but these are so thinly peopled that large central places do not develop; this is the case among the mainland state capitals in Australia, where each of the states was a separate colony prior to federation in 1901. Only in Asiatic Russia has the spread of urban settlement (eastward) resulted in a series of primate-dominated regions similar to that in the United States; only in India does a series of coastal primate gateways serve densely populated hinterlands. Thus apart from the trans-Appalachian area, where the primacy of gateways such as Cincinnati has been largely removed, the settlement of the United States has been similar to that in many other parts of the world. The only major difference is that in the United States more separate regions are amalgamated into a single country and a wider range of environmental conditions influences the nature of the settlement pattern within those regions.

Two features dominate the urban pattern of mercantile capitalism, therefore: primate gateways and central place hierarchies; the two play complementary roles in the articulation of international, interregional, and intraregional trade. They also provide the settlement framework within which industrial capitalism has evolved.

4

INDUSTRIAL CAPITALISM

AND THE

URBAN SYSTEM

UNDER MERCANTILE CAPITALISM, wealth originates in the rural areas, whereas its expenditure takes place in the urban settlements. To a considerable extent, then, the towns are parasitic on their hinterlands, although it is also the case that rural wealth would not be increased—even realized—in the latter areas were it not for the urban markets. Without an urban system, the American frontier would not have developed. Thus mercantile capitalism produced an urban-rural symbiosis, but that probably was less beneficial to the countryside than to the towns, because it was in the towns that the merchants and the capitalist investors (other than farmers) lived. With the shift to industrial capitalism, the town becomes much more independent, although still ultimately reliant on the food supplies produced in the country.

Mercantile capitalism is based on the buying and selling of the products of labor. Industrial capitalism involves direct investment in labor by the capitalist, who is an employer of contracted workers rather than a bargainer with independent producers. There are employees under mercantile capitalism, of course—on the farms, in the warehouses, and in the craftsmens' workshops—but they are few in any one workplace. The situation is changed under industrial capitalism, which creates a system that depends on large numbers of employees performing routine tasks in factories.

The growth of industrial capitalism in the United States was stimulated by several factors. One was the drive to increase agricultural productivity, so as to meet the demand for foodstuffs and other raw materials at home and abroad. Despite the high rate of immigration, farm labor was in short supply, and it was necessary to increase the productivity of the existing workforce by providing better tools. Their manufacture required large-scale production from factories rather than the limited activities of craftsmen, whose labor was also in short supply; this led eventually to the establishment of large factories for the manufacture of agricultural implements; such as the McCormick plant that opened in Chicago in the 1840s.

Independence from Britain was another major stimulus. During the colonial period manufacture from American raw materials was legally prohibited, except for some processing and the production of a few goods that could not be imported; for all but a few basic commodities America was legally dependent on European suppliers, though the law was not observed completely. Once the colonial link was broken, processing of and manufacture from local raw materials was an obvious avenue for the investment of local capital, producing goods destined for the expanding local market and also for export. As mercantile capitalism expanded on an indigenous base, greater prosperity (fewer profits were being remitted overseas) led to a larger, more viable local market to be exploited by local entrepreneurs, and more mercantile profits that could be reinvested in manufacturing.

Industrial capitalism necessarily produces urbanization since it is based on the concentration of productive activity, which occurs in factories. Factories are the descendants of the craft workshops of the mercantile settlements; the factory labor force lives in housing away from the rural areas. The towns of mercantile capitalism are closely linked with the countryside, therefore, whereas those of industrial capitalism exist separately. In addition, the town continues to serve as the center for the consumption of the profits of capitalist investment; thus, whereas under mercantile capitalism the town has two main functions—consumption and the articulation of trade—under the industrial mode there is a third, factory production, which is related to the other two.

INDUSTRIAL LOCATION
AND URBAN SYSTEMS

Industrial capitalism developed out of mercantile capitalism; trade provided the capital to be invested in labor. Thus the spatial manifestations of industrial capitalism were built on the settlement pattern of its predecessor: a new urban system was not created; the existing one was the foundation for the new. To study how the urban system was modified by the introduction of industrialization it is necessary to look at the main influences on the location of industry.

Industries are established to make profits for capitalists through the manufacture of salable commodities. A factory could be located virtually anywhere, within the constraints of the physical environment, but most potential locations are never considered since they would not be very effective places at which to carry out manufacturing. Industry must be efficient, which involves making the commodity cheaply, at least relative to its price. The raw materials must be assembled, the labor force and the source of power put to work on them, and the finished products supplied to consumers at the least cost possible, given an accepted product standard. With a fixed price being paid for the product, the cheaper the production process the more profit that is made. Thus industries are not restricted to the cheapest location, but as they approach that position, their profitability rises.

This analysis assumes that the price cannot be affected by the producer. For the early stages of industrial capitalism this was a reasonable assumption, because there was a large number of sellers. The only exceptions were in industries located in relatively isolated towns and with no competitors, because of the costs of "importing" products made elsewhere; such spatial monopolies were quickly destroyed by the rapid development, and the decline in relative costs, of transportation media. But the premise is not the same for late capitalism, as discussed in Chapter 5. Under that later mode of production a wider range of locations is potentially profitable.

Efficiency in production is achieved by choosing locations for factories that keep the costs of making the commodity down. According to traditional geographical theory, this involves minimizing the costs of moving the various materials and products. A factory is at its least-cost location when the total bill for the movement of raw materials and other inputs to the factory, the movement of the product to the market and the costs of labor, power, and capital is the lowest possible.

Location with respect to raw material sources is crucial to the success of many factories because of the nature of those materials. In heavy industries, such as the manufacture of iron and steel, the raw materials are extremely bulky and expensive to move. A considerable proportion of the bulk may be lost in the initial stages of manufacture, so that the finished product is much less expensive to move, because it is smaller. Thus it is extremely wasteful of effort and cost to move large volumes of iron ore many miles to a furnace when the process of smelting reduces its bulk so much. It is sensible in least-cost terms, and hence from the standpoint of profitability, to locate the furnace on the iron-ore field. For heavy industries that require inputs in great bulk, therefore, location at or close to the source of the raw materials is highly desirable.

Many industries require more than one raw material, of course; iron furnaces need coal and limestone as well as iron ore. If all of these are found in the same general locale, then the site for the industry is clear. Usually they are not, however, and the least bulky has to be moved to the others or, in some cases, all the materials have to be moved to some central point for manufacture. The movement of materials in bulk is almost always cheaper by water than overland (that is, by road or rail), because the unit size of ships is much larger and the transport costs per ton consequently lower. As a result, ports are often the sensible locations for heavy industries when some movement of raw materials is necessary.

Changes in technology loosen the constraints of location relative to raw material sources; less coal is needed now to produce a ton of steel than was the case a century ago, for example, and the relative advantages of waterborne transport are not great. At certain stages of technical development, however, some materials were virtually immovable and had to be consumed where they were produced. Power obtained from falling water was immobile. Without an efficient means of storing and transmitting that power, industries using it had to be located at the point of production. Coal could be moved before being burned to produce power, but this was expensive and many industries using much coal power were virtually tied to the coalfields. Until a means was developed for moving electricity, therefore, many industries had to be located near a power source, and the urban development at such a location often constrained later development, as is discussed below.

The market and raw materials are opposing forces influencing the location of industry; the closer a factory is to the consumers of its products, the lower the cost of moving the commodities to them. The importance of market forces varies according to the characteristics of the commodities. Some finished goods are bulkier than the raw materials from which they are made, and so in terms of efficiency it is sensible to pay transport costs on the materials rather than on the products. Others are perishable once produced, and must therefore be moved to the customer quickly; the greater the distance between factory and consumer, the less feasible, and hence the less profitable, this becomes. (Perishability here refers not only to goods that decay physically, such as foodstuffs, but also those that require almost immediate consumption, such as newspapers.) Still other goods must be produced near the consumer, since their purpose is to meet specific consumer desires; jobbing printers and custom tailors are examples of this type of activity. Just as raw materials impose constraints on location, changes in technology, particularly the relative decline in transport costs, have reduced somewhat the importance of location close to the market, but again the initial development often imposes a major constraint on later location decisions.

ECONOMIES OF SCALE

Being close to the market has two general types of advantages to manufacturing industries, advantages generally known as economies of scale. The first type is the *internal economies of scale*, which are largely a function of factory size. The larger a production unit, the more efficient it can be, for two main reasons. First, its labor force can be used more effectively. In very small concerns, there may be insufficient work of a particular type to employ a person full-time, and so he must perform several tasks. The more goods that are produced, the greater the degree of specialization, and since specialization usually requires training, if an employee can work full time at his particular expertise he can probably produce more per day than if portions of his time have to be spent at a variety of tasks. Second, most manufacture involves the use of equipment. If equipment is being used full time, then its cost is being met rapidly by the returns on its production; if it lies idle for periods, it takes longer to recoup its costs and its use is relatively inefficient. Thus large factories involved in large-scale production can use their equipment more intensively and their workforce more efficiently than their smaller counterparts can, and earn larger profits for the industrial capitalists. To operate such a large factory requires a large market for its product, however, and so factories close to major concentrations of population are the most profitable, all other things being equal.

External economies of scale are the second type of advantage of proximity to the market. Very few factories take a single raw material, process it, and produce a commodity that is ready for consumption by the general population. Most require a range of inputs, many of which are not raw materials in the sense of having been taken from the environment. The majority of inputs that factories use are partially processed materials that have already been through one or more other factories, and it is with other production units that most of the backward or input links operate. Similarly, as a logical sequence of this, most factory products go on to other factories for further processing before they reach the final consumer. There is a long line of linkages, therefore, from the initial processing of raw materials to the fabrication of a finished good for general consumption, and the length of this chain is increasing as technology advances and the products of industry become more complex and sophisticated. And it is not only the flow of goods among factories that is multifaceted. Most plants contain a range of machinery that is manufactured elsewhere, and most manufacturing companies depend on a range of other businesses for legal, financial, equipment repair, insurance, trading, and other services. Very large companies can provide some of these services for themselves and maybe even manufacture some of their own machinery, but because of the lack of the necessary internal economies of scale, most find it cheaper to rely on other firms, which service a number of factories. If those factories involved in the same type of activity are in the same area, all the links become that much more convenient, so a large market for the products of one type of factory can lead to a concentration of related plants; the result is a particular type of industrial complex.

All these interfirm links are most efficiently articulated when the various companies involved are close together, making the costs of movement between them low. Since to a considerable extent firms are each other's markets, large agglomerations are the most efficient locales for manufacturing enterprises (which is why external economies of scale are often known as either agglomeration or urbanization economies). A large consumer market which purchases the final products of certain factories is likely to be conducive to the development of such an agglomeration of linked firms; it is also likely to generate the capital needed for further rounds of industrial investment.

So far this discussion of the location of industry has focused on the influence of the flows of materials on the siting of factories. Materials are only one of the factors involved in production, however, and the others—labor and capital—also influence location. (Economists often refer to materials as the land input, completing the triad of factors of production—land, labor, and capital.) Clearly, access to a labor force is vital to an industrialist. This often involves not just a pool of workers available for hire but a specific level of certain skills. If the available labor force is not prepared for a particular form of work it will have to be trained, which can be expensive to the industrialist, and every time a worker leaves a replacement will have to be trained. Thus a pool of skilled labor is often desirable, and this is another agglomeration economy. A place where a certain type of work is already performed is more likely to offer skilled workers for either a growing or a new factory than one with no tradition of a particular activity.

Labor is a cost of production, and this cost may vary from place to place. The greater the demand for a given group of workers, the higher the wages it can ask; where there is a pool of unemployed labor, so that supply exceeds demand, wages are usually relatively low. If spatial variations in other costs are negligible, therefore, the industrialist may be faced with a choice between a high labor cost location, where the potential workforce is skilled, and lower-cost locations where employees will have to be trained. The importance of the training might then be a crucial factor in the factory location decision.

Finally, what of the locational pull of capital? Of the three factors of production, capital should be least important in determining location since it is the most mobile, as its transfer involves only an accounting procedure. But many investors prefer to put their money where they are sure it is safe, and for them this may be in their home town or its surrounding area. Investment at a distance involves risks, or is perceived to, because of uncertainties about environments and likely returns. When industrialists generate their own capital out of profits capital is a negligible influence on their location decisions; when they depend on borrowing capital from others, this is made easier if the factories are close to the investors' scrutiny. Again, availability of investment capital can be an agglomeration economy.

Manufacturing industry requires an infrastructure, a major component of which is a transport system. Much of the growth of industrial capitalism occurred when the railroad was the main transportation medium, and so the location of lines had a strong influence on the location of industry. Railroads were built by private capital, either encouraged or subsidized by the state (as illustrated in Chapter 2), and their function was to make profits for investors; the more profitable routes were likely to be those carrying the most trade, which in turn were likely to be those linking the main centers of production and consumption. During the mercantile period, railroads opened up production potentials; in the industrial period they consolidated the existing pattern, so that although many routes were constructed to pioneer new traffic, most investment took place where good returns were likely. In this way, a transport infrastructure was frequently yet another part of the agglomeration economies, and its development was encouraged by those seeking to boost local expansion; for example, the Chicago City Council assisted in the building of the Illinois Central via the provision of a lakeshore breakwater.

THE IMPORTANCE OF
LEAST-COST LOCATION

The argument presented thus far in the chapter is based on the assumption that transport costs are a major component of the total cost structure of manufacturing firms, which will therefore locate their factories so as to minimize those costs and maximize profits. This is undoubtedly a less valid assumption now than it was even a few decades ago, for the relative costs of transport have fallen considerably. (The costs of fuel have declined in relative terms, at least up until the last few years. More efficient transport technology creates economies of scale in bulk movements, and technological advances in industries mean less dependence on bulky raw materials.) As a result, many firms are now faced with a wide range of possible locations for their plants, particularly those plants whose raw material demands are neither great nor bulky. Heavy industries are still very much restricted to locations either at points where the needed resources are supplied (though electrical power can now be transported efficiently over long distances) or at ports where various resources are brought together cheaply. But these heavy industries have declined in their relative importance; an increasing proportion of industries are involved either in processing small volumes of inputs or in assembling final products from the output of other industries, and for these industries agglomeration economies are the important locational influences. For some, there are few, if any, locational influences of any importance with regard to land, labor, and capital; these are often known as footloose industries, whose location is influenced mainly by the owners' desires.

A further assumption about least-cost locations is that the individual producers have little control over the price of their product when it is sold, so that if they occupy inefficient locations they are very likely to be forced out of business. Although not completely true, this position reasonably approximates the situation under industrial capitalism, in which many small producers compete in the market, but not under the later stage of late capitalism. If firms are competing in a market, then those that incur the lowest transport costs in getting products to consumers should prosper. The inefficient will suffer, so that in the long run those firms that choose the least-cost locations, or nearly so, are likely to survive. Hence, since decision making with regard to location may be imperfect, as many manufacturers choose relatively inefficient locations for their factories, the pattern that eventually emerges should reflect the optimal pattern of locations, though it will almost certainly not be the optimum. (Of course, as technological conditions change and the distribution of population is altered, the optimum changes too.)

Since establishing a factory is a considerable investment, once it is installed at a location a firm is unlikely to move until that investment has been paid off, although competition may drive it out of business if a very bad decision has been made. Many firms can survive bad decisions, however, because they have the initial advantage over any competitor who may come in at a later stage in a move to a "better" location. An area may be able to support only one factory of a particular type, for example. The first established will then capture the market. It may not occupy the most efficient location in terms of transport costs, but it will have obtained a labor force, generated some urban growth, and earned the good will of customers. Another location might be slightly better, but it would be a risky investment to build a factory there and compete with the firm with the initial advantage. A somewhat imperfect location decision may remain on the horizon, therefore, since other capitalists will not wish to challenge it; other potential investments are less risky. In this way, the location of industry is part of the structuring of the economic geography of an area, and is not totally subservient to it.

INDUSTRIAL LOCATION
WITHIN THE URBAN SYSTEM

Factories are urban phenomena, because of their labor requirements and their need for accessibility to large markets for agglomeration economies. Industrial capitalism followed mercantile capitalism, however, so that there was already an urban system in existence when factory production began. Where, then, have factories been located within the American urban system?

It is suggested here that industry has had two impacts on the urban system. The first process accepts the given urban pattern and builds on it, producing urban industrialization on a mercantile base. The second brings about changes in the urban pattern, producing new settlements specifically for industrial purposes. The first process does not disturb the pattern that emerged under the previous capitalist system; the latter, which is discussed first, can produce considerable variations in the relative prosperity of settlements.

NEW INDUSTRIAL TOWNS

As stressed already, new industrial towns are likely to emerge where there are concentrations of particular natural resources. Winning of these resources may lead to the initial development of the settlement; their processing will extend its economic base.

Four types of new industrial settlement can be identified. The first type consists of *mining towns.* The most common of these, in terms of permanent settlements in the United States, have been those based on coal, such as many in the Appalachians. A lot of them are single-function settlements, with only the mines plus a few retail establishments and other businesses providing employment. Such places rarely grow to any great size. Their long-term prosperity depends on the supply of and the demand for the commodity mined there. Many mining communities, particularly those based on rare metals such as gold, have declined as rapidly as they have grown because of a limited supply of the resource. But coal-mining towns generally are stable for at least several decades; only since the 1930s have large numbers of communities in the Appalachians and elsewhere declined due to both falling demand and the exhaustion of viable seams. Today there are several boom towns based on mines in the western states, especially Colorado and Wyoming.

Mining towns that have attracted no other industries rarely grow to large relative size within an urban system. *Heavy manufacturing towns* that developed on a mining foundation, at the settlement or nearby, frequently do. Several places in interior New York and Pennsylvania exemplify this, none more so than Pittsburgh. Immense quantities of high-quality coal, fairly close to the surface and very easily mined, plus locally available iron ores, led to massive investments in a local iron and steel industry, which is now supplied with iron ore via the waterway system of the Great Lakes plus a canal from Cleveland, itself a major steel center. Today Pittsburgh has a population of more than 2.5 million people, many of whom work in the industries that generated the city's growth. Nevertheless, only one-third of Pittsburgh's employees in 1970 were working in manufacturing industries, compared to 43 percent two decades earlier.

The third type of industrial settlement is the *water-power-based manufacturing towns* located along the Fall Line of the eastern flank of the Appalachians and the associated mountains of New England. These were among the first of America's industrial towns; they have specialized mainly in the production of cotton and woollen cloth and the commodities manufactured from it. The wool was locally produced, whereas the cotton was imported from the southern states. Manufacturers made use of the available power supply and the humid climate that was necessary for spinning at the current state of technology.

The first cotton mills were established in the ports of Baltimore, Maryland, and Providence, Rhode Island; they were small and added little to the size of the towns. The first large mill, with a permanent labor force, was built at Waltham, Massachusetts, nine miles west of Boston, where the owners found it necessary to open a boarding house for their workers. Waltham was an established town, however. The first specifically industrial settlement in the country was at Lowell, located on the Merrimack River near the boundary of Maine and New Hampshire. The first mill was established there in 1826 to make use of the excellent source of water power; by 1839 there were nine more, and in 1845 there were thirty-three. By 1845 the population of Lowell had reached 30,000 persons, 9,000 of whom (two-thirds of them women) were employed in the cotton mills. Many of the workers lived in boardinghouses built by their employers, as did workers in the other New England textile towns, such as Manchester, New Hampshire, and Lawrence, Maine. Such industrial cities did not grow very large, but with 33,000 residents in 1850 Lowell was the twenty-third largest town in the country (larger than Chicago, Detroit, and San Francisco), so the establishment of it and its neighbors clearly influenced the form of the contemporary American urban system. Today it ranks 152nd.

The fourth type of new town includes the *transport centers,* which were established where necessary on the new modes. Canal ports and railway junctions were perhaps the best examples of settlements whose sole initial *raison d'etre* was to serve the movement of industrial commodities. Many remained small servicing centers only. A few, occupying central positions in the new transport networks, were chosen as suitable locations for industrial enterprises, which resulted in later, self-perpetuating growth (for example, Chicago): centrality on transport networks and industrial growth were closely interrelated. This link between mercantile and industrial urbanization is somewhat artificial, however, though it should be remembered that these two processes overlapped considerably; mercantile urbanization in the West proceeded into the twentieth century, while industrial urbanization began in the East in the first half of the nineteenth century.

The industries that either initiate urban settlement or generate growth in an existing settlement (see below) are often termed *basic industries*. The term "basic" implies that they are the prime sources of income for the settlement, in that most of their production is sold outside and brings money in. This is used to pay the bills—for materials (some of which may have been imported, so the money is immediately exported again: note that imports and exports here refer to trade between settlements and *not* necessarily between countries), labor, machinery ("dead labor"), and so on, and as returns on investment (profits). Some of this money—notably, that paid to the labor force but perhaps also some of that going for materials and machinery—is spent at other establishments in the settlement. These industries are dependent solely on local trade, and do not export. They are therefore termed *nonbasic*; if the basic industries did not exist, there would be no local income to support the nonbasic establishments. Of course, many establishments cannot be associated entirely with one of the two categories; they provide both for the local market and for export, so each has its own basic/nonbasic ratio.

INDUSTRIAL URBANIZATION ON A MERCANTILE BASE

These new industrial settlements added to the variety of the American urban pattern, but few of them (Pittsburgh is one of the exceptions) rose to any prominence within it. The general pattern of urbanization in the period of industrial capitalism was to continue the system developed under mercantile capitalism, with, if anything, the role of the largest cities accentuated during that epoch. There were three types of industry in the large gateway ports prior to large-scale industrialization: (1) entrepôt manufacturing, which processed imported materials, such as sugar, and then exported them to final destinations; (2) commerce-oriented manufacturing, such as ship building and repair; and (3) market-oriented industries catering to local (including hinterland) households, construction companies, and governments. According to Pred, in 1832, 201 of Boston's 994 manufacturing establishments were involved in entrepôt industries (they employed 21 percent of the workforce), 232 (employing 30 percent) were in commerce-oriented manufacturing and 561 served the local market. To a large extent, industrial preeminence occurred there because of the attraction of the large cities for those investing in market-oriented industries—those involved both in processing already treated materials and in assembling commodities for final consumption. (Merchants were for a long time chary of investing in industry rather than in trade or real estate.) Two growth processes were involved in this: import replacement/export diversification based on local linkages, and the urban multiplier.

LINKAGES AND GROWTH

The impact of *local linkages* on growth can be illustrated by the simple, hypothetical example of a town that acts as the regional center for an area of the Corn Belt in the Midwest, and in which three meat-packing plants have been established. These factories "import" (from outside the town) both their raw material—the cattle—and the equipment they use—cutting tools; their product, meat, is exported. As the hinterland develops, a larger volume of meat is packed at the plants, whose expansion creates a greater demand for knives. To meet this demand, capital is invested in a local knife factory, whose production replaces imports. Further factories are also established to use the by-products of the meat-packing industry—the hides—and thus the export functions of the town are diversified by the addition of the sale of shoes and other leathergoods to other places in the urban system.

As development continues, more and more meat is packed in the town. Additional meat-packing plants are established and more knife and shoe factories. Further import replacement takes place when a firm manufacturing the tinplate for the cans is established in the town, and this in turn attracts other canning plants, to use the products of the local plants and to benefit from the pool of skilled labor. Eventually, consumption in the town's industries may expand so much that an iron and steel plant is established at its port. Meanwhile, the expertise developed by the local manufacturers means that knives are produced not only for local use but also for "export" to other towns. New industries may also be spawned; for example, the manufacture of knives and cutting implements for other purposes, including domestic ones.

Many mercantile towns in the United States developed what are known as export complexes in this way. Undoubtedly the prime example is Chicago, whose industrial development was based on meat packing and the manufacture of agricultural equipment for the farmers in its hinterland, plus the backward and forward linkages related to these activities. The large stockyards, covering 320 acres, were opened in 1865 at a site four miles southwest of the city center. They attracted industries covering such a wide range of associated products that a cow going into the yards came out not only as meat but also as glue, gelatin, fertilizer, celluloid, jewelry, cushions, hair restorer, washing soda, soap, and bedsprings. To serve the grain farmers McCormick moved his reaper factory from Cincinnati to Chicago in 1847, and an iron industry was established in the 1850s to serve both the other local industries and the demand for railroad lines. (The country's first steel rails were made in Chicago in 1865.)

Chicago is an extreme example of a mercantile town that also became an industrial city, but a great many of the regional primates both generated and attracted investment in industries that were related to the farming activities in their hinterlands: Cincinnati's industrial growth, for example, was based on entrepôt industries processing local pork, and Buffalo and Cleveland grew on a flour-milling base. And this industrial development was only a part of the process. Because the export complexes were major earners of income for the city, they were its basic industries, without which growth was unlikely. As cities grew, however, these basic industries tended to be overshadowed by the nonbasic industries, those that were attracted largely to serve the local population and not necessarily to become involved in exports. The latter are called import-replacement industries, for obvious reasons: they reduce, if not remove, the settlement's dependence on outside suppliers, and so money remains to circulate in the town rather than being spent elsewhere to the benefit of nonlocal capitalists. Such import replacement industries—or services, such as banking—may thrive and extend their markets beyond the settlement, in which case they broaden its economic base; this related process is termed export diversification.

THE URBAN MULTIPLIER

The process of expansion of the nonbasic industries is known as the *urban multiplier*. The process is governed by thresholds, and so the multiplier is in a sense an application of central place theory to industry rather than to commerce. As a city's population grows, so does the local market for a wide range of manufactured goods. Initially these are imported from elsewhere in the system, from either other specialized industrial cities or the larger centers. Large markets attract investment capital, however, particularly local investment capital, and industries are set up to meet the local demand and replace the imports. Thus, whereas Pittsburgh's initial development was based on iron and glass, it soon had many furniture makers and printers, for example.

Once import-replacement industries are established, every time there is any growth in the basic industries there is an impact on the nonbasic sector; hence the term urban multiplier. Expansion of employment in a basic industry will mean more money circulating in the local economy and more to be spent on the commodities being produced in the nonbasic sector for the local community. In turn, expansion in the nonbasic industries will increase the workforce of the town and create even more demand for its own products. Growth, then, creates growth (beginning with the construction industry). Much of the extra demand in a relatively small place will go to further imports, so that the cycle of the multiplier will not be great. The larger the place, the more self-contained it is, however, and the greater the proportion of the extra demand that can be met locally, through either the expansion of existing nonbasic industries or the introduction of new ones.

Together, then, expansion of the basic and nonbasic industries in a settlement generates further growth via a multiplier process. Figure 4.1 illustrates this. There is an initial multiplier effect, generated perhaps by greater demand for the products of a basic industry. This brings extra income to the town, which is spent by the workers in nonbasic establishments. It also generates activity for the construction and public utility industries, which, together with the expansion in the tertiary sector, create secondary multiplier effects. These may mean that the population growth created by such expansion lifts the town above a critical threshold size that attracts entrepreneurs to establish a new industry with its associated workers. This in turn stimulates another initial multiplier effect and sets the growth process off once again. (The multiplier process is usually discussed in terms of the extra jobs created, and thus as a process of urban population growth. It is, in fact, a process of income and profit generation, some of which may generate further employment. For example, a steel works may improve its productivity and pay its workers more. That extra money is then spent in the local stores. To cope with the greater volume of business the store owners may employ

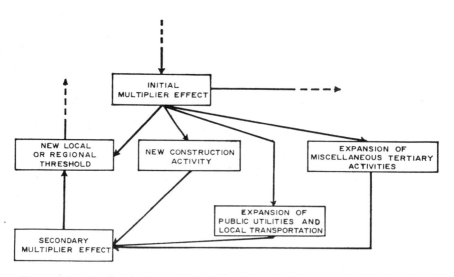

Figure 4.1. The impact of a multiplier effect in a basic industry, showing the various links in the urban economy. Reprinted from A. R. Pred, *The Spatial Dynamics of U.S. Urban-Industrial Growth, 1800–1914*, p. 27, by permission of the MIT Press, Cambridge, Massachusetts. Copyright © 1966 by the MIT Press.

more staff, work themselves and their employees harder, and/or introduce labor-saving devices. Thus not all of the extra basic income in the
town is used to create new jobs; in part it may generate higher incomes
for those already working there.)

INPUT-OUTPUT MATRICES

For those cities and towns with more than one basic industry, the
growth process represented in Figure 4.1 begins in several parts of the
economy, perhaps simultaneously. The various interindustry links involved are represented formally in an input-output matrix (Figure 4.2).
Each row in the matrix represents the origin of a flow, and each column
represents a destination; the entries in the various cells represent the inputs necessary for a certain volume of output. Thus the matrix of Figure
4.2 contains rows for four industries—A, B, C, and D—plus rows for
imports, labor, capital, and profits. The four industries also form columns, as do exports and consumption. Each of the four industries produces $1,000 of goods. For industry A, the first row in the matrix shows
that of this $1,000 worth of outputs, $300 goes to exports, $200 to final
consumption within the town, and the remaining $500 to other indus-
tries as intermediate inputs ($100 to itself). Column A shows that
$1,000 of inputs (including $240 of profits, or a profit rate of 24 percent) goes to produce this $1,000 of goods. Industry A clearly is in-

		A	B	C	D	EXPORTS	CONSUMPTION	TOTAL
			INDUSTRIES					
INDUSTRIES	A	100	100	200	100	300	200	1000
	B	200	300	200	100	100	100	1000
	C	50	50	100	400	200	200	1000
	D	10	20	50	100	700	120	1000
LABOR		100	200	200	100			
CAPITAL		100	200	50	50			
PROFITS		240	100	150	100			
IMPORTS		200	30	50	50			
TOTAL		1000	1000	1000	1000			

Figure 4.2.   A simple input-output matrix. All values are in dollars.

volved in processing imports, with a large proportion of the output for exports. Industries B, C, and D, on the other hand, are linked together in a production complex: B and C are the backward linkages of D, which exports a large quantity of its output.

A great deal of data must be collected to compile input-output matrices, and relatively few have been put together for individual towns. Their value is clearly in displaying the complexity of linkages. They can also be used as predictive devices to show both the potential effects of expansion of one industry on others and what linkages currently external to the town (the imports and exports) await development by local capital. There are problems in using matrices as predictive devices, however, since to do so assumes that the relationships remain the same. A factory may double its output with only a 50 percent increase in labor costs, for example. And as a city grows through the expansion of certain of its industries, the import-replacement process may mean that less is being imported and more bought locally, creating local multiplier effects. Thus the input-output matrix cannot be used as a predictor except in the short run, since it does not incorporate changes in the economic structure of a town that are consequent on growth in one or more of its sectors. An improvement, though basically still having the same problems and involving immense data collection, is an interregional input-output matrix, which subdivides the row for imports and the column for exports in Figure 4.2 according to the location of the relevant source/destination.

A shorter way to establish the multiplier effect in individual towns is the basic/nonbasic ratio. As it implies, this ratio compares the size of the basic industries in the town to the size of the nonbasic industries; size is usually measured as the number of people employed. The larger the ratio, the more dominant the basic industries, which implies a relatively small nonbasic sector, probably indicative of a high level of imports for needed goods and services. Some of the results of various attempts to measure the basic/nonbasic ratio are given in Figure 4.3, which shows that in general the larger the place the larger the number of nonbasic employees. Bigger places are more self-contained; more of the demands of their population and their industries can be met locally, and more of their produce is consumed locally than is the case in smaller places.

Some people recognize another circuit in the urban growth process, in addition to the local linkages and the urban multiplier of Figure 4.1. This is the *innovation* circuit (Figure 4.4). Larger places are those where most of the original developments take place within manufacturing industries. In part this is because they are the homes of the larger firms, which are more likely to have research and development divisions whose purpose is to devise new and better salable products. In addition, it is because the large cities tend to house the more original workers, em-

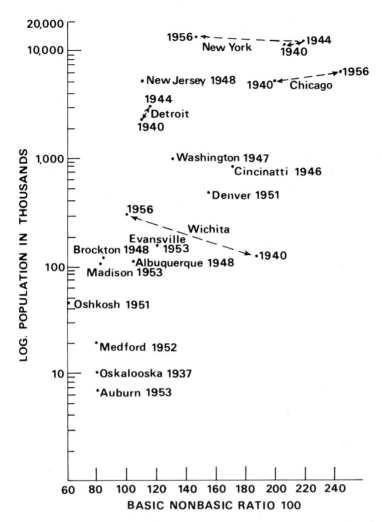

Figure 4.3. The basic/nonbasic ratio for certain American towns and cities. Adapted from Kent Blechynden, "An Economic Base Analysis of Hamilton, 1961," *New Zealand Geographer,* 20, 2, 1964, p. 130, with permission of New Zealand Geographical Society, Inc.

ployed in the already successful factories. Some of these individuals set up their own factories to develop their inventions. In a large city, original minds can more readily come together on projects and can more easily find a capitalist to back them than is the case in smaller places. One index of originality in an area is the number of patents taken out. Thus in 1860 the thirty-five largest cities in the United States produced 44 percent of the country's new patents (they contained about 11 percent of the population): New York alone produced 748 of the national total

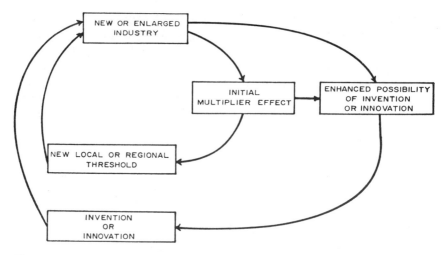

Figure 4.4. The multiplier effect and the invention/innovation circuit. Reprinted from A. R. Pred, *The Spatial Dynamics of U.S. Urban-Industrial Growth 1800-1914*, p. 25, by permission of The MIT Press, Cambridge, Massachusetts. Copyright © 1966 by the MIT Press.

of 4,589 patents; Philadelphia produced 259, Boston 136, and Chicago 49. Fifty years later the same thirty-five cities produced 31 percent of the country's 39,000 new patents (New York 2,768; Philadelphia 953; Boston 352; Chicago 2,016). And of course these innovations and inventions also have multiplier effects, stimulating even more growth.

INTEGRATING THE GROWTH PROCESSES

Together these three growth processes—local linkages, the multiplier, and innovations—all generate urban expansion, in terms of both money income and jobs. They operate everywhere, but since, as shown here, growth creates more growth, those cities that were large at the beginning of the industrial capitalism era are likely to benefit most from the processes just described.

The full operation of these growth processes is illustrated in Figures 4.5 and 4.6. Both depict growth as a cumulative process, but neither shows where it might start. Figure 4.5, however, can be taken as representative of a mercantile settlement whose main functions are related to trade. Thus the most likely starting place for growth is in the box in the upper left-hand corner. Expansion in the wholesale/trading complex generates income and jobs in the town. These in turn create more business for the wholesale/trade complex, via purchases in the town's shops and offices. Some construction work may be generated; new factories may be attracted to the town, and others extended; industrial multipliers may be set in motion; and innovations/inventions may result. But, as shown by the heavier lines in Figure 4.5, the main circuit is that in the upper left-hand corner; the industrial goods that are traded have to be imported, because the mercantile town lacks an industrial base.

The larger the settlement, however, the more attractive it is to industry, and the more likely that the industrial multiplier is set in motion. This phenomenon is illustrated by Figure 4.6. Again growth is assumed to be initiated in the box in the top left. This growth sets off initial multipliers in other industries, in the tertiary sector, in construction, and in the provision of an infrastructure. These generate secondary multipliers (the construction industry needs materials, for example), other existing industries expand, new ones are introduced (thereby replacing imports), and the likelihood of inventions and innovations creating even more new jobs and wealth is enhanced.

Two industrial growth processes have operated in American towns and cities. In those founded on a mercantile base and whose main func-

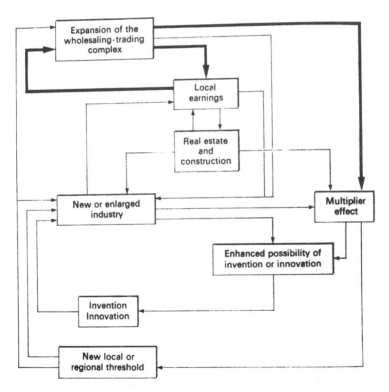

Figure 4.5.   The growth process in a mercantile settlement; heavy lines indicate the major flows of money. Source: A. R. Pred, *City-Systems in Advanced Economies.* London: Hutchinson, 1977, p. 72.

tion was to act as either a gateway or a central place for an agricultural region, the process outlined in Figure 4.5 was the most likely. Most of the growth occurred in the tertiary sectors; some manufacturing establishments were opened to serve local needs, but most factory products were imported. The towns retained their status as trading centers. In those that had grown to major size on the basis of mercantile capitalism (notably the eastern seaboard port cities plus the major inland gateways, such as Chicago), the process in Figure 4.6 was more likely. Some industry was already present; there was a large local market to be served; and capital and skilled labor were available. Thus the mercantile primates became industrial as well as trade centers, based on their initial advantage in the settlement process. Their growth to national prominence was ensured. In 1840, as Pred shows, about $40 million was invested in manufacturing industries in the main cities of the Atlantic seaboard, the Ohio Valley, and the Great Lakes basin (excluding Chicago). Over $11 million of this was invested in New York, with $5 million in Philadelphia and $3 million each in Baltimore and Boston. Inland, the main

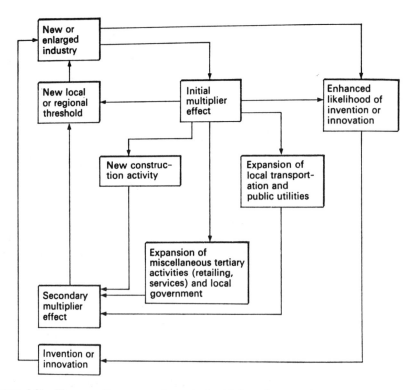

Figure 4.6. The growth process in an industrial settlement. Source: A. R. Pred, *City-Systems in Advanced Economies.* London: Hutchinson, 1977, p. 90.

gateway for the Ohio Valley—Cincinnati—had $7 million invested; the only city of any size lacking a large mercantile base was Pittsburgh, with $2 million. By 1860 the ten largest cities (New York, Philadelphia, Chicago, St. Louis, Boston, Baltimore, Pittsburgh, San Francisco, Cleveland, and Detroit) were responsible for 24 percent of the nation's total value added in manufacturing (value added is the difference between the price a firm pays for its inputs and the price it receives for its outputs); thirty years later the percentage was 38.5.

POPULATION GROWTH
IN INDUSTRIAL TOWNS

Industrial development involving a highly capitalized and productive workforce in factories (and on farms) was necessary in the United States because there was a relative shortage of workers. Labor was being freed from the farms, as increasing mechanization and productivity reduced demands there, but in many places at certain times these processes were insufficient to meet the great demand for labor, which could be met only through immigration. The mercantile period was one of great immigration, but whereas many of the British and north European migrants went to the land as farmers, it was to the towns that the immigrants of the period of industrial capitalism flocked. Thus in 1920 only two-thirds of the German-born lived in towns, for they had been numerous among the immigrants of the mercantile period, whereas 84 percent of the Italians, most of whom were recent arrivals, were urban residents, despite their rural origins; they provided the needed unskilled labor. Similarly, only 55 percent of the Scandinavian-born lived in towns (many of them may have settled initially in rural areas), compared with nearly 80 percent of those from Austria-Hungary, most of whom arrived twenty years later.

The importance of immigrants to the rapidly industrializing cities is shown in Figure 4.7, where the populations of the twenty-eight largest cities of 1840 are categorized by place of birth. Only 12 percent of Milwaukee's population were native whites, and another fourteen cities had less than 30 percent in that category. Many of these were the rapidly expanding industrial cities of the time, whereas the frontier primate cities without much industrialization—such as Omaha, Denver, Indianapolis, and Kansas City—whose main functions were associated with commerce, had much larger proportions of native-born. (These patterns do not necessarily mean that the majority of late-nineteenth-century immigrants worked in factories, though a large majority almost certainly did.)

As has been the case everywhere in the world, many immigrants remained in the port where they landed. Immigrant communities devel-

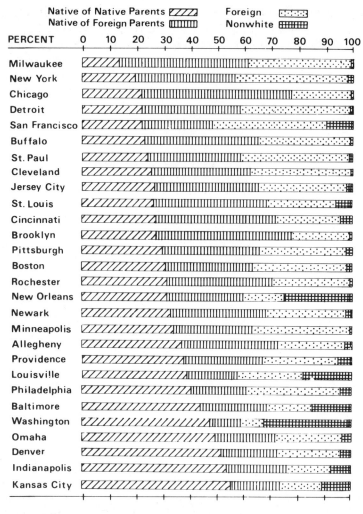

Figure 4.7. Birthplace of residents and their parents in the 28 largest cities, 1890. Source: B. McKelvey, *American Urbanization: a Comparative History.* Glenview, IL: Scott, Foresman, 1973, p. 72.

oped from their initial settlements as information and money were sent back to the homeland and more migrants were encouraged to come to where their predecessors could find them housing and jobs. But many more moved on to the opportunities inland, and again remittances back attracted even more immigrants. The result was a clear geography of migrant origins by destinations, dependent on the timing of the main movements. The Irish, as Ward demonstrated, dominated the migration streams prior to 1860, and many of them went to the new industrial towns of New England; more than 25 percent of the population of Lawrence in 1870 was Irish-born, and another ten New England towns contained more than 15 percent Irish-born. The Germans, on the other hand, dominated the migration streams in the 1850s, 1860s, 1870s, and 1880s, and they settled mainly in the Midwest: 31 percent of the population of Milwaukee in 1870 was German-born, as was 23 percent of the residents of Cincinnati, and more than 15 percent of the populations of Buffalo, St. Louis, Chicago, Cleveland, Toledo, Dayton, and Detroit.

THE MANUFACTURING BELT
AND CITY CLASSIFICATIONS

The two main influences on urban growth during the period of industrial capitalism were the initial advantage of large size achieved during the mercantile era and the location of fixed resources, such as power and minerals. But many industries, and certainly most large industries, were established to serve more than a local market, so for them location relative to other large towns was also important. It was because of this that the main development of industrial towns during the nineteenth and early twentieth centuries occurred in one area of the northeastern United States that is generally known as the Manufacturing Belt.

The success of Detroit and its surrounding towns as the centers of the automobile industry, for example, is not a reflection of the local market alone. Ford, Olds, and the other pioneers of the assemblyline industry were successful there because the Detroit area is close to both the main steel-producing towns, where inputs could be bought, and the major urban markets of the country. Detroit had no special advantages over several other settlements in that area, and the automobile industry could have been established in any one. Detroit's growth reflects the success of the capitalists who chose to invest there, and who were able to gain control over a large segment of the rapidly expanding market for their products. Thus the particular success of Detroit reflects a combination of advantages that it shared with several other places and the particular contribution of its industrialists (whose location could not be predicted.)

ACCESSIBILITY, MARKET POTENTIAL, AND LOCATION

Accessibility to the national market was the key to the growth of the manufacturing belt. This fact was demonstrated by Chauncy Harris in a classic paper published in 1954, in which accessibility was defined using the concept of population potential, a measure of how close one place is to all the others, weighted by their populations, in a system. Figure 4.8

A. TOWNS AND ROUTES

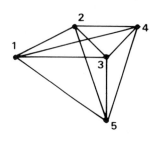

B. DISTANCES (1)

	1	2	3	4	5
1		22	30	41	36
2	22		14	20	32
3	30	14		14	20
4	41	20	14		32
5	36	32	20	32	

C. SUMMED DISTANCES

1	129	2	88	3	78	4	107	5	120

Figure 4.8.   The concept of population potential.

illustrates its measurement. There are five towns, linked to each other by the road network shown in A. (The distances are expressed in B as the costs of movement for one ton of goods.) Summing the distances, one finds that town 3 is the closest to the other four, involving a total travel cost of $18, and town 1 the most isolated. But what if the towns had different populations? This should be an important factor, because a location close to several small towns is probably not as valuable to industries as is one close to a few large centers. And so population is introduced to the measurement of potential, each population being weighted by its distance (travel cost) from the town whose potential is being measured. For the five towns in Figure 4.8 the assigned populations are:

1—200,000; 2—400,000; 3—100,000; 4—50,000; and 5—50,000

The potential of town 1 is now;

$$\frac{\text{Population of town 1}}{\text{Distance to town 1}} + \frac{\text{Population of town 2}}{\text{Distance to town 2}} \cdots +$$

$$\frac{\text{Population of town 5}}{\text{Distance to town 5}}$$

Distance to town 1 is assumed to be a travel cost of one dollar (although other assumptions are often used), so the sum becomes:

$$\frac{200,000}{1} + \frac{400,000}{22} + \frac{100,000}{30} + \frac{50,000}{41} + \frac{50,000}{36}$$

$$= 200,000 + 18,182 + 3,333 + 1,220 + 1,389 = 224,124$$

which is the potential of town 1. Doing the same sum for the other four places gives the following potentials:

1	2	3	4	5
224,124	420,297	141,309	83,584	74,619

Thus, although town 3 is the most central of the five, because towns 2 and 1 are the largest, these two are more accessible to the population as a whole. Expressed as a percentage of the highest these potentials are:

1	2	3	4	5
53	100	34	20	18

These values clearly indicate the superiority of town 2's location for an industry aiming to serve the populations of the five towns.

In defining market potentials (replacing population by purchasing power) for the United States, Harris took the main cities as the points for which potential was measured. A series of concentric circles of given radii was centered on each city, and the total retail sales in each band were divided by the estimated cost of moving one ton over that distance. The sum of these (sales/distance) computations gave the market potential for the place. New York had the highest potential—that is, it was the most accessible place to the national market—and the potential of all other places as a percentage of the New York total is shown in Figure 4.9. The Manufacturing Belt stands out on the map as the area within 20 percent of New York's potential. Over time, as the western states have grown in population, the advantages of the Manufacturing Belt in terms of access have diminished somewhat. But in the nineteenth and early twentieth centuries, as maps of potentials at different dates have shown, this area was by far the most accessible and contained the largest proportion of the American market.

The calculation of potentials can be modified to show the relative cheapness of the Manufacturing Belt in terms of transport costs to the national market. Instead of dividing the market by its distance from the given point, if one multiplies the two values one gets the total cost of moving to that point. For the urban system in Figure 4.8, therefore, the total transport costs from place 1 to all other places are:

$$(200,000 \times 1) + (400,000 \times 22) + (100,000 \times 30) + (50,000 \times 41) + (50,000 \times 36) =$$

$$200,000 + 8,800,000 + 3,000,000 + 2,050,000 + 1,800,000 = 15,850,000$$

which is the total cost of travel if something made in place 1 were to be sold to everybody in the same quantity. For all five towns the total transport costs are:

$$(1)\ 15,850,000;\ (2)\ 8,800,000;\ (3)\ 13,000,000;\ (4)\ 19,200,000;$$
$$(5)\ 23,600,000$$

The cheapest location from which to reach all five is thus town 2. Expressed as a percentage exceeding the total for town 2, the values for the other towns are:

$$(1)\ 180;\ (2)\ 100;\ (3)\ 148;\ (4)\ 219;\ (5)\ 269$$

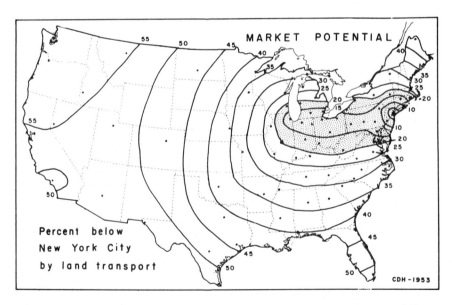

Figure 4.9. The distribution of market potential in the United States, 1948, assuming overland transport only, expressed as a percentage below the potential for New York. Source: C. D. Harris, "The Market as a factor in the Localization of Industry in the United States," *Annals of the Association of American Geographers*, 44 (1954): 320. Reproduced by permission of the *Annals*.

showing just how much more expensive it would be to locate anywhere else.

For the United States, the city with the lowest transport costs to all others, according to Harris's work in the 1940s, was Fort Wayne, Indiana, although this calculation assumed that all movement was overland (Figure 4.10 top). Water transport is frequently cheaper, of course; and allowing that to be used where feasible, the cheapest point not surprisingly shifts to the coast, at Philadelphia (Figure 4.10 bottom). In both cases, most of the area of the Manufacturing Belt was within 10 percent of the cheapest location, again stressing the concentration of the American market in that section of the country.

THE MANUFACTURING BELT

The origins of the Manufacturing Belt lie in the early primacy of the seaports of the northeastern Atlantic seaboard, the focused development of the rich lands of the Midwest on the eastern gateway cities, and the development of the coal and mineral reserves of the Appalachian region in the early decades of industrial capitalism. After a concentration of population in urban markets developed, it was then sustained and extended by the attraction to it of investment in industries that were largely market oriented. As industrial organizations became more complex, and the linkages between plants more numerous, such a concentration offered external economies of scale that were not matched anywhere else in the country. Thus the Manufacturing Belt developed the major concentration of assembly industries, those which take partly processed materials and assemble them into final products for consumption. These industries are identified by the size of the value added—basically the labor—component of their total costs; inputs are a relatively small percentage of the costs of production.

Twenty-three industries were identified by Pred for which more than 70 percent of their costs in value added were identified in the 1958 Census of Manufacturers; seventeen of these had more than 80 percent of their activity in the Manufacturing Belt, as defined in Figure 4.11 The six nonconforming industries (Table 4.1) can be accounted for as follows. Since the demand for newspapers and manufactured ice is widespread and the products are very "perishable," the Manufacturing Belt tends to have about the same percentage of newspaper production (55) as of the country's population (47); it has less of the ice production for obvious climatic reasons.

Two other industries—photoengraving and metal plating and polishing—are very much concentrated in the Belt, but just fail to meet the 80 percent cut-off. Their deviations from the general pattern are not significant, but that of automatic temperature controls is: the main production of this product is by a single firm—Honeywell—which was es-

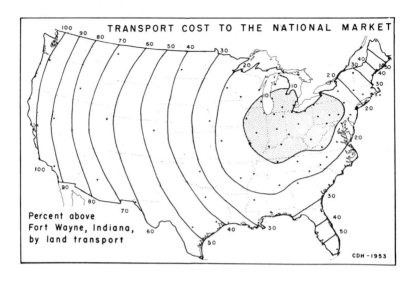

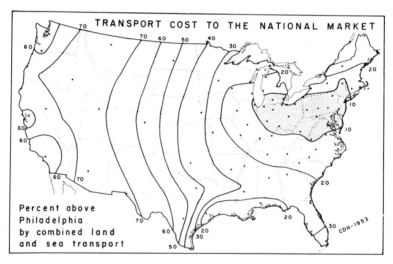

Figure 4.10. Transport costs to the entire United States market in 1948, expressed as the percentage exceeding the lowest value, assuming (top) overland transport only, and (bottom) land and sea transport. Source: C. D. Harris, "The Market as a Factor in the Localization of Industry in the United States," *Annals of the Association of American Geographers,* 44 (1954): 324. Reproduced by permission of the *Annals.*

tablished in Minneapolis in 1885 and, through skillful management, has come to dominate the industry despite its eccentric location relative to its markets. Finally, the structural clay products industry produces items such as tiles and pipes for which demand is widespread, and the industry does not have strong links with other industries.

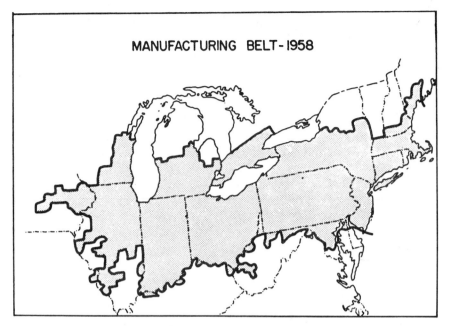

Figure 4.11. The United States Manufacturing Belt, 1958. Source: A. R. Pred, "The Concentration of High-value-added Manufacturing," *Economic Geography*, 41 (1965): 110.

Apart from these exceptions, the main pattern identified in Table 4.1 is that the industries that depend on agglomeration economies, particularly links with the suppliers of inputs and with consumers of outputs (many of these for the producers in the list of Table 4.1 are other industries), are very much concentrated in the Manufacturing Belt. Their links are not necessarily with other factories in the same town, but are usually only a relatively short distance away, so that transport costs are low and delays in delivery are slight.

This was shown by the compilation at the University of Pennsylvania of an input/output matrix for the economy of Philadelphia in 1959. For example, of $69 million in purchases of paper and paperboard for use by Philadelphia factories, only $10 million came from Philadelphia producers, even though the total production of paper and paperboard there was $136 million. The paper mills are not market oriented in that they supply only local firms; instead, their links are complex over a wide area of the Manufacturing Belt, which is a single system rather than a set of relatively independent settlements.

TYPES OF CITIES

The discussion of the ways in which the towns and cities of the United States have developed, and the functions they perform, suggests

Table 4.1
HIGH VALUE-ADDED INDUSTRIES AND LOCATION
IN THE MANUFACTURING BELT

Industry	Value added as Percent of Total Output	Percent of Production in Manufacturing Belt
Safes and vaults	71	97
Furs, dressed and dyed	80	94
Machine tool accessories	71	93
Pharmaceutical preparations	72	91
Vitreous china food utensils	82	90
Cutlery	74	89
Earthenware food utensils	74	88
Electron tubes	74	87
Special dies and tools	75	87
Industrial patterns	80	87
Pressed and blown glass	73	87
Electrotyping and stereotyping	77	87
Bookbinding	73	86
Typewriters	72	85
Typesetters	88	81
Industrial controls	71	81
Engraving and plate printing	73	80
Photoengraving	82	78
Metal plating and polishing	72	74
Structural clay products	71	58
Newspapers	70	55
Automatic temperature controls	78	52
Manufactured ice	73	28

Source: A. R. Pred, "The concentration of high-value-added manufacturing," *Economic Geography*, 41 (1965): 116.

a variety of roles for places within the country's economic system. Some are central places, involved mainly in the articulation of local commerce; some are concerned with manufacturing; others perform both functions. To indicate the various urban activities that result from capitalist investments, several researchers have developed classifications of cities according to their functions.

For one such classification, Nelson took all towns with a population of 10,000 or more in 1950 (897 of them) and divided their workforces into nine categories. (Although Nelson's work is now somewhat dated, its general findings are still valid today. Further, 1950 is a convenient date for categorizing urban functions before the major onset of late capitalism.) Frequency distributions of the number of towns with various percentages in each category were then compiled (Figure 4.12). These

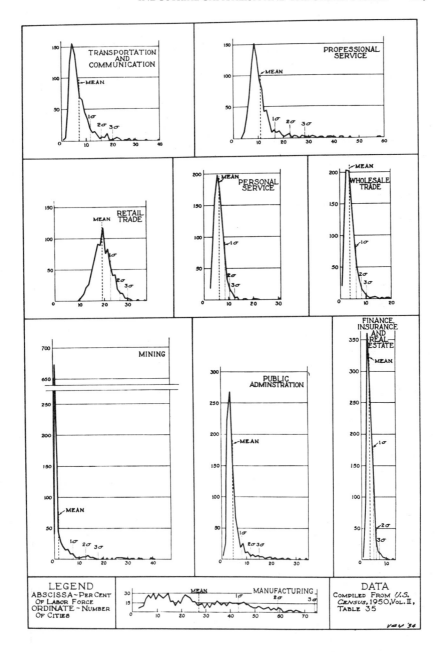

Figure 4.12.   The distribution of employment in nine separate categories in 897 cities, 1950. Source: H. J. Nelson, "A Service Classification of American Cities," *Economic Geography,* 31 (1955): 193.

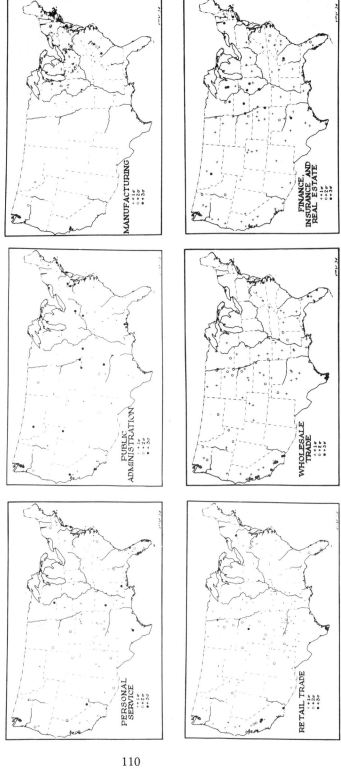

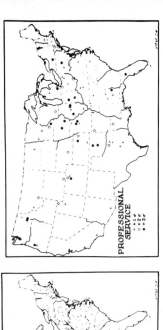

PROFESSIONAL SERVICE

DIVERSIFIED CITIES

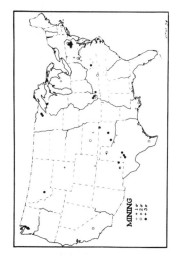

MINING

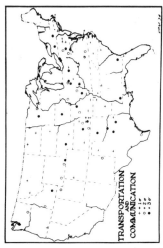

TRANSPORTATION AND COMMUNICATION

Figure 4.13. The distribution of towns in the ten functional classes identified by Nelson. Source: H. J. Nelson, "A Service Classification of Associated Cities," *Economic Geography*, 31 (1955): 197–201.

show, for example, that in the majority of towns no people were employed in mining; in only a few were more than 20 percent so engaged. Similarly, most towns had small percentages employed in transport and communications, in professional and in personal services, in wholesale trade, in public administration, and in finance and insurance. Retail trade (average of 19 percent) and manufacturing (average of 27 percent) were the dominant employment categories, with some places having almost 70 percent of their workforce in manufacturing.

To identify towns specializing in a certain function, Nelson took a measure of distance from the average—the standard deviation(σ). In a normal statistical distribution, about 68 percent of all towns would be within one standard deviation of the mean, so that about one-sixth of all towns should have a percentage in the given workforce category more than one standard deviation above the mean; thus its use here identified the towns with relatively large percentages in the given workforce category. The percentages that qualified a town as specializing in a certain function were:

Manufacturing	43.1	Public administration	8.1
Retail trade	22.9	Wholesale trade	6.0
Professional service	17.0	Finance/insurance	4.4
Transport/communication	11.7	Mining	7.6

A town could qualify for more than one category; Kearney, Nebraska, for example, was in four categories, as it specialized in retail trade, professional service, personal service, and wholesale trade (all connected with mercantile functions; its percentages in the other categories were very low—only 8 percent in manufacturing, for example). Alternatively, a town may have no specialization at all, in which case it was classified as a diversified city, with an employment structure similar to the national average.

Maps showing the locations of the towns in these various categories indicate a major spatial dichotomy between those specializing in manufacturing (Figure 4.13) and the others. The former are concentrated in the area east of the Mississippi and north of the Ohio River—the Manufacturing Belt—whereas the latter are most common west of the Mississippi. (The exceptions to this are mining towns, which are localized near resources, and the diversified towns, most of which have a considerable manufacturing base.) This clear-cut difference points up the development of the urban system of industrial capitalism in the northeastern United States on top of the mercantile base. Elsewhere the mercantile base remains dominant. Manufacturing has developed in towns west of the Mississippi—largely to serve local markets and in the largest cities— but the dominant specializations there are those associated with either central place (notably retailing) or gateway status (for example, wholesaling). The concentration of the diversified cities east of the Mississippi—south as well as north of the Ohio—indicates the greater probability of a wide range of functions for towns that were formerly gateways and/or central places but have been able to attract substantial manufacturing investment because of their location relative to the national market.

CONCLUSION: THE URBAN SYSTEM AND INDUSTRIAL CAPITALISM

No clear dividing line can be drawn between the mercantile and industrial capitalist eras, as they overlapped considerably. Indeed, industrial capitalism was generating urban growth on the eastern seaboard long before the western frontier had been closed by metropolitan expansion. Mercantile capitalism preceded the development of the industrial form, however, and provided the settlement framework within which most of the latter was established; only in the creation of some mining towns did industrial developments outflank mercantile expansion.

The mercantile impact on the urban system of industrial capitalism was very considerable. The large mercantile cities—the ports and the inland gateways—have nearly all remained high in the rank-orderings of cities based on their populations, and were among the major industrial centers of the next phase of American development. Agglomeration economies, the operation of multiplier processes, and the benefits of initial advantage ensured their continued growth. New towns were founded as locations for the factories of industrial capitalism, most of them in the northeastern sector of the country, where the transition from mercantile capitalism first occurred. They are the major additional elements of the settlement pattern created during this second major stage of American economic development and, as will be shown in the next chapter, their prosperity in most cases has been short lived. The enduring prosperous elements of the American urban system have been the mercantile gateways.

5

LATE CAPITALISM
AND THE
AMERICAN URBAN SYSTEM

INDUSTRIAL CAPITALISM IS distinguished from mercantile capitalism by the nature of investment. During the mercantile phase, capital was invested in the products of labor, and profits were earned from the buying and selling of commodities; under industrial capitalism, labor itself became a commodity to be bought and sold, and profits were made from the difference between the value of the product of labor and the price paid for it. No such clear distinction marks off late capitalism from industrial capitalism. Instead, the former was a logical development of the latter, so that their difference is one of degree rather than of kind. Several features are characteristic of a well-developed monopolistic trend within industrial capitalism, however, and these are used here to focus the discussion on contemporary urban patterns.

THE MAIN FEATURES
OF LATE CAPITALISM

CONCENTRATION AND CENTRALIZATION

Capitalist enterprise returns a profit to the investor. Part is spent on consumption, which increases demand in various sectors of the economy and leads to greater production within them. The remainder is reinvested in the search for more profits. Profits are made by firms, of course. If these are owned and operated by individuals, then the split just discussed occurs without any intermediate stages. But most firms, and certainly virtually all large ones, are owned by companies whose managements must decide what proportion of the profits should be reinvested within the firm and what proportion should be paid to the shareholders as dividends. The dividends are either spent on consumption by individuals or reinvested in the search for profits, not necessarily with the same firm. Reinvested profits also lead to an increase in production, since they usually involve payments for more plant and machinery to increase the productivity of the labor force.

To return a profit, investment must be cycled into either the production of salable commodities or the provision of salable services. Within manufacturing industry, this involves either employing a larger labor force to produce more goods or getting greater productivity from the existing labor force. The resulting production from either source must then be sold in order for profits to be realized, so that increases in profits are dependent on increases in sales. If there is an unsatisfied local market for the commodity, such increased sales present no problems and the profits are assured. But if the market is saturated, then the capitalist enterprise faces difficulties.

A major solution to the problem of market saturation is to attempt to expand the market. There may be untapped sales potential, either locally or elsewhere. The population of an area beyond the firm's hinterland may not be consuming the commodity, and so marketing strategies there may result in a possible destination for the surplus product that cannot be sold in the home market. Much of nineteenth- and twentieth-century imperialism was based on this strategy, and currently countries—including the United States—often give foreign aid on the understanding that it must be spent on their products.

Alternatively, consumption in the home market may be accelerated. A product may initially be sold to only a certain segment of the population, so there may be potential for widening the custom, as occurred when the automobile shifted from a luxury item to a general consumer good, if not actually a necessity. (The use of a credit system encourages such sales—and increases the price.) And consumers may be induced to increase their consumption by purchasing a new automobile every two years instead of every three, for example.

Market-expansion policies, both "at home" and abroad, are clearly feasible and are the reason for much advertising, but market saturation is bound to develop eventually. Even before it does, growth in the rate of consumption of a commodity may be insufficient to provide the required level of profits and will lead to investment moving elsewhere. Industrial capitalists and their managers react to this by seeking to increase their firms' share of the market. The production of automobiles may be shared among ten companies, for example, each winning ten percent of the market. If one of these companies could capture some of the sales of the others, it might be able to increase its share to twenty percent, thereby selling more of its products and ensuring a reasonable return on its investments. Competition among companies for more sales is characteristic of industrial capitalism, therefore, as firms strive to increase their profit levels, or even to hold them constant in a situation of market saturation.

The ultimate consequence of competitive strategies is capture of the entire market by a single producer, who thus establishes a monopoly. En route to this situation, each industry will show both a decline in its number of separate firms and an increase in their average size. This major trend is *concentration,* which can come about in a variety of ways. Firms may be driven out of business through intense competition in a "survival of the fittest" contest. Those least able to compete, perhaps because of relatively inefficient production methods, may find the quality and price of their product inferior to those of others. Sales will fall and income will be less than expenditure; the consequence is closure, perhaps preceded by bankruptcy. Investors in the unsuccessful companies will lose their assets; while control of a large share of the market is left in the hands of the successful. Alternatively, a strong firm may either take over or force a merger with a weaker competitor. The latter may find that its market share is falling; by selling to a stronger competitor it avoids bankruptcy and perhaps some recouping of investment, while again concentrating ownership into fewer hands.

Concentration focuses investment into a few firms in any one industry, therefore, and once a small number of strong firms emerge they can act, individually or collectively, to prevent the growth of any new competitors. Their size will undoubtedly mean that they enjoy considerable internal economies of scale, so that their production costs per unit are relatively low, and they can probably either force out, or prevent the potential entry of, any new competitor by (the threat of) price cutting. (The large firms will also have much larger reserves, which could enable them to withstand a loss while countering competition.) Existing firms can protect their position from potential challenges by gaining monopolies over raw materials and other inputs—for example, through buying agreements—and can ensure that sales outlets do not handle a competitor's products.

If competition proceeds to its logical conclusion, then only a single strong firm will survive, establishing a monopoly over its particular industrial sector. In certain monopolistic situations, the problem of market saturation and insufficient returns can be solved by pricing policies. If a firm has a monopoly, and demand for its product is inelastic—so that consumers have no alternative but to buy from it—then within reason it can raise its prices sufficiently to provide the required profit level. But if the product is not a necessity, and demand is elastic, then consumers can react by changing their preferences (drinking tea rather than coffee, for example) and thus reduce the sales of the monopolist. A monopoly brings some advantages, therefore, but it too faces the problems of market saturation.

Concentration frequently does not proceed to a monopoly, because the contest becomes a battle between equals rather than unequals. In the case of the automobile industry, if only one firm expands its portion of the market from the original ten percent, it could eventually cause the extinction of the other nine firms. If more than one firm expands, however, they may eventually reach a stage of three firms having an equal share of the market. They could then try to eliminate each other, but whereas the potential benefits from the movement toward monopoly may be great, the potential risks are perhaps even greater, since it becomes an "all or nothing" game. Rather than risk the nothing option, a firm may settle for a steady one-third share of the market, or thereabouts. A steady state may emerge, then, of an industrial sector dominated by a few firms, but with no trend toward monopoly. Such oligopolistic concentration may be the result of independent decisions within the firms concerned, or it may involve collusion between the firms who agree, for example, not to engage in price-cutting campaigns against each other. Any price rises consequent on increased costs of materials or labor can be passed on to the consumers, in the safe knowledge that the other firms will almost certainly do the same.

Concentration of production in an individual sector, proceeding to either an oligopoly or a monopoly, cannot prevent the eventual situation of a saturated market and sales growing too slowly to ensure the required rate of profit. What will firms do then to achieve the profits they need in order to be able to pay dividends, which in turn will lead investors to buy shares? A common strategy is to expand the production capability into other sectors, either by establishing new plants or by taking over firms in sectors where reasonable profits are available. Initially, this has often taken the form of firms taking over either others that provide inputs for them or those that purchase their outputs. This *vertical integration* reduces the price of inputs, since the entrepreneurs selling them and making a profit are eliminated, and brings a greater proportion of the profits from the final selling price back to the producers, since no intermediate profit-making firms are involved. In this way, interfirm linkages, with profits being made on each transaction, are replaced by intrafirm linkages.

Because of market saturation, vertical integration offers only limited possibilities for improving profits. More attractive is *diagonal integration,* in which firms invest in others whose production is in no way related to their own. (Indeed, they may not be involved in production at all; many of the large conglomerates own subsidiaries in several completely separate sectors of the economy and engage in such activities as land speculation.) Any market that seems especially buoyant with good profit prospects will attract investment from the corporate conglomerates. Thus, not only is ownership concentrated, but it is *centralized*; the central component is usually a holding company, often with its roots in the financial sector. The buying of companies—and then perhaps the selling of the least profitable parts (asset stripping)—is typical of the monopoly stage of capitalism, which brings control of large portions of the economy into relatively few managerial hands. (Ownership, at the same time, is widely dispersed among individual and institutional shareholders, most of whom play no part in the direction or management of the company's affairs, but who are concerned only with its dividends.)

Late capitalism, then, cannot be distinguished from industrial capitalism in the same way that industrial is distinguishable from mercantile capitalism. The switch from mercantile to industrial activity involved a change in the mode of production; the transition to late capitalism occurred gradually, and involved a quantitative rather than a qualitative change. The main characteristics of the phenomenon being studied in this chapter are concentration and centralization, which involve control of much of the nation's economy in relatively few hands (and places).

GROWTH OF THE TERTIARY AND QUATERNARY SECTORS

In his classic work, *The Conditions of Economic Progress* (1940), Colin Clark identified a relationship between the level of economic development in a society and the relative size of its nonproductive labor force. Late capitalism, the highest level to date, is characterized not only by concentration and centralization of ownership of the means of production but also by large numbers of people engaged in service occupations, both the direct operations of buying and selling (the tertiary sector) and the control functions of financial organizations (the quaternary sector). This is shown for the United States in Figure 2.2.

The relative size of the tertiary sector reflects the high levels of productivity in the primary (agriculture and mining) and secondary (manufacturing) sectors. As more and more goods for consumption are produced by fewer people (often absolutely as well as relatively)—a consequence of capitalist investment in machine power rather than labor power—so more people are required for the more personalized functions of selling the commodities. This involves not only the direct process of selling in the store, but also the advertising of products, their transfer from one firm to another (producer to wholesaler to retailer), their transport, and so on. Some economies of scale are possible in such employment, and some replacement of labor is possible (by computers in invoicing, for example, and by self-service stores in retailing), but these have not been as extensive as in the primary and secondary sectors. Consequently, as late capitalism expands, so does the size of the tertiary workforce.

To become more productive, late capitalism must invest as much of the profits from its activities as possible, within the constraints of ensuring that demand for products continues to expand as well. In order to obtain sufficient investment, the capitalist class has extended its facilities to the working class, encouraging them to save money now so as to gain greater benefits later. Much of this effort has gone into the development of insurance and pension funds, whereby individuals invest part of their income now to obtain a guaranteed larger income later. To ensure that this guarantee is fulfilled, the money must then be channeled into profitable ventures, and to organize this a large finance industry that routes money around the economy has been developed. These quaternary occupations are a major part of the nonproductive service sector that has developed under late capitalism.

Apart from the commercial and financial components of the tertiary and quaternary sectors, there is a wide range of other nonproductive occupations that develops to support late capitalism. Scientific research and development is one example. Since firms are forever seeking new products to market, and new ways of making existing products more cheaply, large companies often employ considerable scientific staffs on these problems. Others invest in research rather than conduct it themselves, either at independent research institutes, most of which are organized on a commercial basis, or at universities and comparable institutions.

MATERIALISM

As indicated, industrial capitalism progresses into its late stage when there are problems of market saturation. People have to be convinced of the necessity to consume, and marketing becomes something of a science.

The two basic commodities necessary for human existence are food and shelter. In a developed, industrial society most people are adequately fed and well housed, and more than adequately clothed. Food must be purchased in certain quantities; homes will decay and eventually need replacement, at a slower rate than clothing. The demand for such commodities is insufficient to form the basis for expanded production, which is necessary for capitalist expansion. And so a whole range of other commodities has been, and continues to be, invented, and people have to be convinced, first, of the need to buy them, and, second, of the desirability to replace them frequently. One way of doing this has been to create the whole notion of status symbols—images of the possession of certain commodities as necessary for social respect.

Thus homes become not only places for shelter and privacy but also items of display; automobiles are status symbols as well as means of locomotion; clothing provides an index of the wearer's social position; and so on.

An abundance of commodities has been promoted in order to sustain the productive capacity of industry and ensure capitalist profits—which increasingly, through savings, insurance and pension funds, are for the benefit of all. Many of these commodities are of only indirect concern here, in that they are necessary for the survival of urban industries. A few are more important, however, because of their impact on the urban scene.

THE LARGER ROLE OF GOVERNMENT

The growing role of government under industrial and late capitalism was demonstrated in Chapter 2, with details of the size of government employment and expenditures. The role of government is manifold. In part it acts against capitalist interests—or apparently so—as in its antimonopoly and antitrust legislation, which is designed to protect consumers against producers. But most of its functions are allied to those of capitalism, to ensure its continued health for the good of all, capitalists and working class alike. It educates the workforce, thereby transferring the cost of training to society as a whole; it guarantees minimum incomes, to reduce social unrest; it purchases many commodities, notably defense products; it guarantees prices, especially to farmers; it gives foreign aid, which must be spent on American goods; it insures mortgages to encourage consumption of housing; it builds freeways, which encourage the use of automobiles and the consumption of gasoline; it gives subsidies to ailing large companies (such as the Chrysler Corporation) and it provides a range of incentives for new businesses to be established, especially small businesses that are perceived as the most likely to provide jobs and thus remove the pressing problem of unemployment; and so on.

All these governmental functions involve the raising of taxes, which requires a labor force, and a vast bureaucracy to redistribute that income. These office workers—members of the quaternary sector—are linked one with another in the same way that industrial sectors are, and there are also many links between them and the private sector with which they are allied. Government, therefore, is not an independent sector; it is very much a part of the economy. Without it, the economic system of late capitalism might not fail, but it would almost certainly display more pronounced periods of boom and slump, inflation and recession, than has been the case since the 1930s, when governments accepted the need to inflate the economy by public spending, to reduce levels of unemployment, and to protect businessmen (notably farmers) from falling profit levels.

THE URBAN SYSTEM
UNDER LATE CAPITALISM

Thus far I have identified four distinguishing characteristics of late capitalism: concentration and centralization; growth of the service sector; materialism in consumer goods; and the expanded role of government. All are reflected, separately or together, in the urban pattern.

One of the clearest consequences of these characteristics for the settlement pattern is a tendency toward concentration of population in the large settlements. This largely stems from concentration and centralization, a trend that channels industrial workers into large, assemblyline plants. The large firms most likely to survive to this stage of late capitalism are those in the largest cities which are those probably the most able to benefit from the economies of scale and so become the most productive units. Their initial size advantage is likely to enable them to take over smaller plants in neighboring places.

Take a hypothetical urban system comprising one large center and a number of smaller ones. Each has a brewery serving its local market. All need to expand production. The brewery in the largest town is producing beer at the lowest price, because its larger volume allows it to enjoy greater internal economies of scale. It can then afford to transport beer to hotels in the neighboring towns and sell it below the price of the local product. Some market resistance may be met, but the lower price should eventually enable it to force the smaller local brewery out of business. This process can be repeated at each place, so that eventually a series of small, local monopolies is replaced by one large, regional monopoly. Production is centered on the large-town brewery and jobs are lost in the small towns, although one or two of the others may be kept open after takeovers, perhaps for brewing special beers. In addition, the profits once made by the owners of the small-town breweries are now made by the owners of the large-town brewery. They are channeled away from the small towns, thereby reducing the local urban multipliers, while at the same time accelerating the multiplier at the place(s) where the profits are received by the shareholders of the large firm.

The process of concentration need not be focused on the production unit in a large place; the example of the Honeywell Company serving the national market from its headquarters in Minneapolis was quoted in the previous chapter. Similarly, many large corporations operate multiplant enterprises in several places. But the advantages of scale economies, the accessibility of a larger market, the availability of local capital, the focus of transport routes, and the pool of skilled labor are all factors suggesting the success of large-town concerns in the trend to late capitalism, and a further building on the initial advantage of size that may date back to the original settlement in the early mercantile era.

Beside this concentration, the growth of materialism in consumption suggests a trend toward decentralization or spread of the urban settlement itself. Two factors in particular point in this direction: the increased consumption of housing and the availability of the automobile. The latter in effect is necessary for the former to happen, since new housing can be built only on open land at the edge of the city (unless a large scheme of urban renewal—the replacement of obsolete dwellings—is in progress). Use of the automobile by individual workers adds flexibility to the workplace/residence linkage, and allows for the suburbanization that is discussed in later chapters. Use of the truck by firms affords great flexibility in the movement of goods that a fixed-route network, such as the railroad, does not provide: with it, industries as well as residences can be located in settlements on the edge of the main urban market, rather than in its center, causing no great problems for the movement of goods to and from linked factories and to markets. Movements between metropolitan areas are made relatively easy, both for manufacturers and for commuters; the linking of adjacent metropoli in this way leads to the development of megalopolis.

The trend to concentration in decentralized cities is further encouraged by the growth of the quaternary and government sectors. Offices are very much interlinked in the flows of information between them. Much routine business can now be handled by computers and telecommunications equipment, but the majority of office complexes in large cities developed before those media became available, and again a strong initial advantage must be overcome if concentration is to be countered. In any case, despite the availability of telecommunications media for routine message transmission, much business (as in insurance and home purchase) is still transacted by personal contact. A businessman seeking a contract; a constituent wishing to influence a state politician; a financier seeking information on investment possibilities: all find their tasks much easier by face-to-face contact than by mail, telephone, or telex. The office complex is thus likely to be a major component in the employment structure of the large city, often associating industry, the financial sector, and government.

Late capitalism therefore is likely to be reflected in the continued absolute and relative growth of the largest urban places, albeit in a more decentralized form than in previous eras, with the central cities of some metropolitan areas—and in some cases their suburbs too—having lost population in recent decades. These cities should be the centers of the major industries, the locations of the major office complexes, the nodes of the organizational structure of industry and commerce, and the centers of government activity. Their more diffuse spatial organization suggests the term "city region" rather than city to describe their pattern, however, since city suggests a compact, mononuclear unit, whereas city region indicates a scattered, multinodal complex.

CONCENTRATION
AND DECENTRALIZATION

Concentration trends with negative consequences for small towns have long been a feature of the urbanization process under capitalism. In the last three decades of the nineteenth century, small towns throughout the states of Illinois, Indiana, Iowa, Michigan, Missouri, Ohio, and Wisconsin were losing their machine shops and sawmills, flour mills, agricultural-implement makers, furniture workshops, and brickworks as their markets were invaded by the products of the large

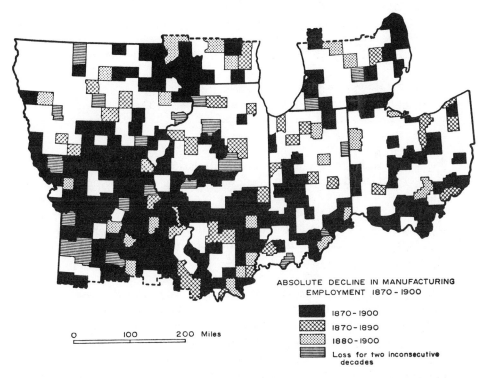

ABSOLUTE DECLINE IN MANUFACTURING
EMPLOYMENT 1870 - 1900

- 1870 - 1900
- 1870 - 1890
- 1880 - 1900
- Loss for two inconsecutive decades

0   100   200 Miles

Figure 5.1.   Counties in part of the Midwest where the employed population in manufacturing industries declined during the last three decades of the nineteenth century. Reprinted from A. R. Pred, *The Spatial Dynamics of U.S. Urban-Industrial Growth, 1800–1914*, p. 62, by permission of the MIT Press, Cambridge, Massachusetts. Copyright © 1966 by The MIT Press.

towns. Indeed, as Figure 5.1 shows, most of the counties of these Midwestern states experienced absolute declines in their number of manufacturing jobs in the last decades of the nineteenth century, at a time when most of their populations were growing and the trend to late capitalism was very slight. And even in those with an increase of manufacturing jobs, at most this was less than the comparable increase in the local cities of Chicago, Cleveland, Detroit, and St. Louis. Indeed, in 1860 Chicago produced only 3.5 percent of America's industrial output in value; by 1900 it produced nearly 25 percent and over that intervening forty years its industrial output had increased two or three times more than its population.

Thus the decline of the small town began a century ago and continues today. Between 1950 and 1960 nearly half the places in Wisconsin with less than 500 residents lost population, compared to one-third of those with 500 to 1,000 residents, and 20 percent of those with between 1,000 and 2,500. These trends were reproduced nationally. The total population change for all places in certain size categories between 1950 and 1960 was as follows:

Size	Percent Population Change
0–1,000	15
1,000–2,500	27
2,500–10,000	32

For individual settlements, the cross-tabulations in Table 5.1 illustrate this general trend. Inspection of the values along each row indicates that in each size category for small, nonmetropolitan settlements, movement up into the next largest category was more likely than movement down into the next smallest; most stayed in the same category, however.

Three factors can be used to account for these changes. The first is the decline in the agricultural population. As this falls, the population of town plus hinterland falls below critical thresholds; businesses close and more people move away. Secondly, the widespread availability of the automobile gives greater mobility to the rural population (two-thirds of Wisconsin households had at least one car in 1960), enabling them to travel easily to the larger centers for their shopping and bypass the smaller towns with their limited choice of goods. And finally, concentration in the retail sector is leading to the decline of the small store and its replacement by a smaller number of large supermarkets and shopping centers in large places, especially geared to shopping by automobile. Together, these three trends cause the urban multiplier to work in reverse in the small towns; just as growth generates more growth, so decline generates more decline.

Table 5.1
**THE CHANGING SIZE DISTRIBUTIONS OF
INCORPORATED SETTLEMENTS OUTSIDE METROPOLITAN
AREAS, 1950 TO 1960 AND 1960 TO 1970**

Population at First Date*	LESS THAN 500	500– 999	1,000– 2,499	2,500– 9,999	MORE THAN 10,000
Population at Later Date					
1950–1960					
New in 1960	338	99	59	25	2
Less than 500	5,002	305	17	1	0
500–999	279	2,064	378	7	0
1,000–2,499	5	132	2,063	281	2
2,500–9,999	0	0	44	1,551	123
More than 10,000	0	0	0	9	546
1960–1970					
New in 1970	344	73	43	23	6
Less than 500	5,220	393	9	1	1
500–999	192	2,050	347	11	0
1,000–2,499	3	129	2,200	229	0
2,500–9,999	0	1	50	1,735	88
More than 10,000	0	0	0	20	653

*New in 1960/1970 indicates settlements incorporated during the previous decade.

Source: G. V. Fuguitt, "The places left behind: population trends and policies for rural America," *Rural Sociology*, 36 (1971): 453.

Some small towns are continuing to grow, however, especially those close to the metropolitan centers. In Wisconsin between 1950 and 1960, classification according to the size of the largest center within thirty miles of the small town produced the following:

Size of Largest Center within Thirty Miles	Percentage of Small Towns Losing Population
0–10,000	62
10,000–50,000	28
50,000–	4

Settlements of all sizes close to large cities have tended to grow, therefore. In most cases this growth represents a change in function, for most of the towns have become commuter settlements feeding the larger place with little or no independence from it. A few may have attracted some industry, but most are residential areas only.

This changing function of small settlements close to the larger cities is part of the general decentralization trend that characterizes metropolitan America today, and is illustrated in Table 5.2. Here large nonmetropolitan settlements are categorized by distance from a metropolitan area and accessibility via the interstate highway system. Clearly, those closest to a census-defined metropolitan area (SMSA) were most likely to grow, especially if they had a highway link to it.

The extent of this trend was first elaborated in a classic study of the northeastern seaboard of the United States. The area stretching from north of Boston, in southern Maine, to south of the national capital in Washington, D.C., was recognized in 1950 census data as one huge megalopolis (Figure 5.2), a stretch of almost continuous urban settlement of more than 600 miles. Much of it is not covered with either housing or factories, of course (indeed, much of it comprises empty, idle land), but all of it is part of the commuting hinterland of one or more of the great cities of the area, which include Boston, New York, Philadelphia, Baltimore, and Washington. Other megalopolitan equivalents, such as Chipitts (the area from Chicago to Pittsburgh) and Sansan (San Diego to San Francisco), have also been identified.

Table 5.2
ACCESSIBILITY AND GROWTH OF NONMETROPOLITAN SETTLEMENTS (MORE THAN 10,000 +), 1950 TO 1960

Accessibility	Distance from Nearest SMSA* (miles)			
	LESS THAN 50	50–100	100–150	MORE THAN 150
Two Interstate Highways in County	27.6	15.0	15.4	14.7
One Interstate Highway in County	16.7	13.6	15.1	17.2
Interstate Highway in Adjacent County	15.5	5.6	10.0	4.2
No Available Interstate Highway	14.6	2.2	6.7	7.1
Total	22.7	10.7	10.9	10.7

*The entries show the percentage of settlements whose populations increased during the decade.
Source: R. R. Campbell, "Beyond the suburbs: The changing rural scene," In A. H. Hawley and V. P. Rock (eds.), *Metropolitan America in Contemporary Perspective*. New York: Halsted Press, 1975, p. 107.

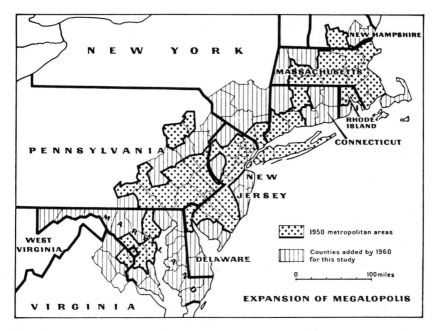

Figure 5.2.   The extent of megalopolis in 1960. From Jean Gottmann, *Megalopolis: The Urbanized Northeastern Seaboard of the United States.* Copyright © 1961 by the Twentieth Century Fund, Inc. Reprinted by permission.

Because of this decentralization, there is now a marked discrepancy between the limits of an administrative city and the extent of the built-up area of which it is the center. (The topic of suburbanization is treated in Chapter 8.) To deal with this problem, the Census Bureau has defined Standard Metropolitan Statistical Areas for the United States since 1910 (not always using the same term). They comprise contiguous counties of high population density, from which at least fifteen percent of the working population commutes to a central city with a population of at least 50,000. There were 219 of these areas in 1963, but by then these underbounded the true extent of the decentralized urban areas.

A new concept was devised in the late 1960s by geographer Brian Berry to define the functional urban areas. *Daily urban systems* are based on commuting patterns, and according to maps of commuting areas to the major cities, a great deal of the country was within a decentralized urban area. Population data for these areas show more clearly the concentration trend of the immediate postwar decades (up to 1970). The main characteristics are:

1. The larger the place, the greater its growth rate during the decade from 1960 to 1970.

2. Places with populations of one million or more generally grew at a faster rate than did the country as a whole; only three lost population.
3. The range in growth rates was greatest for places with between 1.0 and 2.5 million inhabitants, indicating that they were the decade's main growth centers.
4. Most places with less than one million residents grew at less than the national rate.
5. Places with less than 225,000 residents tended to decline in population, as did fully one-third of those with populations between 225,000 and 500,000.

More detailed analysis showed that decline was most likely in those daily urban systems with a high dependence on agricultural earnings, and that growth was most rapid in the centers with high levels of government and office employment.

These twin processes of concentration and decentralization result in a series of backwash and spread effects in the distribution of population and economic activity across the face of America. The *backwash* effects involve the closure of small-town factories and stores and the loss of jobs, which generates a movement of workers to the larger centers. The general pattern of movement is toward a nearby growing place, although the larger the center the greater the area from which it "siphons" migrants. (Thus most of the recent immigrants to the United States—notably the Puerto Ricans, Mexicans, and Filipinos, plus Asian and Cuban refugees—are moving to the large cities of the east and west coasts.) The *spread* effects radiate outward from the growing centers, as in the example presented in Table 5.2: again, the larger the place and the more rapid its growth, the larger the area that benefits from these effects, with influences on population and economic activity.

These changes in population distribution involve large-scale migration; indeed, about one in every five Americans changes his home address each year, though most remain in the same state. The urbanization of the population during the twentieth century has resulted in part from immigration to the cities, especially from southern Europe and, more recently, from Puerto Rico, Mexico, and Asia. And in part it has been brought about by the movement of the rural and small-town population to the sprawling major urban centers. Blacks have moved to the cities in particularly large numbers. In 1900, 20 percent of blacks lived in urban areas and the remainder were in the rural south; by 1950, 62 percent were urban residents, and by 1970, 81 percent lived in the defined urban areas.

The flow of migrants into the United States and from the rural areas and small towns to the large cities is only a small part of a complex pattern of movement. Early in this century, such migrations dominated.

Now, however, the major element of migration in America is intermetropolitan, and instead of comprising mainly low-income people seeking a better life in the burgeoning industrial cities, it is dominated by high-income people moving from place to place to further their career goals, many of them employees of the large corporations that characterize late capitalism. Such movement is occasionally termed the "intermetropolitan circulation of elites."

CENTERS OF ECONOMIC DISTRESS

A consequence of the backwash effects involved in the concentration of population and economic activity is that some areas suffer economic distress, from a decline in their competitive status within the urban system. Such distress may be local in both time and space, resulting perhaps from a general recession in the economy, but much of it is more permanent than the temporary wave of unemployment—16 percent—that hit Detroit in 1958, when the automobile industry suffered a severe recession. Chronic unemployment usually arises in cities that are very dependent on a particular industry whose prosperity has been destroyed by one of a variety of causes. Most often these places are involved in the extractive industries, notably coal mining, and the associated heavy industries. (The location of the steel industry has changed considerably, with a net movement toward the coast and imported ores and away from the traditional centers in western Pennsylvania.) Towns such as Scranton and Wilkes-Barre, Pennsylvania, have suffered, as have several New England towns, such as Fall River, Lawrence, and Lowell, where the traditional industries based on textiles and leather have been hard hit by competition from elsewhere.

An urban system characterized by concentration will have its problem towns, therefore; usually these are smaller centers away from the major expanding cities. To counter the associated problems of unemployment, the federal government has initiated a number of programs in recent years. The Area Redevelopment Act of 1961, for example, was used to designate Redevelopment Areas on the basis of unemployment rates, and the Area Redevelopment Administration provided long-term, relatively low-interest loans to firms wishing to establish in those areas; it also invested in the infrastructure necessary for industrial development. (This and other programs are discussed in greater detail in Part Four.) Similar, but more generous, programs were introduced by the Public Works Act of 1965.

Yet some of the most severe problems of unemployment and low incomes are experienced in the larger expanding cities, as we will discuss in more detail later. In part this reflects the attractiveness of those places for people suffering economic distress elsewhere in the country, including the rural areas where the demand for labor has fallen rapidly. Most numerous among these poor migrants are the blacks, who have moved by the millions from the South to the large cities of the North. They have been both "pushed" from the South and "pulled" to the cities. (Increasingly, it seems, they are returning.) The southern states, for example, are relatively poor and their welfare payments relatively low (in part due to racist beliefs about welfare among generations of southern politicians); the northern states are more liberal, however, so some believe it is better to be poor in New York than in Mississippi. Thus, although most of the problem towns are those in the Economic Development Regions, there are also many problems to be faced in the expanding cities of late capitalism.

CENTRALIZATION AND CONTROL CENTERS

Concentration of economic activity into the expanding, sprawling centers represents one part of the major trend of late capitalism. The other is centralization, which involves the location of the control centers of the economy.

The size of the leading companies in the American economy is legendary. Some are much larger in their operations—number of employees, volume of turnover—than many small countries, and the thousand largest American companies control over half the country's gross national product. As many as 2,000 firms disappear each year through mergers, as the more successful large companies seek to expand their operations and maintain their profit levels. Thus as well as operating its well-known retail outlets, the Sears, Roebuck organization of Chicago manufactures clothing, a wide range of electrical and electronic appliances, household goods, and sporting goods, and it runs insurance companies and restaurants. In all, some 380,000 employees are controlled from the Chicago headquarters, and sales in 1972 exceeded $11 billion.

With the major growth of conglomerates in the late capitalist system, it is clear that many jobs are created in the organizational structure of such firms. The location of headquarters offices is thus a major element in the growth fortunes of cities and has been a significant contributor to the concentration trend of recent decades.

Looking at the largest companies in the country, one finds the clearest feature in the distribution of their headquarters to be the concentration on New York (Table 5.3); that metropolitan area contains about 7 percent of the national population, but about 30 percent of the country's manufacturing firms had their headquarters there in 1972, as did more than 20 percent of the 300 largest nonmanufacturing firms. The area around New York was a major headquarters locale, too. In all, the

Table 5.3
HEADQUARTER LOCATIONS IN METROPOLITAN AREAS

Area**	Manufacturing			Top 50 in Other Sectors*						1972 Total
	TOP 500 1960	TOP 500 1972	NEXT 500 1972	R	U	T	B	I	F	
New York	156	147	108	17	12	8	11	9	15	327
Los Angeles	18	20	26	3	2	5	4	2	6	68
Chicago	52	55	44	7	2	7	4	3	4	126
Philadelphia	22	15	18	3	3	2	4	3	2	50
Detroit	16	13	7	2	1	0	4	0	0	27
San Francisco	16	15	12	2	1	3	3	0	1	37
Boston	8	6	16	3	1	0	1	2	0	29
Washington	0	1	0	1	2	2	0	0	1	7
Cleveland	21	21	20	2	1	3	2	1	0	50
Pittsburgh	24	15	9	0	1	0	2	0	0	27
St. Louis	14	10	9	1	1	2	0	1	1	25
Dallas	7	8	14	1	1	1	2	2	1	30
Baltimore	1	2	6	0	1	0	0	0	1	10
Houston	2	6	10	0	5	0	1	0	1	23
Seattle	3	3	0	0	0	0	1	0	1	5
Minneapolis	7	12	10	2	1	4	2	2	2	35
Cincinnati	5	5	4	2	0	0	0	2	2	15
Milwaukee	9	11	9	0	1	0	1	1	0	23
Atlanta	0	4	6	1	1	1	1	0	0	14
San Diego	2	1	1	1	0	1	0	0	1	5
Buffalo	5	3	2	0	0	0	1	0	0	6
Miami	0	1	3	0	1	1	0	0	0	6
Kansas City	3	2	4	0	1	2	0	1	1	11
Denver	4	2	3	0	0	2	0	0	0	7
Indianapolis	4	3	1	0	0	0	0	6	0	4
New Orleans	0	1	1	0	0	0	0	0	0	2
Tampa	0	1	1	0	0	0	0	0	0	2
Portland	1	4	5	0	1	0	1	0	0	11
Phoenix	0	3	1	0	0	0	1	0	1	6
Columbus	0	0	3	0	0	0	1	0	0	5
Providence	2	1	3	0	0	0	0	0	0	4
Rochester	2	3	4	0	0	0	1	0	0	8
San Antonio	0	1	2	0	0	0	0	0	0	4
Dayton	3	4	4	0	0	0	0	0	0	8
Louisville	0	1	4	0	0	0	0	0	1	6
Hartford	2	4	3	0	1	0	0	5	3	16
Memphis	0	1	3	0	0	0	0	0	0	4
Birmingham	1	1	0	0	0	0	0	1	0	2
Albany	0	0	1	0	0	0	0	0	0	1
Toledo	6	7	1	0	0	0	0	0	0	8
Oklahoma City	2	1	2	0	0	0	0	0	0	3
Syracuse	1	2	1	0	1	0	0	0	0	4
Honolulu	1	1	1	0	0	0	0	0	0	2
Greensborough	3	5	1	0	0	2	1	1	1	11

Table 5.3 (continued)

Area**	Manufacturing			Top 50 in Other Sectors*						
	TOP 500 1960	TOP 500 1972	NEXT 500 1972	R	U	T	B	I	F	1972 Total
Salt Lake City	0	0	1	0	0	0	0	0	0	1
Allentown	2	2	1	0	1	0	0	0	0	4
Nashville	1	2	1	0	0	0	0	1	1	5
Omaha	2	3	1	0	1	0	0	1	0	6
Grand Rapids	0	0	2	0	0	0	0	0	0	2
Youngstown	1	0	2	0	0	0	0	0	0	2
Springfield	1	0	3	0	0	0	0	1	0	4
Jacksonville	0	0	0	1	0	1	0	0	0	2
Richmond	3	3	3	0	1	0	0	1	2	10

*Key: R—retailing; U—utilities; T—transportation; B—commercial banking; I—insurance; F— diversified financial.

**For multicentered areas only the first name is given; places are listed according to population size.

Source: A. R. Pred, *Major Job-Providing Organizations and Systems of Cities.* Commission on College Geography, Research Paper No. 27. Washington D.C.: Association of American Geographers, 1974, pp. 19–21.

Manufacturing Belt contained twenty-seven metropolitan areas with more than 500,000 residents each in 1972, and those twenty-seven housed 616 of the 1,000 largest manufacturing company headquarters. The second most important single location was Chicago.

Between 1960 and 1972 there was some movement away from the centers of the Manufacturing Belt, notably from Philadelphia and Pittsburgh, and this process is continuing. No single major concentration seemed to be developing to counter the strength of the Northeast, however; growth was widely spread in such places as Atlanta, Houston, Minneapolis, Phoenix, and Portland.

This slight decline in the dominance of headquarters in the large cities of the Manufacturing Belt is illustrated by an analysis at the regional level, which shows the distribution of the headquarters of the fifty largest corporations in six sectors for 1956 and 1971. (Table 5.4; the regions are shown in Figure 5.3. Note that the distributions shown are of the corporate assets or sales so that, for example, 1.1 percent of all sales by the fifty largest industrial corporations in 1956 was earned by corporations with headquarters in New England.) For each date, the dominance of the Manufacturing Belt corporations is clear (that is, for those in the Middle Atlantic and East North Central regions, plus New England for insurance), but in several sectors this dominance was some-

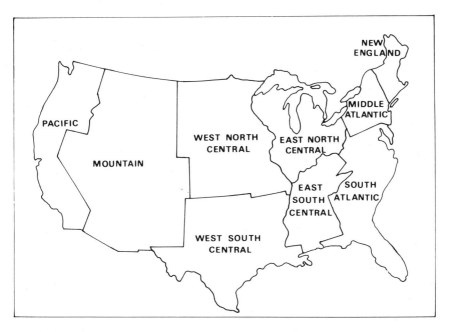

Figure 5.3. The regions used in the analysis of the distribution of corporate headquarters in Table 5.4.

what lower in 1971 relative to 1956. Only in banking, however, does another region (the Pacific) in any way even challenge the corporate hegemony of the corporations in the cities with the initial advantage in the country's Northeast.

An alternative index of the degree of centralization of control over the American economy is given by the numbers of jobs associated with the firms headquartered in the major metropolitan areas (Table 5.5). Fully 8.5 million jobs are controlled by the 327 firms listed in Table 5.3 as having headquarters in New York (an average of 26,000 per company), more than four times the total number of jobs controlled by the two next largest—Chicago and Detroit. (In Detroit the individual firms are larger, however, with each controlling an average of nearly 110,000 jobs.) In terms of growth, too, although many of the larger centers had a slight decline in the number of companies with headquarters there, only Baltimore suffered an absolute decline in the number of jobs controlled. Although the highest growth rates were recorded by the places with few headquarters, there was a clear trend toward further concentration of control among the largest and the growing centers.

Virtually all the employment in the various sectors of the economy is controlled by the largest companies with headquarters in the fifty-five

Table 5.4
PERCENT DISTRIBUTION OF THE FIFTY LARGEST CORPORATIONS BY REGION AND SECTOR, 1956 TO 1971

Region	Year	Sector					
		INDUSTRIAL SALES	TRANSPORT REVENUES	RETAIL SALES	LIFE INSURANCE ASSETS	BANKING ASSETS	UTILITY ASSETS
New England	1956	1.1	2.2	3.0	22.7	2.1	1.7
	1971	2.1	0.0	0.0	24.4	2.2	1.1
Middle Atlantic	1956	54.1	36.9	45.7	59.5	48.0	63.3
	1971	47.4	33.7	38.1	56.0	48.6	60.5
East North Central	1956	35.8	26.8	32.0	8.5	17.4	11.9
	1971	32.2	22.1	40.5	9.5	14.0	7.9
South Atlantic	1956	2.1	12.6	3.0	1.6	0.6	4.6
	1971	1.6	12.4	1.5	1.4	2.1	12.0
East South Central	1956	0.0	2.6	1.0	1.3	0.0	0.0
	1971	0.0	2.9	2.1	1.9	0.0	0.0
West South Central	1956	1.2	0.7	2.9	1.6	3.0	8.3
	1971	5.3	2.5	1.4	1.7	2.4	7.7
West North Central	1956	0.0	11.6	3.6	2.9	2.8	2.1
	1971	1.8	11.8	4.9	3.6	3.2	3.9
Mountain	1956	0.0	5.2	0.0	0.3	0.0	0.8
	1971	1.1	0.6	0.6	0.0	0.8	0.0
Pacific	1956	5.8	1.5	8.7	1.5	26.1	7.3
	1971	8.5	13.1	11.0	1.5	26.7	6.8

Source: Calculated from R. K. Semple, "Recent trends in the spatial concentration of corporate headquarters," *Economic Geography*, 49 (1973):312.

metropolitan areas with populations exceeding 500,000. The percentages are as follows:

Number of Companies	Percent of Employment per Industry
500 largest manufacturing	93
50 largest retailing	100
50 largest utilities	97
50 largest transportation	95
50 largest banking	99
50 largest life insurance	90
50 largest financial	97

Some places specialize in certain of these functions; Hartford, Connecticut, for example, houses five of the fifty largest life insurance companies plus three of the financial companies, and Houston is the headquarters of five of the fifty largest utility companies. In general, however, the main pattern for all kinds of activity is that of centralization into the largest places.

This pattern of centralization has developed throughout the present century. Duncan and Lieberson have shown that, even in 1900, seventeen of the forty largest iron and steel companies had their headquarters in New York, as did twelve of the forty-nine firms involved in the food and liquor trade and forty-one of the ninety-six other companies listed in Table 5.6. One of New York's iron and steel firms alone controlled sixty-five separate plants. No other clear concentrations of headquarters activity were apparent at that date, the main competitors being Chicago and Pittsburgh (the latter reflecting its importance in the heavy industries). Under late capitalism since then, the large cities have prospered in terms of attracting a large portion of the important new white-collar jobs involved in control of the economy that have increased so much more rapidly than have those in other categories.

The pattern of where jobs are controlled is complex. The major metropolitan centers—New York, Chicago, Los Angeles, San Francisco, Detroit—control jobs in most other metropolitan areas, so that, for example, fifty-four of the plants in Atlanta owned by the major industrial organizations have their headquarters in New York, as do seventy-seven of those in Buffalo and twenty-four in Portland (Oregon). There is also an element of local control. Eight of the plants in Atlanta controlled by one of the major firms have their headquarters in nearby Birmingham, Alabama. Maps of the distribution of centers with control of jobs in a particular place for a sample of four places illustrate this combination of

Table 5.5
JOBS CONTROLLED BY MAJOR COMPANIES
FROM LARGE METROPOLITAN AREAS

Area**	Jobs* (Thousands) M	N–M	Area**	Jobs* (Thousands) M	N–M
New York	5802	2706	Portland	87	8
Los Angeles	711	188	Phoenix	76	5
Chicago	1297	876	Columbus	16	9
Philadelphia	394	274	Providence	73	0
Detroit	1683	153	Rochester	164	4
San Francisco	316	332	San Antonio	10	0
Boston	209	110	Dayton	161	0
Washington	4	69	Louisville	21	6
Cleveland	790	103	Hartford	118	147
Pittsburgh	528	12	Sacramento	0	0
St. Louis	415	97	Memphis	16	0
Dallas	229	51	Birmingham	6	4
Baltimore	38	15	Albany	6	0
Houston	177	36	Toledo	163	0
Seattle	113	7	Norfolk	0	0
Minneapolis	334	150	Oklahoma City	13	0
Cincinnati	149	157	Syracuse	35	9
Milwaukee	162	15	Honolulu	47	0
Atlanta	94	62	Greensborough	170	24
San Diego	10	19	Salt Lake City	2	0
Buffalo	44	11	Allentown	120	7
Miami	20	16	Nashville	71	20
Kansas City	28	41	Omaha	17	17
Denver	39	8	Grand Rapids	6	0
Indianapolis	44	0	Youngstown	6	0
New Orleans	29	0	Springfield	17	7
Tampa	28	0	Jacksonville	0	75
			Richmond	73	16

*Key: M—1,000 largest manufacturing companies; NM—300 leading nonmanufacturing.
**For multicentered areas, only first name is given.

Source: A. R. Pred, *Major Job-Providing Organizations and Systems of Cities.* Commission on College Geography, Resource Paper No. 27. Washington D.C.: Association of American Geographers, 1974, pp. 37–38.

Table 5.6
THE LOCATION OF HEADQUARTERS OF
MAJOR INDUSTRIAL CORPORATIONS

Site	All Industries	Iron and Steel	Food and Liquor	Other
New York	70	17	12	41
Boston	4	1	0	3
Philadelphia	5	0	3	2
Baltimore	4	1	1	2
New Orleans	2	0	2	0
San Francisco	5	0	4	1
St. Louis	4	0	1	3
Chicago	18	3	9	6
Pittsburgh	16	4	1	11
Cleveland	6	2	1	3

Source: B. Duncan and S. Lieberson, *Metropolis and Region in Transition*. Beverly Hills: Sage, 1970, p. 73.

national and local patterns (Figure 5.4). Atlanta, for example, has parts of its industrial structure controlled from southern cities, as well as from the national metropoli; Buffalo has links to several New York centers; and Kansas City's contacts are mainly with headquarters locations in the Midwest. San Francisco's pattern is the most widespread, indicating that although that city is near the top of the national urban system it is far from independent of the other places: about 40 percent of the city's jobs that are associated with major organizations are controlled from headquarters in New York (which itself has nearly half a million jobs in industrial organizations with headquarters elsewhere).

The pattern converse to that depicted in Figure 5.4 could be given by mapping the distribution of jobs controlled by organizations with headquarters in particular places. The largest of the centers—the San Francisco/Oakland/San Jose metropolitan complex—has the greatest impact on local economies elsewhere, but many places have jobs controlled from smaller centers, such as Portland and even Boise City, whose population is approximately 120,000. Boise City's pattern is dominated by four firms, a forest-products conglomerate with 29,000 employees, a construction and engineering firm with 21,000, a retailing company with 14,000, and a food processing/fertilizer production conglomerate with 6,000.

The distribution of corporate control illustrated here can be used to suggest that the jobs, and hence the economic and social well-being, of large numbers of Americans are controlled in distant parts of the country (as well as in other countries in the case of European and Japanese multinationals), to which the profits flow. Local autonomy has been re-

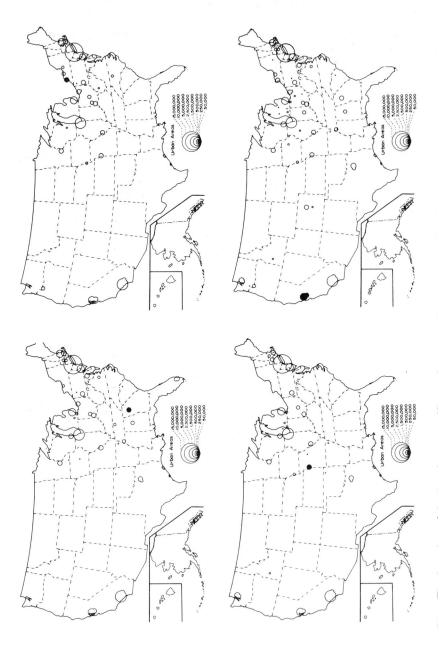

Figure 5.4. The location of the headquarter offices of organizations with plants in four metropolitan areas—Atlanta (top left), Buffalo (top right), Kansas City (bottom left), San Francisco/San Jose (bottom right)—in 1965. Source: Allen R. Pred, *Major Job-Providing Organizations and Systems of Cities.* Washington, D.C.: Association of American Geographers, Resource Papers for College Geography No. 27, 1974, pp. 42, 44, 46, 48. Reprinted by permission.

duced—if not wholly eliminated—by the centralization trend. Indeed, given the multiplier effect of many of the jobs so controlled, it can well be argued that the livelihood of the majority of Americans is controlled, either directly or indirectly, from distant corporate headquarters.

More relevant to the present analysis is the effect of centralization on the cities that house the various corporate headquarters. To a considerable extent these can be classed as basic industries, since much of their income is generated elsewhere in the urban system. Thus they too generate local multipliers (Figure 5.5), which have two components. The first is the general multiplier (the outer loop in the diagram), which is similar to that shown in Figure 4.6. The other is a multiplier specific to the corporate sector. The expansion of the corporate sector contributes to the growth of specialized information regarding business activity (national and international) circulating there. Such information is crucial to successful decision making in large conglomerates, and much of it can be obtained only through personal contacts. Thus the attractiveness

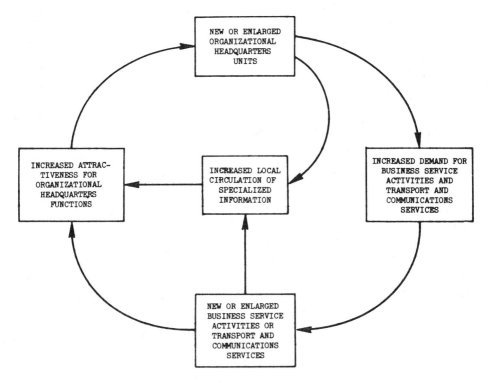

Figure 5.5. The local multiplier effects of corporate headquarters. Source: Allen R. Pred, *Major Job-Providing Organizations and Systems of Cities,* Washington, D.C.: Association of American Geographers, Resource Papers for College Geography No. 27, 1974, p. 24. Reprinted by permission.

of the place for headquarter offices is increased, a fact that is accentuated by the growth in the industries serving the corporate sector; many of these service industries are in the finance sector, and they too add to the attractions of the place. Thus, as with manufacturing under industrial capitalism, growth stimulates growth; in New York alone, 61 million square feet of office space were added to the city's stock between 1970 and 1975.

Growth in one center with a large concentration of corporate headquarters tends to be closely linked with growth in similar centers, through what might be described as an intermetropolitan multiplier process based on information exchange. This is illustrated in Figure 5.6, in which there are two main component parts: C_1, a major corporate center, and $C_2 \ldots C_n$, all the other corporate centers. Each center has its own local multiplier process, shown in the boxes at the left. In addition, however, the interdependence of firms in the two centers means that growth in each also stimulates more trade between the two. This is accompanied by spatially biased flows of specialized information, which means that firms in the major centers are most likely to identify and exploit new business opportunities and spawn innovations and inventions. (The same occurs at the international scale. Most trade is between

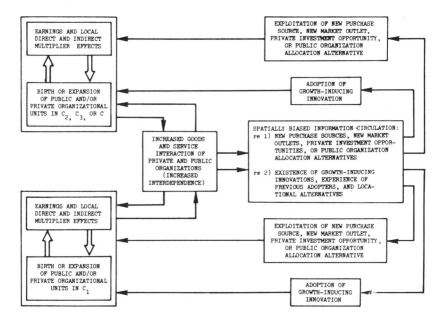

Figure 5.6. The intermetropolitan multiplier involving flows between large cities. Source: Allen R. Pred, *Major Job-Providing Organizations and Systems of Cities.* Washington, D.C.: Association of American Geographers, Resource Papers for College Geography No. 27, 1974, p. 58. Reprinted by permission.

the advanced economies; most capital and information flows between these, too, and these are the major growth economies.) The combined effect of the local multiplier (Figure 5.5) and the shared multiplier (Figure 5.6) very much favors growth in the large metropolitan areas— the corporate centers—to the detriment of the smaller places. The big get bigger.

In terms of the urban system, therefore, centralization has had the same general effect as concentration; it has accentuated the dominance of the larger places. The American economy is becoming increasingly centralized into a relatively small number of major corporations. Many of these choose to have their headquarters in one of only a few large cities—of which New York is by far the most popular—in order to benefit from proximity to each other, to the major elements of the financial infrastructure (such as the New York Stock Exchange and the complex focused on Wall Street), and to the centers of manufacturing activity.

GOVERNMENT AS A BASIC URBAN ACTIVITY

The massive growth in government employment, payrolls, and expenditures in recent years has also benefited certain places by generating jobs and prosperity, both directly and indirectly. Three types of government-generated activity can be identified: federal employment, including defense forces; state and local government employment, most of which is in administration, particularly of various public welfare programs; and federal contracts, the most important of which are those for the supply of military goods.

The main center of federal employment is, of course, Washington, D.C., where 80 percent of all basic employment earnings (32 percent of all earnings) come from the federal government. The federal administration is both highly centralized and complex, and is the keystone of the economy of Washington, which has become the eighth largest metropolitan area in the country, with a population of nearly three million in 1970. No other place is as dependent on federal income for its basic earnings (Figure 5.7), but six others get over 60 percent of their income from that source, mainly through large defense installations. None of these is among the largest metropolitan areas, so that federal employment has slightly modified rather than accentuated the urban system of premonopoly capitalism. All but one of the places shown in Figure 5.7 are in the South.

Many state governments are located in relatively small urban areas, so that the growth of these governments has not contributed to the growth of the large cities that is characteristic of private-sector organizations. Nevertheless, seventeen of the largest metropolitan areas have major concentrations of state government employees (Table 5.7).

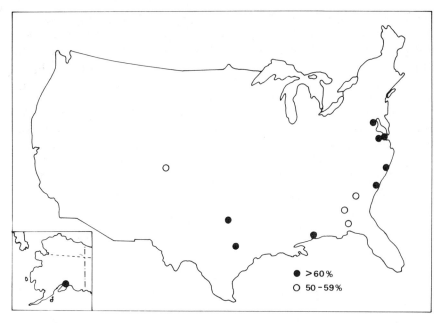

Figure 5.7. Daily urban systems with more than half their basic income coming from the federal government. Source: Data from B. J. L. Berry, *Growth Centers in the American Urban System, Vol. 1.* Cambridge: Ballinger, 1973, Table 1.2.

Notable among these are the capitals of the two most populous states—Sacramento (California) and Albany-Schenectady-Troy (New York)—with controlled employment totals close to 200,000 each. Again, the governmental function is sufficient to generate considerable growth in the local employment base via the various multiplier loops.

Many thousands of government contracts are issued each year and bring employment to various centers. A large number go to the main urban areas, simply because they contain much of the country's manufacturing capability. In 1972 alone the federal government spent $227 billion, of which the largest sum—$77 billion—was for the Department of Defense. Many of the department's suppliers are in the West and South, building on wartime installations. Thus in 1972 defense contractors in the Los Angeles and neighboring metropolitan areas earned $3.1 billion.

Competition for government contracts is great, and one influence on their disbursement is membership of the relevant committees in the House and Senate. Members can lobby for contracts for companies in their states and districts, as part of their efforts to win the votes of their constituents. Within the Los Angeles area, for example, the representative for the thirty-first Congressional District (C. H. Wilson) was the tenth-ranking member of the powerful Armed Services Committee, and contractors in his district received $1.3 billion of work in 1972. Perhaps the best example of a congressman clearly able to help his constituents in this way was Mendel Rivers, who represented South Carolina's First Congressional District (embracing the Charleston metropolitan area) and chaired the House Armed Services Committee from 1965 to 1970; fully 35 percent of Charleston's payroll in the early 1970s came from the Department of Defense, either directly or through contractors, and the district has eleven naval installations. Influential individuals can thus direct government money toward certain areas, which may not always be the largest, so that, as with other government activity, federal contracts do not completely reinforce and support the existing system.

SUMMARY

Although governmental activity does not support the thesis as strongly as private sector operation, in general the consequences of late capitalism for the urban system have been to enhance the dominance of the largest centers. These house the headquarters and the major factor-

Table 5.7
STATE GOVERNMENT JOBS CONTROLLED FROM MAJOR METROPOLITAN AREAS

Metropolitan Area	Jobs Controlled (Thousands)
Boston	65
Baltimore	53
Minneapolis/St. Paul	45
Atlanta	57
Denver	37
Indianapolis	55
Phoenix	25
Columbus	89
Providence	15
Hartford	39
Sacramento	195
Albany/Schenectady/Troy	184
Oklahoma City	39
Honolulu	30
Salt Lake City	19
Nashville	50
Richmond	68

Source: A. R. Pred, *Major Job-Providing Organizations and Systems of Cities.* Commission on College Geography, Resource Paper No. 27. Washington D.C.: Association of American Geographers, 1974, p. 39, from U.S. Bureau of the Census data.

ies of the largest manufacturing companies, as well as the offices of the other large corporations in the country that are not involved in manufacturing. This not only creates the usual multipliers in the large places, with consequences for their growth relative to that of other urban areas, but also makes the smaller places "subservient," in that many of the decisions about jobs there are made in the control centers of the cities with headquarter locations. There is no definite hierarchy of control— New York is itself dependent on other places as well as being a dominant control center—but the ten or so largest centers clearly control a large segment of the national economy. Late capitalism has produced concentration and centralization; which are reflected in urban functions, although they are somewhat difficult to map because late capitalism has also encouraged suburban sprawl and spatial decentralization.

SOME RECENT TRENDS
IN INDUSTRIAL LOCATION

Several of the data sets used to discuss the American urban system in the era of industrial capitalism in the preceding chapter refer to the late 1950s and 1960s. In part the choice of data reflects the information available from completed studies, but mainly they were chosen to illustrate the situation at about the peak of the developments that characterized industrial capitalism. Some of the more recent changes in the urban system represent the transition to late capitalism.

The recent trends can be summarized in one phrase: national decentralization. Since the Second World War, in particular, although the Manufacturing Belt has retained its dominance, there has been growth of employment in the towns of the South and the West, and to a lesser extent in the Mountain States. A variety of reasons accounts for this shift.

One of the most rapidly growing industries of the past few decades has been aerospace. The initial stimulus for the major development of the aeronautical industry was the Second World War. Production of aircraft was dispersed, for defense reasons, and several big plants were established on the west coast, notably in Seattle and its environs and in Los Angeles. The production of armaments and other military supplies also advanced rapidly in the West, and this growth helped make California the major attraction for migrants in the postwar decades, when it could offer jobs as well as climate and scenery. The west coast is now a minor Manufacturing Belt, with a sufficiently large market to attract many market-oriented industries, often branches of companies operating in the Northeast. It has also developed as a major industrial complex based on continued large federal expenditures on defense equipment. Armaments are now very highly sophisticated, so a range of advanced electronic and other technological industries has developed in Los Angeles, San Francisco, Seattle, and their environs.

Alongside the aeronautical and other defense industries has been the massive, although now slackened, development of space and space-related industries. Here again, the West has benefited, building on its expertise in other fields, but so have both the South, notably around Houston and the launching sites in Florida, and areas of the Mountain States, particularly Denver and Boulder. Although the latter places have grown to major size in recent years, many of their industries are still supplied with components from the Manufacturing Belt.

There are several reasons for the establishment of these industries outside the Manufacturing Belt, but like those set up earlier, many have generated the sorts of multipliers indicated in the discussion of Figure 4.1. The basic/nonbasic linkages are the same, as are those related to backward and forward linkages. But perhaps the most important multiplier chain has been that associated with innovation. The aeronautical and space industries have rapidly expanded as highly sophisticated enterprises, associated with the development of the computer and other technologically advanced innovations. These became the boom industries of the post–Second World War era, not only because of their links with the aerospace and defense industries, but also due to their adoption of a wide range of other activities. Not surprisingly, many of these new industries were established as spinoffs in the South and the West, where the advanced technologies were being developed. And again, industrial growth generated more growth. California in particular benefited, and by 1970 it was the most populous state in the union, the flood of migrants enabling it to outstrip New York. (The population of California in 1976 was 21.5 million, compared to 15.9 million sixteen years earlier; comparable figures for New York were 18.1 and 16.8 million. There was a net migration of 2,113,000 people to California between 1960 and 1970 and 623,000 more between 1970 and 1976; New York lost 51,000 by migration between 1960 and 1970 and 640,000 more in the next six years.)

One of the most striking examples of the growth of this "new Manufacturing Belt" in California is the silicon chip industry—the basis of microprocessors—of the Palo Alto/Santa Clara/San Jose area (often known as Silicon Valley) south of San Francisco Bay. The initial factory there was established in 1958 by eight scientists with the backing of the Fairchild Camera and Instrument Corporation. During the next two decades more than forty new companies were established in Silicon Valley by scientists who formerly worked for Fairchild (hence their nickname, the "Fairchildren"). They chose to open plants near their "parent," since there was an established pool of labor, risk capital could be obtained, and it was easier to open a factory near home than to move in order to do so. Hence a specialized industrial complex and the associated multiplier processes developed in exactly the same way as described in Chapter 4. Today, growth in the industry there has slowed, because of competition from elsewhere (including cheaper foreign manufacturers) and the cost of land in the area. Perhaps the rapidity of technological change and the almost irrelevant role of transport costs to such low-bulk/high-cost products mean that industrial inertia and advantage are now much more ephemeral. Today California, tomorrow . . . ?

Newly exploited resources have also attracted industries to areas outside the Manufacturing Belt. Examples are the petroleum-refining complexes of Texas and the industrial developments based on local salt, sulphur and phosphate deposits, and the coal, oil, and mineral resources of the High Plains that brought prosperity for regional centers such as Denver. Local agriculture has also provided the raw material base for industrial development. But a major attraction of the South to other industrial investors has been the availability of relatively low cost labor. For five representative industries, average earnings per hour in 1968 for the country as a whole were textiles $2.21; apparel, $2.21; food $2.80; lumber $2.56; and furniture $2.47; whereas in North Carolina the averages were $2.13, $1.85, $2.00, $1.99, and $2.14, respectively. This cheap labor is especially attractive in industries such as clothing, which are relatively, if not absolutely, in decline, and in which industrial capitalists are seeking lower costs in order to maintain their profit levels. The low cost of labor is in part related to the low level of unionization in the South (Figure 5.8); it is drawing industrial investment away from the traditional areas of New England.

But New England is also relatively cheap compared to most parts of the Manufacturing Belt, and increasingly firms in the electronics industry are opening plants in southern New England; new technological developments allow them to employ relatively unskilled operatives rather than the skilled personnel who were typical of industrial capitalism. Indeed, many industrial firms are opening branch plants in rural areas to benefit from the cheap labor supply (much of it female), and there has been a considerable growth of employment in rural areas as a result, especially in the South; indeed, that region experienced an increase of almost one million jobs (a growth rate of 57 percent) in its nonmetropolitan areas between 1962 and 1978, or more than half the national nonmetropolitan growth during that period. (Interestingly, some of the money being invested in southern growth industries is institutional, including the pension funds of unions whose strength is in the Manufacturing Belt. Paradoxically, these funds are being invested—to earn maximum returns—in industries that are competing with those employing the investors, who may be indirectly putting themselves out of work in order to finance their retirement.)

Two types of industrial development characterize the move to the Sun Belt (see Chapter 1). The first is based on the initial advantages of

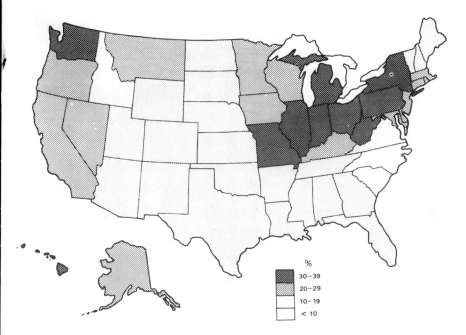

Figure 5.8.   Interstate variations in the level of unionization: percentage of non-agricultural employees who were union members, 1975. Source: Data from U.S. Bureau of the Census, *Statistical Abstract of the United States 1977*, p. 418.

the region, its natural resources (including oil and increased agricultural production) and its acquired skills in the highly sophisticated technology-based industries, focused on defense and space but extending widely now into other fields. These advantages are being built on in the rapid growth of some Sun Belt metropolitan areas, such as Atlanta and Houston (see Table 5.3), which are becoming corporate as well as industrial centers. The second type of industrial development is based on the cheap labor still available in the South, especially its rural areas—although the differential in average income between the South and the North has decreased rapidly in recent years. A third stimulus to growth in some parts of the Sun Belt is retirement migration. Relatively affluent older people are retiring in very large numbers to states such as Florida and Arizona, largely attracted by the climate. Specially designed housing and entire retirement communities have grown up to cater to this demand, which sets up local multiplier effects generated by the investment income and pensions of the new residents; there is also a growing demand for the facilities provided by the Veterans' Administration.

Those industries employing cheap labor are examples of a complex product cycle, with a typical locational pattern that is becoming characteristic of late capitalism. In the industrial capitalism stage, product development was usually carried out by small firms, as part of the innovation/invention cycle identified in Figure 4.4. Increasingly, however, the research and development needed for new products has become a long, large, and expensive process, for which small firms lack the capital and expertise; there were about 6,000 industrial research and development laboratories in the United States in 1975, and 598 firms were responsible for some 95 percent of the "R and D" (research and development) expenditure.

The vast investment necessary for research into the development of new products not only confines such work to large companies, but also suggests that this is likely to take place in the major urban agglomerations where the relevant specialized information is available (Figures 5.5, 5.6). At this stage of a product cycle, the most important influences on location of the relevant activity are specialized information/ability and external economies. Thus one would expect to find major industrial research laboratories in the large cities, especially those (such as Boston, Los Angeles, and San Francisco) that have major technological universities. This is indeed the case. Figure 5.9 shows the metropolitan areas with the greatest concentrations of R and D laboratories and em-

△ Concentration of R and D Employees

○ Concentration of R and D Labs

⊘ Concentration of R and D Employees and Labs

Figure 5.9.   Major research and development complexes, 1975. Source: E. J. Malecki, "Agglomeration and Intra-firm Linkage in R and D Location in the United States," *Tijdschrift voor Economische en Sociale Geografie,* 70 (1979): 328.

ployees; the majority are in the Manufacturing Belt and only San Francisco, Denver/Boulder, Austin, Huntsville (Alabama), and Raleigh/Durham (North Carolina) have well-above-average concentrations (per thousand population) of both laboratories and employees. These concentrations are, of course, multiplier generators.

Much R and D is funded by the federal government (almost exactly half in 1976–1977), and where contracts are awarded can have considerable effects on the economic health of not only companies but also whole cities and regions. In 1976 the federal government spent $9.29 billion on Research and Development, more than half of it on aerospace and another one quarter on the electrical and electronic industries. Together the Department of Defense and the National Aeronautics and Space Administration awarded contracts worth $2.92 billion in the Los Angeles/Long Beach/Anaheim metropolitan area alone in 1977; the next largest recipient was Boston, with less than $800 million. The multiplier effects of such expenditures are immense, although not all of them stay within the areas to which the contracts are granted; Los Angeles contractors granted $256 million of subcontracts to local firms, for example, and $297 million to firms in other metropolitan areas. Nevertheless, the Sun Belt cities, and especially those of the west coast, benefit most from the federal investment in industrial research.

The initial stage of the product cycle—R and D—is very much concentrated in the large metropolitan areas to benefit from the external economies there. (There is some evidence of a slight trend away from the largest centers in recent years, but this is not very great.) Once the new product has been established, the next stage in the cycle is the investment of large quantities of capital in developing production lines; skilled labor is increasingly replaced by machines, and the crucial developmental factor is managerial ability. The new factories are likely to be close to the research and management centers in the major metropolitan areas. But once production methods have been standardized, management skills decline in importance. The manufacturing process is mechanized—capital is invested in machinery and the operations need mainly semi- and unskilled labor. The latter is available in its cheapest form in the small towns of rural America, both those just beyond the fringe of the metropolitan areas and those in the rural areas of relatively depressed regions, such as the South. (The disadvantages of the large metropolitan areas include high taxes, in part a reflection of this decline.) Thus at this final stage of the product cycle a firm is likely to shift the bulk of its manufacturing activity to such cheap locations, establishing branch factories outside the major urban systems. Indeed, one study of new branch factories in rural Kentucky, New Mexico, Vermont, and Wisconsin found that the majority produced either clothing or electronic components (including assembly); both are characterized by their relatively large demands for unskilled labor. Thus the recent industrialization of the rural South reflects its cheap labor; the parallel growth in the southern and western metropolitan areas represents their initial advantages in the current growth industries and the direction of federal contracts (many of them by powerful local politicians) to R and D laboratories there.

CONCLUSIONS

The present chapter has brought the development of the American urban system up to date. The basic theme of this and the two preceding chapters is the stability, especially with regard to the major elements, of that system. The urban centers that emerged under mercantile capitalism formed the framework within which the later stages of industrial and late capitalism have been enacted. The crucial influence on this stability has been initial advantage, a concept expressed in a variety of ways, including market size, access to finance and specialized information, external economies, and the alignment of transport networks.

The role of initial advantage has not been all powerful, of course. Major changes have occurred. As the mercantile frontier was pushed westward, new gateway cities were established, some of which outstripped the older centers of the eastern seaboard, especially those in the South. Industrial capitalism added some new types of town, a few of which also grew large and disturbed the city-size distribution. And now, under late capitalism, the cities of the South and West are experiencing the most rapid growth, benefiting from new types of industry, especially those with few ties to the older centers of the Frost Belt. Yet throughout, New York has remained the national metropolis, and Philadelphia and Boston have retained their places in the second rank. They are the monuments of stability around which, to date, the fluctuations of the American urban system have flowed during the last two centuries. Whether the next few decades will see major changes is uncertain but, I would suggest, unlikely.

SUGGESTIONS FOR FURTHER READING—PART TWO

There are many books on the urban history of the United States, including:
GREEN, C. M. *American Cities in the Growth of the Nation.* New York: Harper & Row, 1957.
MCKELVEY, B. *The Emergency of Metropolitan America.* New Brunswick: Rutgers University Press, 1966.
MCKELVEY, B. *American Urbanization: A Comparative History.* Glenview, Ill.: Scott, Foresman, 1973.

The best summary of urban historical geography is to be found in:
WARD, D. *Cities and Immigrants*. New York: Oxford University Press, 1971.

The most detailed treatment, covering the entire history of the United States, is found in a series of books by Allan Pred:
PRED, A. R. *The Spatial Dynamics of U.S. Urban-Industrial Growth, 1800-1914.* Cambridge: M.I.T. Press, 1966.
PRED, A. R. *Urban Growth and the Circulation of Information.* Cambridge: Harvard University Press, 1973.
PRED, A. R. *Major Job-Providing Organizations and Systems of Cities.* Washington, D.C.: Commission on College Geography, Association of American Geographers, 1974.
PRED, A. R. *City-Systems in Advanced Economies.* London: Hutchinson, 1977.
PRED, A. R. *Urban Growth and City-System Development in the United States, 1840-1860.* Cambridge: Harvard University Press, 1981.

More general statements of the development of America's urban system are offered by:
BORCHERT, J. R. "American Metropolitan Evolution," *Geographical Review,* 57 (1967): 301-332.
LUKERMANN, F. "Empirical Expressions of Nodality and Hierarchy in a Circulation Manifold," *East Lakes Geographer,* 2 (1966): 17-54.

and various publications by Eric Lampard, including:
LAMPARD, E. E. "The Evolving System of Cities in the United States," in H. S. Perloff and L. Wingo (editors), *Issues in Urban Economics.* Baltimore: Johns Hopkins University Press, 1968, pp. 81-140.

The mercantile model for urban development is covered in:
TAAFFE, E. J., R. L. MORRILL, and P. R. GOULD. "Transport Expansion in Under-developed Countries," *Geographical Review,* 53 (1963): 503-529.
RIMMER, P. J. "The Changing Status of New Zealand Seaports," *Annals of the Association of American Geographers,* 57 (1967): 88-100.
VANCE, J. E. *The Merchant's World.* Englewood Cliffs, N.J.: Prentice-Hall, 1970.
BURGHARDT, A. F. "A Hypothesis about Gateway Cities," *Annals of the Association of American Geographers,* 61 (1971): 269-285.

The concept of the primate city was introduced in:
JEFFERSON, M. "The Law of the Primate City," *Geographical Review,* 29 (1939): 226-232.

and central place theory is reviewed in:
BERRY, B. J. L. *The Geography of Market Centers and Retail Distribution.* Englewood Cliffs, N.J.: Prentice-Hall, 1967.
BEAVON, K. S. O. *Central Place Theory.* London: Longman, 1967.

The role of banking is discussed in:
DUNCAN, O. D., et. al. *Metropolis and Region.* Baltimore: Resources for the Future, 1960.
DUNCAN, B., and S. LIEBERSON. *Metropolis and Region in Transition.* Beverly Hills: Sage, 1970.

and in a number of publications by Michael Conzen, including:
CONZEN, M. P. "A Transport Interpretation of the Growth of Urban Regions," *Journal of Historical Geography,* 1 (1975).
CONZEN, M. P. "The Maturing Urban System in the United States, 1840-1910," *Annals of the Association of American Geographers,* 67 (1977).

A broad review of the literature on urban systems is to be found in:
BOURNE, L. S., and J. W. SIMMONS, editors. *Systems of Cities.* New York: Oxford University Press, 1978.

Industrial location is treated in a number of general texts, including:
SMITH, D. M. *Industrial Location: An Economic Geographical Analysis* (second edition). New York: Wiley, 1981.
ISARD, W. *An Introduction to Regional Science.* Englewood Cliffs, N.J.: Prentice-Hall, 1975.
SMITH, R. H. T., E. J. TAAFFE, and L. J. KING, editors. *Readings in Economic Geography.* Chicago: Rand McNally, 1967.

For a more general treatment, see:
JACOBS, J. *The Economy of Cities.* New York: Random House, 1971.

Multipliers and linkages are covered in the books by Pred already referred to; input-output matrices are described in the book by Isard listed above. For a local input-output matrix, see the work on Philadelphia by Karaska, found in the volume edited by Smith, Taaffe, and King. The geography of innovations is discussed by Pred.

For a general treatment of urban growth under industrialism, see also:
THOMPSON, W. R. *A Preface to Urban Economics.* Baltimore: Johns Hopkins University Press, 1965.

For case studies, see:
ESTALL, R. C. *New England: A Study in Industrial Readjustment.* London: G. Bell, 1964.
MAYER, H. M., and R. C. WADE. *Chicago: Growth of a Metropolis.* Chicago: University of Chicago Press, 1969.
HELFGOTT, R. B., et al. *Made in New York.* Cambridge: Harvard University Press, 1962.

For city classifications, see:
BERRY, B. J. L., editor. *City Classification Handbook.* New York: Wiley, 1972.

Detailed surveys of American urbanization under late capitalism are included in:
STERNLIEB, G., and J. W. HUGHES. *Post-Industrial America: Metropolitan Decline and Inter-Regional Job Shifts.* New Brunswick: Center for Urban Policy Research, Rutgers University, 1975.
BRUNN, S. D., and J. O. WHEELER, *The American Metropolitan System: Present and Future.* New York: Halsted Press, 1980.
YEATES, M. H. *North American Urban Patterns.* New York: Halsted Press, 1980.
LONSDALE, R. E., and H. L. SEYLER, editors. *Nonmetropolitan Industrialization.* Washington: Winston, 1979.
BERRY, B. J. L., editor. *Urbanization and Counterurbanization.* Beverly Hills: Sage, 1976.
BERRY, B. J. L., and Q. GILLARD. *The Changing Shape of Metropolitan America.* Cambridge: Ballinger, 1977.
BOURNE, L. S. "Alternative Perspectives on Urban Decline and Population Deconcentration," *Urban Geography,* 1 (1980): 39–52.
MASOTTI, L. H., and J. K. HADDEN, editors. *The Urbanization of the Suburbs.* Beverly Hills: Sage, 1973.
PERRY, D. C., and A. J. WATKINS, editors. *The Rise of the Sunbelt Cities.* Beverly Hills: Sage, 1977.
TABB, W. K., and L. SAWERS, editors. *Marxism and the Metropolis.* New York: Oxford University Press, 1978.

Population decline in small places is treated in a number of papers by Glenn Fuguitt, including:
FUGUITT, G. V. "The Places Left Behind: Population Trends and Policy for Rural America, *Rural Sociology,* 36 (1970): 449–470.

whereas urban sprawl is discussed in:

GOTTMANN, J. *Megalopolis*. New York: Twentieth Century Fund, 1961.
GOTTMANN, J., and R. A. HARPER, editors. *Metropolis on the Move*. New York: Wiley, 1967.

For discussion of the growth of the tertiary and quaternary sectors and the geography of control centers, see:

ARMSTRONG, R. B. *The Office Industry: Patterns of Growth and Location*. Cambridge: M.I.T. Press, 1972.
BORCHERT, J. R. "Major control points in American economic geography," *Annals of the Association of American Geographers,* 68 (1978): 214–252.
SEMPLE, R. K. "Recent Trends in the Spatial Concentrations of Corporate Headquarters," *Economic Geography,* 49 (1973): 309–318.
ARMSTRONG, R. B. "National Trends in Office Construction, Employment and Headquarter Location in U.S. Metropolitan Areas," in P. W. Daniels, editor, *Spatial Patterns of Office Growth and Location*. London: Wiley, 1979, pp. 61–94.

The topic of growth poles and the related spread and backwash effects is covered in:

BERRY, B. J. L. *Growth Centers in the American Urban System*. Cambridge, Mass. Ballinger, 1973.

The role of the state in the geography of the United States is discussed in:

JOHNSTON, R. J. *The Geography of Federal Spending in the United States*. London: Wiley, 1981.

PART THREE

The INTERNAL STRUCTURE of URBAN AREAS

CASUAL INSPECTION OF any urban area in the United States reveals a complex organism. A large number of separate units—individuals, households, firms, and governments—make decisions that determine the morphology and organization of these densely occupied tracts of land. Some of these decisions are relatively few in number, are usually influenced by only a small proportion of the population, and yet probably have the most important long-term consequences; these decisions involve the locations of factories and office blocks, for example, as well as the construction of new housing and the zoning of land for different uses. In other cases many more people are involved in the decision-making process—where to live is the best example—and although these decisions are not as permanent or as significant in

their effects they have considerable short-term, local influence on urban patterns. Finally, there are the frequent decisions that involve the majority of people. Where to shop, how to travel to work, whether to dine out (and, if so, where) or at home: these determine the ebb and flow of people and vehicles that characterize the city as a living organism.

The great range and number of separate (though far from independent) decisions being made in American urban areas could clearly produce immense chaos, unless a set of organizing influences ensured that this did not occur. Indeed, the internal spatial structure of urban areas is highly ordered. The distributions of different land use types and different household groups are far from random fashion, for example. They are carefully arranged in patterns that have features in common across most settlements—although each place also has its unique characteristics. These features reflect the operation of two basic processes: congregation and segregation. Congregation involves clustering in space for mutual benefit; segregation involves the exclusion of certain land uses or users from particular areas, thereby restricting their locational choice and confining them to prescribed districts only.

The current geography of American cities and towns reflects the interplay of these two forces of congregation and segregation, within the constraints of an existing pattern created when the processes were operating during an earlier phase of development. Three sets of forces produce these two processes—social, economic, and political. The three are, of course, highly interdependent, as separate but linked parts of the capitalist system. But for purposes of exposition they are treated separately here, although the relevant links are not neglected. Thus the next chapter deals with the social geography of the urban area, with its residential districts: its focus is the class and other divisions of American society introduced in Chapter 2, and how they are reflected in the urban mosaic. Chapter 7 discusses economic geography, focusing on the nonresidential land uses and the features of late capitalism that influence their distribution patterns. Finally, Chapter 8 looks at the political geography, with special reference to suburbanization and the nature of municipal government, emphasizing the role of the state in the creation of America's urban geography.

6

THE RESIDENTIAL MOSAIC

IN MOST URBAN areas, residential land use is the major category in terms of acreage occupied, especially where local streets are considered part of the residential environment. The great extent of housing, much of it at very low densities, is mainly a twentieth-century phenomenon, built on an eighteenth- and nineteenth-century base that itself developed from very small settlements without much spatial order. In the latter, rich and poor, employers and employees, young and old, and members of the various ethnic groups lived in high-density, spatially nonsegregated residential districts, many of which also contained much commercial and industrial land use. Today, these various groups are spatially separated from one another, to a greater or lesser extent. This transformation, from a pattern of residential heterogeneity to one of homogeneous separateness, is the subject of the present chapter.

FROM MERCANTILE
TO INDUSTRIAL CITY

The lack of any observable pattern in the small, early mercantile settlements is a reflection of both their size and the nature of their society. Among the population, there were marked differences in social and economic status, reflected in the distribution of incomes and wealth. But three characteristics of the society made congregation and segregation largely unnecessary, unlike the situation today. The first was that the society was relatively static: people "knew their place" in the social and economic scale, and knew everybody else's, too. Many did not accept their position as permanent, of course, and were determined, through their own efforts, to achieve a higher station. But the relatively affluent did not feel threatened by such ambition; there was room in an expanding economy for it, and their own positions were secure. Secondly, the level of technology was such that long daily journeys were impossible, especially given the length of the working day, and so very high-density living was necessary. Finally, although even in a settlement of only a few thousand people most residents would know, and be known to, only a small number of other persons, the status of most "unknowns" could be identified easily and social distances could be maintained, where appropriate, without the reinforcement of spatial distance that was introduced later.

In the earliest settlements, many people lived at their place of work, with perhaps some spatial compartmentalization of different functions in the larger places. (Some of this compartmentalization was made necessary by demands on the physical environment: an obvious example is the location of functions related to shipping.) Merchants and shopkeepers often ran their businesses from the ground floor of their homes, for example, while living in the upper stories, and many craftsmen operated workshops within the family residence. Further, many employees lived with their employers, usually in separate quarters (along with domestic servants) but sometimes sharing certain facilities, such as the dining room. The staff of most businesses was small and could be accommodated in this way (especially for unmarried workers), albeit often in conditions that were far more crowded than those of their masters.

Not all employees lived at their workplace. Some rented accommodations, either for themselves alone or for their families as well, usually close to the workplace, in order to reduce the effort involved in traveling before and after a long day's work. Rental dwellings were built by those who saw the ownership of such housing as a profitable investment; the nature of the accommodations provided was determined by the ability of the renters to pay. Other workers rented rooms, some dwelling with families who owned their own homes but needed the income from the rents, and some subletting from renters. Thus there was a degree of residential separation that reflected income differences. In addition, some of the affluent households—those of the main merchants—were located away from business premises, and in general these merchants chose to live apart—in separate streets with superior accommodations—from their paid employees.

The small mercantile settlement was not characterized by a total absence of residential separation—of employers and employees, of well- and poorly paid, even of employed and unemployed/underemployed. Its extent was small, however, relative to the developments during industrial capitalism, when the processes of congregation and segregation became dominant influences on the form of the residential mosaic. The growth of the major mercantile cities, the introduction of industries (as opposed to craft workshops), and rapid immigration were the sources of the transformation. Technological improvements, notably in transport, facilitated and speeded the transformation. The result was, at a smaller scale and still relatively high density overall, the mosaic that has persisted to the present.

As firms—whether mercantile or industrial—grew, workforces became too large for most employers to provide with housing, certainly in their own homes. Separate accommodation was needed. In some early industrial towns, notably those in New England, employers provided either barracks for single workers or separate dwellings. This reflected a combination of necessity (if a labor force was to be obtained), paternalism, and relatively close employer-employee ties. (Some towns, such as Pullman, south of Chicago, were founded by a single employer, whose employees were the only ones able to obtain housing there.)

But as settlements grew, and more firms were established in them, the need for employers to provide housing ceased. The various firms were competing for workers, either in the same occupation or for use of the same basic skills, encouraging employees to change jobs, especially if they could earn higher wages in the process. Thus linked housing became an encumbrance to the mobility of labor. No longer required to provide it, employers preferred to invest their capital elsewhere, in more fruitful ventures. Employees became responsible for providing—or at least obtaining—their own accommodations.

Provision of rental housing for employees occurred in two ways. First, as will be described in detail below, many members of the employer class decided to vacate their homes in or near the city center. Some of these homes were bought by intending landlords, who rented all or, in most cases, parts of the dwellings to individual families: some were subdivided into many small dwellings, often consisting of only a single room, with most basic utilities having to be shared. (This allowed considerable rental income to be obtained; the congestion, poor quality of housing, and health hazards that were created usually prompted other members of the employer class to move away from the area, thereby putting more of such accommodations on the market.

This process could provide relatively few homes, however, especially in a rapidly expanding settlement. The majority of the housing was provided by capitalist investors who built homes, mostly blocks of tenements, that could be rented by the working class. Again, many of the dwellings were small, poorly serviced, and occupied at high densities, both per room and per acre; only in this way could the needed return on capital (the most rent for the least expenditure) be assured. Some investors built large blocks and rows of such housing, but much construction was undertaken by small firms, and a varied, if uniformly drab and low-quality, townscape was produced. Even so, in many places the supply of housing did not meet the demand (which allowed rents to be kept high). Some urban residents, almost always the poorest and usually including many of the most recent arrivals, found it necessary to build homes for themselves. Some became squatters in shanty towns on the edges of the built-up area and were displaced from about the mid-nineteenth century on as transport improvements made these areas desirable for the relatively affluent.

Not all the housing built to make profits for landlords was of low quality and intended for the low paid, the unskilled, and the recent immigrants. Some of it was substantial, usually constructed of superior materials, and occupied at lower densities; some was built for sale. The employer class resided in such areas, as did the more skilled and better paid of their employees, plus the many small businessmen (including the landlords of the workers' housing) who benefited from the economic boom of the expanding nineteenth-century cities, especially the port and inland gateways.

Thus by the middle of the nineteenth century most American cities contained the elements of an ordered residential mosaic. The constraints of commuting on foot meant that much of this mosaic comprised very high-density, low-quality dwellings, most of them tenements. For example, it has been estimated that the average journey to work for those who lived away from their workplace in New York in 1840, was 0.33 miles for machinists, 0.43 miles for bakers, 0.66 miles for printers, and 0.99 miles for engravers. Most of the last group worked in an area just north of Wall Street, and the majority lived nearby (Figure 6.1); those who traveled long distances used either the horse-drawn omnibus (the daily fare was 12.5 cents, and there were 25,000 users, mainly merchants and prosperous artisans) or the horse-drawn New York and Harlem Railroad.

This pattern in New York reflects the onset of industrialization. Previously, the more usual situation was to find the central areas occupied by the higher-status groups (the merchants) and the outer zones by their employees. A model of such a pattern is shown in the top part of Figure 6.2. It has been tested for Charleston, South Carolina, in 1860, when the city was still in the preindustrial, mercantile stage. For the analysis the city was divided into six concentric zones focused on the main intersection, and the distributions of four occupational groups across these zones are shown in the bottom part of Figure 6.2. These graphs show that, in both absolute and relative terms, there was clear spatial segregation. The city's elite—the merchants and managers, the planters and professionals—were concentrated in the inner zones, along with their domestic servants, whereas the manual workers lived in the outer zones. There were some deviations from the general pattern, how-

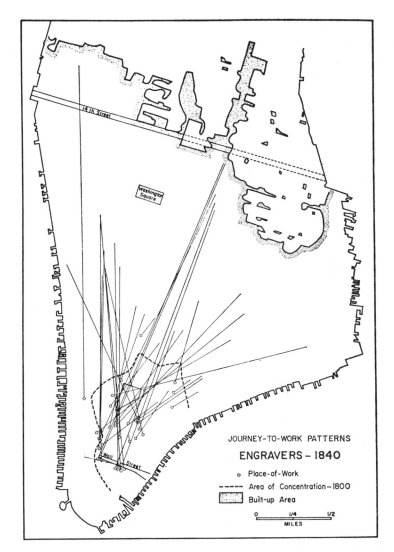

Figure 6.1.   The journey-to-work pattern for engravers in New York, 1840. Reprinted from A. R. Pred, *The Spatial Dynamics of U.S. Urban-Industrial Growth, 1800–1914,* p. 212, by permission of The MIT Press, Cambridge, Massachusetts. Copyright © 1966 by The MIT Press.

ever, notably the concentration of some manual workers in the inner zone near the wharves, marking the initial stage in the development of the more typical industrial urban pattern.

The basis of residential separation was the different level of rewards received by groups within the employee class—as well as, of course, between the employee and the employer classes. The more income that

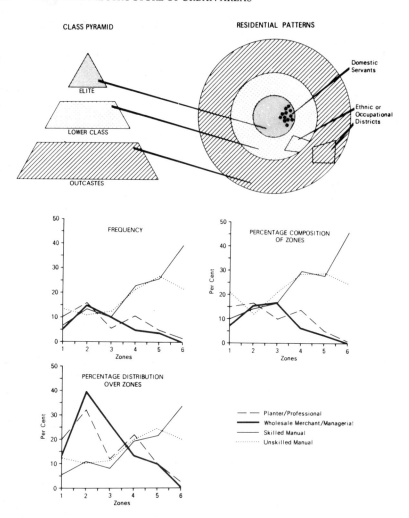

Figure 6.2. The distribution of occupational groups in preindustrial Charleston, South Carolina: top, a model of the residential pattern; bottom, the distribution of four occupational groups across a set of six zones. Source: J. P. Radford, "Testing the Model of the Pre-Industrial City: The Case of Ante-Bellum Charleston, South Carolina," *Transactions, Institute of British Geographers,* NS4 (1979):394, 399.

people received, either from investments, from the sale of their labor, or from their skills as craftsmen, the larger and the better the dwellings that they could afford for their families. Thus a range of dwellings was provided to meet these different demands, and the construction industry promoted the dwelling as a status symbol, as a means of attracting investment and rents. Increasingly, as indicated above, these different types of dwellings were provided in spatially separate areas to meet the growing desires for congregation and segregation.

Much construction of high-density tenements and similar housing for the lowest-paid groups was around the industrial nucleus, an area increasingly emptied of higher-income residents: apart from some small enclaves, the central residential areas of American industrial cities were the preserve of the lower classes, who dominated the local social milieux. Most of the merchants and other former residents of the large, inner-city homes (including the professionals, such as doctors and lawyers) moved away from the industrial and commercial center. They chose to live in relatively low-density seclusion, on the edge of the built-up area, distancing themselves from their employees—their perceived "social inferiors"—by occupying new homes built for them by a booming construction industry.

This movement from the city center to its edge was a reaction to a number of factors. It is probable, for example, that many employers did not enjoy living in close proximity to their employees. With larger establishments they could afford to employ managers and supervisors, thereby distancing themselves (at home and at the workplace) from the lower echelons of society. The time they spent commuting was not crucial to them, as the minutiae of control were left to the relatively well-paid, senior employees. More important, however, was probably the desire among the well paid to distance themselves from what was to them the increasingly distasteful city environment. Several components of the city were viewed as unsavory. The most prominent was pollution. The mercantile city was a relatively clean place, but as industrialization gathered momentum the factory effluent fouled the air and any available bodies of water; the processes conducted in factories, workshops, and warehouses created a great deal of noise; the horses, which were the main mode of transport, fouled the streets, and the inefficient systems of waste removal created both stench and smell. The city was unpleasant, and, more crucially, it was also unhealthy: the insanitary condition of the streets and the packed tenements made the city a breeding ground for many diseases, and in the high-density areas these spread rapidly. Self-interest demanded escape from such an environment if at all possible; new construction on the edge of the city offered an avenue of escape, open only to those with money.

The inner-city social environment was another push factor that encouraged the employers, the professionals, and the well-paid employees, such as the managers, to flee the inner residential areas. The influx of immigrants brought people of different ethnic and cultural backgrounds into the low-paying occupations and the worst housing areas. These people provided labor that was vital to the expanding economic system, but in many cases their potential social impact was viewed with alarm. Much of the alarm was based on perceptions of the social and other habits of those with different ethnic, cultural, and religious backgrounds that had little grounding in reality. These perceptions rapidly developed into patterns of prejudice (many of them based on myth rather than fact) that were expressed in discrimination, not only between rich and poor but also between segments of the poorer classes. A highly volatile society was thus created in which crime—much of it petty—was rife, and employers and managers sought escape from it.

Distancing, by moving to new homes on the city's edge, was a mechanism that allowed those with wealth and/or high incomes to remove their families from exposure to the negative aspects of the inner city. It also allowed the relatively affluent to respond to a recurrent feature of American culture—the rural idyll (which was very much emphasized by the construction industry that was seeking to attract the rich to new homes on the urban periphery). The city has long been depicted in American literature as a necessary evil: it is in the rural areas, close to nature, where the American dream is realized and the truly American life styles are practiced. Further, the urban periphery became attractive because there people could own their own homes and provide the proper foundation for family life, something that was becoming increasingly impossible in inner-city areas where the demand for land by industrialists, commercial land users, and the builders of high-density tenements was generating a boom in property values. Thus the urban periphery—the suburbs—offered an approximation of the American idyll, the ability to own property and so develop a stake in society, yet was within commuting distance of the main workplaces.

Two preconditions were necessary for this move to the suburbs. The first, as already described, was the existence of a construction industry ready and willing to develop the growing penchant for semirural living. The other was transport. In the 1830s railroads became the first to allow those able to afford the fare to escape the city center and yet commute there rapidly; the development of such communities as Germantown, Philadelphia, illustrates their impact, which was generally slight. Much more important was the introduction of horse-drawn streetcars in the 1850s, which encouraged people to move to the edges of the city, along and adjacent to the major thoroughfares; indeed, in many places streetcar lines were extended into open country prior to residential development, as part of the stimulus to suburban construction and purchase. These streetcars were slow and relatively expensive, however, and after about 1880 were replaced by electric streetcars, which at 15 to 18 mph moved three times as fast. They could serve an area ten miles or more from the city center, and their extending tentacles enabled massive movement to the suburbs (Figure 6.3). The result was that the construction industry capitalized on this new available resource and undertook development programs aimed at attracting the growing middle classes of the expanding industrial system to partake of the suburban idyll. The zonal pattern indicated in Figure 6.2 was reversed.

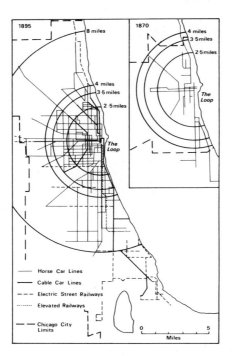

Figure 6.3. The extension of Chicago's streetcar network between 1870 and 1893. From *Cities and Immigrants: A Geography of Change in Nineteenth Century America* by David Ward. Copyright © 1971 by Oxford University Press, Inc. Reprinted by permission.

Further transport developments allowed the continued expansion of low-density suburbia, not in a continuous zone, but along development tentacles. The commuter railroads stimulated expansion along corridors (Figure 6.4A), and once-separate towns beyond the urban center were transformed into dormitory settlements. Then, as more and more people purchased automobiles by the mid-twentieth century, the commuters moved back to the roads. Eventually a new series of corridors was built—the freeways (Figure 6.4B)—which pushed deep into the rural areas but also had cross-metropolitan links, which were not characteristic of the earlier eras. Thus, not only did the freeways allow widespread urban sprawl, but their use also broke the dominance of the traditional urban center as the main workplace.

The transport system was only the means, however. For large numbers of people to move to the suburbs there also had to be an end—housing. Housing was provided by a construction industry that benefited immensely from the transportation innovations and that made great use of the various federal incentives to new home buying. (The freeway system was largely paid for by federal money, too.) But to make suburban development pay, entrepreneurs had to encourage a large seg-

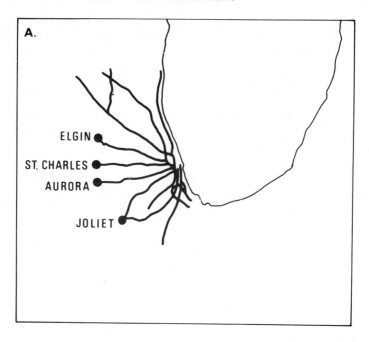

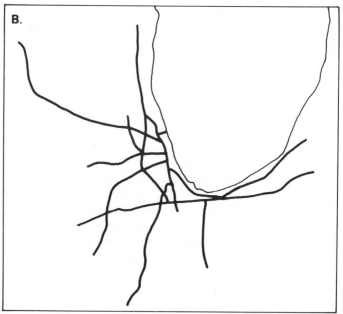

Figure 6.4. Chicago's commuter railroad (A) and freeway (B) networks. Reprinted with permission from B. J. L. Berry et al.,*Chicago: Transformation of an Urban System.* Copyright 1976, Ballinger Publishing Company, pp. 199, 202.

ment of the population—the lower middle classes and some of the better-paid working classes—to invest in home ownership long distances from their jobs. Some developments catered to the rich and pandered to their desires for exclusive residential areas. But others aimed lower down the class scale. Their product had to be cheap, which meant efficiency in its production; efficiency, in turn, meant large scale. Whereas in 1938 only five percent of new homes were constructed by large companies, in 1959 the percentage was 64. The personification of these large firms was Abraham Levitt, who began by building custom-designed homes for the affluent, but who in the late 1940s shifted his activities to the mass production of housing in the first Levittown, on Long Island; 17,000 identical homes were built there, at a rate of 35 per day, and by selling a home for $7,990 (including a profit of $1,000), he could undersell his competitors by $1,500. A later larger Levittown was built in suburban Philadelphia, and his model was followed by several other firms.

DISTANCING, TERRITORIALITY, CONGREGATION, AND SEGREGATION

The discussion in the preceding section suggests that city growth and the transformation from mercantile through industrial to late capitalism resulted in both an increase in the residential separation of classes and income groups and a spatial pattern in which the more affluent lived on the edge of the built-up area. This general picture of the social geography of the American city has been painted on a very broad canvas, however; it remains to fill in the detail, to identify the social and economic processes underlying the patterns.

Employers, according to the earlier discussion, distanced themselves from their employees in the nineteenth-century cities to avoid the physical and social environment of the inner city. They were escaping from *negative externalities*: undesirable elements in the environment, created by institutions and individuals, over which those moving out had no control. They were seeking *positive externalities,* other environmental elements, over which they also had no control, but whose impacts were considered desirable, not undesirable. Pollution was one such negative externality. No one household can, by its own efforts, control the amount of pollution in its local area—it must bear its share of the costs. Collective effort might reduce the costs, but for those with the means to escape (that is, money) the usual solution was to move to an environment where such costs were not imposed. Their destination would offer them the positive externality of (among other things) clean air—which was why the rich often sought to live either on higher land or on the shores of bodies of water upwind of the pollution sources. They then had to ensure collectively that this positive externality was preserved.

Air quality is only one aspect of the environment. Others have perhaps been more important, especially those relating to the social environment. In this section the impact of social factors on residential patterns is examined.

EDUCATION, SOCIAL MOBILITY, AND DISTANCING

As outlined in Chapter 2, a crucial element of all societies is the class system. Differences between societies concerning, for example, the history of land ownership influence that system's nature. Thus, although a land-owning aristocracy, such as that of western Europe, is not a feature of American society, in all societies, including the American, there are major inequalities between groups in the distribution of income and wealth.

The major determinant of one's position in a class system, especially in the later stages of industrial capitalism and late capitalism, is occupation. Initially, the main distinction was between employers and employees. Of the two, the employee class has grown the most and is far more heterogeneous. Within it there are major subdivisions, notably between white-collar and manual workers, between skilled artisans and unskilled laborers, and between executives and clerks. These differences are the result not only of the types of labor involved but also of the differing abilities to bargain for wages and salaries—the rewards paid to labor.

A major influence on the rewards any group of workers can command is the skill they possess, and the relative demand for it. Some skills, such as strength, are innate, but most are learned. These require training—for a period in which income is (at least partially) forgone; the longer the training period, in general, the fewer the number who succeed and the higher the rewards that are demanded, and usually paid, for the skill acquired. Thus education is respected as a passport to high-income occupations. (It is not the only one, though it dominates. Small amounts of capital—inherited, won, or obtained illegally—can be used as the basis for business success by people with acumen but no formal training.) There is a general correlation between occupational skill, education required, and rewards received, and the skilled, high-paying occupations are generally those accorded the highest status by society as a whole.

If success—measured by income or social mobility—is achieved via education, then in a competitive society there will be rivalry to obtain advantages in education, particularly among parents for their children. Very few parents can ensure their children's future by guaranteeing them a certain occupation, since most jobs are obtained by proved or potential ability, not by nepotism. To be sure, under industrial capitalism ownership of companies could be inherited, and this is also true for small firms under late capitalism. But in the dominant corporations, in which ownership is divorced from management, few of the best-paid posts can be passed to succeeding generations. Children must succeed in the educational system.

Education can be bought in the private sector, either individually, from private tutors, or, more often, at private schools, many of which offer excellent facilities (small classes, good equipment, high-quality teachers, etc.) Private education is a major part of the American system; many of the private colleges and universities are among the most prestigious in the country and attract many of the ablest students. Obtaining an education at these institutions does not guarantee fulfillment of career aspirations—exams must be passed—but the chances of success are high. Still, these schools are expensive and most children are educated in the public system, which is supported by taxes, notably local property taxes, and has been provided by the state as both a major aid to the reproduction of the labor force and a means of socializing training costs that otherwise might have to be paid by capitalists.

Two major traditions regarding the American public education system are relevant here: first, that children attend their neighborhood school; and second, that in most states organization and finance are a local issue, under the control of a school board elected locally, though working within guidelines laid down by the state government. For a variety of reasons, these two traditions have produced considerable variations between schools and between school districts in the quality and type of education provided.

This variation both reflects and is reflected in the residential separation of classes and ethnic groups. For parents wishing educational success for their children within the public system, placing them in what is perceived as a "good" school is a paramount concern. "Good" schools are apt to be those in districts with the needed financial resources, that is, those with high property values, which can yield considerable returns at relatively low tax rates. Thus a rich area with control over its own educational system is perceived as more likely to provide good educational facilities than is a poor one; its students are more likely to succeed in the contest for good jobs, and so parents compete to live in its district, to send their children to its schools, and to exclude those families whose finances and attitudes might downgrade the local education.

The formal educational facilities—the school buildings, teaching resources, and teaching staff—are only one part of the students' educational milieux. Another is the social composition of the school and its catchment area (from which it draws its pupils). A school's social ambience is important to many parents because of its role in fostering their children's value systems. Parents will wish their children to be spurred to educational success by competing with others having similar attitudes and will not want their offspring to mix with students whose parents are fatalistic about their life chances and more concerned with early entry into the labor market and enhanced family incomes. Middle-class children, it is feared (and shown by research), become neither as oriented to educational success nor as likely to earn high grades when they attend a predominantly working-class school than when they attend school with their social peers. The reverse also is perceived and occurs: working-class children who attend predominantly middle-class schools achieve more academically than do working-class children attending predominantly working-class schools. Because of the tradition of neighborhood school attendance, parents who wish their children to attend a predominantly middle-class public school must live in a predominantly middle-class area; they must be able to afford the "entry fee," the local property values. Similarly, if they wish their children to attend an ethnically unmixed school—usually all white—then they must ensure that the undesirable groups do not live in the same catchment areas as themselves.

The crucial role of education in late capitalist society and the two traditions of the American public school system mean that school catchment zones are positive externalities if they coincide with the parents' desires (the right social mix; good educational facilities) and negative externalities if they do not. To create the desired positive externalities, the affluent congregate to contribute jointly to the desired educational environment. An outcome of their congregation is segregation, or the exclusion of those perceived to bring negative externalities to an area. The overall result is a continuum of school catchments from the wealthiest to the poorest; those segregated from the most expensive areas congregate to exclude others less affluent and "desirable" than themselves, and so on down the socioeconomic scale.

SOCIALIZATION AND SOCIAL DISTANCING

Educational requirements and the nature of local school systems are strong incentives to a congregation of class groups, with the consequent segregation of various groups into different parts of the residential mosaic. But education is only one part of the general process of socialization, by which children are introduced to the attitudes and values of their parents' social stratum. In addition to the school there are two other crucial agents of socialization: the family and the child's immediate neighborhood peers. The role and the importance of the family are obvious; parents and other close kin are the main models on which children base their attitudes and behavior.

The neighborhood is an important socialization agent because for most children it provides the social milieu for growing up. Most of their early social contacts are made locally, and unless parents insulate them entirely from such contacts, it provides a further set of models to be emulated. To ensure the desired socialization for their children, parents will want those models to be consonant with those provided in the home, since alternatives may lead children to reject their parents' attitudes, aspirations, and values. The best way to achieve this is to select a neighborhood which, according to the known characteristics of its residents (income, race, religion, etc.), comprises people of the desired social and economic background. Thus, neighborhood peer-group socialization reinforces education, as it also requires congregation, with families seeking to distance themselves from those considered alien to their social goals. Segregation naturally follows. Some of those excluded will seek to be included, however: their social aspirations are such that they want their children to live in a "better" neighborhood, and they will seek to achieve this, perhaps by paying a relatively large proportion of their incomes on housing costs.

Beyond the "impressionable" years of basic socialization, a major step in the social and economic life of most young people is marriage. Particularly in the past, marriage was seen as a major potential step up the social mobility ladder, especially for women in a male-dominated society; to marry up the social ladder was very desirable, while to marry below one's station was to harm one's social and economic chances and sometimes was seen as bringing disgrace to one's parents. Parents are unable to arrange marriages, of course. All they can do is manipulate the potential choices.

Even in a highly mobile society, the majority of marriages are between persons who live in the same districts within a city. As Figure 6.5 shows, the number of marriages declines as the distance between the homes of bride and groom increases, despite, of course, an increase in the number of potential mates as distance increases. Whether the distancing that this apparently reflects has any real influence on the choice of spouse is open to some doubt; what is clear, however, is that many parents believe that congregation is sensible if one wishes one's children to do well in the marriage market, and such perceptions are more important to an understanding of people's beliefs than are any "facts" which they appear to ignore.

Apart from the socialization of children, parents—and childless adults, too—are also concerned about their own social contacts. Distance restricts social relations, especially those involving frequent face-to-face contacts, for no other reason than that traveling takes time and costs money. It is possible to live all of one's social life outside the local neighborhood, focused perhaps on the workplace, or even to be a recluse, but many people have the majority of their social contacts (particularly those with nonkin) in the immediate environment of their homes.

Lasting social contacts are based on common interests. These may be very specialized—a particular hobby, perhaps—but many are based on interests, notably the problems of child rearing, which reflect com-

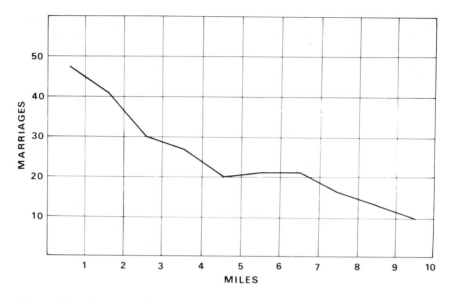

Figure 6.5. Marriage distances in Seattle, showing the number of marriages graphed against distance between the previous home addresses of bride and groom. Source: R. L. Morrill and F. R. Pitts, "Marriage, Migration and the Mean Information Field," *Annals* of the Association of American Geographers, 17 (1967):415. Reproduced by permission.

mon values and life styles. These commonalities, in turn, reflect incomes, occupations, and educational backgrounds. The more similar people are on these criteria, the more they are likely to have in common and the more mutual benefits they are likely to receive from frequent social contact—both formal (local societies, churches, etc.) and informal (coffee mornings, cocktail parties, bridge clubs, etc.). Again, congregation and segregation are obvious means to this end, ensuring that one's neighbors are potentially valuable social contacts, even if that potential is never realized.

People often accentuate this desire for congregation and segregation out of ignorance (or at least partial ignorance). Any large city contains a wide range of life styles and attitudes, most of which are associated with particular groups. Most residents regularly encounter only a small portion of this range, in part because of their relative insulation in homogeneous neighborhoods. Thus they must categorize the other groups —create models of them—based on either incomplete knowledge or second-hand information. This produces stereotypes, many of which stress negative aspects of the unknown groups. A consequence of such stereotyping is a heightened desire to distance one's family from such people and to segregate those identified as deviants into defined, separate areas. This is illustrated by the use of prisons and mental hospitals, in which deviant minorities are forcibly segregated, but in a milder form it applies to the way in which many other minority groups are segregated—in terms of attitudes toward homosexuals, for example, and, until recently, toward divorced persons. Thus intergroup differences are accentuated, and the result is distancing, even on the basis of false stereotypes. For instance, apartment dwellers are widely believed to impose extra financial burdens, via property taxes, on residents of single-family homes, although this is probably not so.

The key to this distancing via stereotyping is perception; groups are categorized as desirable or undesirable by other groups, with consequences in the arrangement of the residential mosaic. Some of these perceptions seem at least partly justified. Studies of what is known as the "neighborhood effect" have shown that individuals are influenced by their social contacts in a variety of ways: attitudes toward schooling; achievement in examinations; political preferences; criminal tendencies —all seem to be individual decisions that, in part, are influenced by what other people are doing locally. But whether or not such effects actually occur—and they are difficult for researchers to disentangle—it is believed that they do. Congregation and segregation are the results; people prefer to live among others like themselves, producing (in ways described below) separate neighborhoods that can be characterized by the occupations, incomes, and education of their residents.

ETHNIC DISTANCING

The discussion so far of social and spatial distancing has focused very largely on socioeconomic criteria, especially those related to success or failure within the competitive capitalist system. As yet nothing has been said about distancing along ethnic lines, although ethnicity is the source of many of the more vivid stereotypes based on ignorance of the sort discussed above. Stereotyping is most apparent with regard to white attitudes toward the blacks who have moved to the cities in large numbers since the 1920s, but it has existed—not only toward blacks but also toward many other ethnic minorities—throughout American history.

Some of the residential separation of blacks and other ethnic groups that is so apparent in American cities reflects their economic position. Most immigrants to the cities have occupied the lowest strata of the occupational scale, at least on their arrival, and their low incomes have limited their residential choice severely. But others of similar occupational status have also separated themselves from the members of the ethnic minorities; similarly, the members of the various minority groups have spread out into different neighborhoods.

Many of the minority groups that have suffered from this additional stereotyping have possessed characteristics—language, religion, cultural practices, and mere appearance—that make them stand out. Stereotyping, largely out of ignorance, accentuates such differences; because the tendency is to focus on perceived negative characteristics, the result is that contact with and among the different groups is shunned. The majority, the white Anglo-Saxon Protestants, wish to avoid contact with the minorities, whether Jews, Germans, Italians, blacks, or Puerto Ricans. (Over time, many minorities have been integrated into American society; there is little active segregation of Jews, Germans, and Italians now.) A clear recent example is the opposition of white parents to school integration because of the perceived threats to the safety of their children that will result from close contact with black students. Such stereotyping leads to social distancing, but because stereotypes are often expressed in extremes, it has resulted in almost complete segregation of the minority groups.

A further argument often used to buttress such social (or antisocial!) behavior is that every society needs at least one scapegoat—an individual or group that can be blamed for society's ills and suffer the main brunt of its economic problems. A distrusted, disliked group is an obvious target. And if that group is not homogeneous, antagonisms will develop within it; thus conflict among the various ethnic minorities will deflect them from conflict with the majority, who are exploiting them, and who—as much social research shows—want little or no contact with them.

The minority groups who suffer this prejudice and discrimination, in housing and labor markets, for example, can seek one of two main avenues of redress. The first is to become inward-looking, to form a cohesive, separate social structure to combat that of the majority society. Economic integration is needed—the minority needs jobs and the majority needs poorly paid, menial labor—but it is accompanied by social and cultural separateness. To maintain the latter, congregation is needed (buttressing the imposed segregation); and boundaries between separate ethnic territories must be defined; these are often stoutly defended, with occasional conflict (some of it violent) accompanying violations of perceived frontiers.

The other remedy is to seek social as well as economic integration, so that eventually the group loses its identity—except perhaps for relatively uncontroversial aspects, such as religion—and becomes assimilated into the larger society. This is largely an individual process. Many minority groups come to the cities in closely knit communities, often via the process of chain migration, whereby money and information are sent back to the place of origin to encourage further migrants; the result is often the transplanting of large parts of whole settlements (Italian villages, for example), which are partly reconstituted in the segregated inner areas of American cities. Assimilation involves the breaking apart of these closely knit, often very protective communities, with members of

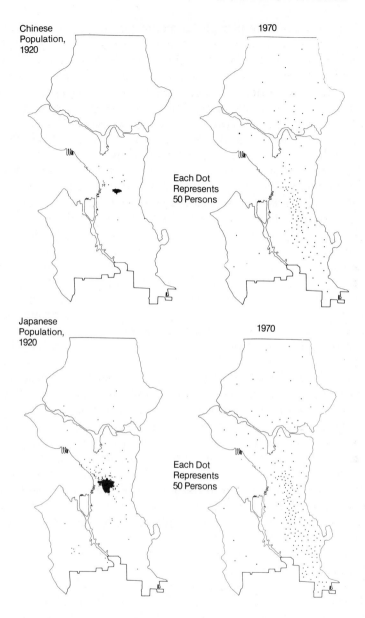

Figure 6.6.   The declining residential segregation of Chinese and Japanese in Seattle, 1920 to 1970. Reprinted with permission from A. P. Andrus et al, *Seattle.* Copyright 1976, Ballinger Publishing Company, pp. 454–5.

the minority becoming part of the majority host society and sharing its value system.

The extent to which assimilation is possible depends on majority attitudes and the state of the national economy. For much of American history, the latter has not been a problem, and rapid expansion has provided many opportunities for immigrants and their descendants to pursue individual assimilation. The result has been a decline in spatial separation; distancing has disappeared with assimilation. Figure 6.6 illustrates the case of the Chinese and the Japanese—in Seattle. The nucleus of Chinese settlement in 1920 was near the city center, which remains the focus of their social life (as well as the main concentration of Chinese restaurants); now, however, members of the group, most of whom have roots in the province of Canton, are dispersed throughout south and east Seattle. Similarly, the Japanese population there has been dispersed, in part because their major inner-city concentration was broken up—for the safety of the Japanese—during the Second World War.

The opportunities to assimilate and escape from the inner-city ghettos that have been seized by members of many minority groups have not so far been made available to many blacks (some of whom have become relatively wealthy). The main reason for this is the strength of the negative stereotype and the depth of white prejudice, both of which are used to bolster discriminatory practices. Many whites believe blacks are genetically inferior (such beliefs are built into some religions), that black-white contact will taint the latter, and that it will destroy American social structure. The result is that blacks have been kept at the bottom of the occupational ladder, while spatially they have been confined to inner-city ghettos; Figure 6.7 illustrates their spatial segregation, showing that while the former concentrations of various immigrant groups in Detroit have been much diminished, blacks have been, and remain, concentrated. Blacks have reacted to this in a variety of ways, including the demonstrations and riots of the 1960s, whose distribution reflected the geography of their disadvantage.

HOUSING MARKETS

The preceding sections have presented the social and economic rationale underlying the social and spatial distancing that has resulted in the residential mosaics of American urban areas. Initially, the employer class sought a territory for itself, clearly separate from the employee class. Since then, in a continuous process of sorting and resorting, the various groups within the employee class have sought to distance themselves from perceived negative externalities and establish separate dis-

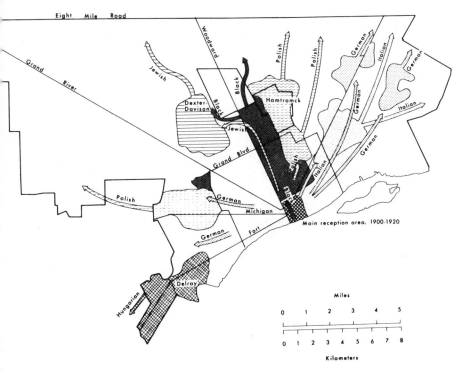

Figure 6.7.   Change in the distribution of Detroit's ethnic communities, 1900 to 1950. Reprinted with permission from R. Sinclair and B. Thompson, *Detroit.* Copyright 1977, Ballinger Publishing Company, p. 299.

tricts within which to protect and enhance their economic and social status. Let us now examine the means by which congregation and segregation have been achieved.

The crucial influence on the sorting process has been income. Housing that varies in quality will vary also in price, which results in the stratification of housing according to residents' incomes. But to many people housing quality refers not only to the dwelling itself but also to its social and physical environment. Thus the more desirable an area, the more expensive its homes, not only because of their quality but also because of the characteristics of their residents. Buyers come prepared to pay a premium to live in areas from which undesirables are excluded by the operation of the free market.

In a relatively static society, the price system may be sufficient to produce the distancing required by the affluent, who feel they have most to gain from it. But in an expanding society, flux is considerable. Newly rich people threaten the characteristics of certain neighborhoods; the demand for housing is such that people may be prepared to pay high prices for homes in areas where they are considered negative externalities. Thus the housing market has a complex organization, which protects the social desires of some groups and advances the aspirations of others.

A major feature in the organization of the housing market in the twentieth century has been the growth of owner-occupation (from 47 percent in 1890 to 65 percent in 1975) and the consequent decline in renting. In the mercantile and the industrial captialist city, the landlord played a crucial role in providing accommodation: landlords are still crucial for the poorly paid, but for the majority it is now the developer, the realtor, and the mortgage lender who are the important elements. Landlords have declined in significance because, compared with other opportunities, the provision of rental housing has not been an attractive investment; most of the properties currently rented are old. Thus to attract investment in rental housing rents must be high. They were not, because people could not afford them. Thus most new construction was of dwellings for sale, whose purchase was financed out of loans on which the interest paid offered an acceptable return, especially to the small depositers, whose money was the basis for many of the loans.

The mechanism by which owner-occupancy has been advanced is the mortgage, or a loan to a householder based on the security of his income and the value of the property being purchased. Such loans are risky; the lender must gamble that borrowers can repay them, with interest, and that if they should default, the sale of the property will produce the needed return on the investment plus the costs of handling the default. In addition, the capital invested is tied up for long periods—mortgages typically are granted for fifteen to thirty years. Thus the security of both borrower and property must be great, if money is to be attracted from depositers in what is potentially a very risky situation.

Thus the risks involved in financing mortgages must be minimized to ensure an adequate supply of finance. Most mortgages are granted either by savings and loan associations or by big commercial banks; the former earned $78.8 billion in mortgage advances in 1976, and had $323.1 billion in loans outstanding, compared to $146.6 billion for the commercial banks (of which only $88.5 billion referred to nonfarm, residential properties), indicating the importance of the S and Ls for home purchase. By offering interest, these institutions attract deposits, which they use to finance loans, again at interest. To ensure that depositers will lend to them, and have confidence that their investments are secure, the lending policies are very conservative. Among potential borrowers, those with guaranteed incomes sufficient to meet the repayments are favored, so that borrowers are restricted by their incomes in the size of the loan, and thus the price of the home that is bought. Similarly, lenders favor dwellings that will not depreciate in value; this means avoiding older buildings, and also those in neighborhoods where social change may cause property values to fall.

Because it is a gamble, mortgage lending is specific to both person and place; it strongly favors the well paid, who hold secure jobs, have stable backgrounds, and buy new or relatively new homes in desirable neighborhoods. As such, it encourages congregation and segregation and discourages neighborhood change (except that which produces above-average rates of appreciation). Certain groups are excluded from many areas because they fail to qualify on income grounds. Furthermore, lending agencies are very reluctant to lend on dwellings in areas they (or their appraisers) perceive as likely to decline in quality and thus in dwelling price. The introduction of perceived negative externalities into an area—black families, for example—may lead to a relatively rapid change in neighborhood characteristics, as residents decide to sell and move. The panic selling may depress prices, with consequences for the lenders if there are any mortgage defaults. Thus in addition to the social reasons for keeping out negative externalities, owner-occupiers and mortgagees have economic ones. The declining prices of homes locally reduce the value of their wealth, the equity they have built up in the home during their repayments, and make it more difficult for them to capitalize on their asset and purchase a comparable or better home elsewhere.

To maintain local property values, residents often act in concert to exclude negative externalities. In many cities, for example, white householders in certain areas have agreed, through local neighborhood associations, to place restrictive covenants on their homes, stating that they will never be sold to blacks. In this way, the potential negative externality is avoided, although attempts to obtain compensation through the courts against those who have broken their covenants have failed, on the grounds that this requires the state to become involved in discriminatory practices that are contrary to the equal protection clause of the Fourteenth Amendment to the Constitution. The covenants are gentlemen's agreements only, but their existence indicates the desire of owners' to protect their economic interests in their homes as well as the social ambience of their neighborhoods.

Others in the housing market are also involved in practices aimed at maintaining property values in neighborhoods. Landlords, for example, may refuse to rent apartments to blacks, for fear of the effects on the desirability of the apartments and their impacts on rent levels; such practices continue despite attempts to outlaw them. Realtors, too, will steer home buyers away from certain areas, to protect prices, and hence their commissions on sales; again, despite attempts to outlaw such discrimination there is evidence that it is still practiced.

Perhaps the most controversial restrictive practice is "redlining." Mortgage-lending agencies, it is assumed, refuse to lend on properties in certain areas because of the risks involved. Usually the areas are older, inner-city neighborhoods and those who suffer from the discrimination involved are the poor and the blacks. Studies of the distribution of mortgage allocations show clear spatial patterns that are in line with other aspects of urban social geography. For example, across the 114 census tracts in the urban area of Sacramento, the ratio of mortgages granted per 100 dwellings in 1975 was closely correlated with the geography of median household incomes. The areas with concentrations of blue-collar employees and minority groups received relatively few mortgages. In itself this is not evidence of redlining, however, for it is not clear that there are neighborhoods in which savings and loans institutions refused to grant mortgages. When their policies discriminate against certain income groups and types of dwellings, then the spatial separation of these tends to produce a geography of mortgage lending, without any need even for an explicit redlining policy.

A final mechanism available to residents of neighborhoods to protect their environments is the zoning plan that is applied in most cities. (One of the few exceptions is Houston, where there is no zoning plan.) Zoning was introduced early in the twentieth century to advance the general welfare by segregating various land users, notably factories and workshops, from residential areas. As the planning profession grew, zoning became used more widely to protect property rights and values by providing the legal backing to the congregation and segregation processes operating in the property market. Homogeneous residential areas were zoned for, not only in small, home-rule suburban municipalities (see Chapter 8), but also within large cities where neighborhood action groups, especially those representing the rich and the politically powerful, were able to obtain zoning provisions that protected their districts from invasion by perceived negative externalities; a good example of this is the zoning achieved by the residents of Beacon Hill, a traditionally exclusive residential area overlooking Boston Common, that was designed to maintain the area's social characteristics.

Neighborhoods do change, of course, despite the efforts of residents. Properties age and become less desirable, so that a process known as filtering can be initiated. In this process, properties move down the social scale, while households move up the housing scale. What was formerly a desirable area for high-income people is replaced by a new development; the high-income households move to the latter, and their former homes are made available to members of lower-income groups.

This filtering process may be hastened by institutions. As already noted, realtors are usually not prepared to introduce black buyers to all-white areas. If they perceive that the neighborhood is changing, however, they may then introduce such buyers, in the hope that the rapid turnover that this induces will bring them a windfall in commissions. This process is sometimes known as "block-busting." Figure 6.8 illustrates its consequences for a small area on the edge of the black ghetto in northwest Detroit. In 1970 the eastern part of this area was almost entirely black, whereas most of the rest was almost exclusively white (top

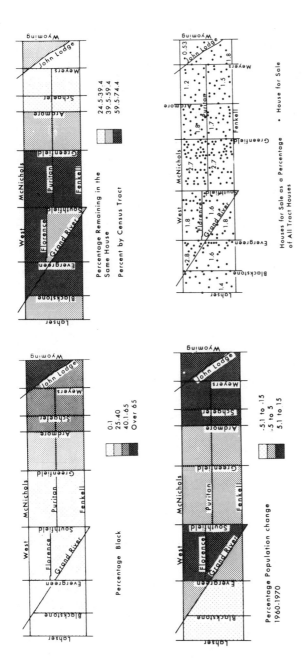

Figure 6.8. Racial change on the edge of Detroit's black ghetto: (top left) percent black, by census tract, 1970; (top right) percent population turnover, 1965 to 1970; (bottom left) percent population change, 1960 to 1970; (bottom right) houses for sale, 1973. Reprinted with permission from R. Sinclair and B. Thompson, *Detroit*. Copyright 1977, Ballinger Publishing Company, pp. 332-337.

181

left). Blacks had been moving to the eastern part since 1965; in the rest of the city, a high percentage of the households were in the same home in 1970 as five years earlier (top right). The black "invasion" was accompanied by a considerable population increase (as much as 15 percent) in the eastern blocks (bottom left) that was followed by an increased desire to sell in the adjacent areas (bottom right), reflecting the wish of whites to escape the approaching negative externality. Many of the blacks who moved to the eastern blocks clearly reached beyond their resources, for the rate of mortgage defaults (up to 7 percent) there in 1973 was very high, and as a result many dwellings were left vacant. The fears of the neighboring whites with regard to the approaching negative externalities were perhaps reflected in the changing commercial landscape: as many as half the stores on the streets in the black areas had protective screens by 1973, compared to less than five percent in the white areas.

Not all neighborhood change involves downward filtering, however. An increasingly common process is gentrification, whereby properties and neighborhoods are improved and values rise accordingly. Gentrification involves the movement of the relatively affluent, especially the young, into inner-city areas, displacing the relatively poor and exacerbating their housing problems. The gentrifiers have rejected low-density suburbia and long commuting journeys and are attracted to the substantial older homes of inner areas, which, when restored and remodeled, became extremely attractive. In Philadelphia, for example, the area of Society Hill near Independence Hall contains streets of colonial homes that have been revitalized; individual homes now are sold for six-figure sums, and the district has the second highest median income in the entire city.

THE STATE AND THE HOUSING MARKET

During the present century, the various interest groups involved in the property market—notably the construction companies, the savings and loan associations, and the realtors—have grown into a powerful lobby that has strongly influenced federal housing policy. These lobbying activities have been aimed at ensuring a favorable financial situation for depositers—to maintain a regular supply of mortgage funds—and at obtaining concessions for developers—the provision of an infrastructure (roads, utilities, etc.) for new construction.

Pressure was applied for suburbanization, for policies that would favor the building of new homes in the urban fringe and would back the aims of the construction industry in convincing Americans, especially middle-income families, that a single-family dwelling in a low-density suburban setting was their "American dream." To sell these homes, mortgage money was required; deposits had to be attracted, and on secure terms. The lending institutions thus sought special status, and they obtained valuable concessions. Their deposits are guaranteed, which has eliminated the gamble of placing money in them. The Federal Housing Administration has insured mortgages, when they are considered reasonable risks, with the result that the institutions have been able to make larger loans—relative to the price of the property—over longer periods and at lower rates of interest. Further, the mortgage lenders are able to sell the mortgages to other federal agencies (at a discount) if they qualify for FHA insurance, thus enabling them to recycle their deposits and make further advances. (This "creates" money, of course, and so is inflationary.) Other federal assistance to the mortgage/construction complex has included loans to war veterans for the provision of infrastructure in certain areas; FHA "seals of approval" for builders and realtors; FHA advances to builders, especially large firms; FHA refusal to underwrite mortgages in the inner city; federal highway construction that has provided the needed central city-suburb links; and federal income-tax deductions for owner-occupiers.

This subsidized boom in suburban home building since the Second World War has inflated property values so that they have consistently outpaced other prices. As a result, the debts that mortgagees take on are increasing, which has made them even more determined to protect the equity they have tied up in housing and land. Conflicts over perceived negative externalities, such as apartment construction in areas of single-family housing, have increased.

There have been negative consequences, too. Many people have been socialized into aspiring to own their own home, but the combination of price inflation and the decline of the rental sector has caught them in the pinch; they cannot afford a mortgage on a conventional home but have nowhere else to go. A major solution for relatively low-income households has been the mobile home. This is defined officially as "a portable structure built on a chassis and designed to be used without permanent foundations as a year-round dwelling when connected to utilities." Indeed, few are transported once they have been parked on a permanent site. Immediately after the Second World War, about 60,000 mobile homes were being built annually; the number increased rapidly, and a peak was reached in 1972 when 576,000 were constructed, about 20 percent of all new homes in that year. In 1962, mobile homes made up 22 percent of new housing, and 33.7 percent of new single-family housing. Many of the mobile homes are located on the fringes of urban areas; many are in unincorporated portions of counties, although a few incorporated municipalities have zoned large areas for such homes. The typical residents are young, blue-collar families who lack the resources to make the large down payment needed to buy a conventional home. Though the mobile home is attractive because of the relatively small initial payment needed, because the mortgages or other loans are usually for shorter periods than are those for conventional homes (mobile homes have shorter life expectancies), the monthly payments are often as high as those for a conventional mortgage.

Another problem caused by inflation in home prices in recent decades has been the inability of certain income groups to afford mortgages for single-family homes, especially those built at low densities for which the land value is a major part of the total price. This has led to greater demand for owned apartments, including various cooperative ownership plans, such as condominiums. Multifamily dwellings reached a peak of 45 percent of all new homes built in 1973 (by 1976, the percentage had fallen to 25), and many of these were in the suburbs, reflecting the combination of a desire to live there and an inability to afford the costs of a mortgage on a single-family income.

Federal encouragement of owner-occupied housing has been to the detriment of the rental sector, where two groups, the young and the poor (especially the black poor), are concentrated. The young are the more catered to, in that they can afford fairly high rents, whereas the poor suffer considerably. Provision of rental housing is not an attractive proposition for capital, and most of the rental dwellings available are relatively old and in poor condition (twice the percentage of rented as opposed to owned homes lack plumbing and/or are dilapidated): most of the new units built (490,000 in 1973 but only 154,000 in 1976) rent for $200 or more per month. Thus the poor are restricted to dilapidated, inner-city slum or near-slum properties, either those built as such or those that have filtered down the housing scale. Nevertheless, the rents that they can afford are insufficient to provide a reasonable return to landlords, let alone cover the rising costs of maintenance. Increasingly, landlords are abandoning properties, especially in the older cities of the Manufacturing Belt, which rapidly fall into an advanced state of dereliction.

Abandoned dwellings merely serve to depreciate the quality of inner-city environments further and restrict the options of the poor and the disadvantaged. At the same time, some of the more attractive rental properties are being taken out of the market, to meet the growing demand for ownership apartments and condominiums. In part this reflects a famine of mortgage money for single-family homes, a consequence of restrictions on the interest rate ceilings imposed on savings and loans associations in some states during a period of very high general interest rates. Tenants lacking security of tenure are being evicted, left to search for alternative homes in a dwindling market.

Although new suburban construction has catered to the upper- and middle-income groups and has resulted in very high accommodation standards for a majority of urban Americans, this channeling of money toward certain groups and areas has starved others of funds, with consequences for minority-group housing. Inner-city residents are denied conventional mortgages, and landlords are not prepared to provide properties for them. For many, it seems, the only solution is to enter the house-purchase market through what has been termed the "underworld of real estate finance," usually at a relatively high price and at disadvantageous terms. Some, especially low-income whites, are able to obtain loans from local inner-city institutions. But most, particularly low-income blacks, are forced to seek loans elsewhere. The most common source has been the installment contract. This has involved buying from a seller in monthly payments, but with no mortgage; in effect the seller lends the buyer the money to purchase the dwelling, and the client does not get title to it until the last payment has been made (after, say, fifteen years). Because there is no mortgage, interest rates are not controlled and high rates can be charged; further, any default in payment can cause the dwelling to be repossessed, and the defaulter receives nothing of the payments made until then. The excessive interest rate is known as the "black tax" to the many poor persons who are forced to buy in this way. Often it is paid to a speculator, someone who buys the dwelling on a conventional loan (perhaps even on a mortgage) and then sells it on an installment contract for a large profit. Attempts to stop this practice have involved the provision of FHA loans in areas where conventional mortgages are denied (the presence of FHA loans in such areas has sometimes been taken as evidence of redlining), but these were used by local speculators to force prices up in such neighborhoods, with later high default rates (as indicated earlier in the discussion of racial change in Detroit).

One final area of state involvement is public housing, but this has been used very little in the United States, compared with other late capitalist nations. The number of low-rent public housing units in the country in 1976 totaled only 1.3 million (out of a total of more than 80 million units), and of these one quarter were designed and built specifically for the elderly, the disabled, and the handicapped. Apart from the elderly, most households that are public housing tenants are poor (in 1976 the average income was only $3,400 for those allocated homes, compared to the national median family income of $15,000), non-white, living on public assistance, and include no permanent member of the labor force. But the number of homes provided does not meet even a small proportion of the housing demands of the poor and underprivileged. (The problems of housing the inner-city poor are considered further in Chapter 10.)

HOUSING CLASSES

The provision of housing in American towns and cities reflects the reactions of capitalist interests (notably the construction industry and money-lending institutions, in alliance with the state) to the desires of the population—desires which those interests mold to suit their own ends. The desire for distancing and its consequences—congregation and segregation—are general in capitalist societies, while the responses to them, and the patterns created, are particular to each society. Thus in the United States there has been extensive suburban low-density sprawl and little public housing; in the United Kingdom, almost exactly the reverse has occurred.

The operations of the housing market have created a series of housing classes. The concept of class, as introduced in Chapter 2, usually refers to a person's position in the division of labor and describes his or her relationship to the mode of production. A housing class, however, is a group of people with common modes of consumption. Access to the various housing classes is very largely a function of income, and therefore of economic class; control of access is exercised by a series of ''urban managers'' or ''gatekeepers,'' including the realtors, who try and steer buyers toward particular areas, appraisers who ''determine'' the value of property and therefore the loan that can be made for it (if at all), the mortgage lenders who decide whether an applicant is eligible for a loan, and how much, and the various government and other agents involved in the business of insuring mortgages, in what is generally known as the ''secondary mortgage market.''

Four main housing classes can be identified in American cities. Each is subdivided on a number of criteria, the most important of which is property value.

1. Outright owners and purchasers by mortgage or other loans. These form the majority class and are subdivided according to the value of their home, the type of home (house, apartment, or mobile home), the source of the loan, and so on. Each subdivision tends to be spatially separate from the others, producing a detailed mosaic of residential areas whose geography is reflected in a map of personal and family incomes.
2. Renters from private landlords. Again, there is a division by quality and price, although the majority are of relatively low quality.
3. Renters of public housing.
4. Those who share a dwelling with others, subrenting a room or part of the dwelling or apartment.

In addition, there are those who have no permanent home.

For most people, these four classes can be placed in a single rank-order of desirability: ownership is the most desirable state, and so it is the most difficult to enter. In general, membership of the ownership class is reserved for the relatively highly paid in society, and because ownership is a title to wealth, it serves to accentuate the financial inequalities between those in different parts of the labor market.

THE RESIDENTIAL PATTERN

The processes described so far in this chapter produce a set of housing classes that are spatially separate from one another. Further, there is separation within the classes, especially the largest, reflecting social and economic distancing and its role in both heightening social inequalities and minimizing interclass conflict. These processes rarely produce complete segregation of certain groups—the main exception is the black ghetto, which is virtually exclusive to that group. Some overlap, especially within the ownership housing class, is to be expected, for several reasons. For one, many households can exercise some choice as to the proportion of their income that they devote to housing, and thus where they live. It is often observed, for example, that members of white-collar occupational groups are more status conscious and more prepared to spend money on living in a "desirable" area than are some blue-collar households whose skilled members receive higher incomes; there is no perfect correlation between income and home value, therefore. Further, the inheritance of a home, or money derived from the sale of an inheritance, may allow families to live in areas that they could not afford on the basis of current incomes. Thus position in the labor market and income are major determinants of what a household can afford, and where, but they are only constraints within which preferences may be expressed. Variations in preferences lead to some spatial overlap of income groups within housing classes.

Much work—reviewed briefly in Chapter 1—has been undertaken to identify the level of residential separation and the degree to which individual areas of cities are socially, economically, ethnically, and demographically homogeneous. This shows, not surprisingly given the rest of this chapter's discussion, that the more similar two households are the more likely they are to live in the same residential area. What these studies do not show is where within the urban settlement that area is likely to be. Some discussion of the answer to that question has already been presented here with regard to suburbanization and inner-city neighborhoods. The rest of this chapter considers spatial arrangements in greater detail, given the operation of the processes that result in congregation, segregation, and housing classes.

The discussion that follows is based on two research traditions, both of which have their roots in urban sociology. One is concerned with the disposition of different types of districts within the residential mosaic. The other is concerned with identifying, via statistical analyses, the number of ways in which districts differ. Four basic ways have been identified: (1) by the economic and social status of the residents; (2) by the ethnic status of the residents; (3) by the life style of the residents; and (4) by the age and family structures of local populations.

THE SPATIAL MORPHOLOGY

So far in this chapter the vital geographical question of "where?" has been of only secondary importance, because it cannot be answered without prior discussions of "what?", "why?", and "how?". Having answered those questions, it is now possible to turn to the spatial morphology.

A major stimulus to studies of the arrangement of the urban residential mosaic was the seminal work of a group of sociologists working at the University of Chicago in the 1920s. One of them, Ernest Burgess, developed a model of social patterns in a typical American city, which he organized as a series of five concentric zones, the innermost of which (the CBD) contained no residences. Burgess gave the zones a variety of names in his several publications (Figure 6.9), but the salient feature of his work is the general statement that the economic and social status of

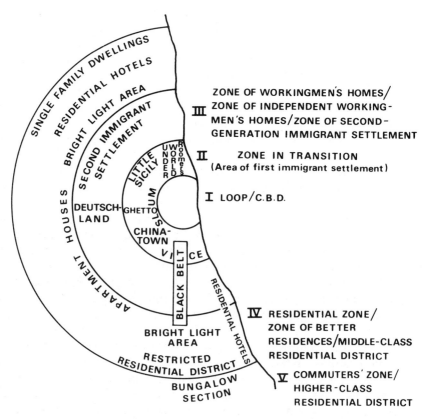

Figure 6.9. Burgess's model of the social geography of the American city, showing the various names used for the different zones.

zones increases with distance from the city center; the higher-income groups live in zone V, and the most recent immigrants in zone II.

Burgess offered his model as a growth model. The main component of urban growth, he argued, is immigration. The vast majority of immigrants enter at the bottom of the occupational ladder and so live in the poorest housing in zone II. As the demand for housing in zone II increases, the existing stock is unable to cope—beyond a certain threshold of increased densities—and the zone expands outward into the next. The process, described earlier as "block-busting," involves the higher-income residents of zone II seeking to escape the increased negative externalities there (introduced by the expansion of industry and commerce as well as the demand for residences) by moving into zone III. Those who move are the earlier immigrants and their descendants who have become assimilated—hence the term "zone of second-generation immigrant settlement" used in one of Burgess's papers. Their movement into zone III creates negative externalities there and generates a further round of outward moves that ends with the highest-income residents in zone V feeling obliged to build new homes on the urban periphery.

The entire process, akin to the filtering process described earlier, was termed invasion and succession by Burgess. A group from an inner zone "invades" the territory of a higher-status group farther out. Those invaded, in turn, react to the perceived negative externality by invading the next zone, and their vacated homes are taken over by other members of the invading group, who thus complete the succession process. In some cases, the process is slow; in others, where the invasion involves a group widely perceived as a serious negative externality, succession may be complete within just a few years.

Burgess's model received considerable criticism on a number of points. Many critics claimed that it was overgeneralized, and they argued, at least implicitly, that so simple a model of urban social geography was impossible, given the complexity of the subject matter. One of the most constructive criticisms was made by Homer Hoyt, a Chicago-trained economist whose detailed field studies of 204 urban areas during the 1930s were the basis of certain generalizations regarding, in particular, the creation of high-status residential areas. His basic argument was that cities are organized not into zones according to the economic status of area residents but rather into sectors. Figure 6.10 is the most frequent representation of his ideas, which Hoyt himself never presented in cartographic form. Hoyt also suggested that the process of growth need not be invasion and succession. The filtering process could be initiated from the city center, as Burgess suggested, but it could also be generated by developments on the periphery, as the urban elite sought to replace their aging homes with new ones, perhaps stimulated

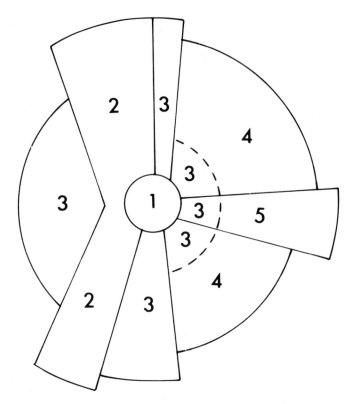

Figure 6.10. The usual representation of the location of different types of residential area, according to Homer Hoyt. Key: 1—CBD; 2—wholesale and light manufacturing; 3—lower-class residential; 4—middle-class residential; 5—upper class residential.

to do so by the marketing pressures of the construction industry. Thus he allowed for zones within sectors.

The ideas of both Burgess and Hoyt have been criticized as simplistic in their social base and too mechanistic in their view of how society and its constituent groups have acted and reacted. Some groups resist invasion, it was pointed out—such as the residents of Boston's Beacon Hill mentioned earlier—and sentimental and other ties to certain areas prevent the realization of the filtering sequences. (Defense of neighborhood—or turf—is a frequent political activity today.) Nevertheless, Burgess's and Hoyt's spatial models of cities organized into zones and sectors have provided the basis for a half-century of empirical investigation, and no general model has been produced to replace them. Furthermore, in broad terms their ideas have stood the test of time, especially in cities with no major topographical features. Hoyt did point out that high-income groups prefer high land and attractive waterfronts, and one of Burgess's students wrote a thesis on Chicago's Gold Coast, on the shores of Lake Michigan immediately north of the CBD which is an anomaly in terms of Burgess's model.

Figure 6.11 shows the spatial pattern of socioeconomic status by census tract for the Minneapolis-St. Paul urban area in 1960. Clearly the highest-status areas were in the outer zones, mostly beyond the central city boundaries (see below and Chapter 8). There was a sectoral pattern too, with relatively low-status sectors extending north and east. In both, status increased with distance from the city center, creating zones (or at least a gradient) within the sector. But there are anomalies to the zonal pattern, notably the high-status node on the Minneapolis-St. Paul border, on the river bank. This is common to many American urban areas; some of the most prestigious and expensive areas are in an intermediate zone occupying an attractive site, having resisted invasion and been out-flanked by a development of large suburban tracts for the middle classes in recent years.

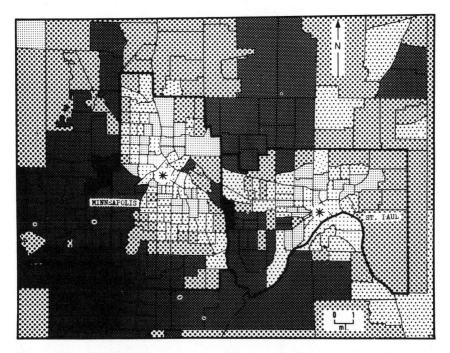

Figure 6.11.   The spatial pattern of socioeconomic status areas in Minneapolis-St. Paul, 1960. The darker the shading, the higher the incomes and the greater the educational achievements of the area's residents. Source: P. H. Rees, *Residential Patterns in American Cities, 1960.* University of Chicago, Department of Geography, Research Paper 189, 1979, p. 195. Copyright 1979 by Philip H. Rees.

In the 1960s an attempt was made to account for the pattern described by Burgess in economic rather than in social terms. The argument was based on a model of intra-urban land values which postulated that these would decline with distance from the city center, in reaction to the increased costs of commuting to and from the more peripheral locations. Higher-income households, it was argued, will prefer the outer zones because they can afford the commuting costs and can indulge their desires for low-density living, whereas low-income households will prefer the more accessible inner locations. In general terms this model is also fitting, but its explanation overlooks the operations of the housing market and assumes a demand for space among the affluent. As the earlier discussion of gentrification showed, when the affluent prefer to live elsewhere they can outbid any other potential residents and can use their political power to achieve their ends. Thus the zonal pattern reflects a certain set of preferences, molded by the construction industry and its allies. It illustrates that the rich are able to impose their preferences on the poor but does not indicate that these will always produce the zonal pattern identified by Burgess and modified by Hoyt (who also located the affluent in the outer zones of his sectors).

Some of the most extensive, although now slightly dated, analyses of spatial patterns in American cities have been reported by Leo Schnore. He divided the built-up area into two zones only—the central city and the suburban ring (see Chapter 8 for more details)—and sought regularities in the relative concentration of status groups between these two.

Schnore identified two main types of urban areas. In the first, the lowest-status groups are relatively concentrated in the central city and the highest-status groups in the suburbs; in the second, the highest *and* the lowest status groups are concentrated in the central city, with the middle-status groups in the suburbs. (The other types contained many fewer urban areas; the only one of any significance had the reverse of the first pattern.) Looking at which urban areas were in which type, he found that the first pattern (that consonant with Burgess's model) was typical of the large, old cities of the Manufacturing Belt, whereas the second was more typical of the younger, usually smaller urban areas of the Sun Belt. The small Sun Belt cities lack the extreme negative externalities in the central-city physical environment that have forced the affluent out into suburbia, and their recent growth has been allied with the provision of mass suburbanization for the middle classes. Thus the highest-status groups have been trapped in intermediate zones, which are likely to be in the central city rather than the suburbs, because of the more active annexation policies of Sun Belt than of Frost Belt cities (see Chapter 8).

Thus the pattern of socioeconomic status areas in the residential mosaic reflects the early Burgess and Hoyt proposals, modified with re-

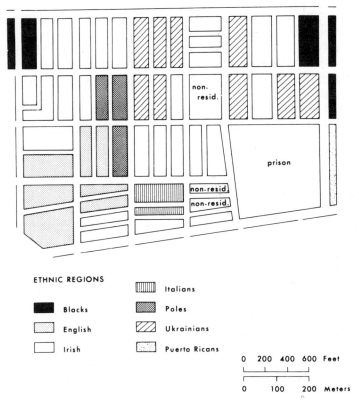

ETHNIC REGIONS

|||||| Italians

■ Blacks

▒ Poles

English

▨ Ukrainians

Irish

Puerto Ricans

0   200   400   600   Feet

0   100   200   Meters

Figure 6.12.   The racial composition of street blocks in the Fairmount district of Philadelphia, 1970s. Reprinted with permission from P. O. Muller et al., *Metropolitan Philadelphia: A Study of Conflicts and Social Cleavages.* Copyright 1976, Ballinger Publishing Company, p. 240.

spect to the mass production of suburbia for the affluent middle classes in recent decades. With regard to ethnic groups, Burgess and Hoyt were both generally accurate in forecasting sectoral ghettos (Burgess's "Black Belt" in Figure 6.9) and spatial spreading consequent on social assimilation (Figures 6.6 and 6.7). Within central cities where several ethnic groups are concentrated, territorial boundaries are firmly defined. In the Fairmount district of Philadelphia (Figure 6.12), for example, most blocks are dominated (70 percent or more in several cases) by a single ethnic group, producing a very fine-grained social geography at the local scale. Some of the ethnic concentrations are extremely large, of course, especially the black ghettos, whose populations may exceed one million. Within these, as in the white residential areas, there is considerable spatial separation of the poor and the (relatively) affluent: in its social and spatial structure the ghetto is a microcosm of the entire urban area.

The models developed by Burgess and, especially, Hoyt referred largely to the distribution of socioeconomic and ethnic groups. They referred only in passing to the differences between areas in terms of life styles, ages, and family structures. Regarding the first, three major life styles have been identified: familism, which stresses family life, child rearing, the wife as homemaker, and the desire for a spacious suburban home with garden; careerism, which is centered on occupational (especially professional) attainment; and consumerism, with its concentration on hedonistic values. The three are extreme ideal types and may overlap in individual households. In general it is assumed that the familism orientation is associated with a desire for a single-family home in suburbia, whereas consumerism and careerism are more likely to be associated with apartment rental. This suggests a simple zonal dichotomy that is matched by the stereotypes of suburbia on the one hand and, for example, Greenwich Village on the other. But several factors are breaking down this simple dichotomy. Among them are the increased building of apartments in suburbia; the aging of the population and the smaller size of families, releasing many persons from their parental responsibilities twenty-five or more years before their death; and the greater overlap of life styles, in part reflecting the increased participation of married women in the labor force (see Chapter 2). Thus a greater spatial mixture is likely in the future than heretofore, as new life styles and family structures take hold.

The familism life style remains the most common. Within it there is a characteristic life cycle associated with bearing and rearing children. Child rearing is still generally associated with low-density suburban living, and so most urban areas have a typical zonal form, with the youngest families in the outer zones (Figure 6.13). Again, however, the changing nature of the family cycle may see this simple pattern somewhat destroyed in the future, as people adopt alternative life styles and as the parents of grown children move to custom-built premises for smaller households. At present, suburbs and their populations tend to age together; the relationship may not be as strong in the future. (Already, for example, many single-parent families—especially those with a female parent—are being forced by relative poverty into the inner-city housing market.)

MOBILITY AND THE MOSAIC

Americans have always been highly mobile. According to one survey, only 51.5 percent of the population over age five lived in the same dwelling in 1975 as they did in 1970; 17 percent were living in a different county and 9 percent in a different state. And in the single year 1975–1976, 17 percent moved home, including 8.3 percent who changed address *within* a metropolitan area. Such high mobility rates are not new; if anything, people moved about even more in the nineteenth century.

Intra-urban migration reflects people's adjusting their housing to meet their requirements (and in some cases having to do so, because of eviction). Mobility rates are generally highest in two type areas. The first, not surprisingly, includes newly developed housing areas, especially the outer suburbs. The others are in the inner cities, where most people are renters with fewer ties to dwelling and area and fewest impediments to movement (it is harder and costlier to buy one home and sell another than simply to change landlord and address.)

The filtering processes inherent in the Burgess and Hoyt models suggest that most moves are away from the city center within a defined sector. The bulk of the evidence supports this and shows that most moves are over short distances. Several reasons for this are suggested. According to one explanation, once people decide to move, they look outward from their existing homes until they find one that meets their needs; most succeed relatively quickly and so do not have to move far.

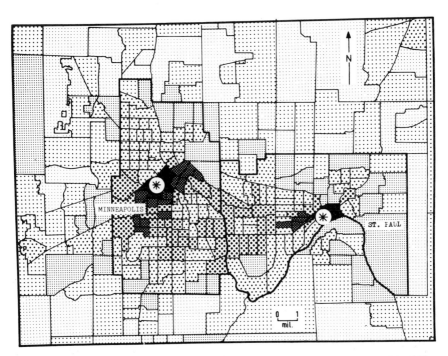

Figure 6.13.   The spatial pattern of family status in Minneapolis-St. Paul, 1960. The lighter the shading, the younger the average age of the population. Source: P. H. Rees, *Residential Patterns in American Cities, 1960.* University of Chicago, Department of Geography, Research Paper 189, 1979, p. 239. Copyright 1979 by Philip H. Rees.

Another states that the city is large and complex and most people know only one part of it, their home area. The majority will be unwilling to move to an unknown area where they will know no one and where they will be relatively ignorant of social, educational, and economic conditions; they will prefer to stay in an area which they know and in which they are known. Finally, it is argued that the constraints of the housing market are such that choice is limited to a certain area and that unless a household's economic circumstances change markedly, most are already occupants of that area; they have nowhere else to go. For some people, the constraints may be very tight. Especially in a large urban area, others may have considerable choice within their ability to pay, in which case they can express their preferences. Most seem to do so by not moving far, unless they are going from an inner-city apartment to a new, outer suburban home.

The high levels of mobility in most districts of American urban areas suggest a degree of change (although most of the immigrants are very similar in their characteristics to the outmigrants whom they replace) that is not conducive to neighborhood stability. Indeed, the concept of community as a description of most residential districts is irrelevant. Although many people rapidly develop social contacts with their new neighbors (perhaps encouraged by semiformal neighborhood organizations and by business-sponsored ''welcome wagons''), these contacts rarely develop into close and lasting bonds. A true community is rare; the main examples are some of the stable, inner-city ethnic neighborhoods. Social contact is plentiful, if it is desired, and local groups may develop close ties to face a common threat, such as the potential invasion of a perceived negative externality. But the state of flux is such that most links are ephemeral and there is no enduring community, only a transitory sharing of common interests.

CONCLUSIONS

This chapter has dealt with a major topic of urban geography; the residential mosaic of the individual urban settlement. The argument offered here is that the prime mover for such a mosaic in an industrial capitalist society is a series of social desires for distancing, congregation, and segregation among the various classes and interest groups within that society. These social desires are closely tied to economic ones, however, and together the two are a powerful force for the development of different residential areas for various class and ethnic groups. The morphology of that development reflects the operation of other economic factors, notably the investment in an intra-urban transport infrastructure and the power of the construction industry to obtain financial and other concessions for its operations. These economic forces are peculiar to the United States (along with the political factors discussed in Chapter 8) and have produced its characteristic residential mosaic; the more general social and economic forces are typical of all capitalist societies. Thus the necessary conditions for distancing, congregation, and segregation are general; the mechanisms by which they are put in place are specific to individual capitalist societies.

7

NONRESIDENTIAL
LAND USES

ALTHOUGH THEY FORM the major land use within urban settlements in terms of area occupied, homes are not the focal points of the urban system. The major nodes are the factories, offices, shops, and warehouses. Each is linked with the residential mosaic, via the flows of people, goods, and messages, and there is a multiplicity of links between and among the nonresidential uses. As part of the general evolution of the intra-urban spatial organization, these different land uses have become separated, both from each other and, within each, by function; again, the processes involved are the mutually reinforcing ones of congregation and segregation.

Some land use separation was a feature of mercantile cities, notably in the dock areas of the ports and around the main transport nodes in the inland centers; both were dominated by clusters of warehouses and workshops. But it was in the industrial capitalist stage that the separation became marked. This was aided later by the introduction of zoning policies whose major aims included reducing, if not entirely eliminating, the mixture of land uses in local areas. In the mercantile settlements, as indicated in the previous chapter, many buildings performed two or more separate functions, one of which was usually residential. The firms occupying these premises were almost invariably small, with many, especially those operating workshops and small trading establishments, employing only the owner and perhaps members of his family. It was only as the average size of firms increased, and as the division of labor within firms increased accordingly, that the separation of land uses became a major characteristic of intra-urban spatial organization.

The spatial separation of the manufacturing industry from commerce was thus the major feature of the growing industrial capitalist settlement, a separation that paralleled—and in part produced—the removal of residential uses from many inner-city areas. This separation reflected the operation of two processes. The first was the growth of separate firms, with most of the industrial firms no longer being involved in selling their products directly to the consumer. Separate establishments were opened in the wholesaling and retailing trades, with the former buying products in bulk from the manufacturers and selling them in smaller consignments to the retailers. This separation did not occur at the same time in all sectors, of course. Many small workshops—especially those involved in the specialized manufacture of commodities with no mass-production counterparts—remained selling as well as manufacturing concerns, as did those making commodities that had to be purchased soon after production; bakeries were an example of the latter, and they were dispersed throughout the buying population. In addition, some manufacturers, again usually those with small workshops, had a direct link with a particular retail outlet and did not use the middleman services of warehouses; custom tailoring is a good example of this type concern. Thus while the growth of the factory introduced a new element to the urban scene, it did not immediately replace the workshop; rather it rapidly outgrew it in importance (measured by volume of production). Workshops remained, particularly in certain industries like custom tailoring and certain aspects of jewelry manufacture; even today the workshop quarters of most large cities are still near the central business area.

The second process leading to land use separation was the development of different locational requirements. Accessibility was important to all forms of land use, to allow efficiency of operation, but it involved accessibility to different groups within the urban area. Thus the retailing functions had to be made accessible to customers, in order to attract trade, whereas for most manufacturing industries the links were more with other industries and with the warehouses through which many of the inputs and outputs were channeled. (An accessible labor force was also needed.) Retailers therefore needed the most accessible locations, so that when trade and manufacture were separated it was trade that remained in the city center, whereas manufacture shifted to its edge.

LAND VALUES
AND LOCATION

Twentieth-century locational analysts have suggested that there is a close correlation between accessibility and business success. Assume a city with a radius of two miles around its focal point. The closer a retail store is to that central point, the closer it is to the entire population of the city. (This can be established—assuming that the population is distributed relatively evenly across the urban area—using the concept of population potential introduced in Chapter 4.) Assume, too, that the more people have to spend on traveling to the store, the less money they have available to spend there. It follows that the closer the store is to all of the population—that is, the higher the population potential of its location—the greater its volume of turnover. Thus the more accessible a store's location, the more business that is transacted; this, in turn, should mean greater profits and the store will be prepared to pay more to obtain such a central location. A simple equation is thus suggested: greater accessibility equals greater trade profits equals greater land values. From this, one can deduce that land values decline with distance from the most accessible point.

So far, the assumption has been that the trade volume of each shop is independent of that of its neighbors. For some there is an inverse relationship—if one grocery store is doing well, another next door to it will probably not. But others obtain mutual benefits from being neighbors or near-neighbors: a grocery store brings in customers, who might then be attracted to shop at a nearby butcher, and vice versa; a dress shop might generate business for a nearby shoe repair shop; and so on. Thus stores benefit from agglomeration economies in the same way that factories do (Chapter 5), which is a major reason why they cluster together. Each store in a cluster enhances the trading prospects of its neighbors, thereby improving their potential for making profits and increasing the price they are prepared to pay for their premises.

For manufacturing and nonretailing commercial establishments (offices, warehouses, etc.) accessibility is not as important as it is to retailers. Nonretailers need accessible locations, in order to serve their customers efficiently, but they do not need locations at or near the peak point of population potential as much as retailers do. Their volume of trade is affected less by such minor variations in location, and their profit levels are affected only when they occupy relatively inaccessible locations. Thus, while retailers will be prepared to pay more for a piece of land the closer it is to the city center, they will not outbid retailers for the most central locations.

The brief analysis given thus far suggests a simple geography of land values that can be represented graphically by plotting distance from the city center (the most accessible point) against the price that various land users are prepared to pay for sites. This is shown in the left-hand diagram of Figure 7.1a. The steepest graph is for shops, which value accessibility most highly and outbid all other users for the central locations. The next steepest is for industries, followed by one for residences. (Individual households benefit from accessibility too, but the benefits that they receive are relatively small so they cannot outbid shops and factories.) Finally, agricultural activities that serve the local urban population (notably truck farming) also benefit from being accessible to their market, but individual farmers cannot outbid urban land users.

These graphs suggest two urban features. The first is a clear-cut geography of land values within the city, with a negative correlation between values and distance from the center that has been found in many empirical studies. The second is that if the graphs are rotated 360 degrees, they suggest that the urban area is spatially organized as a series of concentric zones. Again, empirical evidence generally confirms this pattern.

The highly generalized pattern in Figure 7.1a (several major land users have been omitted for simplicity of presentation) is typical of the relatively small, industrial capitalist city. In larger places and in most modern cities the pattern is more complex. For a variety of reasons, detailed later in this chapter, the city center may not be the accessible location preferred by all. Other nodes may be relatively attractive, and some uses may be drawn to locations on major transport arteries rather than at particular nodes. Finally, changing transport technology has reduced the importance of the central point. This produces the sort of pattern presented in simplified form in Figure 7.1b, in which both shops and industries outbid residential users in parts, according to the upper diagrams, of the residential zone. The result is a more complex pattern, al-

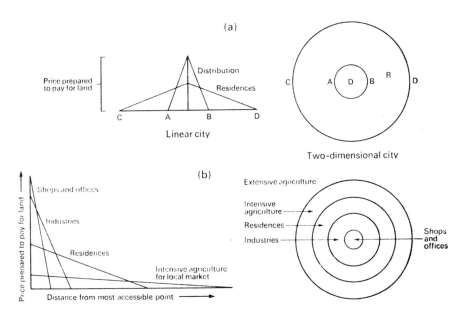

Figure 7.1. The relationship between accessibility and the price paid for land, with its resulting land-use zonation in (a) industrial capitalist cities and (b) late capitalist cities.

though the underlying logic of the relationship between accessibility, desirable locations, and land values remains the same. The rest of this chapter will examine how this pattern evolves from that shown in Figure 7.1a.

MANUFACTURING INDUSTRIES WITHIN THE CITY

Industrial capitalism is usually identified with the factory, and with the implicit assumption that manufacturing dominated the economy and the labor force. That assumption is not true, however: Except in very small industrial settlements (plus a few larger ones dominated by a single firm), employment in manufacturing has rarely occupied a majority of the urban labor force, although it may have been the largest single sector in the local economy. Certainly by 1950, according to the classification of settlements used in Chapter 4, an average of only 27 percent of the labor force was employed in manufacturing. (This, too, can be considered an overstatement, since as many as one-third of the employees in manufacturing firms are not actually involved directly in the productive processes but are in managerial, service, and other jobs.) Nevertheless, the commercial and other functions in many cities depend on the basic employment in the manufacturing sector.

Areas of two main types developed for industrial locations in the capitalist city. The first was focused either on a major transport artery, or—in many places—was at the junction of two such arteries. At the ports, this was the dock area, usually adjacent to the city center, at which marine transport was linked to the railroad network. (In some cases, there were links to canals; today, freeways have at least partly replaced the railroads.) In the inland cities, the railroad was the focus, with industries concentrated around the major freight yards. The industries located in these areas were those that relied on the transport links for the movement of materials and products. This was particularly the case with the ports, with respect to imported materials: factories were established to process bulky material, such as refining sugar, either for reexport or distribution to local consumers. Inland the links were used to move both inputs and outputs; in midwestern cities, for example, the railroads were used both to bring the cattle in for slaughtering and to move out the packed meat. These industries attracted others to serve them, notably the various ship building, repair, and provision establishments of the dock areas. Some of the establishments, especially those linked to the major functions, were small, but a major characteristic of the basic industries was the large size of plants. This has remained the case, especially at the ports. Indeed, the growth of large industries and industrial complexes (such as iron and steel and petrochemical com-

plexes) there has often resulted in the development of separate port facilities for each industry at custom-designed sites, which are usually
some distance from the original docks that are near the city center and
now in economic and physical decline.

The other type of area is a collar of industrial premises around the
city center, separating the commercial and residential areas, in which
factories, workshops and warehouses are interdigitated. In the early development of this industrial collar, most of the firms were small and
specialized, occupying premises that were designed for other purposes.
(Many were in converted dwellings, or parts of dwellings.) Custom-built
factories were later developments. Many of the firms were linked with
several of their neighbors, and each performed a specialized task within
the manufacturing process.

Figure 7.2 shows the extent of this industrial collar in Baltimore in
1860. Up until then, the main industries in the city served the local
community. For example, in 1833 there were thirty-one flour mills,
along with fifteen textile factories and ten iron and copper works. But

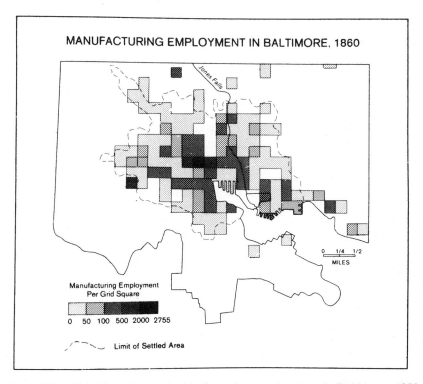

Figure 7.2.   The distribution of manufacturing employment in Baltimore, 1860.
Source: E. K. Muller and P. A. Groves, "The Emergence of Industrial Districts in
Mid-Nineteenth Century Baltimore," *Geographical Review,* 69 (1979):171.

these relatively large establishments, many either in the port district or along the line of the major river, comprised only 30 percent of the city's manufacturing premises; the remainder were small workshops, half of which were in the central business area just north of the docks. Twenty-seven years later there were 1,147 establishments, 786 of which were small workshops employing 5,017 of the 16,122 manufacturing employees. (The largest sector consisted of 46 clothiers, who employed 5,164 persons, three-quarters of them women.) These small firms were clustered around the city center, where, as Figure 7.2 shows, the highest densities of employment were recorded.

The distributions of two of these typical inner-city industries are shown in Figure 7.3. The boot and shoe industry was characterized by small establishments; nearly 90 percent of the 236 workshops employed fewer than 10 people. The clothing industry comprised both a number of large firms (one-fifth employed 100 or more; most of these firms were concentrated just west of the center and occupied large, multistory buildings designed for the industry) plus a number of small workshops to which work was assigned. In contrast, some of the largest employers were either in the dock area, which included a number of large shipbuilding and iron foundry works as well as a lot of small artisan workshops, or on the main railroad link: the works of the Baltimore and Ohio Railroad (forming the main cluster of workers on the eastern edge of the built-up area; Figure 7.2) employed 990 persons.

These two types of areas, as exemplified by Baltimore, illustrate the importance of linkages in industrial location. For the first type, the links are forged via the transport arteries; for the second type, there were many links among manufacturers, warehouses, and customers that involved the movement of small consignments (often of semifinished goods) by hand. Because of the intensity of the links in the latter case, establishments tied together in manufacturing and marketing chains congregated in certain parts of the inner collar, as Figure 7.3 illustrates. Clothiers, boot and shoe manufacturers, jewelers, jobbing printers— each concentrated in a particular area (perhaps one or two street blocks only). Within the clothing industry, specialized subdistricts developed in the largest cities, such as the fur district in midtown New York. These clusters not only facilitated the flow of goods, but they also allowed contact between members of the industry and eased the flow of communications, vital to industries in which changes of style or the need for rapid delivery were crucial.

Another feature of the congregation of manufacturers within the industrial collar—and one that accentuated the congregation—was its role in fostering new establishments (as suggested in the innovation/invention elements of the urban multiplier in Figure 4.4). The inner area was a seedbed, where new firms were being established, some merely extending the number of firms in a particular industry but others

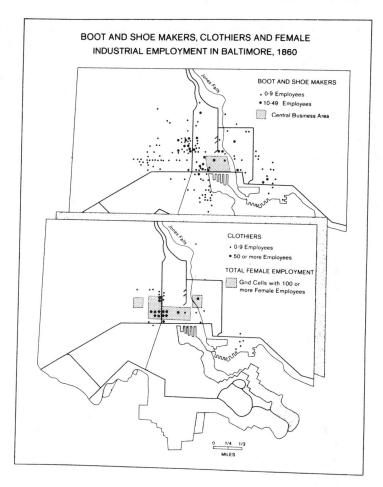

Figure 7.3.   The distributions of boot and shoe makers and clothiers in Baltimore, 1860. Source: E. K. Muller and P. A. Groves, "The Emergence of Industrial Districts in Mid-Nineteenth Century Baltimore," *Geographical Review*, 69, (1979):174.

widening the range of products manufactured. The opportunities to sell in a growing economy attracted individuals to set up businesses on their own—fulfilling a part of the American capitalist ethos of which every employee dreams: first, of being his own boss and, second, of being a big businessman. Most opened establishments in the trade that they had learned from their previous employers. To do this, they needed capital and premises. They may have been able to borrow some capital, but many depended largely on their own savings and resources. Some of this money had to be spent on machinery (although in many industries there were firms that rented machinery, thus reducing the need for initial capital outlay). Few persons could afford to buy premises; most were restricted to renting. Since special premises were not necessary in the industries concerned, a few rooms in a workshop area were sufficient. These were available in the industrial collar and could be obtained through the information networks operating within each industry. Thus growing industries spawned new establishments within and on the edge of their existing concentration. A good example of the seed-bed process associated with innovation is the development of the brassiere in the 1920s. A New York seamstress invented it to accompany her dresses, and gave it to her customers. It proved popular; she found a partner and some capital and established a factory that produced brassieres. The company grew, developing a demand for new skills, involving hooks, eyes, and the like. The firm took the name of the Maidenform Company and transferred its operations first to Hoboken, New Jersey, and then to West Virginia, where labor was cheaper.

Many of these seed-bed firms failed, for various reasons often involving the incompetence of their owners as managers, who returned to being employees. Their vacated premises were available for other budding self-made men. Other firms survived, but did not expand. A few were successful, however, and grew. The more firms that succeeded, the more pressure there was on space in the collar. To expand, especially if they wanted to build their own premises, industrialists had to extend the collar, displacing, in particular, residential areas through a process of invasion and succession similar to that described in the previous chapter. Thus in a growing city, the residential areas were in constant retreat from the swelling tide of workshops, factories, and warehouses; at any one time, their intermixing formed the transitional zone of Burgess's model (Figure 6.9).

Growth also occurred in the transport-artery type of areas. Increasingly, as space demands grew, as the problems of congestion, land values, and outdated premises in the inner collar got worse, and as movement of both goods and workers was eased by transportation developments so firms were attracted to move from the inner collar to locations alongside the main transport arteries. Clearly, bigger factories needed space, and this was more easily obtained on the edge of the built-up area, at sites that rail and road developments made sufficiently accessible. (In general, the larger the plant, the less its need for close links with others.)

The development of noncentral industrial districts began more than a century ago. The main difference between this process and the process operating in the inner collar was that whereas in the latter changes were spontaneous and *ad hoc*, the new, outer developments were specifically designed, often by land development companies. The Union Stockyards in Chicago, for example, were established in 1865 and attracted milling and meat-packing plants. Thirty or so years later two organized industrial districts opened next to the stockyards, offering the basic utilities needed by industries—land for factory building and expansion, and links to the railroad network.

The railroads were the prime movers of industrial decentralization within urban areas, but the greatest stimulus to this trend was provided by the truck, and later by the freeway. Changes within industry have also required the development of low-density, custom-built premises away from the city center. The large size of production lines, the need for storage areas, the replacement of labor by machinery needing, in some cases, specially constructed buildings: these and several other factors impelled the suburbanization of industry as the transformation from industrial to late capitalism gathered pace. Not all the firms either moving to the suburbs or newly established there (a group including migrants plus branch plants) have been large. Many are, but many of the large factories that dominate the modern industrial scene require the services and specialized products of small plants, which also move to the suburbs, either to be near their main customers or to be able to reach them quickly (via the freeway networks and, for some specialized industrial services, via the airways; major airports such as O'Hare in Chicago have attracted considerable industrial development in their environs).

The suburbanization of industry is not a recent phenomenon but its pace has quickened rapidly in recent decades. In most metropolitan areas, manufacturing employment is now growing much more rapidly in the suburbs than in the central cities (details of the political geography are given in the next chapter), and some central cities are losing jobs in large numbers. Not surprisingly, this decentralization is most apparent in the older, larger cities of the Frost Belt. Between 1947 and 1972 metropolitan areas with populations exceeding 1 million suffered a net loss of 880,000 jobs in manufacturing, while their suburban rings experienced a net gain of 2.5 million; of those that achieved metropolitan status before 1950, the central city loss was 1.4 million jobs and the suburban gain was 2.3 million. Wholesaling has moved out, too: for the metropolitan areas with populations exceeding 1 million, the central cities lost 302,000 jobs net between 1947 and 1972, while their suburban rings had a net gain of 798,000.

These changes reflect three factors. First, many of the growth industries in the economy are relatively new, and so are concentrated in the suburbs. Second, new factories in advanced capitalist industries are large, and they too need suburban, not inner-city, locations. Finally, firms are moving to the suburbs. In 1970 alone, forty-three companies in metropolitan St. Louis moved their premises away from the central city. In the New York region many firms are moving to Westchester County, New Jersey, and Connecticut, from where they can serve the regional and national markets, moving their products mainly by road. An early example of this focus on freeway locations was the movement of firms from central Boston to industrial areas along Route 128, a circumferential highway about ten miles from the city center that was completed in 1951. In the late 1950s about 40 percent of Boston's new jobs were located along Route 128.

It is easy to view this decentralization as a "natural" process, reflecting the needs of industries. To a considerable extent it is. Like the decentralization of residential uses described in the previous chapter, however, it is also a manipulated process, part of the dynamic of urban change impelled by the construction industry and its allies (including the state; the federal government pays 90 percent of the operating costs of the interstate highway system, much of which serves suburban areas). The key to this manipulation of industrial location has been the development of planned industrial districts, or industrial parks, in the suburbs. There were only 35 of these in the United States in 1940, but over 2,500 by the early 1970s; Chicago alone had 356 in 1972.

Early industrial parks were developed by the railroad companies, and now account for about one quarter of all those in operation; such developments were aimed clearly at increasing freight traffic on the declining railroads. Most have been developed by nonprofit organizations, including local governments, to provide jobs and property-tax revenues for communities; about a third are operated as profit-oriented ventures. Some are aimed at specific types of industry, as are the science industry parks like the Stanford Industrial Park in Palo Alto—but most are open to all industries though few attract heavy industrial firms.

Figure 7.4 shows the industrial parks in the five-county metropolitan area centered on the city of Atlanta, Georgia, in the early 1970s. Most of the fifty-five shown are in the suburbs, near the freeways. (The major cluster in the south is near Atlanta's international airport.) In all they occupy some 35,000 acres, with the largest covering 3,000 acres and, even when only half completed, containing more than 100 firms. Manufacturing and warehousing are intermingled in these parks. Some offer prestige locations and include services such as the nine-hole golf course around which one park in Chicago is built.

INDUSTRIAL LOCATION AND COMMUTING

Thus far the discussion of industrial location has focused on the linkages between factories, suppliers, and customers. One significant linkage that has been ignored up to now is that with the workforce. Factories need an accessible supply of labor, and the movements that they generate create the peak traffic flows within most urban areas—in the early morning and in the late afternoon/early evening.

In the mercantile and early industrial cities, most jobs were concentrated in or near the city center. Most residential areas, especially

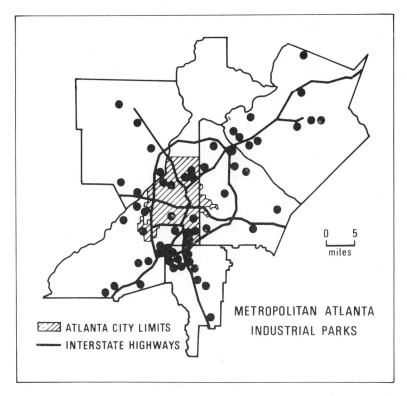

Figure 7.4. Industrial parks in metropolitan Atlanta. Source: T. A. Hartshorn, "Industrial/Office Parks: A New Look for the City," *Journal of Geography*, 72 (1973):40. Reprinted with the permission of the *Journal of Geography*, National Council for Geographic Education.

those for the blue-collar workers, were adjacent to this industrial collar, permitting relatively easy journeys to work on foot. As the urban area expanded, the concentration of jobs could be serviced more readily by a public transport network that focused on the city center. In general, the lower the status of the worker, the lower his income and the longer his hours of work. Together these financial and temporal constraints (together with the spatial structure of the housing market) required a residential location near the workplace, so that the commuting journey was both cheap and short. Proximity to workplaces was especially important to those without permanent jobs (as was the case in some occupations, such as on the docks, where casual labor was important), who needed to search for employment frequently and who found that living close to the possible sources aided the gathering of information about potential openings.

At the other extreme of the employment scale were the well paid, who worked shorter, and sometimes more flexible, hours. They could afford to live farther from their place of work, indulging their desires to escape the negative externalities of the inner city and own a suburban home. Thus employers and well-paid employees traveled longer distances to work, a fact that reflected their positions in the labor market and in the developing residential mosaic. The development of public transit systems accentuated this pattern. The result was the funneling of workers into the city center each morning, with a close correlation between type of job and distance traveled.

As industrial decentralization proceeded, this simple pattern was modified, but not entirely destroyed. For the movement of goods, extensive decentralization depended on the truck and the freeway network; for the movement of workers, increasingly it became necessary to be an automobile owner. Some of the earliest industrial areas beyond the inner city could be reached by public transport from at least part of the urban area, and so a local labor market was created (at least for the blue-collar workers, especially females, who relied on public provision). But the widespread dispersion of modern industrial parks oriented to the freeway network militates against such provision. There are some bus routes linking industrial parks to residential areas, but the development of the parks assumes that the majority of employees have automobiles, or at least access to a ride in one. For those with cars, rapid freeway driving allows for long-distance commuting, which, compared with that to the central city, does not channel everyone toward the same destination. Suburbanization has produced a complex pattern of cross-city, intersuburban flows, whose intersections often create major traffic problems.

As industrial decentralization has proceeded, the major commuting flow—from suburbs to central city in the morning and the reverse in the afternoon—has become much less dominant. In 1960, for a set of 101 metropolitan areas, more than three suburban residents had a central-city job for every one central-city resident working in the suburbs; ten years later the ratio was about two and a half to one. One related consequence of the suburban shift of jobs has been to make finding employment much more difficult for the poor (especially members of minority groups) trapped in inner-city housing and lacking the means to commute to a suburban industrial park. Only half of Chicago's black households owned cars in 1970, for example, compared to 80 percent of white households. As the jobs moved away from the inner-city ghetto, its residents' chances of holding them declined, too.

The contemporary commuting pattern of manufacturing workers therefore is complex. The simple, industrial-city pattern of most jobs being in or near the city center and drawing workers from the entire urban area (the higher their status, the longer the distance traveled), plus a few suburban centers drawing mainly on a local district, has been considerably distorted. The decentralization and widespread suburban dispersal of jobs, combined with widespread use of the automobile at nearly all status levels on the occupation scale and a system of intra-urban freeways that can move large volumes of this traffic, means that the urban area now has much less focus to it.

THE OFFICE SECTOR

Together, the tertiary (mainly retailing) and quaternary sectors form the largest portion of the current office workforce in the United States, and the location of the main office centers is a crucial element in the spatial organization of the country's cities. The trends in that location pattern are similar to, though lagging behind, those for the manufacturing industry.

Offices developed as subsectors of manufacturing, mercantile, and retail companies, in many cases through the spatial separation of, for example, the clerical and executive functions from the warehouses in a mercantile concern or the administrative components from the factories in a large manufacturing company. In addition, as the capitalist economy developed, new office functions emerged to provide previously unavailable services, such as many aspects of banking, finance, and insurance. The former type of office was separated from the other sections of the company because the need for links with other establishments was greater than for links within the company, thereby requiring a separate location. For the latter type—the new office functions—interfirm linkages were in many cases crucial influences on location, as between, for example, many finance companies and the Stock Exchange.

Separate office quarters developed in the hearts of nearly all cities within the collar of industrial land uses described in the previous section. They were adjacent to, but in almost all cases clearly separate from, the retailing area, which had greater requirements regarding accessibility to the general population. The land occupied by offices is expensive, being near the population potential center, and is used intensively, more so as land values have escalated. This required the development of a technological solution to the problem of getting maximum use from often small but expensive plots of land. The answer was the skyscraper, made possible by advances in construction methods and design, including the elevator. For the largest companies, requiring a great deal of office space, custom-designed skyscrapers have been built, some with particular features identifying them with the company, which thus gains a status symbol as well as a workplace.

Relatively few firms need a whole building and so many skyscrapers have been built by speculators, aiming to cash in on the growing demand for office space through profitable leasing or renting. The rapid growth of the quaternary sector in recent years has made such speculation extremely attractive, and rents have risen sharply. In some places at some times, however, developers have produced an oversupply, leading to temporary high vacancy rates. Nevertheless, adequate demand seems to persist over the longer term. In the New York metropolitan area alone, 111 million square feet of office floor space was constructed between 1960 and 1975—out of a total of 370 million in the nineteen largest metropolitan areas—and another 2.6 million was under construction in 1975; Manhattan alone had 227 million square feet in 1975 (11.5 percent of it vacant), which was an increase of 84 percent over 1960.

The concentration of offices into relatively small, densely occupied areas of the urban core reflects the importance of linkages within this sector of the economy, especially during the period when such concentration was developing. In part, some of the need for proximity has been removed now with regard to routine administrative work, since modern telecommunications equipment allows almost instantaneous transmission of messages over considerable distances. But for the decision-making sectors of the office industry, contacts are nonroutine and mostly oriented outside the firm. In these instances, business often involves face-to-face contacts; deals are discussed and agreed in the intimacy of an office, or at a nearby restaurant, and not through the relative anonymity of a telephone call.

When a large volume of even the most routine business was conducted face to face and many firms employed messengers, proximity was very important for contact. Thus not only did offices cluster within the urban core, they congregated into separate subclusters according to their dominant linkage patterns. This is illustrated in Manhattan, which has two distinct office cores. At the southern tip of the island—Lower Manhattan—is the international finance cluster, focused on Wall Street and containing the main offices of banks and dealers in stocks and shares, plus the accountants, lawyers, and other professionals who serve them. The second area is in Midtown Manhattan, south of Central Park, which is dominated by the headquarters of manufacturing companies. Much more space is available for further development in this area than in Lower Manhattan, which is virtually saturated, as the skyline suggests; two-thirds of the recent office construction in Manhattan has been in Midtown. Within the major clusters are minor centers of particular functions; advertising companies on Madison Avenue are one good example.

Some of the ties to particular locations are not as strong now as they have been in previous decades, which allows for some slackening of the intense concentration of office functions, except for those (like the Stock Exchange) still operated by personal, immediate contacts. But the inertia of the established pattern is considerable, especially for companies that have made considerable investments in buildings as status symbols. Thus decentralization of offices has been much less rapid than that of industries, and the increase in office employment downtown has off-set the loss of manufacturing jobs. One of the major ties has been with the workforce. Offices, more than many factories, depend on female workers, who in turn are more reliant than male workers on public transport systems for commuting; thus the Midtown Manhattan office cluster is close to the termini of the main suburban railroads.

Decentralization of offices within metropolitan areas is proceeding at an increasing pace, however. The high costs of maintaining routine operations in expensive center-city buildings are convincing firms of the desirability of reducing their central staff to a minimum, moving other functions—if not the entire office—to suburban sites. This is associated with the centralization and concentration trends in the economy as a whole. The giant corporations are much more self-contained than their predecessors were and have less need for links with other firms; they may retain a presence within the city center, and a suite of rooms for in-tercompany meetings, but most of their operations can be conducted from a pleasant suburban location. Developers are catering to this shift in demand by creating office parks. Atlanta, for example, has a number of these (Figure 7.5), the first having been developed in 1964. As with the industrial parks (Figure 7.4), location close to a freeway is clearly a considerable attraction (especially for commuters); almost all of Atlan-ta's office parks are in the northern suburbs, which are generally of higher socioeconomic status than those in the south.

The distribution of offices is changing, therefore, much as that of industry has, and suburbanization is clearly acceptable to the workforce. Nevertheless, it is not certain that office decentralization will proceed as far as industrial decentralization. Offices are now not only the major central-city employers, but the major sources of property-tax revenue, and so pressures to retain the downtown office core will be intense. Fur-thermore, to date decentralization has been very selective. Many of-fices—banks, insurance companies, brokers, advertising agents, and various other services—need the advantages of proximity in the high-density core, and much of the movement to suburban office parks is by large companies, in many cases their regional headquarters (the nation-al office being in a major metropolitan center, probably Midtown Man-hattan). A dual pattern thus appears to be emerging, reflecting the dif-ferences between office types in the need for access and linkages.

The inner-city office sector is also closely linked to the local labor market. Although many of its workers commute long distances from the suburbs, large numbers live relatively close to their workplace. In partic-ular these are the young employees, many of them female, who are responsible for the routine, nonexecutive tasks, and who live in the apartment blocks of the inner zones. There is also a great deal of em-ployment for lower-status workers, in custodial duties for example, and

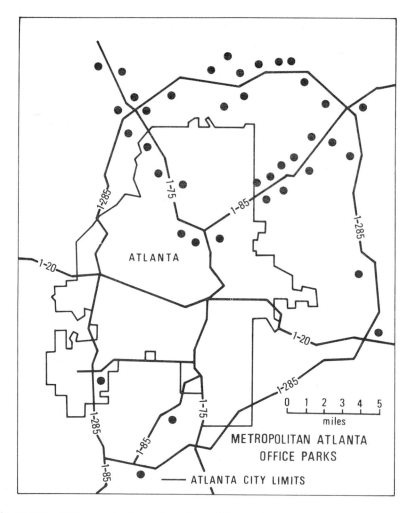

Figure 7.5. Office parks in metropolitan Atlanta. Source: T. A. Hartshorn, "Industrial/Office Parks: A New Look for the City," *Journal of Geography*, 72 (1973):43. Reprinted with the permission of the *Journal of Geography*, National Council for Geographic Education.

many of these people are restricted to the inner city by their housing class position. To some extent, these segments of the labor force cannot be duplicated easily in the suburbs, which is a further (though perhaps minor) influence maintaining the vitality of the central core. Finally, some of the gentrification trends discussed in Chapter 6 involve office executives moving closer to their downtown jobs and to the inner-city environment that they prefer.

THE RETAIL SYSTEM

Retailing is probably the intra-urban land use pattern that has received the most attention from urban geographers, due to the wide interest in central place theory. Retailing has traditionally occupied the heart of the American city, in what is generally known as the Central Business District (CBD). It attracts the greatest volume of pedestrian traffic and contains the peak land values. Initially, it contained virtually all the retail establishments in the urban area; the settlement was small and most people went to the CBD to do their shopping. As the population grew, the range of establishments and types of goods sold increased. The existing stores were duplicated, and new, more specialized ones were introduced.

All these new stores could have located in the CBD and competed for trade with those already there. Many did. But others located outside the established center, leading to the development of a hierarchy of shopping centers. Two processes were involved in this retail decentralization: one involved entrepreneurs seeking to serve only a spatially delimited portion of the market, and the other involved entrepreneurs who followed the "market leaders" and sought to capitalize on proved locations.

The search for a spatially restricted portion of the market involved entrepreneurs who preferred the possibility of a local monopoly to competing with similar stores in an established center. In a large place, many stores—notably those providing the frequently purchased convenience goods, such as food—require only a very small share of the total market in order to be viable. They do not need to be in the CBD, with its high land values; a small area of the city (perhaps only one or two blocks) might produce enough business, and if an entrepreneur could convince the local population to use his store, its viability would be ensured. (The assumption is that a substantial proportion of the population buys from the nearest available outlet.)

General stores, retailing food and other daily needs, were the first to desert the CBD and seek a local market within the residential areas. Many were opened by residents of those areas, involving some conversion of their home premises; the high-density districts of nineteenth-century cities contained a great number of such stores. Others followed their example, perceiving that there was sufficient trade in local areas to justify the relatively small risk of opening a shop. For many, the most sensible location was near an existing store—a "market leader"—where the local population shopped regularly; the existence of a neighboring outlet, selling a different range of goods, should attract them to buy there, too (another example of linkages and congregation). Different types of stores need different numbers of people to support their operations, however, because of variations in the frequency of purchases. If there were fewer of these stores than general stores, they sought the best locations of those already pioneered. Usually these are at nodes in the street system, points of relatively high local accessibility. Large clusters of stores developed around these points.

Over time, therefore, a hierarchy of shopping centers developed within the built-up area, with a structure much like that of the inter-urban settlement pattern (Chapter 3). A great many locations were pioneered by entrepreneurs seeking local markets. Many of these were attractive to a few others; a few attracted a large number and became major suburban centers, subsidiary to the CBD, which contained the full range of establishments, including types not available in the smaller centers.

In general, this hierarchical system was used as such by most shoppers, who obtained their daily needs from the nearest neighborhood centers, their less frequent needs from the nearest regional center, and made an occasional visit to the CBD. Over time, as tastes changed, so did the composition of the centers; developments in banking and in radio and TV, for example, were reflected in the spread of branches and stores, and some of the firms with big stores in the CBD opened suburban branches as spending power grew. They too acted as market leaders, their choice of a particular center being a considerable stimulus to trade and attracting other stores. Thus entrepreneurs could be divided into those prepared to gamble and pioneer a new location (either a virgin site with no stores at all or a small center to be upgraded substantially) and those locational followers, who accepted the leaders' decisions. Many of the latter were restricted to that situation since they could not, like the large department stores, generate sufficient trade on their own to justify a pioneering step; they depended on being the beneficiaries of positive externalities when shoppers at certain stores in a center decided to patronize others there also.

The largest of the centers in these intra-urban hierarchies had their own typical internal spatial pattern. In most, the main stores—those that differentiated the centers from their smaller competitors and that attracted the most business—occupied the most accessible and expensive sites, just as in the city as a whole (Figure 7.1). On a grid plan, this usually meant a location at a major intersection, usually one with streetcar lines in both directions. Lower-order establishments, those providing more specialized goods and services and perhaps competing both among themselves and with the market leaders, clustered around the peak land value; the convenience goods stores, serving the local population only, were on the edge of the center. In addition, and especially in the CBD, there were clusters of particular types of stores. Some of these involved complementary functions—such as dress and shoe shops, which attracted trade from each other. Some were competing, using their window displays, for the same market—again, often in clothing. Still others had particular requirements, such as the space needs for furniture stores, which led them to concentrate on relatively cheap land. There was a similar arrangement of different functions within individual department and variety stores, where the separate counters were arranged so as to gain the most business. Goods for which people made a special trip, such as furniture, would be as far from the door as possible, whereas those that people bought on impulse would be located to catch the eye of passing shoppers. In the CBDs, too, there were local concentrations of restaurants and theaters. Not all functions clustered, however. Some were fairly uniformly distributed throughout the center, to obtain the local trade, both of passing shoppers and of CBD employees: news vendors, drugstores, pharmacists, and tobacconists are good examples of these.

PROCESSES AND PATTERNS OF RETAIL CHANGE

It has been reasonable to apply the concept of a central place hierarchy to intra-urban shopping-center patterns, at least until the past few decades. Most people were restricted to a nearby, if not the nearest, center selling a particular good, and the whole system was dominated by the CBD. As cities grew, more trade was conducted in the regional centers, and the relative importance of the CBD declined. In 1935, for example, Chicago's CBD handled 26 percent of all sales in the city, by value; in 1958 it handled 14.8 percent. But this was only one symptom of a major change underway in intra-urban retailing.

Two forces have combined to produce this change. One is the increased mobility of the consumer, based on the automobile. The other is the changing corporate structure of retailing. Of the two, the latter is the more influential, although its impact could not have been as great as it has been without the former.

The changes have been evolving for some time, and increased consumer mobility has interacted with new types of retail provision to produce novel commercial patterns. Thus a Chicago study of 1960–1962 identified the two types of retail provision in addition to the traditional hierarchy. The first of these comprised the highway and street-oriented ribbons of commercial development, of which there were some 500 miles, containing more than 35,000 establishments. Some of the business strips served highway traffic, providing motels, restaurants, and service stations. Most served customers traveling by car to a particular establishment, which the customers wished to park near, and many of them—such as used car lots, garages, furniture stores—required large areas of relatively cheap land. Some located on streets to attract passing trade for convenience goods. The second type was the specialized area, a complex—some planned, many unplanned—of establishments in the same functional area. Automobile lots often cluster in particular places; medical services tend to do likewise; and there is a wide range of specialized entertainment districts, including "drive-ins."

These early trends have continued, but they have been overshadowed in recent years by major changes in methods of retailing and by the development of large, planned shopping centers, mostly in the suburbs. The changes in methods have been stimulated by the capitalist drive to boost profits and by the consequent concentration of retailing into a relatively small number of large firms operating large stores: the small, family-owned and operated store is not dead, but it is significantly less important now than it was a few decades ago.

To increase their profits, retailers had to capture more trade and operate their stores more efficiently: the two went together. Greater efficiency meant reducing costs relative to turnover, and this was achieved by replacing labor by space, notably and initially in food retailing. Counter service was replaced by self-service, in which the customer moves past the merchandise (carefully laid out following the principles used in department stores), makes his or her choices, and then pays at a checkout. For this to be efficient, a large floor area is needed, and a large volume of trade must be handled. Sites within the traditional centers were generally too restricted for such expansion, and so the new supermarkets were opened on vacant land, in accessible locations and with large parking areas. Location and parking were needed to attract customers in sufficient number, and shopping by car was essential, in part because there was no other means of access to many of the stores, and in part because of the need to remove goods in bulk.

As supermarkets grew, so they broadened their range of merchandise, taking over what were once the separate functions of grocers, butchers, delicatessens, greengrocers, and so on. Their large trade volume meant they could buy in great bulk—especially the firms that operated chains of supermarkets—which allowed them to undersell the smaller stores, which purchased in smaller quantities and had little room for storage. Continued growth led to the development of large supermarkets with their own attached warehouses; the middleman was thus eliminated and business efficiency was increased via vertical integration. The range of goods sold was extended, and other types of "supermarkets" were introduced, both specialists (for example, in furniture) and those dealing in wide ranges of merchandise (the discount stores). All these changes resulted in economies of scale, making the new stores more efficient and cheaper, and selection and purchasing easier for the customer. The new stores were able to undersell their small competitors by a considerable margin and hasten their demise.

Although these new large stores captured much of the trade, especially in convenience goods, there is still a need for small stores. This need exists in part because there are certain types of merchandise—espepecially very specialized goods—which the supermarkets find it not worthwhile to provide (turnover is insufficient to warrant floor space) and in part because people still prefer to make some purchases from smaller outlets, which are often quicker for small purchases, as checkout lines are avoided. But the traditional locations for these smaller outlets are no longer viable, because the market leaders have taken the passing trade elsewhere. They need to be accessible to the large markets generated by the new mass-sales outlets. This accessibility has been provided in planned shopping centers.

The first planned center was opened in Baltimore in 1907, and by the mid-1960s there were over 8,000; most of these were built after 1950. Chicago alone had sixty-two planned centers by 1962, and three typical sizes. The regional centers had more than 500,000 square feet of selling space, a total ground area (including parking) of 40 acres, and a market area that could accommodate over 250,000 people; each was focused on a department store as the market leader. The community centers, focused on a small department store or variety store, had 150,000 to 300,000 square feet of selling area, 20 to 40 acres of land, and served 30,000 to 90,000 people. The average neighborhood center, focused on a supermarket, had 50,000 square feet, 5 to 20 acres, and a market of 20,000. By the mid-1970s there were 15 regional centers in metropolitan Chicago (Figure 7.6)—all of them in the suburbs—plus more than 100 smaller centers.

These centers were carefully planned by private developers, who sought large profits as returns on their investments. To ensure success, they needed to attract large stores as market leaders, without which neither the smaller stores nor the customers would come: indeed, if the developers could not get a large store to agree to establish in a center before it was built, their plans would probably have been abandoned. The firms owning major CBD department stores have been prepared to move into such centers, however, to meet the new demands of the automobile shoppers, who avoid the congestion and hazards of the inner city.

The suburban centers are the replacements for the CBD for many people. Careful planning makes them attractive places to visit as well as to shop in, and developers have stringent rules regarding their tenants' use of shopping space. Thus the CBDs are now in absolute decline, especially in the largest cities; in metropolitan areas with 3 million or more residents, the number of establishments in their CBDs fell by 26 percent and their sales (holding the value of the dollar constant) increased by only 12.1 percent between 1954 and 1967, compared with increases of 29.9 and 132.2 percent, respectively, in the suburbs. In the smallest metropolitan areas, sales fell in the CBDs by 7 percent. Employment declines have naturally followed these trends. Between 1947 and 1972 the thirty-three metropolitan areas with populations of one million or more lost 565,000 retailing jobs from their central cities,

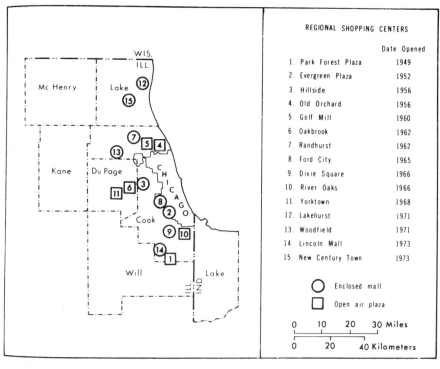

Figure 7.6. Regional planned shopping centers in the Chicago metropolitan area, 1974. Reprinted with permission from B. J. L. Berry et al., *Chicago.* Copyright 1976, Ballinger Publishing Company, p. 229.

while their suburbs gained 2,360,000. The biggest declines were in the oldest cities of the Frost Belt. Growth occurred in the suburbs, with the different municipalities vying with each other, and with the central cities, via zoning schemes and utility provision to attract large centers and the consequent broadening of their tax base.

Thus the old hierarchical system is being replaced by a new set of shopping centers, to which people travel long distances by car. The changes in scale produce price savings for those who can shop at the new centers. For those who cannot—notably the inner-city poor, who have neither cars nor nearby large centers—such savings are not available. The remaining small stores are relatively expensive, with the result that "the poor pay more," in the remnants of the older system.

This structural and spatial concentration has been countered in recent years by the development of new chains of convenience goods stores that are more accessible to the general population. The number of grocery stores declined between 1939 and 1974 from 427,000 to 198,130. To oppose this trend, the new convenience stores—compact supermarkets of about 2,500 square feet and handling an average $210,000 of trade a year—have increased from 5,000 in 1965 to 22,700 in 1974; their share of total grocery sales has increased from 1.1 to 4.1 percent. Most are linked to a franchising chain (such as the 7-Eleven chain) and benefit from economies of scale in buying. They have filled the holes in the spatial system created by the demise of the traditional stores and the rise of the supermarkets. In the inner city these gaps were caused in part by urban renewal; of 641 stores displaced in the Hyde Park-Kenwood project in Chicago, 207 were liquidated, 233 were relocated, and the remainder were liquidated shortly after relocation. By 1972 urban-renewal programs across the country had displaced some 120,000 small businesses, of which one-third were immediately liquidated. Outside the inner city many areas never had a local convenience store.

Like the changing patterns of industrial and, to a lesser extent, office location within cities, the major trends in retailing have been decentralization and a less simple spatial ordering. Major remnants of the previous system remain, and attempts have been made to revitalize many CBDs (through pedestrianization, in downtown Philadelphia), in part to maintain local tax bases. But many fewer people now use the center nearest their home for many purchases than was the case a few decades ago, and many of those who do are among the poorest, who are restricted to shopping at high-price stores. A majority now shop by car, favoring the large centers where goods are cheap and can be bought in bulk. Many people commonly make cross-town and cross-suburban trips to planned retail centers, which are space extensive and labor intensive, compared to the space-intensive/labor-extensive system that is slowly being replaced.

OTHER LAND USES

The above sections have covered all the major land uses within urban areas except residential (treated in the preceding chapter) and open space, which is provided by both the public and the private sector. Private-sector space is the less important; it comprises mainly sporting clubs, of which the most extensive are golf clubs, concentrated in the higher-income residential areas, especially in the suburbs.

Public open spaces—parks and gardens—have their own geography, which is a simple distance-decay gradient away from the center. In general, the farther from that point, the greater the provision of public open space per unit area within residential districts. The city center itself may contain one or more major parks, such as Central Park in New York City, plus specialized facilities, such as botanical and zoological gardens. But the inner residential areas are virtually devoid of open space—except in urban-renewal projects—for either active or passive recreation. The developers of those areas were interested only in cramming in as much housing as possible, to maximize their returns from lower-income tenants, and little or no concern was paid to the physical environment. Only where topographical controls prevented residential development—such as the deep valleys in Washington—was open space left. Farther out, however, in the higher-income areas and in districts developed under the stricter planning controls of the mid- and late-twentieth century, private open space is relatively plentiful and is a positive externality whose value is reflected in property prices. (Properties facing parks generally bring slightly higher prices than those a little distance away.)

The public sector is one of the largest institutional users of land. In the CBD and its surroundings, it occupies office buildings; elsewhere its main properties are schools and hospitals. As with public open space, the amount of undeveloped land associated with a school tends to increase with distance from the CBD, a fact that is also usually correlated with the quality of the premises. The older schools without land in the inner residential areas often occupy obsolete buildings, especially with regard to current educational methods. Other measures of school quality vary accordingly, as is outlined in the next chapter.

Health facilities are provided by both private and public sectors, with the former dominating in the provision of primary care by physicians. Trained doctors are free to establish practices where they wish. Four locational criteria are common: (1) maximizing income, which involves serving affluent patients; (2) living in environments conducive for child rearing; (3) living and developing practices in areas with social prestige; and (4) working close to others to maximize professional contacts. The four overlap and point in the same direction: physicians prefer to practice and live in the higher-status, more affluent residential areas. Thus there are considerable intra-urban differentials in access to primary care; in Chicago in 1970 the ten most affluent community areas averaged 2.1 physicians per 1,000 population, whereas the ten poorest averaged only 0.26. (Twenty years earlier the ratios were 1.78 and 0.99 so the differentials are widening.) As a result, the poorer residents of the underserved areas are forced to seek primary care at the large, free hospitals in the public system; travel to these is often expensive, waits are long, and the general level of health consequently suffers. It is, of course, the black population that suffers disproportionately from this imbalance in supply; in 1970, for example, the Watts area of Los Angeles had a ratio of 33 physicians per 100,000 people, compared to the national average of 178 per 100,000.

For certain types of illness, of a mental rather than a physical nature, sufferers have usually been confined to special hospitals (as is also the case for criminals). In recent years, however, it has been argued that rehabilitation for sufferers of mild complaints is more rapid if they are either not removed from the general community or are returned to it quickly. Some can be released to kin for care. Others have no available kin, however, and provision for them has been made by opening community houses in which the patients live and from which they move out into the community. Such houses are widely considered negative externalities, however, and have been opposed by neighborhood populations. The best organized, and the most likely to succeed in their protest, have been the middle- and upper-income districts. As a result, the community homes are concentrated in lower-status neighborhoods, an indication of the political power that is frequently associated with income and status: congregation and segregation rule.

Finally, there are the facilities provided by local governments for public protection and health: fire and police services; street maintenance, garbage removal, and sewage disposal. As with education, there can be considerable disparities in the level of provision and protection within the constituent areas of a local government's territory. Some classic cases indicate clear discrimination against black neighborhoods, but overall the reasons for the disparities are not clear. Clearly, the affluent and the powerful are generally not the underprivileged.

CONCLUSIONS

The main theme of this chapter on nonresidential land uses in urban areas is clear; during the past few decades there has been a massive decentralization, especially of manufacturing jobs and retail facilities. The favored areas are, in general, the suburbs; the deprived are the older, inner residential areas in which jobs are now hard to find and prices in the remaining shops are high. The automobile is crucial for obtaining access to most needs in the modern American city; those without cars suffer considerably, as will be demonstrated further in the final section of this book.

8

SUBURBANIZATION
AND THE
POLITICAL GEOGRAPHY
OF METROPOLITAN AREAS

THE PRECEDING TWO chapters have illustrated how in recent decades a clear dichotomy between the central city and the suburbs has developed within American metropolitan areas. In almost all cases, this dichotomy reflects the political division of territory, a division that arises from the operation of the individualistic, self-interested policies of firms and individuals. The result is that most metropolitan areas, and especially their suburban rings, form a complex mosaic of overlapping independent territorial authorities, most with taxing powers and control over certain aspects of land use. Understanding the origin and operation of this complex mosaic involves a study of the political geography of metropolitan areas. Without it, many of these patterns cannot be understood.

SUBURBANIZATION

The general processes of suburbanization have been outlined in Chapters 6 and 7 and will be summarized only briefly here. Any growing urban place must, almost of necessity, expand its built-up area. New housing must be built on the periphery, creating a series of annular rings of differing widths, depending on the current demand and the ability of the construction industry to satisfy that demand at prices that can be afforded. New industries need large tracts of cheap land, which again are available only at or beyond the fringe of the built-up area, and increasingly other forms of land use are finding spacious, suburban locations attractive. Meanwhile the inner-city area is often in relative decline, as jobs and households move away from its negative externalities. The result is not necessarily a "metropolitan doughnut" with a void in the center, but the inner areas of central cities are usually—with the exception of some business districts and concentrations of civic facilities—showing many signs of physical decay and relative deprivation of their populations.

The pace and form of suburban extension reflect a variety of influences, of which one of the most important is transportation technology. The first phase of major expansion was based on railroads, which produced discontinuous patterns of development clustered around stations; later, the interstitial areas close to the original core were infilled as streetcar services were provided. But the latest phase has been the most explosive, based on the automobile and the truck. This has resulted in extensive sprawling low-density developments, incorporating much undeveloped land.

Although suburbanization may be interpreted as a realization of the American dream, in terms of residential preferences and the most efficient solution to locational problems for most manufacturing and other business establishments, it could not have occurred without a great deal of investment, both private and public. Such investment had to be perceived as a sensible use of available money, given alternative uses to which it might be put.

In the private sector, three main groups of investors are involved. The first is the construction industry, which builds the homes, the factories, the streets, roads and freeways, and the networks of public utilities. The second consists of the sectors of manufacturing industry that benefit the most from this particular form of development; this group is dominated by the automobile and oil industries, but also includes those industries that produce the consumer goods that fill the new homes. Finally, there is the speculative sector within the finance industry, which invests in land prior to its development as a means of realizing profits from sales for land uses that pay much more per acre than does agriculture.

These three groups cannot produce suburbia on their own. A basic ingredient of the suburban way of life is movement: homes and workplaces, shopping places and schools are widely separated, and the necessary trips can be undertaken only if transportation media are available. Industry can provide the automobiles, but not the roads. (This is the case today. Early suburbanization was stimulated by private investment in railroads and streetcar lines that was undertaken for the profits that fare income would produce. Freeways are not private investments, however.) Thus the suburban interest groups have needed government investment in a road system—notably the interstate highway network, ninety percent of which is paid for by federal grants—to provide the arteries through which they would pump the blood. Further, the construction industry could not provide homes at prices that would be profitable to them unless many of the buyers were subsidized. Again, the federal government has come to the rescue with its various policies, described in Chapter 6, that have enabled large numbers of households to enter the suburban owner-occupier/mortgage market.

Suburban development involves an alliance between private-sector interests and the state, therefore. Its success has ensured that speculators provide the needed land, albeit at high prices—which makes even greater demands on the federal purse. Speculation in land is nothing new, of course, and often it produces an oversupply. In the nineteenth century, for example, much land in Chicago was subdivided either just before or immediately after the opening of an adjacent transport route, either by the original owner or by a speculator who bought the land in the hope of selling it at a higher price once the transport route had stimulated demand. But many sales of individual lots occurred only long after the routes were opened. Between 1848 and 1855 a large length of plank roads was laid, opening up some forty-seven miles for development. Five years later only 2.5 square miles of the land subdivided (within half a mile of a road) had been sold as individual lots. The same occurred with the cable-car routes; a 37.5-mile network was opened between 1882 and 1893. Five years later only 22 percent of the land subdivided in relation to this network had been sold as individual building lots. Speculation often failed to produce the hoped-for returns, therefore, because of an oversupply of land. Between 1868 and 1873 alone, enough land was offered for sale as building lots within the city to house one million people; the current population of Chicago was less than 400,000. The time lag between subdivision and sale was often considerable: only 32 percent of land was sold within ten years of subdivision and 27 percent experienced a lag of at least thirty years. The land may not have been completely idle in the intervening years, but it failed to provide the expected immediate returns, and many speculators lost heavily. The public sector also was involved in much unproductive investment, since to support the subdividers it installed networks of public utilities that were underused for many years, and thus produced very small returns, while deteriorating.

Suburban development today is dominated by large building companies, and speculators are more concerned with selling large tracts of land than with subdivision and the subsequent sale of individual lots— either to small building firms or to households. Thus large investors are needed to assemble the needed tracts and then sell them to the developers. Tax concessions have encouraged high-income individuals to engage in investment. Institutions and large corporations also see such investments as very attractive, if urban development is assured. Much of the assurance comes from zoning, and there has been much collusion—

even corruption—involving speculators and municipal planning boards.

Suburbanization is in the interests of several groups in the private sector of the American economy that have won concessions from the state for their activities. Using these advantages, they have molded public opinion so that suburban development is considered highly desirable. To do this, they have had to ensure that suburbia meets the social and economic desires of both households and firms discussed in the preceding two chapters. (These desires can, of course, be shaped by the relevant interest groups acting through the media.) This has been done, to a considerable extent, by using the local government system.

LOCAL GOVERNMENT

Local government is organized in the United States by a series of overlapping territories. At the highest level in this structure are the fifty states, almost all of them much larger than a single urban or metropolitan area. Each state government is responsible for a wide range of functions, many of which it delegates to local jurisdictions. Some of these jurisdictions are independent, in that the local government can decide what it will do; in others, the local government acts within guidelines laid down by the superior authority; in a third category, the local government has no discretionary power and acts simply as an administrative agency for the state at a local level. Although the states are independent in how they organize their system of local government, most, especially in the same region, have identical cultural roots, and so the majority of systems are very similar. Four types of local government area are typical.

The most basic of these four types is the *county*, a form of local government present in all but one state (Rhode Island). Counties were established on the British model early in the settlement of most of the original colonies, and they were used as the framework for settling the interior, providing a regular grid pattern of administrative boundaries across much of the country. In rural areas counties are very much administrative arms of the state, providing the minimum services necessary for the dispersed population—law enforcement, judicial administration, maintenance of roads, supervision of public health, administration of public welfare programs, and in some cases the organization of agricultural extension services. Where population densities are larger, and the county contains nucleated settlements of some size, further services are probably provided, such as libraries and health facilities. In counties covering urban areas, further facilities still might be required, such as an airport, and a range of cultural and recreational institutions; controls on land use will be needed; and streets will have to be paved and lit, water provided and sewage and garbage removed. All these services may be provided by the county government, although not necessarily directly. Some may be bought, from other local governments or from private companies.

Within the counties, twenty-one states (most of them in the Northeast) have a network of *townships*, subdivisions of the superior bodies. Their functions are usually very few and relatively unimportant, although they vary considerably from state to state: in Michigan, for example, the township governments provide cemeteries and volunteer fire departments, water supplies, and street lighting, whereas in Illinois they are responsible only for road maintenance, property assessment, and the support of indigents.

Much more important within the counties are the *municipalities*, densely populated areas that have been legally incorporated under a variety of names, such as cities, towns, and villages, to provide local government services independent of those of the encompassing county. Incorporation is by the state government as a consequence of public petition and support for such action through a poll of the affected voters. The functions of the municipal government are specified in its charter; there may be a separate charter for each place in the state, but it is more likely that all places of a similar size will be given the same powers under a general charter. Large municipalities may completely replace the county, but in most cases they provide, sometimes even duplicate, only part of the administration supplied by the encompassing body.

The final type comprises *special districts*, most of which are *ad hoc* bodies created for a specific function. Unlike the previous three, they operate in a very complex overlapping set of territories, many covering all or part of several municipalities, some over whole metropolitan areas. The most common form of special district is the *school district*. In twenty-three states these have complete control over education within their territory, and only four states grant no local autonomy in the provision and operation of education. (Nebraska has the most decentralized system. In 1960 it had 3,264 separate school districts; in 1977 it had 1,195.) The other special districts cover a wide range of functions, of which fire protection, drainage, and the provision and maintenance of parks is the most common. (Illinois had 2,313 such districts in 1967, including 704 fire protection districts and 811 drainage districts.) These districts are created for a variety of reasons, including:

1. Limits set by state constitutions on the taxing and spending powers of local governments make *ad hoc* special districts necessary if certain services are to be provided.
2. Local governments in many states cannot levy different tax rates in separate parts of their territories, so special districts are best able to meet the needs of particular areas, when there is clear spatial variation in the demand for particular services.

3. Special districts can operate on a "pay as you go" system, which is more in line with "business-like" views of local government, whereas the general local governments are largely financed through taxes levied on everyone, users and nonusers alike.
4. Federal aid for certain functions is obtainable only if certain criteria are met, such as a metropolitan-wide planning or airport authority, and special districts are acceptable for this, eliminating the need for a consensus among a whole host of other local governments.
5. Special-interest groups feel they can best maintain their independence by acting through special districts, such as those districts that have replaced the former volunteer fire departments.

The United States thus has a very large number of local governments—79,862 according to the census in 1977 (an increase from 78,218 five years earlier). This means that there are 37 separate local government units for every 100,000 Americans. There were also 490,265 elected local government officials in 1977, an average of 6.1 per unit or one elected official for every 441 persons. Illinois had the most separate local governments, 6,620 (of which 5,522 had separate taxing powers); they comprised 102 counties, 1,274 municipalities, 1,436 townships, 1,063 school districts, and 2,745 other special districts.

Many of these government units are very small. Of the municipalities, for example, only 58 of the country's 18,862 housed more than 250,000 people; 9,614 contained less than 1,000. Metropolitan areas contained many of these small units, as Table 8.1 illustrates. Thus nearly every central city of a metropolitan area is surrounded by a halo of separate municipalities, some large, many small. Figure 8.1 shows this for the Denver SMSA in 1979. The City and County of Denver were also surrounded by a large number of school and special districts; the number of constituent authorities is given in Table 8.2. The data in the two tables also indicate the number of small metropolitan school districts. (In addition, in 1977 there were also 35 metropolitan school districts that operated no schools and served no pupils.)

CITY GROWTH, ANNEXATION,
AND SUBURBAN INDEPENDENCE

Whereas the laying out of a system of counties and, where relevant, townships, was a requirement in all states (in some of them before any permanent settlement), municipal government was established only when the affected populations considered it necessary. Coming after the establishment of county and township government, the original municipalities obtained independent government for the whole of the

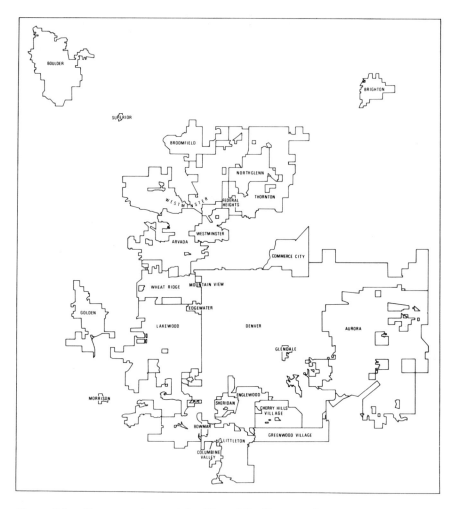

Figure 8.1.   The separate municipalities of the Denver urban area.

built-up area (except in cases where this crossed a state line). And as the towns and cities grew, so the municipal boundaries were extended to keep pace. In some cases extension was necessary prior to the urban development, so that the needed utilities and other services might be provided. Some cities annexed very large areas of undeveloped land in the nineteenth century.

The process of annexing new land to the expanding municipalities was handled differently in the various states, although it was basically controlled by the state government. The usual course was for the city government to request an extension of its area to cover the land required, and for the state legislature to act as arbiter of its claims, in many cases with the aid of a poll of the residents of the area concerned.

Table 8.1

GOVERNMENTAL UNITS WITHIN SMSAS, 1977

	Inside SMSAs	Outside SMSAs		Inside SMSAs	Outside SMSAs
A. Number of Units			B. Population of Municipalities		
Counties	594	2,448	50,000 or more	391	2
Municipalities	6,444	12,418	25,000–49,999	374	140
Townships	4,031	12,791	10,000–24,999	744	468
School Districts	5,220	9,954	5,000–9,999	779	682
Special Districts	9,580	16,382	2,500–4,999	915	1,089
			1,000–2,499	1,262	2,409
			0–999	1,979	7,635
C. Pupils per School District			D. Schools per School District		
100,000 or more	25	1	20 or more	481	119
50,000–99,999	49	0	10–19	732	539
25,000–49,999	132	2	3–9	2,653	3,487
12,000–24,999	357	57	2	667	1,783
6,000–11,999	721	312	1	1,253	4,526
3,000–5,999	1,074	818			
1,200–2,999	1,562	2,096			
300–1,999	1,269	3,667			
50–299	492	2,293			
1–49	105	1,208			

Source: U.S. Bureau of the Census, *Census of Governments 1977. Volume 1. Government Organization.*
       Tables 5 and 13.

Until the late nineteenth century, there was very little opposition to the territorial claims of the large, expanding municipalities. A resident of a new development on the edge of Boston would consider himself a Bostonian and not be averse to his home being situated in that city. Some very large annexations took place, therefore, some of them predating residential development by many years. But increasingly residents of these new areas realized that their interests were better served by incorporating separate municipalities and resisting the annexation activities. From about 1870 on, a wealthy resident living on the edge of Boston began to feel that being a Bostonian was costing him money, and an industrialist realized that he would benefit more from a suburban location. The system of local taxation was responsible for this shift of opinion.

For more than a century, the functions and responsibilities of local governments have increased considerably, and many of these new activities have to be paid for, at least in part, from local revenues. The main contributors to local revenues are the payers of property taxes. These taxes provide the bulk of local government revenues in most states. Commercial and industrial property owners make considerable contri-

Table 8.2
GOVERNMENT UNITS IN THE DENVER SMSA

A. Number of Municipalities, by Population Size		B. Number of Other Units	
50,000 or more	5	School Districts	20
25,000–49,999	5	Special Districts	264
10,000–24,999	6	(with property	
5,000–9,999	3	taxing power)	258
2,500–4,999	5		
1,000–2,499	3		
0–999	12		

Source: U.S. Bureau of the Census *Census of Governments 1977. Volume 1. Government Organization* Table 14.

butions to many local budgets; of the residential users, the owners of the expensive properties pay the most—these are the high-income households. In general, therefore, the rich pay more in local taxation. They do not receive more, however. Many of the facilities of the urban area are provided equally for all (parks, for example), but many more, through the various welfare programs, favor the relatively poor; both a rich and a poor family may send their children to a city's public schools, where they receive the same education, but the rich pay part of the costs for the poor. If rich and poor were segregated into separate school districts, however, this redistribution of income would not occur, and the rich would have to pay only for themselves.

The rich were predominant among those moving to suburbia during the late nineteenth and early twentieth centuries. If, instead of agreeing to the annexation of their land to the city, they were to petition for it to be formed into a separate municipality, they could avoid any responsibilities for paying the costs of city administration, much of which went to provide facilities for the relatively poor. In this way the class conflict came to be represented in the political map of the city, and the mosaic of small suburban municipalities ringing the central city of a built-up area was initiated.

THE BENEFITS OF SEPARATE INCORPORATION

Incorporation of separate municipalities in the county areas surrounding central cities, rather than agreement to annexation with those cities, brought direct financial benefits to the residents of the new municipalities. They need pay nothing in their property taxes toward the costs of running the cities, on which they were dependent for jobs and many other facilities. Responsibilities could be avoided, and money saved. Since it was only the affluent who could afford the move to sub-

urbia—at least until recently—the city government was thus quite im-
poverished.

Separate incorporation brought other benefits. It enabled the residents of the suburban municipalities to escape being subject to the political machines of the central cities, many of which were dominated by
a corrupt combination of big business and immigrant groups. Since the
late nineteenth century there has been a strong movement for the reform of local government that has most of its support among the relatively affluent. This movement was against partisan politics in local
government. It favored what it defined as "good" government, which
included (1) greater direct power for the electorate through the use of
the referendum and the initiative; (2) simpler voting procedures and at-
large rather than ward elections; and (3) replacement of political rule by
the operation of local government as a business, stressing efficiency.
The role of local government in municipalities, it was argued, is to provide services, a function that requires a business approach, not a partisan one. Thus the traditional system of government by an elected mayor
and council was to be replaced by either an administration by a small
body of commissioners (one per department), elected at large and not
by wards, or an administration by an appointed manager whose work
was overseen by a small council, elected at large. Greatest success for the
reform movement has been achieved in the suburban municipalities
(not necessarily the smallest) in the metropolitan rings.

A further benefit of separate incorporation is control over land use,
and thus over the contents of the municipal area, both social and economic. Many municipalities have been incorporated for this purpose:
one in suburban Los Angeles, for example, was established to prevent
an adjacent municipality from building a sewage treatment plant within its boundaries; another was established to allow a circus owner to
zone a large tract of land for the winter quarters of his entourage. It is
the control of the zoning process that is crucial here. The "home rule"
elements of municipal charters in most states means that their local governments alone can decide on the zoning plan, and thus which users can
and cannot be allowed in the area. Negative externalities can be excluded.

For a high-income group this exclusion of unwanted neighbors involves not only zoning for no industries but also zoning out the poor
(and thus the blacks). The latter is achieved by setting minimum standards that are so high that only the affluent can afford to buy into the
municipality. Such exclusionary zoning, as it is called, frequently uses
minimum densities—half-acre lots or more—which act to keep out all
but high-income people. It has been estimated that as much as 82 percent of the land in the New Jersey suburbs of New York was zoned in
the 1970s for a minimum of a half-acre of land per single family home,
whereas in the Connecticut suburbs at least 75 percent of the unbuilt

suburban land was zoned for minimum densities of more than one acre per lot. In suburban Philadelphia, one-third of the land was zoned for minimum densities of two acres per lot.

Minimum lot sizes clearly abet the exclusionary intent of municipal zoning authorities, since they force prices up beyond the reach of low- and even middle-income groups. Many municipalities also seek to exclude the less affluent by prohibiting apartments; 38 percent of municipalities in the Philadelphia suburbs have no areas zoned for apartments. It is widely believed that because of their relative poverty, apartment dwellers impose costs that must be met by their more affluent neighbors. This belief applies to the costs of education in particular, so that many municipalities that do allow apartments restrict the number of bedrooms so that only small families can be housed. This practice (sometimes termed hysterectomy zoning) is used by 42 percent of those Philadelphia suburban municipalities which do allow apartments.

Use of zoning power allows residents of municipalities in suburban rings to gain considerable control over who can and who cannot live among them. It also gives them access to a public school system other than that provided by the central city. Some suburban school districts have been incorporated to serve a single municipality, whereas others serve a group of adjacent ones. Since adjacent suburban municipalities are usually similar in social composition, this ensures that most suburban school systems are socially exclusive, which, as detailed in Chapter 6, is a prime consideration for many residents. (Not all states have separate school districts at a very local level. Especially in the South, public schools are provided at the county scale—though not by the county governments—making escape to an exclusive school district more difficult, especially after the school integration rulings of the 1950s on.)

Local control of local government—as opposed to being a small part of a large city—allows the population to have much more say over what services government will and will not provide. Many communities opt to provide virtually none themselves, but to buy from outside, either from private contractors or from other local governments, including the central city that they have avoided living in. The advantage to the residents is not necessarily the relative cheapness of the services but rather the power to control the social exclusiveness of their residential areas; many are prepared to pay relatively high property taxes and user charges for services for the right, via the zoning process, to exclude negative externalities.

It is not only the affluent who benefit from the separate incorporation of suburban municipalities and the powers that this brings to control local character. Nonresidential land users can benefit in similar ways. There are many examples of exclusive, usually small, municipalities that are predominantly nonresidential in their land use. This use may be a pleasure park, a shopping center, or even a cemetery.

Two good examples of exclusionary zoning by nonresidential municipalities come from the Los Angeles metropolitan area. The City of Vernon lies on the eastern edge of the city of Los Angeles itself. Initially it developed a reputation as a somewhat liberal municipality among relatively Puritan neighbors, with Sunday sporting fixtures in its stadiums and liberal licensing laws. Early in the twentieth century it was taken over by industrialists, and over three-quarters of its area was zoned for industrial use. At present it houses only a few hundred residents but has factories providing tens of thousands of jobs. By zoning out any provision of residential areas on a large scale, the industrialists, who are the major taxpayers, have avoided having to pay for the infrastructure that is common in a residential suburb—such as libraries—whereas the costs of sidewalks, street maintenance, and street lighting are very low. The workers must pay their own costs from their own taxes elsewhere, without any contribution from their employers: as a result, the property tax rate in Vernon is one of the lowest in the state of California.

The other example is found to the southeast of the metropolitan center, straddling the boundary between Los Angeles and Orange Counties. Before the suburban sprawl reached this area, it was dominated by dairy farming. When urban development did arrive, some of the local dairy farmers incorporated three municipalities—Dairyland (1955), Dairy Valley, and Cypress (1956)—as a defensive strategy. They zoned most of the land for dairy farming, and the population density remained one-half person per acre. The lack of any residential areas prevented any complaints about flies, odors, and noise, and the zoning meant that property values stayed low, since land had no speculative value, and the farmers were not forced out by high taxes. (Dairyland and Dairy Valley were exclusively agricultural; Cypress zoned two-thirds agricultural and one-third industrial/commercial.) Meanwhile the tide of residential development moved farther out, so that the three cities became oases of farming in a suburban desert. The speculative value of the land was extremely high, should rezoning ever occur, but meanwhile the farmers and their cows were protected.

Industrialists and the affluent were the first to realize the potential of exclusionary zoning policies and obtain the necessary petitions and votes to incorporate separate municipalities. But as the data for Denver discussed earlier show, not all suburbs either house the affluent or are nonresidential enclaves. As affluence, mobility, and the activities of large developers made it possible for middle- and even some low-income families to escape the central city, the range of suburban types increased. Many municipalities were incorporated for these people and their policies were not as exclusionary. Industrial and commercial areas were zoned, and nonresidential users were encouraged to move in, to provide revenue from their property taxes that would "subsidize" some of the services desired by the residents, as well as provide jobs for them. Many of these are among the larger suburban municipalities, which compete for the developments that will bring the needed tax base. And of course the suburban fabric ages, just like that of the inner cities, and its housing may be filtered down the social scale.

Although much of suburbia is of a relatively high socioeconomic status, especially in the Frost Belt, it is not entirely so. The affluent suburbs are the most exclusive, however, and so there is considerable class segregation between municipalities. The map is complex, however, although the sectoral patterns of the central city usually extend into the suburban ring.

One additional element of the complexity relates to nonincorporation and annexation. In some parts of most suburban counties, residents prefer not to incorporate their neighborhoods as separate municipalities but to remain unincorporated areas directly controlled by the county and, where relevant, township governments. This presumably implies satisfaction with the quantity and quality of services provided. (In some cases, it indicates that incorporation is now impossible. This is so in the state of Maryland, for example, so that much of Washington's suburban ring—outside the District of Columbia—is unincorporated territory.) Incorporation can bring responsibilities and costs, and if there is no defensive need for it, then it may not be petitioned for.

The major defensive need is against annexation, either by a central city or by a suburban municipality. Both seek to annex territory for the same reason; to incorporate newly developing areas that will add to the property-tax base and increase fiscal resources. Incorporation is a defense against this and against paying the high property taxes typical of central cities. Annexation is still proceeding rapidly, however, for a variety of reasons. The residents of some areas see no need to incorporate against it; the residents of others are outvoted by developers, who may be offered concessions by the city government if they agree to annexation; and in some states the procedure is extremely easy and defense against it difficult. (In Texas, strip annexation along highways is allowed, so that municipalities can connect themselves to tracts that they wish to annex.) Indeed, annexation is now the principal source of growth for central cities. Between 1900 and 1950, central cities of SMSAs gained 5.4 million inhabitants, 4.8 million by population increase within their 1900 boundaries and 0.6 million by annexation. In the last three decades for which data are available, the figures are (in millions):

Years	Total Population Growth	In Situ	Annexation
1940–1950	5.644	4.256	1.388
1950–1960	4.551	0.468	4.083
1960–1970	3.593	0.066	3.527

Without annexation, the population of the suburban ring would have increased on average by another 15 percent each decade. Most of the annexation has taken place in the Sun Belt; the older Frost Belt cities are almost completely surrounded by incorporated municipalities.

FISCAL DISPARITIES

A major consequence of the political subdivision of most metropolitan areas into a single large central city and a large number of independent suburban municipalities, school districts, and special districts is the development of major fiscal disparities betwen territorial authorities. These have come about because of the dependence of those authorities on property taxes for their revenue. Transfers from the federal and state governments are making an increased contribution, but local taxes—of which the property tax is the main one—remain the dominant source of income for local governments, especially in the Frost Belt.

The suburban municipalities that incorporate in order to operate exclusive zoning policies and to keep out all perceived negative externalities generally have the highest property-tax base per resident. The others are in competition with the central cities, notably for those uses that will add substantially to the local fiscal resources—industries and large shopping and office centers. The processes of suburbanization described in Chapters 6 and 7 suggest that the suburban municipalities are winning and the central cities are losing.

The simplest index of these fiscal disparities is the fact that central city residents pay more of their income in local taxes than do suburban residents. In 1972 residents of central cities paid on average 4.7 percent of their incomes in local taxes (3.5 percent in property taxes, and 1.2 percent in other taxes), whereas suburban residents paid on average 2.5 percent (1.8 percent property, 0.7 percent others). The differential (approximately 2:1) was the same in all regions, but the percentages varied considerably; in the Northeast (that is, the Frost Belt) central-city residents paid 9 percent of their incomes on average in local taxes, compared with 3.4, 3.4, and 4.0 in the South, North Central, and West regions, respectively. (The suburban percentages—the data refer to suburbs with populations of 50,000 or more only—were 4.8, 2.0, 1.9 and 2.0.) Since central cities in general house the lowest income groups, this means that the poor pay more in relative terms. Furthermore, evidence suggests that they get less value for their money, that suburban governments are more efficient providers of services than are their central-city counterparts and are able to provide a greater range and higher quality of service.

These data suggest very strongly that the political geography of the American metropolitan area is structured to place the greatest burdens on those least able to pay. Many of the residents of the central cities, especially those in the Frost Belt, are trapped there because of their low incomes and their position in the housing markets; they have no alternative but to pay for the constraints on where they can live. Most suburban residents, on the other hand, have been able to opt out of paying central-city taxes; they have much more choice. And yet central cities have larger demands on their tax bills, because they have to service the CBD and provide facilities for those dependent on a variety of social welfare programs; suburban residents avoid contributing directly to these services (except when they shop in the central city and have to pay a local sales tax).

It is not only with regard to the services provided by general local governments—the municipalities—that fiscal disparities benefit suburban residents. The same occurs with many of the special districts, notably the school districts, which spend large sums on what is to most people one of the most important local government services. Fiscal disparities between special districts can be measured using the property-tax base per pupil; the greater the value of the property in a district per pupil to be educated, the more resources that are (potentially) available to pay for that education and the cheaper it is likely to be, relative to residents' incomes. Figure 8.2 illustrates such disparities between the many elementary school districts in the suburban ring of Cook County, for 1966. The richest districts have more than three times the available resources than do the poorest. Interestingly, not all of the richest are high-income areas. Some relatively low-income residential districts are in the same school districts as industrial areas, whose contribution to the property tax aids in paying for schooling.

Suburban residents benefit, therefore, in that most of them live in areas with relatively large fiscal resources and, except for the educational service, relatively small demands on them. They escape any commitment to redistribute income toward the central-city poor. Furthermore, many suburbanites increase the burden on the urban poor, by "free riding." Many more suburban residents work in the central cities than vice versa and travel on the city roads when commuting. The central-city government thus has disproportionately high road and street maintenance costs, though to some extent suburban residents indirectly pay their share of the costs because their workplaces add to the property tax base of the central city. More important, central cities provide a range of cultural and other facilities, such as art galleries, museums, and zoos, which are not found in the suburbs. User charges rarely cover the full costs of these facilities' use by visitors, so their use by suburbanites is subsidized by the poorer central-city residents. Calculations made for Detroit in the late 1960s suggested that perhaps as much as six percent of the City's budget—amounting to $80 per resident household—was spent providing services for suburban residents, and similar suburban

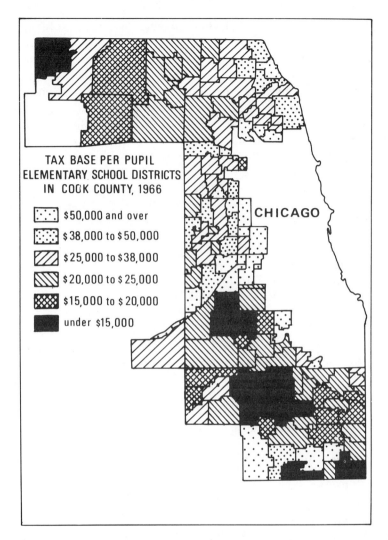

TAX BASE PER PUPIL
ELEMENTARY SCHOOL DISTRICTS
IN COOK COUNTY, 1966

$50,000 and over

$38,000 to $50,000

$25,000 to $38,000

$20,000 to $25,000

$15,000 to $20,000

under $15,000

CHICAGO

Figure 8.2   Fiscal disparities between elementary school districts, suburban Cook County, 1966. Source: R. L. Morrill and J. M. Dormitzer, *The Spatial Order: An Introduction to Modern Geography*. North Scituate, Mass.: Duxbury Press, 1979, p. 399.

exploitation of poorer central-city neighbors has been reported elsewhere. Part of the exploitation is repaid; business generated by the suburban residents generates central-city taxes and stimulates multipliers, and some state taxes are redistributed to local governments on a per capita basis. But the net balance favors the suburbanites.

CONCLUSIONS

Chapters 6 and 7 outlined the forces of congregation and segregation within American society and discussed the social and economic mechanisms used to achieve the desired ends. This chapter has demonstrated how political manipulation of space is also used to achieve distancing and in the conflict between and within capitalist classes. There can be very little doubt that even without the political mechanisms described here congregation and segregation would occur. The spatial arrangements might be slightly different, but the end results would be the same. Those for whom congregation and segregation are desirable goals will seek methods with which to achieve them; most American state constitutions have provided them with such methods in their local government systems. Thus the social, economic, and political geographies of urban areas in the United States are inextricably intertwined.

SUGGESTIONS FOR FURTHER READING—PART THREE

The literature on the internal structure of United States cities in the nineteenth century includes:

PRED, A. R. "Manufacturing in the American Mercantile City: 1800–1840," *Annals of the Association of American Geographers*, 56 (1966):307–339.

WARD, D. "The Internal Spatial Structure of Immigrant Residential Districts in the Late Nineteenth Century," *Geographical Analysis*, 1 (1969):337–353.

VANCE, J. E. "Housing the Worker: The Employment Linkage as a Force in Urban Structure," *Economic Geography*, 42 (1966):294–325.

RADFORD, J. P. "Testing the Model of the Pre-Industrial City: The Case of Antebellum Charleston, South Carolina," *Transactions, Institute of British Geographers* NS4, (1979):392–410.

RADFORD, J. P. The Social Geography of the Nineteenth-Century US City. In D. T. Herbert and R. J. Johnston (eds.) *Geography and the Urban Environment*, vol. 4. New York: John Wiley, 1981.

Suburbanization is treated in:

WALKER, R. A. The Transformation of Urban Structure in the Nineteenth Century and the Beginnings of Suburbanization. In K. R. Cox (ed.) *Urbanization and Conflict in Market Societies*. Chicago: Maaroufa Press, 1978, pp. 165–212.

HARVEY, D. The Political Economy of Urbanization in Advanced Capitalist Societies. In H. M. Rose and G. Gappert (eds.) *The Social Economy of Cities*. Beverly Hills: Sage, 1975, pp. 119–163.

CHECKAWAY, B. "Large Builders, Federal Housing Programmes, and Postwar Suburbanization," *International Journal of Urban and Regional Research*, 4 (1980): 21–45.

MASOTTI, L. H. (ed.) "The Suburban Seventies," *The Annals of the American Academy of Political and Social Sciences*, Vol. 422, 1975.

Particular examples are:

WARNER, S. B. *Streetcar Suburbs*. Cambridge: M.I.T. Press, 1962.

GANS, H. J. *The Levittowners*. New York: Vintage Books, 1967.

Studies of the residential separation of various social and economic groups within urban areas are very numerous. The classic statements include:

PARK, R. E., E. W. BURGESS, and R. D. MACKENZIE, *The City*. Chicago: University of Chicago Press, 1925.
HOYT, H. *The Structure and Growth of Residential Neighborhoods in American Cities*. Washington, D.C.: Federal Housing Administration, 1939.

Detailed collections include the following volumes by sociologists and geographers:

THEODORSON, G. A. (ed.) *Studies in Human Ecology*. Evanston, Ill.: Row, Peterson, 1961.
BOURNE, L. S. (ed.) *The Internal Structure of Cities*. New York: Oxford University Press, 1971.
SCHNORE, L. F. *The Urban Scene*. New York: Free Press, 1965.
SCHWIRIAN, K. P. (ed.) *Comparative Urban Structure*. Lexington, Mass.: Heath, 1974.
HERBERT, D. T., and R. J. JOHNSTON (ed.) *Social Areas in Cities* (two vols.). New York: Wiley, 1976.
TIMMS, D. W. G. *The Urban Mosaic*. Cambridge, England: The University Press, 1971.
JOHNSTON, R. J. *Urban Residential Patterns*. New York: Praeger, 1971.

For a discussion of the segregation of ethnic groups, see:

DUNCAN, O. D., and B. DUNCAN. *The Negro Population of Chicago*. Chicago: University of Chicago Press, 1957.
TAEUBER, K. E., and A. F. TAEUBER. *Negroes in Cities*. Chicago: Aldine, 1965.
SCHNORE, L. F. *Class and Race in Cities and Suburbs*. Chicago: Markham, 1972.
ROOF, W. C. (ed.) *Race and Residence in American Cities. The Annals of the American Academy of Political and Social Science*, Vol. 441, 1979.
ROSE, H. M. *The Black Ghetto*. New York: McGraw-Hill, 1971.

The concept of housing classes was introduced in the British literature, and is discussed in:

PAHL, R. E. *Whose City?* (2nd. ed.) Harmondsworth: Penguin, 1975.

For a discussion of the operation of the housing market, see:

STERNLIEB, G., and J. W. HUGHES (eds.) *America's Housing: Prospects and Problems*. New Brunswick: Center for Urban Policy Research, Rutgers University, 1980.
AARON, H. J. *Shelter and Subsidies*. Washington, D.C.: Brookings Institution, 1972.
STONE, M. E. "The Housing Crisis, Mortgage Lending and Class Struggle." In J. R. Peet (ed.) *Radical Geography*. Chicago: Maaroufa Press, 1977, pp. 144–180.
HARVEY, D. "Class Structure in a Capitalist Society and the Theory of Residential Differentiation." In R. Peel et al. (eds.) *Processes in Physical and Human Geography: Bristol Essays*. London: Heinemann, 1976, pp. 354–372.
HARVEY, D. *Society, the City, and the Space-Economy of Urbanism*. Washington, D.C.: Commission on College Geography, Association of American Geographers, 1972.

The topic of stereotyping is covered in:

SENNETT, R. *The Uses of Disorder*. London: Allen Lane, 1971.

Individual cities are discussed in a recent four-volume compilation by the Association of American Geographers:

ADAMS, J. S. (ed.) *Contemporary Metropolitan America* (four vols). Cambridge, Mass.: Ballinger, 1976.

It contains essays on each of the following twenty metropolitan areas:
Volume 1—The American City; Boston; New York; Philadelphia; Central Connecticut.
Volume 2—Baltimore; New Orleans; The Cities by San Francisco Bay.
Volume 3—Pittsburgh; St. Louis; Northeastern Ohio; Chicago; Detroit; Minneapolis-St. Paul; Seattle.
Volume 4—Dallas/Fort Worth; Miami; Houston; Atlanta; Los Angeles; Washington.

For a discussion of migration within and among urban areas, see:
MOORE, E. G. *Residential Mobility in the City.* Washington, D.C.: Commission on College Geography, Association of American Geographers, 1972.

The basic model of land values in urban areas, and their relationship with land-use patterns is found in:
ALONSO, W. *Location and Land Use.* Cambridge: Harvard University Press, 1963.

The topic of industries in urban areas is covered in:
PRED, A. R. "The Intra Metropolitan Location of American Manufacturing," *Annals of the Association of American Geographers,* 54 (1964):165–180.

The tertiary sector is discussed in:
DANIELS, P. W. (ed.) *Spatial Patterns of Office Growth and Location.* New York: Wiley, 1979.

For a discussion of commuting, see:
TAAFFE, E. J., and B. J. GARNER. *A Geographical Consideration of the Journey-to-Work to Peripheral Employment Centers.* Evanston: Transportation Center, Northwestern University, 1963.
BERRY, B. J. L., P. G. GOHEEN, and H. GOLDSTEIN. *Metropolitan Area Redefinition: A Re-evaluation of Concept and Statistical Practice.* Washington, D.C.: U.S. Government Printing Office, 1968.

Brian Berry and his students have reported most of the detailed research on retailing, including:
BERRY, B. J. L. *Commercial Structure and Commercial Blight.* Department of Geography, Research Paper 85, University of Chicago, 1963.
SIMMONS, J. W. *The Changing Pattern of Retail Location.* Department of Geography, Research Paper 92, University of Chicago, 1964.
COHEN, Y. S. *Diffusion of an Innovation in an Urban System.* Department of Geography, Research Paper 140, University of Chicago, 1972.

Central Business District studies are treated in:
MURPHY, R. E. *The Central Business District.* London: Longman, 1972.

Local government in metropolitan areas, is covered in:
TEAFORD, J. C. *City and Suburb.* Baltimore: Johns Hopkins University Press, 1979.

Financial aspects are dealt with in:
McMANUS, S. A. *Revenue Patterns in U.S. Cities and Suburbs.* New York: Praeger, 1978.
DANIELSON, M. N. *The Politics of Exclusion.* New York: Columbia University Press, 1976.

General coverage of political issues is given in:
COX, K. R. *Conflict, Power and Politics in the City.* New York: McGraw-Hill, 1973.
COX, K. R. (ed.) *Urbanization and Conflict in Market Societies.* Chicago: Maaroufa Press, 1978.
COX, K. R. *Location and Public Problems.* Chicago: Maaroufa Press, 1979.

COX, K. R., and JOHNSTON, R. J. (eds.) *Conflict, Politics and the Urban Scene.* New York: St. Martin's, 1982.

For a discussion of representation, see:
TAYLOR, P. J., and R. J. JOHNSTON. *Geography of Elections.* New York: Holmes and Mayer, 1979.
JOHNSTON, R. J. *Political, Electoral and Spatial Systems.* New York: Oxford University Press, 1979.

PART FOUR

URBAN PATTERNS
and PROCESSES
and the URBAN CRISIS

To ALMOST ALL observers, commentators, and analysts, whatever their ideology and political opinions, the capitalist world is currently experiencing a period of great crisis, best exemplified in the twin problems of high inflation and high unemployment. As a leader of the capitalist world, the United States is sharing in the crisis.

The origins of this crisis are far from completely understood and solutions to its many related problems are proving extremely difficult to identify. A number of the problems are irrelevant here, since they have no particular bearing on the urban patterns and processes described in the second and third parts of the book. But the United States is a highly urbanized country, and so most of its current problems are experienced by urban residents, either directly or, as

with problems initially related to agriculture, indirectly. Thus it could be argued that this final set of chapters should deal with all aspects of the crisis, since they—and the urban system that reflects them—are entirely interdependent. But this approach has been rejected in favor of a more narrow focus on the particular problems facing urban Americans.

No attempt is made here to suggest that the concept of urban problems is in any way novel to the present situation. There have been problems at all stages of capitalist evolution, and there are similar problems in the noncapitalist countries of the world today. As was made clear in Chapter 2, the basic features of capitalism include competition, conflict, and change. These are bound to produce difficulties. Each period and place has its unique characteristics and problems; the intention here is to outline those that are currently most relevant to the study of urban America and the changes and accommodations that are presently taking place.

THE NATURE OF URBAN PROBLEMS Many problems are perceived to exist in American cities simply because most Americans live there. If this fact were the sole cause of the problems, then there could be no urban problems as such; the urban area would be locale of the problems simply because it is the home of most Americans. Clearly, however, this is not entirely the case. There are many variations—in poverty and unemployment rates, and in pollution and crime indices, for example—between rural and urban areas, between small towns and large cities, between Chicago and Los Angeles, between inner cities and peripheral suburbs, and so on. This chapter and the next look at those variations, at their sources, and at the potential for their removal.

PROBLEMS IN AND OF THE CITY Although the argument presented at the beginning of the preceding paragraph is not entirely valid, it does suggest the need to distinguish carefully the causes of the various problems. Two major categories are identified here. The first comprises the _problems in the city._ In its pure form, a problem in this category would in no way be a consequence of the existence of urban areas. Instead,

it would indicate some failure in the economy or society as a whole and would be represented in the urban areas only to the extent that it is in the entire population (or in some segment of the population —the young, perhaps—who are the only ones liable to experience the problem). To take a simple, hypothetical example, in a given year five percent of a country's population may commit, and be convicted of, indictable crimes. Eighty percent of these crimes occur in the country's urban areas, which may suggest the existence of an urban crime problem to the casual observer. But seventy percent of the national population lives in the urban areas, so there is only a slight overconcentration of criminal activity there, relative to the distribution of population. The country's towns and cities are the homes of its population and its criminals in almost equal proportions. There may be a national crime problem, but not an urban crime problem.

The other category comprises the _problems of the city_. In its pure form, a problem of this category would not exist at all outside urban areas. A simple example is the modification of local climates produced by urban areas that is due to the concentration of dwellings and other land uses. But all man-made structures influence microclimates, as does human interference with natural vegetation cover in nonurban areas (sometimes with drastic effects, as in the dust bowl phenomenon). The urban area has a particular influence, because of the density and intensity of land use and human activity there, and so its effect on the local climate is pronounced, producing a problem of the city. (This assumes, of course, that the existence of such modifications is considered problematic; some people may consider it a good thing.)

The distinction between these two categories, problems in the city and problems of the city, is the distinction between the two extremes of a continuum rather than between two polar groups into one of which every problem must be assigned. It would be extremely rare to find a problem that could be located at the continuum's end points; the majority lie somewhere in between. Ninety percent of the indictable crimes of a hypothetical society may be committed in its cities, which house only fifty percent of the population. Thus, the overrepresentation of criminal events in the cities implies that crime is, at least in part, generated by some particular characteristics of the urban place. It may be that cities attract the criminal elements of society in disproportionate numbers relative to rural areas, or there may be some qualities of the urban environment that induce people to act as they would not if they lived elsewhere. Teasing out the relative importance of urbanization as the generator of social and economic problems is thus a major, and difficult, area of research. It is a crucial one, too, for those who wish to improve urban society.

Without an understanding of the genesis of the current conditions, their cure is impossible.

The dichotomy between problems in and out of the city is, in the final analysis, artificial. It is valuable as an illustrative device, directing attention to the causes of problems, and then to potential solutions. A major reason for introducing it here is to stress the basic point—introduced in Chapter 1 and kept in focus throughout the book—that urban areas, and hence urban problems, cannot be studied independently of the economic, social and political context. Any bland introduction of the notion of an "urban crisis" is facile. If there is a crisis, it is seated in capitalism itself, just as crises in socialist societies reflect problems relevant to socialism at the relevant level of development. Urban areas will reflect, deflect, and perhaps accentuate the crisis—hence the study of urban problems—but causes and cures will not be found in the urban phenomenon alone.

FOUR TYPES OF URBAN PROBLEMS There is a large literature—academic and polemic, political and popular—that focuses on the identification of urban problems, and, perhaps to an even larger extent, on the promulgation of remedies and cures. This part of the book is not a review of the first section of that literature, however, nor a summary of the second. Instead, attention is concentrated here on four types of problems, which incorporate most of those that have been individually identified.

The four types presented here group together those that are similar in both their origins and their geography. They are presented and discussed separately, but they are not independent. They interact to a considerable extent, as the text shows, and the separation, although justifiable on generic grounds, is largely for presentational convenience. The categorization is:

1. *The problems of inequality and poverty* within urban areas and their concentration in the inner city districts. Many of these problems center on the provision of what are generally considered basic necessities of life in an advanced capitalist society, such as adequate housing and neighborhood facilities for a high standard of physical and mental health; security from personal assault, invasions of privacy, and violations against personal property; access to good educational facilities; and adequate facilities for recreation, leisure, and personal satisfaction. Many of these goods and services are purchased in the marketplace in a capitalist society, so adequate incomes are needed, which in turn requires access to satisfactorily paid employment. The lack of one or more of these is perceived, both by the sufferers and by outside observers, as a problem. Associated with such problems are the various forms of racial and other discrimination, since members of certain minority groups are disproportionately represented among the sufferers.

2. *Problems of government and political representation.* The United States is a democracy, which, since the ratification of the Thirteenth, Fourteenth, and Fifteenth Amendments to the Constitution in 1865, 1868, and 1870, respectively, has recognized that all its adult male citizens are equal and entitled to the same legal protection; females were granted full equality with respect to voting rights only by the Twentieth Amendment in 1920, and the age of majority for both sexes was reduced to 18 by the Twenty-sixth Amendment in 1971. (The Equal Rights Amendment has yet to be ratified, however.) Whether this equality before the law operates in reality has been seriously contested in recent decades, with several crucial cases being decided by the Supreme Court. A number of these relate to the government of urban areas and the political inequalities within the nation's towns and cities.

3. *Problems of the urban environment.* The existence of urban areas influences many aspects of the physical environment, especially in the hydrosphere and in the atmosphere. It introduces other effects, too, such as those related

to noise and traffic. All these effects are perceived as problems by at least some urban residents.

4. *Problems of urban growth and decay.* The discussion in Chapters 3, 4, and 5 showed that the economic fortunes of urban areas wax and wane. When there is a downturn, there is often a concentration of economic and social problems in particular places or groups of places. At the same time, other places are growing rapidly, and this too can create problems. Together, the patterns of growth and decline raise the issue of whether the current distribution of population in America's cities is the optimal one, an issue which raises major questions about optimal for what.

SPATIAL ENGINEERING AND THE SOLUTION OF URBAN PROBLEMS Having outlined a series of problems that characterize modern American towns and cities to greater or lesser degree, I now turn to a consideration of possible solutions that may lead to a general improvement in the quality of life for urban Americans, and especially those who are currently at a considerable disadvantage. The arguments are based on two assumptions. The first is that all the problems are at least partially problems *of* the city. If, using the dichotomy introduced at the beginning of the previous section, one can identify a pure example of a problem *in* the city,

then it is logical to suppose that there is no available solution that would merely involve reorganizing in some way the geography of American urban areas. On this argument, if poverty and unemployment were perceived purely as problems in the city, then there could be no spatial solution that would improve job chances and incomes—the solution would be entirely external to the urban system. The presentation of the cycle of poverty shows that unemployment and poverty are unevenly distributed among social groups, in part because poverty tends to breed more poverty. The cycle has clear spatial coordinates, in which case its components have a problem *of* the city element in them, and some alleviation might be found through spatial solutions. It is assumed that this is the case for all of the problems identified here.

The second assumption relates to the system within which the problems have been generated. Here I assume that it will continue, that late capitalism is certain to remain the driving force of the American economy and society. The task, therefore, is the widely recognized search for "liberal" solutions. The basic features of capitalism are accepted, but efforts are to be made to avoid the extreme disadvantages that they might bring for some urban residents and the major problems that they might cause for urban society as a whole. The major institution involved in this problem solving is the state, whose function is to mediate between capital and labor, protecting the relatively weak in both camps: capitalist firms are to be aided in their search for profitability and so to maintain their provision of employment; the poor, the unemployed, and the otherwise disadvantaged, who are unwitting victims of the system and not of their own fecklessness, are to be protected and supported, so that they are ensured a basic quality of life and so that they do not seriously question the current situation. As shown in the first chapter of this book, the state has already taken on a major set of mediating roles along these lines; the sorts of programs and proposals reviewed here could well lead to an enlargement of those roles.

The programs and policies to be discussed normally are considered under the umbrella title of planning, although the alternative term "spatial engineering" is sometimes used to indicate more precisely exactly what is done; many of the solutions are sought through alterations of the spatial form of the urban system. In liberal-democratic, capitalist societies, most of this spatial engineering is pragmatic in outlook and implementation; it largely comprises a set of reactions to the present situation rather than the definition of a utopian situation that is to replace the present, with probable major upheavals involved in getting there. Even in a period of rapid growth, it has to be accepted that the current urban environment is the framework for what will exist in the next twenty, thirty, even fifty years. Buildings and road systems have long lives and the capital invested in them is not written off rapidly. Planners must accept what is given, therefore, and seek to modify it, not to propose its wholesale replacement.

Geographer Brian Berry has offered a classification scheme that recognizes four types of planning:

1. *Ameliorative problem solving: planning for the present.* Planners identify and isolate problems, analyze their causes, and then suggest policies that will either eliminate, or, more likely, ameliorate them. Resources are redistributed toward people and places with particular difficulties, which in turn modifies the trends that were producing the future. Such modifications are likely to have unexpected side effects, creating a new generation of problems, or at least problem places, for a new generation of planners.

2. *Allocative trend modifying: planning toward the future.* Having identified trends within the urban system, resources are then allocated by planners so as to accentuate those that are perceived as the "best," thereby steering the urban system toward a particular form. This is a procedure of gentle modifications that tries to identify likely problems and thus prepare for their avoidance.

3. *Exploitative opportunity-seeking: planning with the future.* Like the previous

category, this type of planning involves the identification of ongoing trends and attempts to make the most of them, avoiding predicted problems, but making no recognition of others that might arise as a result of the trend modification. Whereas trend modifying has a clear goal in mind—the best possibility out of those to which the system may be heading—opportunity-seeking merely aims to reap benefits while they are there, and to a much greater extent lets the future take care of itself.

4. *Normative goal-oriented planning for the future.* A desired future form of the urban system is designed, with reference to the current form and trends. Policies are then enacted that will shape the form to that end; such policies are usually long term in content and implementation.

Of these four, the first is the most common, and the second is often aimed for. The first is perhaps simply planning by muddling through, taking each problem as it comes. Two reasons can be suggested for its dominance. First, although most problems slowly emerge rather than suddenly appear, they are usually unforeseen. Second, the temporal horizons employed in planning are usually fairly restricted. This does not apply to professional planners, who often conceive schemes that fit the fourth type in the classification. It is their employers, almost

invariably politicians, who have the limited vision, since their eyes must always be set on the next election, which for many is never more than two years away. For them, the solution of immediate problems has much more potential for vote winning than do utopian ideals about the long-term future, when most of the voters will be dead in any case. Side effects, even those that might emerge in a few years, are often irrelevant—to the cynic, they provide the next round of problems, for the next round of plans, with which to win the next election but one. Trend modifying, as with zoning schemes, might be seen as likely to bring short-term gains, but the risk-taking of opportunity-seeking is usually left to the private-sector capitalist (who may be subsidized to encourage his gambles), while utopias are for dreamers, not practicing politicians.

In this final part of the book, therefore, the focus is very much on proposals to ameliorate present problems and to rectify current trends, which are seen as leading the system toward an undesirable end in the near future. The discussion follows the format of the previous chapter, concentrating in turn on the four types of problems—inequality, urban governance, the environment, and problem cities. Again, this is an artificial division, which is convenient but obscures the interactions between the types. The nature of the interactions will be made clear in the discussion, however, since solutions relevant to one area have implications, either negative or positive, for others.

CONCLUSIONS A wide range of problems and attempted solutions are identified here. Despite their interrelationships, they are treated separately for convenience of presentation. The problems are divided into two groups. The first concerns the closely related issues of the cycle of poverty and the government of metropolitan areas, and are discussed in Chapter 9. The second considers urban environmental problems and the problems of urban growth and decline; these are the subject of Chapter 10.

In each of these chapters, the solutions that have been proposed and implemented are discussed, immediately after the nature of the problems is presented. In each case—with the partial exception of the environmental problems—it is shown that the attempted solutions are ameliorative and pragmatic rather than normative. Few problems are solved. Most are rearranged, so that they reappear in a slightly different guise. This is because almost all of the problems are the product of a society in which inequalities of income, wealth, and power are inherent. The inequalities cannot be eradicated unless the nature of the society is to be radically altered; they can only be rearranged. Even with the environmental problems, in which normative standards can be set, the costs of solution affect various groups differentially, as illustrated in Chapter 10. An urban crisis is an endemic state, therefore. The nature of the urban crisis may vary from time to time and from place to place, but while problems in and of the city remain —as they are bound to in an unequal society—urban crises will, too.

9

THE CYCLE OF POVERTY
AND THE GOVERNANCE
OF URBAN AREAS

MANY URBAN AMERICANS are poor: their incomes are insufficient to allow them access to dwellings and many of them are unable to obtain regular employment. Because of this, they are confined to the lower strata of society, out of which they—and, perhaps more important, their children—find it almost impossible to escape. Further, most of them are concentrated spatially, in the inner-city areas. These areas, in most metropolitan units, suffer from problems generated by the nature of the local goverment system, which tends to exacerbate the problems of their residents. Together, these problems are at the heart of the difficulties of urban America.

THE INNER CITY
AND THE CYCLE OF POVERTY

The inner-city areas are generally considered the main foci of America's urban problems. Many pathologies illustrate this. Infant mortality rates are generally highest there; diets are often poor—some in bulk, some in balance, some in both—to sustain healthy bodies and minds; housing is in many cases inadequate, in size, state of repair, and the facilities provided; health care provision is insufficient; crime rates are high and the police are unable to cope; jobs are few and poorly paid, and unemployment levels are high; and educational facilities are generally below standard. These problems are not new to the inner city,

253

nor is their intensity necessarily greater now than ever before. But in an affluent society they are major sores (and eyesores).

The extent of the inner-city problem can only be hinted at by general statistics, such as those in Table 9.1, which compare entire central cities of metropolitan areas with their suburban rings. Since nearly all central cities contain areas of relative affluence and nondeprivation, such averaging understates the intensity of the problems in the innermost areas of old, dilapidated housing. Indeed, for some indices—such as those relating to unemployment—there is no clear-cut city/suburb difference; extremely noteworthy among these, however, is the very high 1970 unemployment rate for black male youths, the vast majority of whom lived in the central cities. Indeed, by focusing on relative numbers, the table understates the concentration of the deprived, since few blacks live in the suburbs.

More graphic portrayals of the extent of inner-city deprivation are given in maps of Detroit (Figure 9.1) The first of these shows infant mortality rates by health districts and with each rate cites the name of a country with a similar rate. The other shows the area in which rats were frequently sighted in 1971 (it was estimated that there were 600,000 rats in all) plus the locations where babies were bitten by rats. Both maps refer only to the city of Detroit; the high infant mortality rates in the inner city (which is also the core of the black ghetto) are indicative of the extent of the problems of social well-being there.

The various problems identified here, such as poor housing, low incomes, few jobs, and high crime rates, are intertwined and cannot be analyzed separately. Figure 9.2 presents the nature of the interrelationships by introducing the concept of a cycle of poverty. Though far from comprehensive, this diagram shows how the problems are linked in a cumulative causation chain that is hard to break. It says nothing of why people in that cycle are spatially concentrated. (Most are, in the inner cities. Because this book is about urban America, it should be pointed out at this stage that there are similar concentrations, most involving fewer people, in rural areas, especially the South.)

For analytical purposes, the point at which to break into the cycle is at *poverty* itself. In a capitalist society, the competitive drives involving individuals and firms create losers as well as winners. When the economy is not operating at full capacity, those who are losers in a relative sense—the poorly paid—are joined by the losers in an absolute sense—those unable to find employment who are dependent on whatever social welfare payments and subsidies are available from the state. Whichever situation holds, any city will contain those who are paid less than others—because they have few skills in short supply—and, perhaps, are unable to organize themselves effectively into labor unions to counter economic and other discrimination. Alongside them are those with skills and market power, who in addition to having higher

Table 9.1
CENTRAL CITY-SUBURBAN DIFFERENTIALS

| | All Metropolitan Areas | | Metropolitan Areas | | | |
| | | | 1,000,000 + | | 1,000,000 – | |
	CENTRAL CITY	SUBURBS	CENTRAL CITY	SUBURBS	CENTRAL CITY	SUBURBS
Incomes						
Median Family 1973 ($)	11,343	14,007	11,373	14,940	11,313	12,728
Mean Earnings, 1973 ($)						
Males	10,197	11,839	10,379	12,582	9,988	10,704
Females	5,110	4,970	5,547	5,259	4,259	4,509
Housing						
Median Rooms, 1970	4.7	5.3				
Median Value, 1970 ($) Owner Occupied	16,400	20,700				
Median Rent, 1970 ($)	90	113				
Unemployment Rate, 1970 (%)						
Male	5.9	4.3	6.6	4.4	5.1	4.3
Female	6.4	5.8	6.8	5.8	6.0	5.8
Male 16–19	18.4	15.6	19.9	15.7	16.8	15.4
White male 16–19	13.6	14.4	13.6	13.9	13.7	15.0
Black Male	10.6	10.7	10.7	11.7	10.4	9.0
Black Female	9.1	9.7	8.5	9.0	10.0	11.0
Black Male 16–19	37.7	35.3	36.5	—	41.3	—
Families (%)						
Both Parents Present	78	88	76	88	80	99

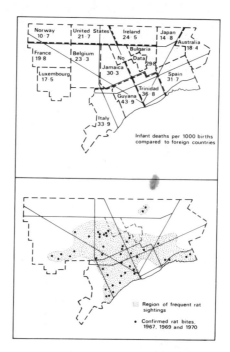

Figure 9.1.   The inner-city problem in Detroit in the late 1960s and early 1970s. Top: The infant mortality rate, 1969; bottom: The area of rat sightings and confirmed rat bites on babies, 1967, 1969, 1970. Source: W. W. Bunge and R. Bordessa, *The Canadian Alternative.* Geographical Monographs, York University, Toronto, Ontario, 1975, pp. 297, 298, 326, 288.

incomes also receive indirect payments such as subsidized meals, transport, housing, vacations, and education for their children. Those in the cycle of poverty are the poorest paid who are employed plus those who receive no regular earned income.

The largest single item of expenditure for households is housing, whose cost varies markedly. Because those with the lowest incomes cannot afford high rents and almost never qualify for mortgages, their poverty is closely associated with living in *poor housing*. In a well-ordered, affluent society, even the lowest-paid should achieve a housing standard that is adequate for the local physical environment—warm and dry, with sufficient room for all and with exclusive use of such basic facilities as a piped water supply, a bath or shower, and toilet and cooking facilities. Much of the housing occupied by those in the cycle of poverty falls below these criteria and yet (relative to their incomes) is expensive for the occupants. This fact reflects a number of influences: the general high cost of dwellings, which filters through the whole housing market; punitive terms (interest rates, length of loans) for those forced to seek a loan to buy a home outside the conventional mortgage market; high rents asked by landlords with oligopolistic control of housing supply and a desire to maximize income; and so on. Furthermore, landlords often fail to keep properties in good repair—it is not in their financial interests to do so—and some abandon housing that rapidly becomes derelict, blighting the neighborhood as well as denying a home to a family in need.

The nature of the housing market and the concentration of those in poverty to certain housing classes leads to the spatial concentration of the poor. They are restricted to certain districts only, to the old, rapidly deteriorating, often poorly constructed homes of the inner city. Certain groups within the cycle, notably blacks and the members of other disadvantaged minorities, are even further restricted by the discriminatory practices that operate even at the lower end of the housing market.

Poverty, directly and through its relationship with poor housing, creates *stresses and strains* for the individuals concerned, who are unable to afford satisfactory diets, shelter, and clothing. The anxieties created by the need to live on an insufficient income are compounded by the problems of an unsatisfactory environment, especially for child rearing. These problems lead to *ill health*; some of it chronic, much of it common. Physical ill health follows from a combination of poor diet and poor living conditions (dampness, cold, exposure to vermin, and so on), and the high densities (both of individual homes and of whole districts) encourage the rapid spread of many diseases, which are often endemic in certain inner areas (hence the pattern in Figure 9.1B). Mental illness results from the problems of coping in such situations. It too can be accentuated by crowding, in which people are in continuous close contact and denied privacy. Many problems of intrafamily strife and family dis-

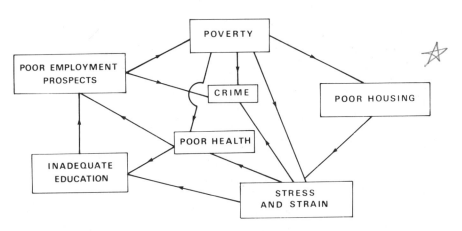

Figure 9.2.   The cycle of poverty

solution follow from, feed on, and exacerbate these mental health problems (many of which go unrecognized, for the sufferers have neither physical nor financial access to treatment).

Unhealthy children are less likely to perform to their full potential in the educational system than are those who are well fed and housed, so that the products of the cycle of poverty are further disadvantaged in that they suffer from *inadequate education*. Their individual characteristics are only a partial contribution to this inadequacy, and they are further disadvantaged by their home situation. The lack of privacy and other resources makes studying difficult; instability in family affairs is disconcerting; and a general sense of fatalism leads many parents to devalue the worth of education and encourage their children to leave school at the earliest opportunity in order to earn extra income. The family in the cycle of poverty cannot invest in the possible long-term gains from education as an affluent family can, and its children may be working after school to aid the family budget.

Much research in recent years has sought to identify the relative influence of personal characteristics, the home environment, and the school on pupils' educational performance and attitudes. Evaluation is difficult, because children from the poorest backgrounds commonly attend the least well-endowed schools. In general, however, it has been found that school quality (measured by spending on resources and teaching) has only a marginal effect, except for that very small number of cycle-of-poverty children who are fortunate enough to attend a predominantly middle-class school and are not alienated by the experience. A good school can in part offset some of the difficulties of the home situation, but in the inner cities such schools are rare. The premises of inner-city schools are obsolete, and they lack modern teaching facilities; they are unable to attract high-quality teachers, because of competition with the suburbs; and the financial resources available to the school boards are relatively meager. Thus inner-city schools are predominantly one-class schools, with poor educational prospects for their students.

An inadequate education means that school graduates from the cycle of poverty are poorly prepared for the world of work; they lack the basic skills and have *poor employment prospects*. This factor is of growing importance in the increasingly polarized labor market of late capitalism with its advanced technology. The blue-collar sector is being "deskilled," as advanced machines replace the skilled craftsman and artisan. Those machines are designed by highly trained, white-collar workers, are operated by a small number of, at best, semiskilled machine-minders, and are maintained by a small group of skilled engineers. Thus without educational qualifications, most of the school graduates of the cycle of poverty can expect entry only to menial unskilled and service occupations, which pay poorly and offer no career prospects. And thus the cycle is closed. Poverty breeds more poverty.

The employment prospects of those in the cycle of poverty are not enhanced by the location of their homes. Manufacturing industries have been fleeing the city in large numbers in recent years, as we saw in Chapter 7. The new suburban jobs are often inaccessible to the inner-city poor. Similarly, employment in offices and shops is now moving out—the movement not only removing jobs but also leading to the poor paying higher prices for what they need to buy.

This discussion has circled the cycle of poverty and has therefore avoided its central element, *crime*; many people see this as the distinguishing characteristic, both of the cycle and of its spatial concentration. Crime rates, as suggested in Figure 9.3, are influenced by many of the other elements of the cycle. Two types of crime can be identified. The first comprises economic crimes, or those against property, many of which involve petty larcenies only. Poverty itself is likely to stimulate such activity (although some would argue that affluence stimulates much more, in terms of tax evasion, and so on), as is the idleness that comes with long spells of unemployment. The stresses that result in mental instability can lead to the second type, crimes against the person. Child- and spouse-battering are very common in the cycle of poverty, and many homicides take place within the immediate family, as indirect consequences of both poverty and living in depressing and debilitating environments.

Just as poverty begets poverty, so crime often generates more crime, through the neighborhood effect discussed in Chapter 6. Criminal activity in an area is perceived by nonparticipants, who may be drawn to emulate it, either by joining an established gang or by operating alone. In some cases (especially with children) participation in criminal activity, much of it petty, is often virtually forced on individuals by their peer groups. Participation is seen as more sensible than incurring the sanctions and reprisals that may result from opting out. Thus the neighborhood effect is particularly important in juvenile delinquency. Youths hang around in gangs, on street corners, in drugstores, in bars, in parks, even in schools. They draw in others and stimulate the development of opposing gangs. Intergang rivalry and "warfare" may become rife: turfs are delimited as gang territories and are defended, both ostensibly by graffiti and occasionally in physical attack. Some inner areas are divided into a mosaic of territories, with "no-man's lands" in-between. Other residents may become very wary of entering certain territories.

The result of these processes is a concentration of criminal activity in certain parts of urban areas (Figure 9.3) associated with the cycle of poverty. (Because so many members of that cycle are black, many people believe that blacks are a more criminal race.) Some observers suggest that its generation is accentuated by certain aspects of the physical environment, especially in public housing projects characterized by high-rise apartment dwellings. Many public areas are not part of any one in-

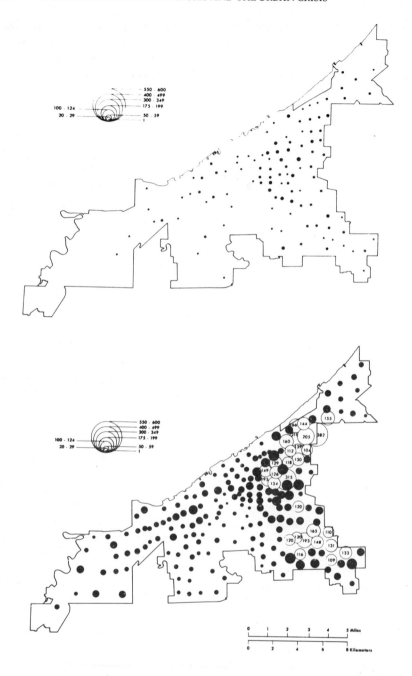

Figure 9.3. The distribution of (top) homicides and (bottom) burglaries in the city of Cleveland, 1971. The data refer to census tracts. Reprinted with permission from G. F. Pyle, "Geographic Perspectives on Crime and the Impact of Anticrime Legislation" in J. S. Adams (ed.) *Urban Policymaking and Metropolitan Dynamics.* Copyright, 1976, Ballinger Publishing Company, pp. 273–274.

dividual's or household's territory, and are not overlooked (and thus surveyable) from homes. Thus the corridors, elevators, and stairways, for example, form no-man's lands where residents and others can be harassed, if not criminally attacked. Bad design can create an environment in which crime will thrive, therefore. Whether it generates crime is dubious.

Crime is tackled by policing, but rarely to good effect in the inner city. Many of those crimes related to mental stress are committed in the home, for example, and conventional policing is largely irrelevant in such cases, although social work may help to reduce the crime. Most economic crimes—and a large number of personal assaults—either occur in public places or involve illegal entry of property. But underfinanced central-city police forces lack the manpower to prevent such crimes merely by the presence of patrol cars.

Inner-city residents are thus the victims of the cycle of poverty, from which their chances of escape are relatively slight. Initial relative failure in the competitive world of capitalism, (a failure that is almost certainly not self-induced and could be completely out of the individual's control) condemns them to low incomes and to lives in the worst housing areas, where conditions are poor and not conducive to a healthy life, where social, economic and physical constraints to personal development are severe, and the possibilities of either or both a good education and a well-paying, secure job are remote. Deprivation is transmitted from generation to generation; in some cases it becomes depravation.

RACE AND THE CYCLE OF POVERTY

Some groups within American society suffer more from the cycle of poverty than do others. This relative suffering may be temporary, as part of the integration and assimilation processes for immigrants in periods of labor shortage. It has been possible for many individuals, if not entire groups, to break out and join the prosperity of mainstream American society. But certain groups have been stuck in the cycle of poverty for many decades, and seem destined to remain there. They have three common characteristics: (1) their color; (2) their relatively recent arrival in the big cities; and (3) active prejudice and discrimination against them by members of the majority society. Most numerous in this set are clearly the native-born blacks; they have been joined in recent years by Puerto Ricans, Chicanos, and East Asians.

The members of these groups have entered the American system at the bottom of the labor market. Prescriptions on where they can live and discrimination in most other aspects of life have kept them at the bottom. A few have escaped, some as successful entrepreneurs, a few as academics and politicians, and a few as sports and entertainment stars, but their success has not been followed by a later mass, upward movement.

Most have remained an economic underclass stuck in the cycle of poverty, condemned to ghettos in the same way that criminals are condemned to prisons and the mentally ill to asylums. They endure appalling housing, suffer from the slightest recessions in the labor market more than other groups, endure stresses that generate many family problems—producing high rates of family dissolution, are driven to crime, and are numbed into a fatalistic acceptance of their position. Occasionally, however, the stresses, strains, and frustrations exceed some threshold, and they are goaded into action to protest against the racist discrimination that suppresses them. Their partial alienation from society is made clear by their attacks on it, in both individual acts and, occasionally, mass riots. Thus the cycle of poverty is not exclusively black or colored, but the particular positions of these groups, and the attitudes of most whites to them, make them its major victims.

CONCENTRATION AND THE CYCLE OF POVERTY

The cycle of poverty depicted in Figure 9.2 refers to individuals and households, and has no inherent spatial component. Frequent references in this section have implied that the members of the cycle within urban America are almost all concentrated in the inner city—creating what to many people is an inner-city problem. This concentration comes about because of the concentration of the poor in certain housing classes—notably the private rental sector of relatively outmoded homes, most of which are in the inner, older parts of cities. Such concentration is not necessary although, given the nature of externalities and the congregation and segregation tendencies discussed in Chapter 6, it is extremely likely; only where gentrification is active is there a major divorce between the cycle of poverty and the inner city.

A major related issue, already touched on here, concerns the potential impact of spatial concentration on the members of the cycle of poverty. The concept of the neighborhood effect suggests that at least some elements of the cycle are exacerbated by this concentration, such as "crime breeding crime," the poor facilities of inner-city schools, and the suburbanization of employment. To some extent, therefore, the cycle of poverty is a problem *of* as well as *in* the inner city.

TACKLING
THE CYCLE OF POVERTY

Poverty is probably best classified as very largely a problem in the city, although there is a circular causation inherent in this classification. Given this fact, there are few, if any, ways in which spatial planning can be used to improve incomes in any direct way. Accordingly, this discussion of planning and the cycle of poverty begins with a consideration of the second step in the cycle:housing.

HOUSING

The housing conditions of the poor can be improved in two basic ways: by the provision of superior housing for them by governments and by government policies that will improve their competitive position within the housing market. The former largely involves the provision of public housing for rental by a government agency.

Public housing is not as important in the American housing market as it is in comparable countries. In 1972, for example, there were just over one million low-rent public-housing units in the nation (approximately 1.5 percent of the total number of units, compared to some 35 percent of the total in the United Kingdom). The public-housing program was initiated in 1937, but two wars (World War II and Korea) inhibited any large-scale chaneling of funds in that direction, and the Republican administration of the 1950s was not sympathetic to its aims; Federal Housing Administration policies directed toward home ownership were much more popular. Only 414,000 units had been built by 1955, and 478,000 by 1960; almost half of all the currently occupied low-rent public housing units were constructed after 1965.

Construction of public housing is undertaken by *ad hoc* authorities established by local governments; the federal government provides the total costs of construction ($798 million in 1972), but makes no contribution to operating costs and maintenance. Until 1969, maintenance had to be paid for out of rental incomes, which meant that rents had to be kept high relative to the incomes of potential residents; those poor households that were allocated such dwellings often had to pay relatively large proportions of their incomes in rent, with consequences for their financial situation in the cycle of poverty, despite the improvement in housing conditions. Furthermore, such a policy encouraged insufficient attention to maintenance by the housing authorities. In 1969, however, Congress ruled that tenants should pay no more than one quarter of their weekly incomes in rent (still a large proportion for the relatively poor) and that any residual loss incurred by the housing authority, up to a maximum sum per unit, would be reimbursed from federal funds. One consequence of this, it has been charged, is inefficient management.

The criterion for accessibility to public housing has been income, and almost all housing authorities have had more potential tenants than dwellings to fill. They have been able to select their tenants carefully, therefore, and to choose between helping the poorest, who are in the most need, and housing those who can afford the rents. Most agencies appear to have followed the latter course, thereby protecting their own solvency. Since the policy innovations of 1969, greater flexibility in accepting the very poor has been possible, and indeed evidence suggests that more of them are being offered tenancies. Particular beneficiaries of this trend in recent years have been the elderly, for whom specially designed homes have been constructed in increasing numbers: in 1960 there were 110,000 such units; in 1972 there were 232,000 (about one quarter of all public housing occupied).

A basic aim of public-housing policy has been the elimination of slums, and the 1937 Housing Act required authorities to demolish one slum dwelling for every public-housing unit built; in 1969, the policy was reversed, requiring one new public housing unit for every slum dwelling demolished. Until this policy reversal, much slum clearance activity did not lead to public housing being built. Many authorities acquired slum properties, cleared them, and sold the land to developers, at a loss; the federal government covered two-thirds of that loss. The developers then built medium- and high-income housing projects, often encouraged by the authorities, with the aim of attracting the affluent back to the central cities and boosting their flagging municipal finances. During the 1950s and 1960s, therefore, urban renewal decreased the stock of housing available at low cost and deepened the problems of the cycle of poverty; 439,000 units were demolished to be replaced by only 124,000.

Slum clearance, urban renewal, and public-housing policies are implemented by *ad hoc* authorities set up by local governments (sometimes by a consortium of adjacent governments). Because they have few problems requiring such policies, and because they have no wish to encourage the poor to live in their areas (especially the blacks, who are major consumers of public housing), suburban municipalities have not been willing either to initiate such policies or to cooperate with neighbors, notably central cities. As a result, most public housing has been constructed in the central cities, where land is in short supply, expensive, and difficult to obtain by buying up slum properties in urban renewal areas. Thus authorities have been obliged to provide high-density public housing, in blocks of apartments, as have the private developers who in recent years have worked out schemes in cooperation with the authorities. Combined with the problems of operating and maintenance costs, this has often resulted in a relatively poor standard of design, especially with regard to the environment external to the apartments. A number of public-housing projects have thus rapidly become slums themselves, such as the notorious Pruitt-Igoe project in St. Louis. First occupied in 1954, the project was 27 percent empty by the early 1960s, and was demolished in 1975. Most of its residents liked their apartments, which were superior places in which to live relative to their previous accommodations, but they were very critical of aspects of the project's design and of the vandalism and crime outside.

A second approach to the housing problem has been through policies aimed at improving the housing situation of those in the cycle of poverty by influencing their position in the competitive private market. For many years it was believed that this could best be achieved by improving housing conditions for everybody, a solution that involved the filtering mechanism discussed in Chapter 6. If new housing is built for the affluent, then the housing they vacate can be handed down to lower-income groups; each group will move up one step, and the poorest housing will be vacated and leave the market.

Filtering failed for several reasons. First, the affluent felt satisfactorily housed and not enough people could be persuaded to move frequently enough; the demand for high-cost housing was fairly low, therefore, but developers would not build lower-cost units because they did not offer a satisfactory return on capital. Investment was directed away from housing as a result. Second, metropolitan areas were growing rapidly in population, and what housing was made available by the initiation of filtering chains was taken up by relatively affluent immigrants from the towns and cities. The filtering process, when it operated, rarely reached the poorest groups, who, as they too increased in numbers, were confined to the worst conditions. Third, the trend in the last few decades has been for the number of separate households requiring dwellings to increase more rapidly than the total population. Many of the newer households are in the higher-income groups, and they have taken up much of the available housing, again preventing the filtering process from reaching the families in the poorest dwellings. And finally, when filtering has penetrated the entire market, often the poor have hardly been able to afford the housing made available to them. They have had to occupy it at high densities, in multifamily situations, in order to meet the costs, and so their housing conditions have scarcely changed.

The failure of filtering as a "natural" process meant that measures were needed that would stimulate the building of homes for, and their purchase by, middle-income groups. Programs aimed at making housing easier to obtain for the members of these groups have been in operation since the 1930s, mainly those run by the FHA, assisted for some groups by the Veterans' Administration (VA). These two institutions insure loans; they do not make them. Their role has been to enable households that otherwise could not afford the offerings of credit institutions, or would be considered poor credit risks, to obtain loans; the better terms that they obtain for their clients include smaller down payments, longer repayment, and the ability to purchase dwellings that otherwise might not have attracted mortgages. More recently, a number of government agencies—the Federal National Mortgage Association, Government National Mortgage Association, and Federal Home Loan Bank—have been engaged in diverting money to the mortgage institutions from other areas of the financial market, thereby subsidizing home buyers. And since 1968 those with incomes just too high to qualify for public housing can obtain directly subsidized mortgages; they commit no more than 20 percent of their incomes to the repayments and may get a subsidy of up to 50 percent of the total cost.

These various programs are not aimed directly at those in the cycle of poverty, but if they work they should open up housing for those people through the filtering mechanism. For the lowest-income households, other plans have been introduced to improve their conditions. Prior to the mid-1960s the main one involved subsidies to landlords who built new blocks of apartments to rent. The subsidies lowered their interest repayments and enabled them to charge lower rents, but their charges were still too high for the very poor. In the mid-1960s a program of rent supplements was introduced by which recipients paid no more than 25 percent of their incomes on a sliding scale (Johnson asked for a 20 percent ceiling), as long as they were paying at least 38 percent of the total rent; the rest was covered by the government. The aim of the program was to stimulate the building of new apartment blocks by developers and landlords, but relatively little has been achieved.

Many of these programs have tackled the problem of housing for the poor only indirectly, therefore, by hoping that the poor benefit from policies that produce general improvements in housing conditions. Only public housing is aimed directly at those in the cycle of poverty, and although the standards of the dwellings themselves are generally high, the quality of their environment in the inner-city renewal areas usually is not. In the private market, the problem for the government has been both to stimulate investment in housing by capital, which means that it has to obtain a satisfactory rate of profit, and to enable relatively low-income households to buy or rent what is offered. In a period of rapid inflation, these two aims are almost incompatible. Property values have increased very rapidly in recent years (by 45 percent between 1967 and 1973 for new single-family homes, when general living costs increased by only 31 percent, and by another 32 percent between 1973 and 1976), and this has led to demands for greater and greater subsidies. In general, it might be concluded that those in the cycle of poverty have not been helped much to improve their housing conditions during the last three or four decades, nor, judging by the increased numbers of trailer homes, have those whose incomes put them just outside the cycle.

The impact of these programs can be illustrated by the situation in one of the nation's largest cities—Chicago—where in recent years the amount of home construction (nearly 500,000 units during the 1960s) has outpaced the increase in the number of households (260,000 in the same period); the result was a substantial improvement in the housing conditions of many of those at the bottom of the ladder. However, levels of crowding and percentages of housing units in poor condition fell only slightly (in part because of another decade of deterioration).

Low-rent public-housing projects in Chicago are in the black ghetto that extends south, west, and, to a lesser extent, northwest of the Loop (Figure 9.4 left). This pattern led to a court case in which it was claimed that public-housing construction was discriminatory in that it accentuated residential segregation. The case was won, and the ruling upheld by the Supreme Court; the Chicago Housing Authority was required to build three housing units in white neighborhoods for every one built in a black neighborhood. Needless to say, this ruling was the cause of political controversy, and the planned distribution of the 700 units that the Authority was ordered to build was attacked widely. In the end a

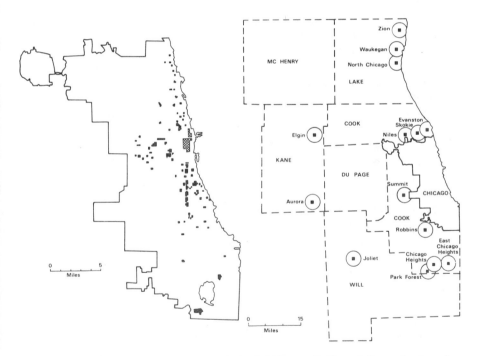

Figure 9.4. Public housing in the City of Chicago (left) and the suburbs of Chicago (right) in 1972. Reprinted with permission from J. Mercer and J. Hultquist, "National Progress toward Housing and Urban Renewal Goals," in J. S. Adams (ed.) *Urban Policymaking and Metropolitan Dynamics.* Copyright 1976, Ballinger Publishing Company, pp. 126, 129.

compromise was reached, and most of the construction in white neighborhoods was in those having either a large number of public-housing units for the elderly or those where many landlords were involved in leasing arrangements that subsidized rents. Outside the central city, very little public housing has been built, in only a few municipalities (Figure 9.4 right). This too was the subject of a court case (*Hills v Gautreaux*), in which the Supreme Court ruled that it was discriminatory for HUD to concentrate its allocation of funds for public housing in the central city; it was not aiding poor blacks to move to the suburbs where they wanted to live. However, the court ruling did not state that suburban municipalities were required to zone for such low-income dwellings!

Subsidized rental housing and subsidized ownership housing are also spatially concentrated. Within the city, the former are concentrated in the neighborhoods with large percentages of the elderly and, to a smaller extent, with middle-class blacks; in the suburbs, the relatively few units are mostly in the small number of municipalities with relatively large nonwhite populations. Finally, the subsidized ownership units in the central city are largely in areas occupied by higher-income blacks, and in the suburbs they are concentrated in lower-status areas, notably south and northwest of the city itself.

The result of the operation of these programs by the Chicago Housing Authority (a special district) is that the metropolitan black ghetto has been joined by a metropolitan public-housing ghetto; the two overlap considerably, of course, since much public housing is occupied by blacks. (The main exception is the public housing for the elderly, a considerable proportion of which is occupied by whites.) Public housing and state-subsidized housing may be improving the absolute standards for some of those trapped in the cycle of poverty and allowing them to keep a larger slice of their incomes for expenditures on other goods and services, but it is not—in Chicago or anywhere else—reducing the spatial concentration of that cycle and the concomitant residential segregation of blacks.

HEALTH CARE AND OTHER FACILITIES

As suggested in the previous chapter, some of the health problems of those in the cycle of poverty are induced by their housing conditions, so that successful housing policies should reduce their demands on the health care system. There are further contributory factors, however, and housing is probably less important than others, such as poor and imbalanced diets and inadequate training in personal health care. The demand for the services of doctors and other medical practitioners from the inner-city poor is considerable, but these demands are far from completely met.

Because medical care is a commodity to be purchased, those in the cycle of poverty are at a great disadvantage. They are often unable to afford medical bills and so avoid consulting doctors when it is really necessary. They also cannot afford the regular payments to medical insurance plans. Medicare and Medicaid were introduced in the 1960s to meet the medical bills of the old and social security recipients; 25 percent of all payments to physicians are now made by these funds, as are half the payments to hospitals. There are major interstate discrepancies in the operation of the programs, however. (Some states did not operate them initially.) And the security of payment that they offer has clearly not induced doctors to practice in the inner cities. Major hospitals and other facilities have not substantially improved their delivery of health care. Other countries, such as the United Kingdom, have policies aimed at forbidding the establishment of new practices in areas with enough doctors and offering financial inducements for doctors to move to the more disadvantaged districts. For a well-paid profession, however, the nature of such inducements is insufficient to attract doctors to areas in which they do not wish to live.

If the feasibility of policies that allowed the location of health care facilities to be determined by public agencies were accepted, then procedures are available that would allow their locations to be tailored to where they were needed. These procedures involve linear programming models which, given the spatial distribution of demand for a service, pose the question: What is the distribution of service outlets that will minimize the total transport bill for either the delivery of the service (if it is delivered to the consumer's home) or the movement of consumers to the outlets? The solution is the most efficient distribution, that which makes every consumer as close as possible to an outlet. Various restrictions can be built into the procedures, such as ensuring that each outlet has a minimum and maximum use, as well as arranging the distribution so that no consumer is more than a certain distance from an outlet. The aim is to minimize the total travel bill (which can be measured in time as well as monetary units). Every consumer cannot have equal access, so it is assumed that each will use the nearest available resource, and then a distribution of services is designed so that accessibility is as equal as possible. (People may choose not to use the nearest available facilities, but the aim is to offer them as good a service as possible; if they choose to use the system in a particular way, that is up to them.)

The demand for health care facilities, or any others, cannot be determined exactly, of course, and so assumptions have to be used in order to arrive at the optimal distribution. However, reasonable predictions of what the demands for services will be in different areas at different times can be made (particularly for services that are age dependent, such as maternity, neonatal, and geriatric services), and constraints can be built in to take account of, for example, the lesser mobility of the poor and the old. Given the will, a reasonable distribution of health care facilities could be produced.

These linear programming procedures can be used for the efficient spatial allocation of a wide range of facilities, particularly those provided by public bodies, such as libraries, fire stations, police stations, branch offices of social and other welfare agencies, parks and playgrounds, swimming pools, and planned shopping centers. (The public body determines the locations of the centers, but does not build them.) The key to the procedures is the central position it allocates to accessibility; the farther people live from a facility, it is argued, the less benefit they will get from it, either because they use it less frequently or because it costs them more (in time, money, and energy) to visit. The aim is to ensure that facilities are located as close to their clients as possible, within various limits related to the size of the facilities and the maximum distance that people can travel. (It may be a requirement, for example, that no home be more than a five-minute drive from a fire station, in order to give it adequate protection.) It is assumed that people use the nearest available facility; if they do not, this represents their personal choice, but planning should aim to provide as much equity in accessibility as possible and should ensure that there is no overt discrimination against particular groups in particular places.

For many public services, facilities are much larger than was the case in the earlier decades; as with so many aspects of late capitalism, the trend has been to close small facilities and centralize provision at a few locations. Doctors have closed their individual offices, for example, and joined colleagues in neighborhood health centers, where they benefit from sharing secretarial, paramedical, and other services, and can arrange for colleagues to cover their patients during time off. But such concentration means that on average patients have to travel farther, so that the efficiency of operation through the economies of scale that concentration allows runs counter to the equity of accessibility that dispersion provides. The linear programming allocation procedures can allow for economies of scale, but the balance between these and dispersion requires value judgments of the degree to which efficiency should override equity in the provision of services.

Many of the services being discussed here are or could be provided by government bodies, and they are commonly known as public goods. Some of these services are equally available to every resident so that there is no spatial discrimination in their provision; national defense is the best example of such a public good. National public broadcasting services approach the same goal of universality. These are known as pure public goods. Others, known as impure public goods, are not provided equally for all.

Two types of impure public goods can be identified. The first are subjects of overt discrimination. Case studies have shown that in some cities the residents of areas who suffer the cycle of poverty, especially blacks, often experience such discrimination in, for example, the quality of street upkeep and the frequency of trash collection. But most cities show interneighborhood variations in the quality of various public goods. In many cases it is suggested that the provision of such services is imperfectly controlled through the political mechanism, and as a result prices are often higher than when services are contracted out by municipal governments to private firms. Such "flabby monopolies," as they are termed, are most common in the large central cities where the poor must pay more for their public goods, relative to their more affluent suburban neighbors.

The second type of impure public goods comprises those services that cannot be provided everywhere. Instead they are provided at certain points, and customers expend energy in reaching them, or, as in the case of fire, police, and ambulance services, energy must be expended in dispatching the service to the consumer. The greater the accessibility to such services, the more benefits one gets, or could get, from the provision of public goods.

The consumption of public goods contributes to the social welfare of urban residents. Addition of this consumption, evaluated in monetary terms, to their earned incomes produces what is known as their real incomes. Not all public goods are spatially allocated (social security benefits are not, for example, although states vary considerably in their level of payments), but many are. Thus some people, living in some places, receive more benefits from impure public goods than do others. The full accounting procedure for any one urban area, aimed at identifying the spatial distribution of real incomes, would require extensive research, and interpretation of the results would be difficult. Fragmentary evidence suggests that it is the poor in the inner cities, especially the poor blacks, who suffer relative deprivation in real incomes; the aim of spatial planning through linear programming allocation procedures is to correct such deprivation and, where necessary, redress past inequities.

EDUCATION

Education is one of the major public goods utilized by most individuals at some time in their lives and is certainly a dominant item of expenditure for local government. There is little doubt that this is an impure public good, since the authorities providing the service—the school districts and, within the large districts, the individual school boards and schools—differ in the resources available to them which they can translate into educational benefits for their students. The resources, including buildings, equipment, and the number and quality of teachers, vary widely from place to place, even from school to school.

Equalization of resources is a major task for governments aiming to provide a satisfactory basic education for all children in their jurisdictions. Such equalization was attempted by the litigants in a Texas school district case, but they failed. The court ruled that variations in the fiscal resources available to school districts were not prohibited as discriminatory under the Fourteenth Amendment.

In some states, rulings under state constitutions have indicated that interdistrict inequalities are unconstitutional and that equalization of resources is required. This was the finding in *Serrano v Priest* in California. The state government there is now trying to produce a politically acceptable plan to redistribute resources—at a time of dwindling public revenue. Another court decision, *Hobson v Hansen*, found that discrimination within Washington, D.C. schools favored the white residential areas and disadvantaged the black ghetto. The school board was required to redistribute teacher resources to remove this inequality.

Federal programs were initiated by the eighty-ninth Congress to provide grants for needy schools and pupils. But education is more than buildings, equipment, and teachers. It also involves motivation and environment. Improvements in the public provision aspect may have marginal effects on children's education, but evaluation and measurement are extremely difficult. Whether educational achievement, and thus employment prospects, can be substantially enhanced by more public investment alone remains an open question.

One aspect of the provision of education has been ruled as discriminatory under the Constitution. In two classic cases (*Brown v Board of Education*, 1954 and 1955), the Supreme Court found that it is unconstitutional to segregate black and white children in separate schools, even though in every respect, such as equipment and the quality of teachers, the schools are equal. The Court required all schools within a district to have approximately the same racial balance. Initially, the ruling applied only to the separate black and white school systems in the South. Blacks and whites were segregated in northern city schools because of neighborhood segregation. Later Court rulings stated that integration must be undertaken in these cities too, where it was shown that the drawing of school district areas indicated intent to segregate blacks and whites. To achieve the necessary integration, city school districts have had to abandon the practice of students attending their nearest neighborhood school—which, because of spatial segregation in housing markets, ensured racially segregated schools.

As residential segregation has not declined, and seems unlikely to, policies have had to be sought that would allow the prescribed racial balance in the schools. One policy approved by the Court involves the busing of white children to schools in black areas, and vice versa. Implementation of this policy has been very slow. Not surprisingly, it has been resented and resisted by many whites who see school integration as a means of devaluing the quality of education obtained by their children—and therefore reducing their competitive status in the job market—as well as mixing them with members of an "undesirable" race. In some cases, as in Boston in 1976, resistance has led to rioting. The greatest integration has, in fact, been achieved in the schools of the South, where segregation was initially almost complete, and racial separation in schools is now the most marked in the cities of the Northeast. As yet there is little evidence that desegregation policies in schools are having a noticeable impact on either scholastic achievement or race relations.

The process of school integration has been hampered by several factors, including the reluctance of many governments required to enact the policy. One way white parents have resisted it is to move their children into private and parochial (religious) schools. Whites have also avoided integration by creating new patterns of residential segregation. Since the school districts are not changed, there is no discriminatory intent in district boundaries. The Court has ruled that such "resegregation" is not unconstitutional. More significant, the spatial engineering proposed has been hampered by municipal balkanization in urban areas. To avoid integration with blacks, many white families who can afford to have moved to the suburbs, where the independent school districts have very few blacks, and so integration is not an issue. The lack of school districts for whole urban areas, especially outside the South, hinders implementation of the Supreme Court rulings. Although there are a few cases of integration policies involving the amalgamation of city and suburban school districts, the Supreme Court has ruled that cross-municipal boundary school integration cannot be legally enforced.

Education is one part of the social process that enables people to improve the quality of their lives; schools are one part of the educational process. Provision of excellent school facilities may overcome some of the problems of the home environment, and thus help people break the cycle of poverty. But, as white flight to the suburbs indicates, those not in the cycle of poverty will always act to protect their position by countering compensatory policies in ways that will ensure that education for the lower classes in a society does not enable them to challenge (let alone surpass) the positions of those currently holding economic, social, and political power. Indeed, white flight serves to accentuate the cycle of poverty by abandoning the city almost entirely to the poor and needy.

EMPLOYMENT PROSPECTS

As the data in Table 9.1 indicate, one of the major problems facing inner-city residents, and especially black youths, is finding employment. The central cities of metropolitan areas have recently suffered from a major decline in jobs. Industries have moved to the suburbs, where spacious industrial parks offer attractive working environments and a location convenient to the homes of the executives; suburban wives can be employed as low-cost labor on assembly lines; and municipalities impose relatively low property taxes that enable property owners to avoid paying for the public goods consumed by the employees, let alone the poor.

In a period of high unemployment in the nation as a whole, inner-city residents appear to suffer most, for a variety of reasons. Their childhood in the cycle of poverty suggests that they have neither the skills nor the discipline that employers require; also, their homes are far from the available jobs so that travel would often cause added difficulty. The inner city is something of a job desert. Unskilled service jobs are still available in the CBD, although the movement of shops and offices to the suburbs is reducing their number; most (for example, cleaning hotels and offices) are poorly paid and insecure, and may involve working at "unsocial" hours. They do not provide the basis for escaping from the cycle of poverty; indeed, improvements in education that give inner-city youths the requisite skills for modern industry may merely increase their frustration with and alienation from society, rather than allow them to capitalize on their potential.

The spatial imbalance in the distribution of people and jobs in American metropolitan areas reflects a failure of spatial planning. In itself, this is a consequence of municipal balkanization and the separation of the functional urban area into a large number of independent authorities that make their own decisions about zoning for land-use patterns. Suburbanization initially involved the movement of people. People were then followed by jobs, as employers sought the benefits of the suburban environment. Those who could not afford to migrate were left behind, lacking in choice if not in jobs. The establishment of suburban industrial areas, in those municipalities that preferred such land uses, led to the provision of some suburban housing for lower-income workers, usually close to the industrial sites. The low-income workers did not have much choice where to live, however.

These problems of imbalance could be tackled if the metropolitan areas were planned as single functional units, with jobs and residences allocated so that all workers had a reasonable choice from available opportunities, especially if public transit were provided. Once again linear programming procedures can be used. But such planning is extremely rare, as the discussions of municipal balkanization below indicate, and American metropolitan areas continue to maintain inequities in spatial access to jobs. At present it is extremely difficult for the central cities to compete in the provision of jobs. Modern industries involve large factories and require lots of space, unlike the workshops that were characteristic of inner-city areas in the past. Such space is rarely available in sufficient quantity in the densely occupied inner areas (the former Chicago stockyards are a clear exception), so that, along with high taxes and unattractive environments (including traffic congestion), there is little to draw industrialists into the inner areas. Interestingly, recent research has shown that a large proportion of the new jobs in manufacturing industry are being created by small businesses, not by the giant corporations. This evidence suggests that the potential for inner-city jobs still exists if the small firms can be attracted there by tax concessions and other benefits.

CRIME, THE NEIGHBORHOOD EFFECT, AND THE BALANCED NEIGHBORHOOD

To the pessimist, the problems of inner-city crime appear to be insoluble. Two approaches to the problem are possible, one involving ameliorative problem solving, and the other normative goal orientation. For the first, the aim is to apprehend criminals and, if possible, prevent criminal acts. If, as studies of the geography of crime suggest, some areas have both more crime and more criminals living there, then these areas should be more intensively policed. The high density of officers would allow both the apprehension of criminals and the prevention of further crime. Of course, not all crime could be dealt with in this way, especially the large proportion that occurs in the home and is out of the immediate reach of the crime-prevention officer.

The success of such ameliorative policies that accept the perpetrators of crime and merely attempt to mitigate the consequences of crime depends on the quality of policing, notably of the personnel provided by often financially deprived police authorities. The assumption is that much crime occurs not as the immediate response to a perceived temptation but as a result of a cost-benefit analysis by the potential criminal, who weighs the possible gains to be obtained from the crime against the likely sanctions if caught, incorporating the probability of being caught. Much crime may indeed be the result of such calculations, so that more police activity could lead to its reduction. Major crimes, however, are not those that lower the quality of life within the cycle of poverty. Other crime, much of it petty but important to the sufferers and to those who fear it, is the result of an immediate stimulus. Very high densities of patrolling officers would be needed even to counter it, let alone eliminate it from the areas where it is rife.

The second type of policy has as its goal a crimeless society, in which temptations are not succumbed to, since there is no need. This assumes an ideal state in which there is no deprivation, no feeling of relative deprivation, no feeling of alienation, and no stress. Such ideals seem unrealistically utopian in a society that emphasizes competition, from which there must be losers, and which encourages much quasi-illegal activity, such as tax avoidance (in contrast to illegal activity, such as tax evasion). Spatial planning would seem to have little role in the preparations for such a utopia, though it could bring us closer to it. Many studies have shown that crime rates increase with population densities, presumably because of the greater range of accessible opportunities which these imply. Lower-density cities might discourage crime, therefore, or at least those crimes which are stimulated by the perception of an opportunity.

Some people argue that the social environment may be an important causative influence on crime rates through the operation of what is called the neighborhood effect. Juvenile delinquency and other crime are especially likely to be affected in this way. Clearly, spatial planning might be instrumental in reducing this neighborhood effect if there were a policy of dispersing the likely leaders and separating them from the easily led. This, of course, is not an argument for prisons. If the relatively deprived were less spatially concentrated, they would not come into contact with each other so easily. They would then be less likely to lead each other into criminal activity, which might begin at a petty level but develop into more severe offenses. This pattern may be true, although it is not clear what the threshold density is, and whether the presence of only a few potential leaders can draw others, who otherwise might be law abiding, into the web of criminal activity. If the threshold is indeed low, then dispersal could have the effect of introducing even more people to criminal life than occurs with concentration, although other factors clearly are important, like the availability of other outlets such as clubs for the interests of youth. In other words, the potential for success with dispersal policies would depend on whether crime and delinquency are inherent to some people in certain situations, such as the deprivation characteristic of the cycle of poverty, so that only the ameliorative problem-solving approaches to crime are feasible.

The pattern of criminal activity is only one example of the probable operation of the neighborhood effect, which has been studied with respect to educational aspirations and achievements, racial attitudes, voting decisions, and a wide range of other aspects of social behavior. Spatial engineering could have important effects on many aspects of social life, therefore, if it could capitalize on this neighborhood influence by bringing people of different backgrounds into the same residential area, assuming that all the effects that such policies produced were positive for the society as a whole.

Many authors from a wide range of disciplines and backgrounds have argued for the spatial mixing of different groups in residential areas to produce the following consequences:

1. Members of the lower classes who are brought into contact with their ''social and economic superiors'' will perceive a better ap-

proach to life that they will wish to emulate. Neatness, cleanliness, and a desire to plan for the future are among the suggested attributes that the lower classes may adopt.

2. Social diversity will have an overall aesthetic effect, producing a mixture of homes that will relieve the current uniformity and boredom of so many residential areas.

3. Mixture will bring people from different cultural backgrounds into contact and engender cross-cultural fertilization.

4. Mixture will increase opportunities for the relatively deprived, putting them on the first rungs of the educational and social ladders, which can lead to economic advancement, especially for their children.

5. Close contact among people from different cultural backgrounds will promote social harmony and reduce the tensions in society, especially those between different racial groups.

6. Contact with people from different backgrounds rather than only with people from similar backgrounds will expose the individuals to conflicting influences. Resolution of those influences through mutual accommodation will produce a more mature person, and thus a more mature society.

7. Mixture will provide all areas with leaders, with a range of job opportunities, and with the full range of public goods; the physical and thus the social functioning of the whole urban area will benefit as a result.

8. Different kinds of housing in an area will enable people with changing needs to move, yet remain in the same district, and thus increase neighborhood stability.

9. The modern urban area comprises a wide range of very diverse groups. Mixture of these groups will improve their awareness of each other and create a more knowledgeable and compassionate society.

Some of the main proposals regarding social mix in residential districts of American cities concern racial issues. In particular, such spatial engineering was put forward as a policy that would avoid repetition of the race riots of the late 1960s. Segregation, it was argued, is largely a consequence of immaturity. We create models for what we do not know or understand about life and then act as if those models represent the real world. Often such models reflect a general fear of the unknown and thus emphasize perceived negative aspects of those things about which we are ignorant. As a result, we tend to avoid contact with what we fear because of our beliefs regarding the possible negative effects they would have on ourselves, and particularly on our children. If we were mature, we would not be ignorant and would not shun the unknown. Most interracial prejudice, the argument continues, is based on ignorance and the immature construction of models which emphasize the potential for harm that contact with an "inferior" race would engender. Therefore we retreat from the unknown. In American cities this means that whites separate themselves from blacks and establish territories with relatively impermeable boundaries to prevent what they assume will be the negative effect of contact with blacks. If, on the other hand, blacks and whites were made to live together in small areas, both groups would gain maturity as each realized the errors in their models and sought an accommodation with the other. The need for group territories would disappear, and major conflicts would end. Residential desegregation would lead to a mature, integrated society.

More generally, the same argument has been advanced for the desegregation of all social groups, by the "opening-up" of the suburbs. When placed in areas dominated by the middle- and upper-income groups, the poor would be introduced to a better life style that they would strive to achieve for themselves and for their children. Motivation and hard work would allow the poor to emulate their richer peers, again with the result being a more integrated society in which class conflicts are removed.

The aim of spatial engineering policies involving mixture of people from different backgrounds in residential neighborhoods is the removal of certain differences within society. There are two recognized processes that lead to that end. The first is the complete process of assimilation, by which one group totally loses its identity and is merged with its host society. The group's initial characteristics may disappear entirely, as with a language, or some of them may be adopted by their hosts, in which case assimilation involves a mixing of unequal forces. Full assimilation of a group can only occur if it is given equal access to all sectors of economic, social, and political activity. The alternative process is the more restricted one of integration, in which a group loses some of its characteristics but retains others. Usually it joins the wider economy of the host society and maintains certain social characteristics, such as religion and language. An element of selection is suggested; the group may be free to change or it may be restricted by law or custom to enter certain areas of society—for example, persons not born in the United States cannot become president. The separateness may involve continued residential segregation, either enforced by the hosts or desired by the minority.

In the past, a number of minority groups, many of whose members may have spent some time in the cycle of poverty, have been assimilated into the mainstream of American society, usually passing through an interim stage of economic integration but social separateness. As already pointed out, however, these groups have been assimilated at times of marked labor shortages when rapid economic and social mobility has been highly desirable for capitalist development. Furthermore, the groups were not generally considered so inferior that assimilation was strongly resisted by the majority, although the religious issue has remained well into the twentieth century, as seen in John Kennedy's presidential campaign of 1960. In several cases it took a number of generations for the complete disappearance of prejudice. (Traces of such prejudice still exist—against the Jews, for example.) Finally, there was always a supply of cheap labor among the immigrants. Since the 1920s black migrants to the cities have replaced immigrants from Europe at the bottom of the urban labor market. Their movement up through the social and economic systems has been blocked for most of the time since by a relative lack of opportunities. The exclusion, legal in some cases and quasi-legal in many others, of the black population from the American mainstream because of prejudice and discrimination eventually led to the riots of the 1960s.

Assimilation requires a lack of intergroup prejudice, therefore, which is not the case for at least half the population currently trapped in the cycle of poverty. Consequently, spatial engineering is unlikely to be successful, and integration is all that can currently be expected. Attitudes may not be as harsh now as they were when slavery was abolished, but white Americans have found many ways in the last century to keep the black population in inferior social and economic positions. One result has been a growth of black frustration and black consciousness, so that for some blacks assimilation is no longer a goal. Integration is probably widely acceptable, though not entirely on the white man's terms, but for some blacks separateness is the goal, best achieved by territorial separation. However, many blacks, through long years in the cycle of poverty, have developed strong feelings of fatalism and despondence.

Many efforts have been made to eliminate overt discrimination in recent years, both by blacks and by whites who identify with the black cause and oppose all racial discrimination. Open housing is an example of this. Initially the removal of barriers to certain housing areas was determined separately by each municipality through open housing referenda. Later all discrimination in the housing market was prohibited by federal legislation. But access to better housing requires money, which is not available to poor blacks. To locate poor blacks in balanced neighborhoods among people with much higher incomes is to invite frustration and alienation if the blacks are unable to achieve similar status rapidly. The social assimilation that is the aim of such policies requires equality in jobs and incomes, and if blacks must remain at low levels in the American economy they cannot be expected to accept a clearly inferior social status to that of their neighbors. A lasting solution to breaking the cycle of poverty requires removal of income and job-access differentials.

All of the arguments just advanced with regard to the possibility of solving interracial problems through social integration in balanced neighborhoods apply equally well to proposals for mixing together other population groups. In order to emulate others, a group must have either resources equal to those others or a clear opportunity to obtain such equality, usually through education. Furthermore, the others must be prepared to grant them equality of opportunity. In general terms, in a capitalist society in which most aspects of social and economic life are dependent on income, there must be some groups that are better off than others. Thus, as we suggested above with regard to nineteenth-century European immigrants, one group can be assimilated only when there is another group to occupy the lower echelons of society, for whom only partial integration is possible. Such groups, which are at the bottom, may be racially different—they are more easily identified and thus discriminated against if they are—but whether they are or not, if they cannot be accepted as economic equals, then their presence in residential areas among their "betters" will be opposed by the latter, who, if necessary, will move away to avoid integration.

The neighborhood effect is thus not easily manipulated, for certain conditions are necessary to its successs. For the isolated individual schooling among a higher-status population may bring many benefits and assist him or her to come out of the cycle of poverty into a secure, well-paid occupation. But for large groups, social opposition and economic difficulties will prevent assimilation into the mainstream of society.

BREAKING THE CYCLE

All the policies outlined above, some of which have never been put into operation and are probably inoperable, deal only with parts of the cycle of poverty—usually the less crucial parts. They are attempts at ameliorative problem solving and do not involve normative goals. The basis of the cycle of poverty is poverty. Improvements in housing conditions, in health care, and in the provision of educational and other facilities may give those trapped in the cycle a better quality of life and perhaps provide a surer basis for further development, but it is steady employment and a regular income sufficient for a certain standard of living that is the absolute necessity.

Capitalist society is competitive. It must have losers, although it may be possible for a nation to ensure that all of the losers live in other countries (Sweden, for example, is sometimes referred to as one large suburb of international capitalism.) In the United States there must always be some losers, at least in a relative sense. Some would argue for the primacy of the term relative, for even the poor and the deprived who suffer the worst conditions in American cities are among the best-off on a world scale. But for those poor and deprived, the reference groups against which they compare their own quality of life are their neighbors, the rich of the suburbs, and the happy, successful, predominantly white Americans who appear in advertisements in the mass media. If the poor are to have their status improved in absolute terms, the wealthier will wish to preserve their relative positions. If they do not, capitalist growth is likely to slow, with important consequences for employment and incomes for all. Particularly when the economic situation is depressed, the relatively affluent will act to defend what they have and to prevent others from encroaching on it: affluence must be protected by maintaining relative poverty. In addition to the cycle of poverty identified in Figure 9.2 there is a cycle of affluence (Figure 9.5). The members of the latter benefit from their high incomes, good housing, good health, good education, and good housing prospects, advancing both their own and their children's positions in an unequal society. Breaking the cycle of poverty involves more than just the social mobility, both up and down, indicated in Figure 9.5; it implies an equality of

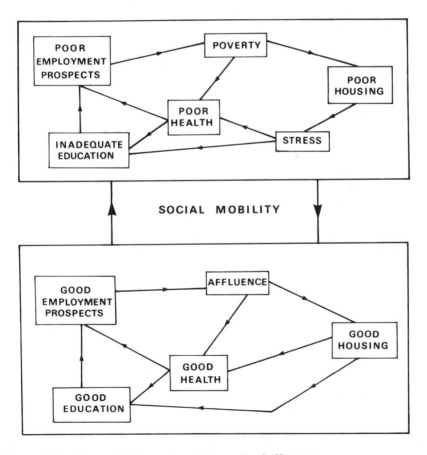

Figure 9.5.   The cycle of poverty and the cycle of affluence.

opportunity that is counter to the competitive drive of capitalism. The absolute conditions of those in the cycle of poverty can be improved; the only cost is financial. But a capitalist society is built on "positional goods," the supply of which must be limited if status is to be maintained. The cycle cannot be broken to the extent of ensuring that such positional goods are available to all: good homes for the poor, yes, but equal opportunities of getting the well-paid jobs, no.

Spatial ameliorative problem-solving may provide better absolute conditions for the poor. From a humanitarian view this clearly should be done, even if it costs the affluent a little and slows the rate of capitalist growth slightly. But there always must be the relatively poor in a capitalist society. While housing is both a status symbol and an investment in the future, as well as a shelter and base for living, then the relatively poor are likely to be confined to certain residential areas. These need not be in the city centers. They will almost certainly be in the areas of oldest housing, unless the United States constructs very large public housing programs on the European model. Thus there will always be an area that contains people living in a cycle of poverty. Spatial engineering will be able to improve the quality of their lives in many ways, but not their position within society as a whole. Relatively poor they and their children are likely to remain.

THE ELDERLY

As indicated in Chapter 2, a major demographic change of recent decades has been the relative decline of children, balanced by the large relative and absolute increases in the number of elderly people. A considerable number of the elderly are on the edge of the cycle of poverty; many others require special facilities and treatment because of impaired mobility and other handicaps. Among the affluent elderly, a considerable number retire to the Sun Belt, many of them to communities specifically designed for retirement. (The population aged 65 and over increased by 79 percent in Arizona between 1960 and 1970, involving a net inmigration of 46,000 elderly. California's comparable population increased by 30.9 percent, a net inmigration of some 143,000. In Florida the state's elderly population increased by 78.9 percent, a net inmigration of 366,000.) But most of the elderly cannot afford such a move to the Sun Belt: between 1960 and 1970 the largest net outflows were 203,000 from New York and 105,000 from Illinois, but these were only 10 percent of each state's 1970 elderly residents, indicating a net outmigration of some 9 percent over the decade.

The characteristics of the elderly vary widely and differ considerably from place to place. In 1970, for example, three-quarters of the elderly residents of New York City were renters, as were about 60 percent of those in Chicago and Los Angeles; about two-thirds of the Philadelphia and Detroit elderly were owners, however. Whether owners or renters, the modal income was less than $5,000 annually for husband and wife families in all five cities, except in New York, where the largest class of owners had incomes in excess of $15,000. In all five cities about 20 to 22 percent of the elderly were below the defined poverty level; for unrelated individuals living alone or together with others (including in institutions), the percentages below the poverty level ranged from 34 to 50.

Many of the elderly continue to live in their preretirement homes, some until their death. Many others move, some to a retirement home in a resort or other preferred area, others either to be near or to live with friends and/or kin. Increasingly, some are moving to designed communities in which the elderly are spatially segregated. Five types of communities have been recognized: (1) the retirement village, usually self-contained and expensive; (2) the retirement hotels, which vary considerably in quality but seem to be typified by older buildings that can no longer be run profitably for tourists—perhaps because the resort itself is run down; (3) the trailer village, a low-income concentration of mobile homes run for profit; (4) the low-rent, public-housing blocks of separate apartments with some communal facilities that include janitors and others who meet tenants' needs; and (5) congregate housing, combining separate sleeping/living apartments with communal facilities for meals. The advantages of such segregation are security, especially in closed places from which others are excluded, an ability to socialize with people in a similar situation, allowing the old to maintain their traditional values (outside a rapidly changing society), and the economies of scale involved in providing for their needs at a central location. The major disadvantage is a separation from the wider society, which some claim is an infringement of human rights.

The elderly form the most rapidly growing segment of the American population; their growth will continue, at least for the next few decades, as will the problems of catering to an increasingly incapacitated population group. As noted here, many of the elderly are below the poverty level (although parts of the cycle of poverty are irrelevant to them). Occupational pension plans may improve their relative situation in the future, but many will continue to fall below the poverty line. How to house them, and whether they should be spatially segregated, will be increasingly important social issues in the next few decades.

GOVERNMENT, POLITICS, AND REPRESENTATION

Urban areas have always been the fulcrum of the American economy, and since the 1920s they have dominated the distribution of population. But they have never dominated American political life to nearly the same extent because of two factors; rural dominance of federal and state electoral machines until the 1960s and the local government system.

URBAN REPRESENTATION

Urban areas were underrepresented in the federal and state Congresses until the 1960s. This underrepresentation has resulted from widespread malapportionment in the allocation of congressional seats. Rural areas have had more representatives, relative to their populations, than have urban areas; rural U.S. Congressional Districts, State House Districts, and State Senate Districts have traditionally contained fewer voters than have those serving urban areas. Consequently members from rural areas have been able to dominate the various legislatures. In the early 1960s, for example, the populations of Idaho U.S. Congressional Districts varied from 257,000 to 410,000 and in Texas the variation was from 216,000 to 952,000: in both cases, and in most of the other states, the rural districts had the smaller electorates. (The U.S. Senate is also biased against the urban areas since each state has two Senators no matter how densely or sparsely populated.)

Malapportionment was practiced because of the ability of the entrenched rural interests in the state legislatures to protect themselves against the growth of the urban electorate by denying the latter equal access to political representation. In state senates this was usually because—paralleling the federal Senate—each constituent territory (in this case usually a county) was entitled to one senator, irrespective of its population. In state lower houses initial rural dominance reflected the population distribution. But as urbanization proceeded, the rural areas were not forced to yield their distribution of seats and thus their control over the house; in many states the differences between urban and rural populations just increased. In some states rural dominance continued because district boundaries were defined in state constitutions that could only be changed by a two-thirds majority in both houses; neither house was going to vote to change its district boundaries and pass political power to new urban-based interests. Rural predominance was legally institutionalized. In other states district boundaries could be redrawn, but responsibility for this task lay with the legislature, and thus with its rural majority. Again, the legislatures were not going to redraw district boundaries to put members out of work. In Idaho, for example, there was no redistricting for the lower house of the state legislature between 1911 and the 1960s. This was not party politics in the sense of Republicans versus Democrats, although outside the South Republicans generally benefited most from the status quo. It was partisan politics—rural interest groups versus urban interest groups, with the former having the initial advantage and the latter virtually powerless to redress the imbalance. A similar imbalance occurred at the federal level, since the boundaries for congressional districts were drawn up by the party in power in the state legislature. Redistricting was needed every decade in most states, because seats in the House of Representatives are reallocated among the states after the announcement of the results of each decennial census. Those in power favored their own constituents, producing districts with unequal populations, with the rural districts having the fewest people.

This urban underrepresentation in federal and state legislatures for most of the history of the United States, certainly for most of the twentieth century, has meant that the urban areas have been relatively deprived of funds with which to tackle the sorts of problems outlined in the previous section. Until recently federal aid has provided only a very small proportion of total city revenues. The data shown in Figure 9.6 underestimate the federal contribution, since they ignore federal money channeled via state governments, but they are indicative of the slight federal involvement in solving the problems of the cities.

Since the New Deal realignment of the 1930s most of the representatives from the nation's cities, but not the suburbs, have been Dem-

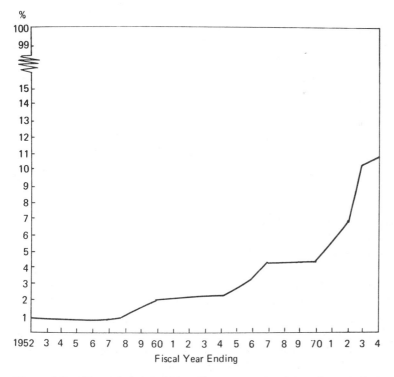

Figure 9.6.   Direct federal aid to cities as a percentage of general expenditure by cities of populations exceeding 300,000 (excluding Washington, D.C.).

ocrats. Within the federal Congress they have joined with the traditional-minded southern Democrats to have a majority in nearly every Congress. But southern Democrats are ideologically very different from urban northern Democrats. On many issues, including those relating to aid to cities, the southern Democrats tend to vote with the fiscally conservative Republicans. Thus much pro-urban legislation has been defeated, despite considerable pressure from the executive. In the eighty-seventh Congress of 1971–1972, for example, the partisan line-up was: northern Democrats, 159; southern Democrats, 104; Republicans 174—the northern Democrats were 59 votes short of a majority and Kennedy failed in many of his legislative efforts, including the establishment of a federal Department of Urban Affairs and Housing. The eighty-ninth Congress (1975–1976) was elected on the coattails of Johnson's landslide victory over Goldwater. The partisan balance was: northern Democrats, 203; southern Democrats, 92; Republicans, 140. The northern Democrats were able to win the fifteen votes needed from the other camps to establish the Department of Housing and Urban Affairs, to pass the Elementary and Secondary Education Act, and to institute such programs as Medicaid, rent supplements, and model cities. In 1981, President Reagan's tax plan was carried in the House by a majority of Republicans and (conservative) Southern Democrats.

Similar anti-urban biases were common in the state legislatures. In Florida, for example, the Senators from twenty-two of the state's smallest counties were known as the Pork Chop Gang. These counties contributed only 14 percent of the state's tax revenues during the 1950s but received 27 percent of the state expenditure. Some tax receipts were divided equally between counties. The racing tax was, for example. It provided 20 cents per resident to the government of Dade County (which houses 20 percent of the state's population, including much of metropolitan Miami), but $61.07 per resident in the smallest county, (where it covered 43 percent of the cost of the educational service).

Malapportionment ended in the 1960s. After refusing to deal with the issue for several decades, the Supreme Court ruled in 1962 (in *Baker v Carr*) that malapportionment contravenes the equal protection clause of the Fourteenth Amendment. A series of rulings applied this to the House of Representatives and to both houses of the state legislatures. Districts now have to be approximately equal in population, giving voters in all areas equal power over the legislature. However, partisan districting still continues through gerrymandering by the parties in control. This is more difficult to contest legally since intent has to be proved. Thus New York State's legislature is still controlled by the Republican party, although statewide the Democrats usually get more votes. Nevertheless, in general urban underrepresentation has been much reduced. The reapportionment revolution came too late for the central-city portions of urban areas, however, for two related reasons.

First, the new urban representatives did not quickly gain great power. The dominant positions in federal and state legislatures are held by committee chairmen; these posts are almost all held by senior members who have been reelected many times. Some of these retired and others were defeated after reapportionment, but many were reelected and retained control until new coalitions within the parties were able to counter entrenched rural interests. Seniority is now not the only path to legislative power, notably among the Democrats in Washington, but its possession by the rural interest groups was used to delay the impact of the electoral changes of the 1960s.

The second reason is that by the time reapportionment became effective, dominance of most legislatures, including the House of Representatives, was no longer possible for the city members. In 1970, 69 percent of all congressional districts were in metropolitan areas, compared with 54 percent in 1950; the predicted percentages for 1980 and 2000 are 77 and 85, respectively. But in 1950, of the 238 metropolitan districts 109 covered central-city constituencies, 76 were entirely suburban, and 52 were a mixture of both. By 1970, the suburbs had 145 districts, compared with 96 for central cities and 58 mixed, and for 1980 the predicted number for the suburbs is 202 of the 338 metropolitan districts. (By 1990 the suburbs should have a clear majority—240 of 435— of all seats in the House of Representatives.)

Analysis of the attitudes and voting records of suburban representatives suggests that they are neither as liberal as their counterparts from the central cities nor as conservative as the rural Republicans. They are unlikely to give too much support for federal aid to the central cities, since many suburbanites move from those areas to avoid paying to ameliorate urban problems. Thus the future of the inner cities does not look bright. Presidents, because of the operation of the electoral college, are more likely to be sympathetic to the problems of urban voters, but it is not clear how much they can achieve without a similarly sympathetic Congress.

MUNICIPAL BALKANIZATION

The nature of this problem was outlined in Chapter 8 on suburbanization and urban government. In brief, it arises through the interaction of two variables: the existence of many separate local government territories within metropolitan areas, notably their suburbs, and the great reliance of those local governments on revenue from property taxes to finance their activities. Furthermore, the ability of households to choose between the various territories when they are selecting their homes is restricted by a number of factors, the most important of which is income. Many of the suburban and rural-urban fringe municipalities in a metropolitan area are comprised almost entirely of relatively expensive homes in low-density areas from which residents commute long distances. The exclusive character of these municipalities is protected by the zoning laws that they have enacted. And so the relatively poor are effectively excluded from much of suburbia. This does not mean that suburbia comprises only very affluent families. Many of its residents are in the middle-income brackets. They are prepared to accept some of the high costs of suburban living in order to get the sort of physical and social environment that the suburbs offer—particularly, for many, the all-white, high-quality public schools.

As suggested in Chapter 8, the separation of income groups into different political territories has an important influence on the distribution of costs for publicly provided services. Table 9.2 illustrates this point with hypothetical figures. An urban population is divided between two independent districts, A and B. The average annual incomes of families with properties of different values is given; district A comprises mostly relatively poor households, living in low-value homes, whereas district B is dominated by affluent occupants of expensive housing.

Each of the two districts has a population of 200 children to educate, at an annual cost of $1,000 each, which has to be met entirely from revenue raised through property taxes. In district A, the total value of properties is $5,750,000, so to raise $200,000 requires a tax of $1 for every $28.75 of property value (a rate of 3.48 cents per dollar). The second block in the table shows how this tax burden is distributed, both per property and as a percentage of the average income of each property owner. In district B, total property value is $9,500,000, so a tax rate of only 2.11 cents per dollar ($1 for every $47.5 of property value) is required to raise the needed $200,000. The table shows that the sums involved in B are much smaller percentages of the residents' average incomes than is the case in A.

Three main conclusions can be drawn from the first two panels of Table 9.2:

1. In both districts use of the property tax means that the relatively poor pay relatively more (as a proportion of income) for the same service.
2. To provide the same expenditure for a service (which may or may not mean the same type and standard of service) costs relatively more in the poorer districts.
3. The higher the average income in a district, the lower the percentage of its income that any group has to pay in property taxes for the given service, because of the "subsidy" provided by the wealthier households. Districts with few or no affluent households do not have this "subsidy," and so in them the poor must pay the full costs of the service.

Table 9.2

THE FISCAL RESOURCES OF TWO HYPOTHETICAL DISTRICTS

	Property Values			
	Up to $10,000	$10,000–15,000	$15,000–20,000	20,000–25,000
1. Fiscal Resources				
Mean Property Values ($)	7,500	12,500	17,500	22,500
Mean Income of Residents ($)	1,000	2,000	3,500	6,000
Distribution of Properties in				
District A	200	200	100	0
District B	50	50	100	300
Total Value of Properties in ($)				
District A	1,500,000	2,500,000	1,750,000	0
District B	375,000	625,000	1,750,000	6,750,000
2. Costs of Raising Taxes to Pay for Education Service				
Total Cost per Property ($)				
District A (tax rate 3.48¢/$)	260.87	434.78	608.69	
District B (tax rate 2.11¢/$)	157.89	263.16	368.42	473.68
As Percentage of Residents' Incomes				
District A	26.1	21.7	17.4	
District B	15.8	13.2	10.5	2.1
3. Taxation if Districts are Amalgamated				
Total Cost per Property ($) (at 2.62¢/$)	196.50	327.50	458.50	589.50
As Percentage of Residents' Incomes	19.65	16.38	13.10	9.83

These conclusions suggest two alternative consequences of the balkanization of local government and the spatial segregation of income groups. Either the relatively poor pay more, as a proportion of their incomes, than do the relatively affluent for the same service, or, more likely, the relatively poor must accept a lower volume of expenditure, and thus presumably a lower standard of service, because they cannot afford the large costs of the full service. In either case, for the poor there is a large fiscal effort, a greater taxing of their meager resources.

What would be the case if there were no balkanization, if districts A and B were amalgamated to form a single jurisdiction? Households in each income group would then all pay the same tax rate, and the relatively poor of former district A should be "subsidized" by the wealthier residents of former district B. The total value of property in the combined districts is $15,250,000. To raise the $400,000 needed to educate the 400 children would require a tax income of $1 for every $38.125 of property value (a tax rate of 2.62 cents per dollar). As the final panel of Table 9.2 shows, in comparison with the second panel, this combined tax rate results in a considerable fall (about 25 percent) in the percentage of their income paid in taxes by the residents of the former district A, and a comparable rise for the inhabitants of what was district B, with the rich households there being hardest hit, because they now have a much larger poor population to "subsidize." The few poorer households in B do lose slightly, but these are small in number; overall there appears to be much more equity in the allocation of taxation by what is basically a regressive rather than a progressive taxation system.

This simple example has contrasted two districts in their provision of one service; metropolitan areas comprise many districts providing a range of services. In general, it is the central cities, which invariably have the largest populations within their metropolitan areas, that, for a variety of reasons, have to provide both the greatest range and volume of services. Traditionally, as the hubs of the metropoli, they have provided services, such as art galleries, museums, and zoos, which are rare in the suburbs (few small suburban municipalities have their own zoos), and which are used by more people than the residents of the cities alone. Such services usually do not have their full costs covered by user charges, so that their enjoyment by outsiders has to be subsidized by the central city taxpayers. In addition, the central-city authorities must serve the business center, which requires more street cleaning and trash collection than do residential areas, as well as more police and fire service personnel and equipment. The city is also responsible for the roads which lead into its hub. These roads are used by outsiders, although their activities in the city contribute to its prosperity and to its taxable potential.

Perhaps more important for the costs of city services is the concentration in cities of the poor—for whom a wider range of services and facilities, and a greater density of some, such as policing, must be provided. The demands of the more affluent suburbs are less. Thus the poor in the cities must finance the relief of their own poverty, while their affluent neighbors in suburbia can escape the responsibility of any contribution to the poor, although property taxes could be used to assist the urban poor. As pointed out in Chapter 8, suburban residents can to some extent take a free ride on the backs of their poorer brethren who do not have the choice of moving to the pleasanter environments on the urban edge.

The figures presented in Table 9.2 are hypothetical but are not unrepresentative of the differences between districts in metropolitan areas. In Detroit, for example, the twenty-five suburban school districts raise on average $500 more per pupil in property tax revenues than does the district for the City of Detroit, where one-third of the public schools were built during the presidency of U.S. Grant in the 1870s. And in New Jersey, one school district had an assessed property value of $5.5 million per pupil, whereas the figure for a neighboring district was only $33,000 per pupil. Given the benefits of such exclusionary policies for the rich, there is little wonder that segregation between municipalities is increasing. For metropolitan Philadelphia, coefficients were calculated to show the percentages of the population with various characteristics that would have to be moved to another municipality if all groups were to be represented in the same proportions in each constituent municipality. These indices of segregation (Table 9.3) for income groups, for the value of owner-occupied dwellings and for dwelling rentals, all indicate increased segregation over the twenty-year period from 1950 to 1970; the rich, it would seem, are escaping even more from the need to "subsidize" the poor through the property tax, and

Table 9.3
INTER-MUNICIPALITY SEGREGATION IN PHILADELPHIA

	Index of Segregation		
	1950	1960	1970
Income Groups (Families)			
Lowest Eighth	8.6	21.6	24.2
Highest Eighth	23.5	35.5	39.7
Value of Owner-Occupier Homes			
Lowest Sixth	32.2	37.9	50.4
Highest Sixth	64.6	65.2	65.7
Monthly Rentals for Homes			
Lowest Sixth	20.7		21.3
Highest Sixth	20.2		39.3

Source: O. P. Williams and K. Eklund, Segregation in a Fragmented Context: 1950–1970. In K. R. Cox (ed.) *Urbanization and Conflict in Market Societies.* Chicago: Maaroufa Press, 1978, various tables.

the latter are being left to suffer alone. (The derivation of the indices is described in Chapter 1.)

A final example of the effect of balkanization on the provision of education services, a major item of expenditure of local government and the most crucial for many families, is given in Table 9.4 (This table was used as evidence in a court case brought in Texas to prove discrimination against children in school placement under the Fourteenth Amendment. The Texas court accepted the argument, but it was later overruled by the Supreme Court.) As the first column shows, districts in Texas in the early 1970s differed by a ratio of more than 10:1 in the average value of property per pupil. In the more affluent districts, a tax yield of $585 could be raised at a tax rate of only 31 cents per dollar, but in the least affluent a tax rate which was more than twice as high produced a yield of only $60 per pupil.

Such disparities do not only arise within metropolitan areas, of course. Between-area disparities are also large, reflecting the position of a place in the urban system and its general level of prosperity, and there are major interstate variations in economic health. Incomes are on average much lower in the states of the South; for example, in Mississippi the median family income in 1969 was $6,068, compared with $11,808 in Connecticut. The governments of the wealthier states can raise more in income and other taxes to pay their contributions to the various social welfare programs than can those in the poorer states. (Parts of these payments are met by federal grants that are on a sliding scale, so that the higher the benefit the smaller the relative federal contribution.) As a result, the poor and unemployed of Mississippi may find it beneficial to move to richer states like New York, joining the cycle of poverty there, but receiving the higher social welfare benefits. There is little evidence, however, of migration just to receive greater social welfare payments.

The balkanization of local governments, and its concomitant spatial separation of rich from poor and black from white, also influences the political muscle of the various groups. In general, the richer and the better-educated are much more able to use the governmental and legal systems for their own ends than are the poor. Furthermore, it is much easier to organize and to create a consensus of opinion in a small group than in a large one. Thus small groups are politically more cohesive and stronger. The rich in their small suburban municipalities are much better placed than the poor in the large central cities. The latter have been manipulated by political machines for several decades, producing greater benefits for a few politicians and for big businesses than for the poor residents of the slums and the ghettos. So while the middle class has been able—through use of the reform movement—to gain political control of suburbia and to orient government toward its own ends, the poor have suffered relative political impotence. Many development and redevelopment plans have been implemented in the central cities

Table 9.4
FISCAL DIFFERENTIALS BETWEEN TEXAS SCHOOL DISTRICTS

Property Value per Pupil per District ($)	Number of Districts	Tax Rate per $100 ($)	Tax Yield per Pupil ($)
100,000 or more	10	0.31	585
50,000–100,000	26	0.38	262
30,000–50,000	30	0.55	213
10,000–30,000	40	0.72	162
10,000 or less	4	0.70	60

Source: R. L. Lineberry and I. Sharkansky: *Urban Politics and Public Policy*. New York: Harper and Row, 1974, p. 233.

(including road construction) that have had major negative impacts on poor and black residents, but those residents have been unable to counter the proposals and protect their lives and livelihoods. There have been recent attempts to stimulate political consciousness. Participation in political activity assumes that the participants have three options open to them: exit, which involves them leaving the territory if its government does not conform with their desires; voice, by which they express their concerns and attempt to influence policy making; and loyalty, which involves acceptance of the final decision. But voice is not a very viable option if exit is not possible, and as most of the poor residents of central-city neighborhoods have no alternative to living there, their voices, unless very voluble and perhaps backed by other action, are unlikely to make much impact.

INTRAMETROPOLITAN POLITICAL CONFLICT

The great fragmentation of suburbia in most metropolitan areas, and its affluence relative to the central city that it surrounds, is the cause of much political conflict. The exclusive suburbs, for example, which zone only for low-density (thus high-income) single-family dwelling units are not only a source of envy for lower-income residents elsewhere but also a cost to others. If such suburbs refuse to construct public-housing projects and pay part of the costs of these out of local taxes, then the demands for such housing must be met elsewhere within the metropolitan area, usually in those jurisdictions with lower per capita property valuations. Thus a low-income resident of a central city can claim that he is in part being required to pay high property taxes because his city is required to meet a very large proportion of the costs of public housing. The rich, he can claim, are making the poor poorer.

In addition to the exclusive suburbs, many others are in competition with one another and with the central city for land uses that will contribute considerably to the local tax base and thus reduce the burden somewhat on the domestic property taxpayers. Thus many suburban municipalities where moderate-income residents live seek large shopping centers and industrial and office parks that will bring in tax revenue. They may offer a variety of incentives to obtain that revenue— subsidizing the developments from local income in the short term to obtain long-term benefits. In most cases, they will be careful to attract only those developments that will not create major negative externalities for residential areas; and the location and design of industrial, office, and shopping areas will be carefully planned.

Perhaps the greatest intrajurisdictional conflict for land uses at present is that between central city and suburbs. There has been a major erosion of the central-city tax base in recent years with the flight of jobs to suburbia and beyond and the decline of CBDs. This has created what has been termed a fiscal crisis for the central cities: demands on cities have been increasing but the tax base on which they can draw has been declining. The city authorities have worked hard to obtain federal funds and to attract large tax-base uses into the central areas. Regarding federal funding, some were quite successful in the late 1960s/early 1970s in obtaining program grants for urban renewal and other projects—some of which were used for gentrification projects, designed for residents with higher incomes than those replaced because of the potential benefits for the property tax base. In the later 1970s, the replacement of program grants (which were applied for) by more general revenue-sharing policies have resulted in a diminished flow to the central cities.

In seeking to revive inner areas—especially the downtown shopping and office districts—the central cities have been in direct conflict with suburban municipalities for new developments. To attract developers central cities have had to offer tax and other incentives, which means that—in the short run at least—the low-income, inner-city, domestic property taxpayer has had to subsidize development plans, including those for highly profitable, multinational companies. In many cases the central cities have lost, however, and developers and others have preferred the advantages of suburban environments. The central cities have, in general, been unable to reverse their declines and, as the pressures of their budgets increase, they have slid toward bankruptcy; federal and state governments have not been prepared to bail them out and stock market investors have not been interested in their bonds.

GOVERNING
METROPOLITAN AREAS

Two problems with regard to urban government have already been introduced: the almost permanent minority status of urban areas (as opposed first to rural and then to suburban interests) in the state and federal power structure; and the balkanization of local government in metropolitan areas, with its general consequence of poor central cities and affluent suburbs. Most of the discussion in this section focuses on the second of those problems, although the conclusions have implications for the representation problem as well.

Municipal balkanization involves a set of local governments that differ in the needs of their residents and in the resources at their disposal with which to serve those needs. Within most urban areas it is the central cities that have the greatest volume of needs and demands on their resources: they must try to break the cycle of poverty and address the worst environmental problems; they must provide services to be used by the population of the whole urban complex, plus its hinterland, such as some airports; and they are more likely to have populations with conflicting demands and views on how resources should be employed. In addition, relative to needs and the related fiscal demands, central cities have the lowest levels of resources, whether measured as property value per resident (which is the basis for the property tax) or as expenditure per resident (a reflection of income and the base for the sales tax). Most suburbs, on the other hand, have few concentrations of needs—the main exception is for educational services— and are well endowed with resources to provide the basic facilities and utilities demanded by their residents, allowing their governments to make small fiscal demands. In addition, most suburban municipalities are small and have socially homogeneous populations; as a result, they are less likely to be politically divided over the use of resources.

Not every suburban municipality conforms to the stereotype just presented. Some contain relatively low-status and low-income residents and have large demands on relatively small fiscal resources. Most of these are in the inner ring of suburbia, adjacent to the central city, and contain aging housing that has been passed down the filtering chain. Thus of the 17.7 million blacks living in metropolitan areas in 1974, 4.0 million (22.5 percent) lived in the suburbs. Most lived in only a few municipalities, however. Although this presentation stresses that the major aspect of the metropolitan fiscal problem is the central-city/suburban dichotomy, it is something of an oversimplification. There are some suburbs, most of them inner suburbs, which share many of the characteristics of the central city in terms of resources per resident, although the demands on them are usually not as great, since they do not have to meet the needs of a wider population. As inner suburbs age, and their deteriorating housing is passed down the economic and social ladders, so a clear tier of relatively deprived suburbs will be created, and a further division—inner city/inner suburb/outer suburb —will be needed for a full analysis.

A variety of solutions have been proposed that would remove the needs/resources imbalance between cities and suburbs. (These assume a political will to remove the imbalance which is not always present, especially when the needs are those of a minority with little political power.) Alternate sources of finance would remove the property tax burden on the relatively poor, for example. User charges to cover the whole cost of a service could be introduced, but these assume equal ability to pay; if the latter condition is not present, the poor pay relatively more and are denied access, sometimes to necessary services. Taxes on sales are also possible and are widely used (New York City raises about ten percent of its income in sales taxes); again, like user charges, they are income regressive and impose heavier burdens on the relatively poor. Redistribution of monies from other levels of government, especially monies obtained from the more progressive taxes on income, is increasing in importance, both as specific grants and as less restrictive contributions to municipal budgets through the general revenue-sharing program. As pointed out earlier, however, urban areas lack the political weight at federal and state levels to obtain large sums of such money; and the change from specific federal programs (such as urban renewal) for which cities made application to pro rata revenue sharing has not benefited inner cities.

METROPOLITAN ENVIRONMENT

One solution proposed many times is outlined in the hypothetical example of Table 9.2. Amalgamation of all municipalities and unincorporated areas within a metropolitan complex into a single jurisdiction would remove the balkanization that denies the affluence of suburbia to the central city. Local government reform, involving some process of amalgamation, federation, or consolidation, is a commonly suggested solution to the problem of fiscal imbalance in the metropolitan area, therefore.

Very little in the way of metropolitan governmental reform has been achieved, however, because proposals must be approved by a majority of interested voters in most states before they can be implemented. (State legislatures could impose reform in many cases but have declined to do so, for obvious political reasons.) The referenda that have been held and the opinion polls that have canvassed public attitudes have nearly all indicated that no majority exists that supports such moves. This is not surprising, for the proposed reforms would impinge on the special interests of many population groups. Very many local government referenda, and not only those involving possible municipal government reform, are defeated, and this has led to the development of a theory of interest-related voting behavior. In general, there is a U-shaped relationship between income and support for proposals with fiscal implications. Low-income residents tend to be in favor, since the benefits to them are likely to exceed their costs in higher tax bills; their voting is termed private-regarding. Higher-income groups will often also vote in favor, especially if they perceive the issue as a "worthy cause," even though success would probably cost them more in greater taxes than the returns they are likely to get from the greater expenditure; this is termed public-regarding voting. But unless the extra expenditure will bring clearly desirable benefits to them (notably in education) the middle-income groups will usually vote against such proposals, in a self-protecting, private-regarding way. Success for any proposal, therefore, depends on the attitude of the high- income group and the relative turnout rates of different voter groups.

Voting on proposals for metropolitan government reform has largely followed the private-regarding line, with the result that almost all have been defeated. The main concentration of opposition votes has almost always been in the suburbs, and it has been difficult to achieve large turnouts in the central cities. An important reason for the defeat of reform is that the proposals offer long-term benefits, whereas most voters, especially those of the middle-income brackets, are much more concerned with the immediate problems of balancing their household budgets. The majority of suburban residents have expressed general satisfaction with the services that they receive from their government, according to many opinion polls and academic surveys, and see no need for a change that will require them to subsidize the residents of other areas, even if the proponents of the proposal argue that reform will bring economies of scale and more efficient government operation. Among suburban residents, reform does not have grassroots support. (This could account for the lack of state government imposition of local government reform, which could be achieved, probably through constitutional amendments. State governments, as described above, are increasingly suburban-dominated.)

Increasingly, local government reform is being opposed in the central cities as well. Blacks now form a majority of voters in many of these and in recent years have won political control there, particularly through the office of mayor. By 1975, 150 cities had black mayors (still a very small proportion of the total), including twenty-six of the largest, such as Detroit, Gary, Los Angeles, and Washington, D.C. The power that this brings to the black population may be slight, because of the constraints on independent action by the mayor and the fiscal problems of many of those cities. Nevertheless, electoral success in mayoral contests brings status to the black population and some feeling of overcoming their political impotence. Local government reform would undoubtedly destroy these gains, small though they are, for in metropolitan areas as a whole blacks would almost always be in a minority. If assimilation were their goal, this would be irrelevant, although political power might help them to advance their cause. But if integration is the aim, and the black population wishes to maintain control over various aspects of its livelihood—such as its schools—then municipal balkanization has its attractions for them too. A hierarchical system of metropolitan government could overcome this problem, with separate districts within the area responsible for certain functions and the metropolitan authority for others. Experience elsewhere, as in Greater London, has not been very favorable, however, especially if the districts and the metropolitan authority are controlled by different political interests. Amalgamation would reverse the conflict between their interests and could well produce permanently dissatisfied minorities.

Some referenda proposing consolidation plans have been passed, as in Nashville, Tennessee. Perhaps the most widely known involves Dade County, Florida, which encompasses the Miami Metropolitan Area. The plan, which involves a two-tier government with some services provided by the original municipalities and others by a metropolitan government, was established in 1957 after a referendum that passed by 1,784 votes out of 82,064 cast (with a turnout of only 26 percent). Initially only a few services were allocated to the new government, but others have since been handed over, and police, fire, health, hospital, highway and welfare services are now handled at the metropolitan level, bringing important economies of scale; sanitation, sewers, and parks remain under the control of the municipalities.

Reform in Dade County seems to have resulted in generally higher levels of government spending, compared to similar areas where there have been no reforms. This suggests that the economies of scale have not been achieved, but in addition there has been an improvement of services relative to the places where there has been no reform. With regard to the problem of fiscal imbalance, analyses have shown that the largest (Miami) and the poorest of the constituent municipalities have gained most in benefits, whereas costs have been disproportionately large in the richest districts (notably Coral Gables). Consolidation has redistributed some money from rich to poor, therefore, but only slightly; Miami gets only 2.61 percentage points more of the expenditure than it provides of the tax revenue, whereas Coral Gables receives only 0.98 percentage points less than it contributes. The reform has hardly solved the rich/poor dichotomy.

Fiscal disparities may be reduced somewhat by consolidation, but major redistribution of resources is unlikely while those with most to lose have most of the political power and revenue-raising remains largely dependent on the income-regressive property tax. Furthermore, consolidation plans rarely remove, or even propose removal of, the power of individual municipalities to control the pattern of land use within their jurisdictions through zoning regulations. This power allows the basic features of the cycle of poverty and the associated fiscal imbalance to be maintained.

ZONING AND ITS CHALLENGES

As already indicated, the land-use planning powers have been used by many suburban municipalities to produce what is widely known as either discriminatory or exclusionary zoning. In a few cases, it has been used to protect and sanitize industrial and agricultural interests, but its predominant employment has been in the creation of low-density suburban strongholds for the affluent. Some suburbs, mainly the larger and more heterogeneous socially, have not sought such exclusiveness, and in a few others there has emerged what has been termed antisnob zoning, which allows a variety of types of development within a jurisdiction; suburbs with relatively liberal populations, such as Princeton, New Jersey, fall into this category. A number of others allow a small amount of lower-value residential development to provide housing for those who work in local services, such as policemen, firemen and teachers. In general, however, suburbs have used their zoning powers to exclude what their residents perceive as undesirable elements.

Since it is enacted by democratically elected governments, exclusionary zoning is difficult to counter by those who wish to see American suburbs have a more heterogeneous character. The most likely means to greater heterogeneity has been the use of the appeal procedure through the courts (that is; the voice option), claiming that exclusionary zoning is unlawful discrimination under the Fourteenth Amendment. The opinion is divided, but the general consensus is that the court action will fail to produce any real "opening up" of the suburbs. Through the 1960s the National Association for the Advancement of Colored People, the American Civil Liberties Union, and similar organizations attempted to get exclusionary zoning prohibited so that more low-income and black households might move to the pleasanter environments of the suburbs. They were thwarted by the courts. In the late 1960s they were joined by an organization known as Suburban Action Institute, which began a large-scale attack on exclusionary zoning, filing many lawsuits claiming discrimination and proposing low-cost suburban developments in parts of the megalopolis. Most of these lawsuits failed, however, and the institute's planning applications were rejected by the relevant local zoning boards. There was clearly little grassroots support to open up the suburbs.

As zoning plans are enacted under state laws, it is the state courts which hear the cases alleging discrimination, and not the United States Supreme Court, which has refused to rule on the issue since 1926, although it has heard certain cases relating to wider issues, such as one (upheld by the Court) from Long Island in which the zoning plan forbade more than two unmarried adults to live in the same house in a suburb (thereby excluding sharing arrangements among students from a nearby university). There are interstate variations in interpretations, as indicated by a series of judgments in the mid-1970s. In 1975, for example, the New Jersey Supreme Court ruled that the plan produced by the Mt. Laurel Township, which banned all apartments plus all single-family homes on lots of less than a quarter of an acre, was discriminatory. The ruling stated that governments in developing municipalities throughout the state should zone for an "appropriate variety in housing." The Supreme Court in Washington refused to hear an appeal, and thus a clear change in municipal planning is required. Nevertheless, the impact of such a ruling could be slight. The land zoned for apartments, for example, might be next to the municipal rubbish heap, and thus unattractive to developers; also, the absence of federal finance for low-cost housing in suburbs might mean that no private developers would undertake such projects, which offer relatively low financial returns. (Municipal governments can only receive certain federal funds if they follow guidelines set by the Department of Housing and Urban Development with regard, for example, to zoning for low-income housing. They can, of course, opt to remain independent, preferring to receive no federal funds rather than be constrained by federal rules.) The ruling may prove to be a hollow victory for the anti-exclusionary zoning lobby.

Some cases have provided not even a hollow victory. In the San Francisco suburb of Petaluma a plan was produced that aimed to restrict the amount of further residential development, thereby protecting the municipality's small-town character. Litigants claimed that this plan denied individuals the right to choose where they lived and thus was discriminatory: their view was upheld by the local court, but this ruling was reversed by the state appellate court. Municipalities in California, it seems, can determine both the character or number of people who live there. They can also limit the volume of residential development. Paradoxically, the Petaluma plan has in part been self-defeating. Before the introduction of the slow-growth ordinance, it was a relatively low-income town. Since then, land and property values have escalated rapidly, denying access to the lower- and middle-income households who would have moved there. Growth control on the Petaluma model is now practiced in many municipalities.

A final case that is of relevance here involved the U.S. Supreme Court, since it concerned the activities of a federal department— Housing and Urban Development. Litigants from Chicago claimed that HUD funds for building public housing were all being channeled to the central city and thus were being used to maintain racial segregation. They claimed that HUD should spread its funds across the whole metropolitan area, giving low-income blacks the chance to live in the suburbs; the Court upheld this view. But courts have also upheld the right of Illinois municipalities to zone against public housing.

GOVERNMENT REFORM AND INTERMETROPOLITAN DIFFERENCES

The problem of metropolitan government reform has been investigated only insofar as it relates to individual metropolitan areas. But different areas have varying needs and resources with which to meet those needs and frequently differ in their political will to try and match resources to needs. Metropolitan local government reform could produce some intrametropolitan equalization of real incomes, as in Dade County, but would have little impact on intermetropolitan differences. Metropolitan areas are the dominant foci in most states, and state governments determine welfare and other related policies—because of the constitutional provisions which prevent federal intervention in these areas. The amount of federal grant-in-aid money varies considerably from state to state and bears little relationship to the state's needs for such grants. Many states with the greatest needs, notably those in the deep South, make relatively little use of such federal programs as Aid for Families with Dependent Children, in part because they lack the resources with which to provide their matching share of the contributions and in part because there is no political imperative to provide generous welfare benefits. Most of the states which make low payments are dominated by one party in their legislatures: in the South the Democratic party; in parts of New England and the Midwest, the Republican Party. In the regions of one-party dominance, it is argued that politicians do not need to seek the votes of the poor by providing them with large benefits, which would mean higher taxes for the wealthier, more powerful classes. In general, therefore, the most generous welfare programs are in the states where the two parties are most competitive. In addition, state governments in the South are unwilling to make large social welfare payments to beneficiaries, the majority of whom are black, and their relatively weak bureaucracies present no major case for the extension of welfare plans (which would boost their own power).

A centralized, benevolent dictatorship or oligarchy that measured needs objectively and distributed resources equitably in accordance with its findings would seem to be the only answer to the problem of spatial variations in welfare programs by states. Like other proposals reviewed here, such a normative, goal-oriented solution would seem to be a utopian dream, since, among other difficulties, it is contrary to the American Constitution and its guarantee of states' rights. American society is imbued with traditions of individualism and privatism and with the use of sectional politics to further personal and group vested interests. Redistribution is not in the interests of most Americans, and programs, whether of opening up the suburbs, distributing welfare more equitably, or insisting on government for large rather than small areas, will be strongly resisted by the conservative coalitions which dominate most federal and state legislatures. Some battles may be lost, especially where the courts are involved (the evidence of the 1970s suggests that the Supreme Court is less liberal now than it was in the 1960s), but metropolitan politics in general is likely to favor the haves over the have nots, and to resort to ameliorative problem solving only when forced to by external powers or when it is perceived desirable by those holding power. Only when Congress and state legislatures insist will much change occur, but a suburban-dominated legislature is unlikely to impose governmental reform in the states. Certain federal funds do require specific action by local governments—for example, the setting-up of regional planning authorities and other special districts—but these do not affect the basic autonomy of suburban municipalities.

POLITICAL ACTION

To some people, the solution to many urban problems—notably those involving both the cycle of poverty and the separation of city from suburb—is political action. Governments only respond to pressure, it is claimed, so those who suffer from the current situation must exert this pressure. This can be done constitutionally or illegally.

Pressure has been applied constitutionally through the existing political system. The political system clearly has not been a very fruitful avenue—urban votes have long been devalued. The courts have been effective, and they have been used for several decades by organizations such as the NAACP and the ACLU, as well as by *ad hoc* groups and individuals. Important victories have been won—notably in the civil rights campaign—but overall little has been changed, in part because without follow-up congressional legislation the court rulings may prove to be ineffective, and in part because the rich as well as the poor have access to the courts, and the rich have more resources with which to argue their cases. Thus it has been established that referenda which result in discriminatory consequences (for example, the exclusion of low-income housing from a municipality) are not unconstitutional. And it is easier to mobilize the affluent, as in the turnout for California's well-publicized initiatives in recent years that have reduced taxes (especially for the rich) and therefore give state and local government less with which to finance welfare programs. In most local political action it is those with the most to lose—households with children and mortgages—who are most active in protecting their interests.

Legal action that has had the greatest impact in recent decades is nonviolent protest, of which the civil rights campaign has been both the largest and probably the most successful example. Illegal protest is best exemplified by the riots of the 1960s. Some commentators suggest that only the latter have major impact, but even their long-term effect is small. Concessions are made—as in the 1930s with the social security program—but once the pressure diminishes (and it is extremely difficult to maintain mass pressure for long) the benefits gained slowly are reduced, even if they are not removed.

Attempts have been made to involve more people politically. An example of this was the Model Cities program introduced in 1966. It was argued that many of the problems of the cycle of poverty could be removed by a concerted rather than a piecemeal approach to the entire range of poverty issues in a community and this concerted approach should involve community participation. (The term used was "maximum feasible participation.") Some minor successes have been reported, but the program has largely failed to achieve its stated objectives of enabling local residents to have a large say in solving the problems of their areas—outside the usual political channels. The program was supposed to provide for each selected community acceptable leadership, financial and technical assistance, and full information to allow proper local involvement in all stages of planning. The total sum of money provided was small, however, and in some cities there was considerable conflict with the established political system. The local bureaucracy proved to have staying power, and as Washington's interest and funds disappeared community involvement rapidly waned. The politically impotent were not helped out of their condition, and mild protest and a willingness to work constitutionally has not wrested power from the affluent.

10

THE URBAN ENVIRONMENT
AND PROBLEM URBAN AREAS

THE URBAN PROBLEMS discussed in Chapter 9 largely concerned the social divisions within society and their reflection in its intra-urban spatial organization. Thus the cycle of poverty reflects income inequalities, its concentration in the inner city reflects the operation of housing markets—assisted by the nature of local government—and the chances of altering some of these inequalities are impeded by the continuing fragmentation of government in metropolitan areas. Overall, the conclusions were pessimistic; the problems, it seems, cannot be eliminated from American society without major changes in society itself. But the conclusions are perhaps less gloomy for the two problems to be discussed here, which is not to claim any great sense of optimism.

THE URBAN ENVIRONMENT

All human activities have some impact on the environment in which they occur. Most of the impacts are of a short-term duration, and leave no lasting imprint, as with the carbon dioxide exhaled by the human body. But some human activities are major determinants of environmental changes, both directly and indirectly; it is the indirect consequences, often unforeseen, that are frequently the most burdensome and difficult to correct, as with the formation of the Dust Bowl in the Plains states during the 1930s.

Urban areas are major modifiers of the earth's environment. Their existence can influence the course of basic physical processes, such as the hydrological cycle. When rain falls onto nonurbanized land, most of the water does not pass directly into the streams and rivers, but filters slowly to them through the plants and the soil. As a result, there is often a time lag between precipitation and the rise in the water level of rivers as the rain enters them. The rate of infiltration through the soil acts as a regulator that evens out the flow, so that floods are often "prevented" by the slow process of water movement through the soil, and it is only when the soil is either saturated or frozen that the precipitation passes directly into the rivers and causes rapid rises in water level. Urbanization interferes with this process by, in effect, removing the soil and its filtering capacity and channeling all precipitation very rapidly into the river systems. This is particularly the case in high-density urban areas, where almost all the land surface is occupied by either buildings or sealed surfaces, such as roads. In these, runoff into the drains and then the rivers is very rapid, so that heavy rainfall is very soon reflected in river levels.

There are two main consequences of this urban modification of the hydrological cycle. First, the lack of a time lag and regulation of the flow of precipitation to rivers means that heavy rain, even if of only a short duration, is much more likely to cause flooding in urban than in rural areas. To counter this, urban governments must provide large storm-water drains to protect properties from extreme rainfall by draining the water away rapidly. Second, the rapidity with which water levels rise in urban areas increases the erosive effect of streams and rivers, creating greater hazards for the residents of the flood plains. As many urban areas are built on flood plains, these hydrological effects of environmental modifications increase the problems of urban life, at least for the occupants of the affected areas, and add to the costs of city services.

This brief example of the environmental impacts of urbanization illustrates just one way in which the towns and cities, and especially the larger cities, influence various aspects of life for their residents. Urban activities produce great volumes of waste products, often at very high densities, and these may pollute different components of the environment, with possible consequences for human health. They even modify the climate of the areas in which they are sited. The nature of these impacts and their influence on the quality of life for urban residents are the subject of this section.

URBAN CLIMATES

Urbanization affects the atmospheric system above it in a number of ways. One of its major effects is to produce what is widely known as the urban heat island. Over the whole year, a city center is on average about 1.0 °C warmer than the rural areas on its urban fringe, though the extent of the difference between the two is often greater, especially at night and under certain weather conditions.

The two main processes that result in the heat island effect reflect the replacement of vegetation by buildings and paved surfaces. The latter absorb much more heat during the daytime than does vegetation, and because they are drier (a result of the more rapid runoff of precipitation) there is less evaporation from them than from vegetation and soil in rural areas. During the daytime, and particularly in the summer months, the urban areas absorb heat; at night, this is radiated out, making urban areas warmer than the surrounding countryside, where there is much less radiation. In winter, buildings also radiate heat at night, but in this case the heat is more likely to come from heating systems operating within the buildings than from absorbed solar energy. The action of other variables assists in the maintenance of the heat island. Urban air pollution, for example (see below), absorbs some of the radiation back to the atmosphere from the earth's surface, forming a heat dome over the urban area, and the generally lower wind speeds over towns relative to those in the countryside inhibit the spatial diffusion of the heat island.

Urban areas also modify the atmospheric system by affecting the amount of moisture in the air. Despite their very high humidity levels in summer, many American cities are on average about seven percent less humid than their surrounding hinterlands, because of the lower evaporation rates in towns. Perhaps more importantly for many residents, towns and cities tend to be cloudier (5 to 10 percent more) than surrounding rural areas, because of greater numbers of condensation nuclei, greater water vapor content, and more air turbulence over urbanized land. As a result, Chicago, for example, gets 5 percent more precipitation than does its immediate hinterland, six percent more days with some rainfall, and 13 percent more days in summer with thunderstorms.

AIR POLLUTION

The clear-cut differences between town and country on several climatic parameters are not widely perceived by residents, but one urban interference with the atmosphere—air pollution—most definitely is. As relatively few homes in cities now burn either wood or coal for heat, there are only two main sources of urban air pollution: industrial emissions, including those from power stations, and the exhausts of vehicles. These produce three main types of pollutant. Particulates are small particles of liquid and gaseous substances, such as ash from coal burning and other industrial processes and fumes from automobile exhausts, which include particles of lead; some of these pollutants, such as asbestos, are harmful and cause diseases, whereas others act only as irritants unless combined with other pollutants, when they can become noxious. Nitrates are gases that result from combustion, both of liquid and solid fuels; they cause irritation to eyes and nose, restrict plant growth, and act as condensation nuclei for photochemical smog. Sulfates are gases that result from burning, especially coal, that irritate the respiratory tract and can cause breathing ailments, damage most plants, reduce visibility in humid atmospheric conditions, and attack stone and most metals, corroding steel at least twice as rapidly as would occur in rural areas.

Air pollution results from the concentration of industrial processes in urban areas, the high population densities that generate concentrations of fuel consumption, and the use of automobiles and trucks, which produce dense concentrations of exhaust fumes. Thus pollution levels in American cities tend to increase with urban size, with average density of land use and population, and with the amount of gasoline consumed. There are also major variations in the incidence of pollution within urban areas, with a pronounced tendency for them to be greatest in the city center, where land use is most intensive and traffic flows at their maximum, and around the major industrial areas. Most residents seek to avoid such polluted areas. Those who can afford to live farthest from the center and from the main industrial suburbs (particularly those with heavy industires) reap the greatest benefits, whereas those with least choice in the housing market (the inhabitants of the cycle of poverty discussed in the previous chapter) are usually assigned the least attractive areas. Thus a study showed that the mean particulate levels in different types of residential areas in Kansas City were:

Predominantly owner/ occupier	63.9	Predominantly renter	78.0
Predominantly white	64.3	Predominantly nonwhite	83.3

These figures indicate that inner-city, nonwhite renters suffered most from pollution. They suffered not only the irritating, impaired environment but also the ill health it causes (research has shown strong positive relationships between pollution levels and morbidity and mortality rates), the deterioration of property, and the costs of keeping clean.

Air pollution is greater in some places than others, irrespective of differences in size, density, and gasoline consumption. Maximum annual average amounts of particulate matter in the air occur in heavy industrial cities such as Birmingham, Alabama, Gary, Indiana, and Youngstown, Pennsylvania. Other places also have high annual averages, such as Los Angeles, which is notorious for its smog. The sources of pollution in such places are the same as elsewhere; the greater intensity of pollution relative to otherwise comparable places reflects differences in local climate, such as the ponding of stagnant air over Los Angeles's heat island.

WATER POLLUTION

Cities produce a great volume of water pollution too, with major consequences for local river, lake, and marine ecosystems. It has been estimated recently that the average American urban resident consumes 150 gallons of water daily, which is converted into 120 gallons of sewage, almost all of which is dumped into local hydrological systems, some in an untreated form.

Most of the sewage produced in urban areas comes from industrial sources. Some of it is in solid form and may, in combination with water, produce a toxic substance. Other solids use up the oxygen resources in the water in which they are dumped, retarding its "disinfection" and encouraging longer life for disease-bearing and disease-causing organisms; they may well destroy plant and animal life. Some of the organic material in the sewage may be biodegradable, in which case it too uses up oxygen resources in the water, leading to the death of the plant and animal life that is dependent on that oxygen; nonbiodegradable organic matter taints the water, altering its color, odor, and taste. Domestic waste water and the output from some industries, such as milk processing, sometimes carry infectious bacteria, which will taint the water and make its reuse dangerous; toxic agents from industries, such as metals, acids, and radioactive material, have the same effect. Nutrients in waste water stimulate the growth of weeds and algae, which use up all the available oxygen and starve the other plant and animal life, leading to the eutrophication, or "death," of the water body. Heat, as from power stations, also reduces the oxygen content and stimulates eutrophication.

All these pollutants enter the water system of American towns and cities in large volumes. (Other pollutants, such as fertilizers applied to farmland, enter rural waters, often with the same general effect on water quality.) Data on water pollution are neither as widely available nor as detailed as those on air pollution, but those that can be used suggest that it is the larger and more densely industrialized areas that produce the greatest damage to their local water resources. This damage is not only aesthetic. It can have major impacts on the lives of city residents, either those in the place where the pollution occurs, who use the water for a variety of purposes, including drinking and recreation, or those downstream from the pollution source, who rely on tainted imported water, which they must pay large sums to cleanse. The relationships between polluted water supplies and human illness have been well known for more than a century; many epidemics of such diseases as typhoid and cholera have been associated with tainted water, and the declining incidence of these diseases in urban America during recent decades has been closely associated with the adoption of cleansing procedures for supplies of drinking water, such as filtering and chlorination.

SOLID WASTES

By no means are all the waste products of an advanced technological society disposed of through the sewerage system into water bodies; American urbanites also produce large volumes of solid waste matter every day. The total production of solid wastes in the country in 1967 was estimated at 3.7 billion tons, of which domestic users produced 128 million (about four pounds per day per person). Urban and industrial uses, including domestic, produced about 366 million tons in all (almost 10 percent of the total). The industrial wastes are dominated by scrap metal, paper and paper products, rags, and ash; domestic waste includes more than 30 million tons of paper annually, 100 million tires, 30 billion bottles, 60 billion cans, and several million discarded automobiles.

As with air and water pollution, the greatest volume of solid waste per capita is produced in the larger and the more industrial cities. All of it has to be disposed of, otherwise it can have very harmful consequences for human health. Many wastes produced in cities, and especially human fecal material, encourage the breeding of flies that can spread such diseases as typhoid, dysentery, and salmonella; direct contact between such wastes and drinking water can lead to cholera, poliomyelitis, hepatitis, and other diseases, as can contact with animals that consume the wastes and whose produce is eaten or drunk by humans. Other wastes can taint water that is used in the preparation of foodstuffs, and refuse dumps are the breeding grounds for rats and other rodents that may transmit diseases to humans.

The problems that can arise from solid wastes depend not only on their volume but also on the efficiency of their removal. Dumping of industrial wastes quite frequently occurs on open ground and may taint waters and encourage rodent breeding, with consequences for the populations of nearby residential areas. They are likely to be the relatively poor, who cannot afford housing in the pleasanter environments. Inadequate trash removal from streets and backyards will encourage the breeding of flies and the spread of disease; again, this is most likely to occur in the poorer parts of urban areas, where, as suggested in the previous section on metropolitan government, the provision of basic facilities and utilities is often both insufficient and inefficient.

NOISE

This final type of pollution is very much a consequence of the twin processes of industrialization and urbanization. Noise is particularly irritating when it is loud, frequent, and occurs at certain times. Most human activities in a technological society produce noise: dishwashers, refrigerators, food mixers, and air conditioners contribute to indoor noise, for example, as do lawn mowers outside. Above the ambient level, however, two sources produce noise pollution: machines in factories and offices and transport vehicles. Of these two, machinery noise is usually of more localized intensity, although it is often of greater magnitude and more likely to cause harm to sufferers; transport media provide most of the general, outdoor noise pollution.

Of the transport media, the automobile affects the greatest number of urban dwellers. Its pollution varies considerably in spatial and temporal frequency and intensity. Along a major urban freeway, which is heavily trafficked all day and for much of the night, the continual roar of fast-moving vehicles, particularly heavy vehicles, is a major source of noise for a belt of properties parallel to the road. Heavily trafficked city streets, especially those near the city center to which much traffic gravitates, are also very noisy, though on these streets the main sources of noise are associated with starting and stopping, accelerating and decelerating, rather than with continuous fast movement. In suburban areas, on the other hand, away from the major roads the streets are lightly trafficked, and noise is generally of low intensity and intermittent frequency. The main noise impact, therefore, is in inner areas and along major traffic arteries.

Railroads have the same general effect as freeways and roads, except that they are spatially much more restricted and, apart from loading yards, not in continuous use. It is the other major form of transport, the airplane, that is by far the noisiest, and spreads its influence over the widest area, particularly when it is either landing or taking off, activities that are extremely common over parts of most urban areas. Thus the main sufferers from this form of pollution are residents of areas around airports and beneath the flight paths to and from the runways; the noise is not continuous, but can almost seem so in areas adjacent to heavily used airports, such as O'Hare in Chicago and Kennedy in New York.

Noise can lead to hearing impairment, especially when it is of very high frequency and intensity, but its major impact is probably on mental rather than on physical health, and it can generally depress the quality of life where it occurs. Research has shown, for example, that noise can reduce an individual's ability to perform certain tasks, especially those requiring concentration, as well as making communication difficult and sleep sometimes impossible. As a result, properties that are heavily polluted by noise are not very attractive and again are most likely to be those that the poor and underprivileged are constrained to occupy.

TRAFFIC AND ITS PROBLEMS

Traffic causes pollution through its exhausts and noise; it also brings other problems to the urban environment. The growth of the American metropolitan area, characterized by high-density concentrations of commercial and industrial activities—particularly in the traditional city center and its surrounding zone of transition—and low-density residential sprawl, has been based for the last half-century on high levels of personal mobility and the ability to move large volumes of goods from place to place quickly and cheaply. The automobile and the truck have been the main instruments of this city form, replacing modes of transport restricted to fixed routes and thereby adding immense flexibility to the selection of locations for activities and the choice of routes for movement.

Consequences of this type of urban development have been the centripetal force that draws traffic into certain areas of the city at certain times and the centrifugal force that disperses it at others. The journey to work is the prime example of these forces in operation, for commuting trips are very concentrated temporally and, despite the deconcentration discussed in earlier chapters, strongly focused on certain parts of the city. In the morning, most trips occur between 7:30 and 9:00, and in the evening between 4:30 and 6:00. At these hours, both the public transit systems and the roads are heavily congested; outside them, usage is sporadic. In the public transit systems, much of the rolling stock must lie idle for part of the day, depreciating when not in use, while staff are underemployed. On the roads serving the city center, there are many traffic jams and accidents during the peak periods, causing much driver frustration. Very expensive freeway systems have been constructed to cope with this major surge of traffic, involving heavy investment, which is underutilized for much of the time. Traffic is always heavy in large urban areas, of course, as people move about on business and social trips and as goods are moved from place to place, but the volume does not require the massive investment in facilities to carry the commuting traffic generated in a few hours.

The traffic-generating potentials of different land uses have been intensively studied in recent years, to provide bases for predicting future flow patterns within metropolitan areas. Such predictions have indicated the likelihood of greater congestion, unless deconcentration occurs, and policies have been initiated both to provide facilities to cope with traffic growth and to promote a new, less centralized land-use pattern. Each assumes widespread use of the automobile, not only for commuting but also for trips to suburban shopping and entertainment centers, for example. Those without access to automobiles suffer, therefore, as rundown and infrequently scheduled public transit facilities, combined with changing land-use patterns, reduce the accessibility of facilities and opportunities for jobs. The closure of many inner-city stores, for example, means that poor households, who have no way to get to the big suburban supermarkets, have fewer, and generally more expensive, shops to choose from.

At present, the increased concern about possible energy shortages and the price of gasoline is likely to hit those least able to afford long trips. And yet, the bigger the city, the longer the average commuting journey. (Cities with more than 1 million inhabitants have average daily commuting trips of over six miles, taking nearly twenty minutes for auto drivers, compared with three miles and seven minutes in cities with less than 100,000 residents.) As with so many other aspects of life in metropolitan areas, this suggests that the bigger the place, the more expensive it is to live in, and that this greater expense is likely to increase in the future.

ENVIRONMENT AND PEOPLE

Perhaps the most important impact of environmental problems is on human health and well-being. There is much evidence, for example, of the injuries to health caused by breathing the lead-filled exhaust fumes from automobiles and by drinking tainted water. Does this mean that city residents in general have poorer health and lower life expectancies? The main predictors of death rates in cities are the age and the race structure of their populations. For example, the higher the percentage of the population over age 65, the higher the mortality rate is likely to be. There is a similar positive correlation between the death rate and the percentage of nonwhites in the population, a correlation that does not imply that nonwhites are intrinsically less healthy but that they are more likely to suffer the privations of the cycle of poverty. If these effects are held constant, by standardizing for age and race, then one finds considerable correlations between pollution indices and mortality rates, both for different age groups and for various diseases (such as breast, lung, and stomach cancer, diseases of the heart, and birth defects). These higher mortality rates, which particularly affect the populations of the older, denser areas of the city where diets are poor and public health facilities insufficient, imply similar relationships between pollution and morbidity. The polluted cities, and especially their most polluted areas, are relatively unhealthy places in which to live.

An indirect indicator of the impact of pollution of various kinds on human well-being is the pattern of property values. In a capitalist housing market, the property values in a district reflect its relative desirability as a residential area. If pollution creates ill effects, or is perceived to do so, then property values should be relatively depreciated in the highly polluted areas, compared with similar districts with lower pollution levels. Recent studies of Chicago in the late 1960s confirm this view. The average value of land in census tracts fell by about $168 per plot for every increase of one microgram per cubic meter in the sulfur dioxide concentration, and by $110 for every similar increase in the concentration of particulates. For houses, the corresponding declines were $34 and $25. Noise pollution has similar effects, but water pollution levels do not show as much spatial variability within a metropolitan area, and so do not have the same influence. Depressed property values mean that an area is not considered desirable and that those with money to invest in land and houses wish to place it elsewhere; the fact that the geography of values in the city follows the geography of pollution—negatively—indicates that the relatively poor, who do not have much to spend on housing, are restricted to living in the least desirable physical environments.

The evidence presented throughout this section illustrates the contention that there are aspects of big cities that make them unpleasant places in which to live. They are noisy and unhealthy, often foggy, and have high crime rates—features that make large cities less nice than smaller places, and also some parts of a metropolitan area (notably its suburbs) nicer than others (the inner city). In addition, people have to spend more time and money moving about the larger places and have to pay higher taxes to facilitate such movement and to combat the other problems.

Overall, big cities are more expensive places to live in than their smaller counterparts. In 1973, for example, it was estimated that the average four-person family in urban America required an annual income of $11,446; in the metropolitan areas, $11,731 was needed, whereas in the smaller nonmetropolitan cities $10,182 was sufficient. Costs were highest in the largest metropolitan areas (with the exception of Hawaii, clearly a special case because of its location): in New York the required income was $13,179, and in Boston $13,576, whereas in Lancaster, Pennsylvania, it was only $11,197. Some of the differences reflect the climatic variations in the country—part of Austin's low annual income of $9,800 is due to relatively low heating costs for homes there—but the general relationship with size is clear.

One consequence of higher living costs in a place is likely to be a demand for higher wages there; in general, such demands seem to have been acceded to. Thus the basic wage for a female typist (class B) in 1968–1969 was $1.27 per hour, but for every tenfold increase in the size of the city in which she worked it rose by 15 cents. (Thus in a city of 100,000 residents she would earn $1.87, in one with 1 million residents, $2.02, and in a metropolis with 10 million, $2.17.) Similarly, for keypunch operators, the basic wage rate of $1.29 per hour increased by

20 cents for every tenfold increase in the city population, and for automotive mechanics a basic rate of $2.42 increased by 27 cents with a similar change in city size.

These wage differentials indicate that the larger the city, the higher the rate of remuneration. If the American average per capita income is set at 100, then for New York in 1967 it was 135, and for other metropolitan areas with populations exceeding 2 million it was 120; in southern metropolitan areas with less than 100,000 inhabitants it was only 83, and for all nonmetropolitan areas it was 77. (This relationship with size can be documented for the period since 1929; at that date, the figure for New York was 196 and for nonmetropolitan areas 57, so there has been quite a considerable equalization of incomes in the intervening period, an equalization that continues today.)

Some of these income differentials reflect the concentration of the more skilled and highly paid occupations in the larger places; estimates suggest that this factor was responsible for nine of the 35 percentage points that New York was above the national average in 1969. Of the other 26 percentage points, 9 were ascribed to higher living costs, and the remaining 18 were called compensatory payments, intended to compensate the recipients for having to live in a relatively unattractive environment. The larger the city, therefore, the less attractive a place it is to live in, and the higher the income that workers can demand as compensation for the experience of its environment.

TOWARD SOLUTIONS
TO URBAN ENVIRONMENTAL PROBLEMS

The concentration of economic and other activities in urban areas creates a number of environmental problems through the production of pollutants (to air—including noise—and to water), the generation of large volumes of waste material, and the growth of traffic problems. Increasingly, the financial and other burdens that these impose on urban dwellers are being perceived as intolerable, and solutions are being sought to the problems of the urban environment. Some of the proposals are merely ameliorative problem solving, but a number prescribe normative goals and propose methods for their attainment.

REMOVING POLLUTION

For many years the response to pollution problems has been to try and isolate the land uses that produce the major pollutants, through zoning plans that sanitize the "noxious" users. The externalities that these produce often spill over into adjacent areas, however, and so those with power and wealth have ensured that they avoid such costs, by locating their homes or factories relative to the pollutant sources, and vice versa, so that the costs fall on others (that is, the poor and the weak). Increasingly, this solution is proving unworkable, in part because some pollution affects everyone. One example of this is the reuse of water that has been polluted by an upriver source, and the powerlessness of the downriver people over their upstream neighbors leads to hypocritical decision making by those living upstream. The extent of the problems that this has caused has led to demands for much more stringent controls, particularly with the growth of the "ecoconsciousness" movement in the 1960s. Thus in recent years legislation has been introduced to ensure that polluters cannot avoid paying the costs of their activities.

The obvious solution to air pollution is to prevent its generation by imposing standards that require that the emission of pollutants be controlled and, if possible, eliminated. Such a normative, goal-oriented approach was adopted in the United States with the establishment of the Environmental Protection Agency in 1970, which published its national air quality standards in 1971. These standards are of two levels. One is designed to protect public health by ensuring that pollution levels are not so high that they endanger individual life chances and expectancies (these are known as the primary standards, one for each pollutant); the other level—the secondary standards—is set so as to protect public welfare, providing a pleasant environment in which to work. States were required by federal law to develop plans that would ensure that all pollution fell below the primary standards within three years, and to reach the secondary standards within "a reasonable time." The legislation, which included stringent standards for automobile exhaust emissions, was strengthened by a federal court ruling in 1972 that no plan could be approved which would allow a deterioration in air-quality standards, even if it remained below the norms set by the Clean Air Act Amendments.

Control of air pollution involves very large costs to the nation as a whole, as well as to particular individuals and firms. For industrialists, the controls mean that they must reduce the emissions from their factories, which usually involves the installation of costly equipment. Such costs will in most cases be passed on to the consumer, who pays for pollution control not only in the higher price of goods that he purchases (and so suffers a slight drop in standard of living as measured by total volume of consumption) but also in the higher taxes he pays to cover the costs of similar controls in the public sector and also the expenses of monitoring pollution levels, enforcing the codes, and running the Environmental Protection Agency. (The total expenditure of the agency—which deals with both water and solid waste pollution—was $1.14 billion in 1972, including $263 million spent on general operating costs and about $480 million on the air pollution program. The agency's budget was $7.43 billion in 1973, but only $4.63 billion the following year, and $4.92 billion in 1976; its employment increased from 7,133 in 1971 to 10,302 in 1974, and 11,694 in 1977.) These increased costs to the individual should be counterbalanced by smaller medical bills, less expenditure on cleansers and the like, and fewer earnings lost due to illness, as well as by the intangible benefits of a cleaner environment. The employer should benefit too, from less worker absenteeism and ill health, which leads to greater productivity. Calculations that indicate the relative costs and benefits are extremely difficult, of course, even excluding any evaluation of the intangibles that follow from greater environmental cleanliness. Hypothetical curves, such as those in Figure 10.1, suggest that it is impractical to attempt a complete cleansing, since the costs of control are very high and almost equal to those from the damage when there is no control at all. The "happy medium" strategy, which is the cheapest as a whole, suggests that there will always be some air pollution.

Water pollution has been dealt with in a similar way to air pollution with a series of legislative acts culminating in the Federal Water Pollution Control Amendment Act of 1972. Its provisions are overseen by the Environmental Protection Agency, which has set standards to ensure that all bodies of water within the country are cleansed by 1983 and the discharge of pollutants into waters is ended by 1985. The agency is also empowered to ensure that all emission of pollutants into American waters uses the best available control technology. Its major expenditure of funds has been for the construction of municipal waste water treatment works; grants for this were $787 million in 1972 alone.

The prohibition of water pollution means that the waste materials once deposited in rivers, lakes, and streams must be disposed of elsewhere in other forms. In most cases this involves their transformation into solid wastes, which can then be removed along with the many millions of tons of other such wastes produced annually. Today most solid wastes are collected, in most cases compacted, and then dumped at a prescribed location, usually operated by a municipality; over 75 percent of all solid wastes are dumped. Other techniques include incineration at very high temperatures (1,400 °C), which reduces the bulk by up to one-twentieth, although one-third is the norm. If sorting is possible, some waste can be recycled, whereas other parts can be made into compost and sold to agricultural interests. There is still much remaining to be disposed of, however, and the most popular procedure being advanced is known as sanitary infill. The day's refuse is compacted, deposited in trenches, and covered with a thick layer of soil, which allows the land to be reused, for agricultural purposes in most cases. There are no national standards for this disposal, but the Environmental Protection Agency does operate demonstration projects and gives grants for research on disposal methods and on the problems that dumping creates for groundwater use.

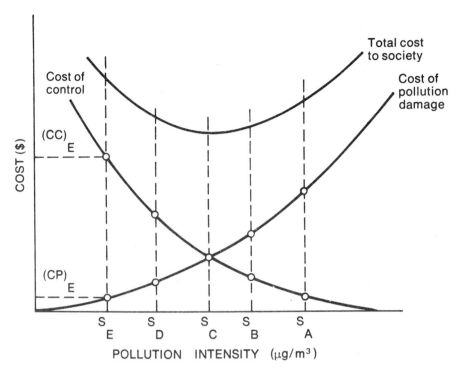

Figure 10.1.   The economics of air-pollution control. Source: Brian J. L. Berry and Frank E. Horton, *Urban Environmental Management: Planning for Pollution Control*, © 1974, p. 138. Reprinted by permission of Prentice-Hall, Inc., Englewood Cliffs, N.J.

The final pollutant discussed here is noise, and for this, like air and water pollution, acceptable standards have been set, initially by municipalities (usually against automobile noise only) and later by the Environmental Protection Agency. The standards for automobiles require them to be fitted with noise-reducing devices, which make the product slightly more expensive. Some authorities have attempted to introduce similar standards for aircraft, which has led, for example, to intense political campaigns regarding the desirability of the Anglo-French Concorde airliner landing at American airports. All noise cannot be removed from the environment, however, and where high levels are unavoidable, insulation standards can be set, if the pollutant sources cannot be eliminated by locational policies.

TRAFFIC PLANNING

With pollution problems, except for solid waste disposal, the response to the stimulus of needed solutions has been the development of normative, goal-oriented policies whose aims have been the creation of a minimal standard environment for all urban Americans. With traffic problems, on the other hand, the solutions proposed have largely fallen into the exploitative, trend-modifying category. The emergence of major traffic problems and the recognition of their rapid growth occurred in the 1950s. The result was a series of major transportation studies—of which that for Chicago was the stereotype—of large cities and metropolitan areas. The basic steps in these studies were as follows:

1. Identify the current land-use pattern.
2. From traffic surveys, establish the traffic generated by each type of land use and the pattern of trips joining different land uses, at different distances from one another.
3. Project future land-use patterns.
4. Estimate the likely total growth in traffic over the planning period, and allocate it to links between the land uses.
5. Plan a road system to cope with the projected volume of traffic between different parts of the urban area.

Highway planning is a state function, so it was possible to set up *ad hoc* authorities to handle this procedure over entire metropolitan areas; the land-use zoning decisions remained with municipalities, however, whose planning had to be integrated if a feasible land-use road system was to be devised.

The basic procedure was made more sophisticated in a variety of ways during the 1950s and 1960s and was the focus of much applied research in a variety of disciplines. Much of the work involved the development of dynamic modeling procedures that would allow the planning of future land-use and transport-link systems simultaneously, rather than taking one of the two as given and using it as the basis for predicting demands on the other. The work of I. S. Lowry and his *Model of Metropolis* (initially developed for Pittsburgh) was fundamental in this context and has stimulated many additional efforts aimed at producing the best land-use distribution to meet certain transport conditions. Whether much of the effort has assisted in the preparation and execution of metropolitan land-use plans is doubtful, however, because of the problems of municipal balkanization. Much road building appears in fact to be only ameliorative problem solving, and, as shown in the previous part of this chapter, much land-use planning is carried out on an *ad hoc* basis by independent municipalities, with little regard for the common good.

The ethos of many traffic plans in recent decades has been to make the best of ongoing trends, such as the move away from public transit toward the use of the private automobile, by attempting to forecast where problems—such as traffic bottlenecks—are likely to appear, and to provide solutions before the system entirely grinds to a halt. Little thought was given to alternative states. More recently, it has been realized that traffic problems are not really soluble within the overriding ethos; a Parkinson's Law of Traffic might well read that "traffic expands to fill the channels available," so that the problems will continually return. As a result, thought has turned to alternative traffic plans, in which the design involves attempting to influence the modal split—the relative use of different modes. A particular aim has been to move traffic from the use of private automobiles on expensive, publicly financed roads (the construction of which benefits some groups in society much more than others) to public transit systems, most of which are rail based. Some plans have been implemented, such as the Bay Area Rapid Transit (BART) system in California and the Washington Metro, but these seem to have had little success in stemming the growth of automobile traffic, let alone reducing its volume. In other places, construction of such systems has been defeated in referenda (as were parts of BART) by self-interested voters who are not prepared to support the immense financial gambles involved in such undertakings. (Los Angeles is an example of one such failure in the mid-1970s.) At the same time, of course, protest is mounting against the construction of more intraurban freeways, and some projects have been halted long after their commencement. In part, it seems, voters want to maintain the status quo in transport systems, as long as they can have free and easy access to where they wish to go. (For example, suburban voters will vote subsidies for local bus services.) Progress in system construction is to be halted, but more automobiles are to be built and driven (if only to maintain viability and jobs in the massive automobile industry).

One major problem facing the designers of new public transit systems is that these are not feasible in low-density suburban areas. If stations on a rail line are to be accessible to most commuters, they must be very close together, which makes for many stations and slow trains; if they are widely spaced, commuters will not use them, because of the problems of either catching buses to them or driving and parking. Furthermore, rapid transit, fixed-route systems are extremely expensive to build, and need to carry large numbers of passengers daily in order to be cost effective; they are only viable for carrying workers to the CBD, which remains by far the largest traffic generator. For the large volume of cross-city and intersuburban movements to the widely dispersed new industrial estates, the automobile is the only realistic mode of transport.

In very recent years, a potential energy crisis has been looming, particularly in gasoline availability. If this comes about, it could have a crucial impact on the quality of urban, and especially suburban, life in the 1980s and beyond. Already planners are proposing more compact urban forms as means of reducing energy consumption, by locating jobs and residences relative to each other so that commuting journeys are on average much shorter than at present, and public transit is a viable mode of transport. Figure 10.2 shows one such proposal, comprising a dominant node central to a multinodal metropolitan area, with a number of major suburban minor nodes, each containing a range of job opportunities for the local population. Adoption of such plans may well be necessary. If it is, there will be many problems. Municipal balkanization and independent planning will be impossible; a major trend in society, toward lower living densities, will have to be reversed; job and other opportunities will have to be restricted, raising problems of spatial allocation relative to the distribution of political and economic power within metropolitan areas; and much of the current fabric of suburbia will have to be refashioned, presumably by the infilling of much low-density housing developments with other residences.

PROBLEMS OF URBAN
GROWTH AND DECLINE

The analysis presented in Chapters 3, 4, and 5 suggested two salient features of the American urban system: (1) the continued growth of the major port and inland gateway cities; and (2) the relative economic instability of the smaller industrial cities (including mining towns) created during the era of industrial capitalism. Each of these features is related to a perceived problem within the urban scene.

 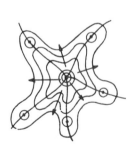 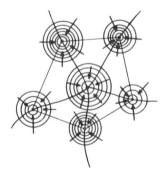

First stage
(pre-World War II):
single employment concentration
causes bidding for central locations
and higher densities toward the
center.

Second stage
(post-World War II to the present):
suburban migration of households
and industry reverses the pattern
and causes sprawl and secondary
suburban nuclei.

Third stage
(suggested future development):
energy conservation causes
more compact development
around the suburban nuclei,
with lower densities in the
areas between the centers.

Figure 10.2.   Stages in the development of a city, indicating a possible urban form compatible with large increases in the real cost of transport. Copyright Pion Limited, London. 1978. Reproduced from *Environment and Planning A*, 10, p. 102, by kind permission of the publishers.

For the second of the features—instability—the problem is economic decline. With the relative or absolute decline of a place's basic industries, a negative multiplier is set in motion; the smaller the number of such basic industries, the more intense the problem. As basic jobs disappear, so the amount of income circulating in the place is reduced, and unemployment is generated. When the whole economy is in recession, this negative multiplier is likely to operate everywhere— although with greater intensity in manufacturing and mining towns than in service centers. But when only certain sections of the economy are in decline, some places will suffer much more than others. Even in a period of general affluence there will be pockets of high unemployment and substantial poverty, reflecting the changing industrial structure of the economy.

Mining centers are the most likely victims of local recessions, either because of a decline in the demand for their raw materials or because the resource has been exhausted (at least relative to price and the exploitative technology). The Appalachian coalfields have provided the largest example of spatially concentrated decline with its related poverty. Industrial centers, both the heavy industrial towns and cities associated with mining and some of the traditional industrial settlements of New England, have suffered too. In 1970, for example, unemployment in the United States stood at 4.9 percent of the labor force; in the Appalachian region it was 5.4 percent, with a peak of 7.5 percent in those parts of Kentucky within the region: in 1978 the respective figures were 6.0, 6.4, and 8.6 percent (the last in Maryland). Related to this, whereas 13.7 percent of the United States population lived below the poverty level in 1969, 18.1 percent of the population of the Appalachian region did with a peak of 38.8 percent in the Appalachian portions of Kentucky: on average, family incomes in Appalachia were only 83 percent of the national median, with a low of 53 percent in Kentucky. (In 1976 the average per capita income in Appalachia was 85 percent of the national figure, with a low of 68 percent in Kentucky.)

The problems of unemployment and poverty in towns spill over into the surrounding areas. The towns do not provide jobs for local residents, who may remain in agricultural employment; the low purchasing power in the towns means low incomes for local farmers serving them, which makes for low profits, little investment, and inefficient operations. Just as growth generates growth, so decline generates decline. The result is a geography of poverty, incorporating the declining towns and their subsidiary regions.

The problems of growth are very different from those of decline. In many places they reflect large size and may comprise either or both of too rapid growth (which strains the provision of a public infrastructure) and simply being too big (producing the environmental problems discussed in the previous section).

At any particular time every economy is experiencing growth and decline. The simplest solution to the differentials created in various parts of the economy is to suggest that the market will operate to produce an equilibrium. Firms will move away from the unpleasant, expensive, big places to seek the cheap labor of the smaller, once-declining towns; to offset this, workers will move toward work (though this may mean they have to sell a house for a low price in a declining center and buy an inferior one in a growing center for much more). Many commentators are dubious about this "free-market solution," and suggest that the market may take so long to produce the spatial readjustment that many people will suffer for a long time. They argue for policies that will both limit growth with its negative effects in large places and encourage it in small and declining places.

ALTERNATIVE URBAN PATTERNS

Two of the dominant current trends in America are centralization and deconcentration, involving widespread low-density suburban sprawl around a relatively small number of large urban nodes. Is this the most efficient and/or the most equitable spatial structure for urban America in the next decades, regardless of whether an energy crisis comes to pass? Investigation of this question will focus largely on economic and related social issues, ignoring those with a cultural base relating to the American Dream. Nevertheless, the cultural base is implicit, since it is undoubtedly the existence of the widely held anti-urban American Dream that has both caused the current suburban sprawl to be an expression of the desire to escape from cities and engendered great interest, among academics and others, in determining the optimum size of cities (which many seem to say is small).

COSTS AND BENEFITS OF URBAN GROWTH

Cities exist because of the benefits which they bring to the capitalist system; spatial congregation facilitates production and profitmaking. Insofar as cities have enhanced labor productivity, through the external and internal economies of scale that they allow, then, as long as some of these benefits are passed onto the workers, the whole society benefits from urbanization. What is unknown is the distribution of benefits among different groups within society.

The benefits that accrue from urbanization are related to city size, since the larger the urban place the more external and internal economies of scale can be realized. What is not known with any certainty is whether the increase in benefits with size is a linear relationship. Almost certainly it is not, and experience with other forms of organization, such as firms whose location decisions produce cities, suggests that with very large size, relatively few extra benefits accrue from growth. Thus hypothetical average and marginal benefit curves have been deduced, as shown in Figure 10.3, to indicate this probable law of diminishing returns. It will be noted that the axes of the graphs in Figure 10.3 are not scaled; the current state of knowledge is such that the size of a city at which marginal benefits from growth commence cannot easily be assessed.

The graphs in Figure 10.3 show several separate aspects of the distribution of costs and benefits. Graph A shows the situation for individual firms. As cities grow, benefits increase, because of the internal and especially the external economies of scale. For the various reasons outlined in Chapter 4, big cities are more efficient places in which to locate. They are also more expensive, above a certain size, because of the congestion, pollution, and other costs discussed here. But it is generally assumed that, although above a certain size diseconomies may

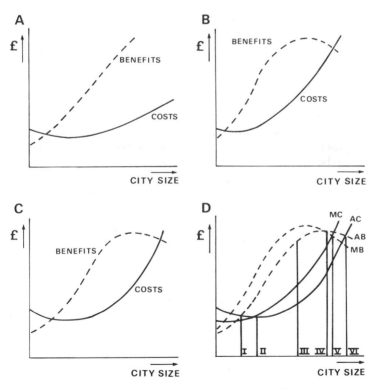

Figure 10.3. Hypothetical graphs suggesting the relationship between city size and monetary costs and benefits. (A) Curves for individual firms. (B) Marginal cost and benefit curves. (C) Average cost and benefit curves. (D) Critical city sizes.

increase more rapidly than economies, the bigger the place the better it is as a location.

Graph B turns attention from the individual firm to the city as a whole. It shows *marginal* cost and benefit curves. As each new firm enters a city—and the city grows—it contributes to the economies of scale, making the city a better place for all firms (because they have more choice of buyers and sellers, more market information, and so on). Above a certain size, however, the marginal benefits introduced by another new firm will begin to fall, as the place becomes saturated with firms and needs no more; diseconomies of scale set in. Each new firm also brings extra costs, in terms of pollution, congestion, and the like. Above a certain level, these marginal costs begin to rise rapidly, until they become greater than the marginal benefits: at that point, the place becomes an undesirable location for new firms.

Residents of a place (individuals or firms) do not have to pay the marginal costs of their arrival there, nor do they receive the marginal benefits. (In some municipalities new homes must pay an impact tax to cover the costs of utilities, and so forth.) The relevant curves for them are therefore *average* costs and benefits, which are shown in graph C of Figure 10.3. These have the same general shape as the marginal curves but, as comparison of graphs B and C shows, the average costs are farther to the right. This is because the marginal costs and benefits generated by the new firm are shared with all those already there: for example, a new firm may require extension of the city's street network, an extension that is paid for out of general revenues (that is, the property taxes all resident firms and individuals pay).

Finally, graph D in Figure 10.3 combines the four curves in graphs B and C. (It should be stressed that, although it is believed that their general shape is correct, these curves are based on best estimates only; there is no detailed information behind them.) Together they show that as city size increases from a small start, costs fall, because of the initial economies of scale. As growth continues, diseconomies set in, and costs rise. Benefits also rise, as firms benefit from the large market and their external links and as individuals benefit from the range of jobs and facilities available. Eventually, at some unknown size, costs exceed benefits. Six critical city sizes are identified on the graph:

I.   The minimum viable size, below which average costs exceed average benefits.
II. The cheapest size, at which average costs are lowest.
III. The most profitable size, at which the gap between average costs and average benefits is widest.
IV. The most productive size, at which marginal benefits are greatest.
V.   The "growth is self-defeating size," at which marginal costs exceed marginal benefits.

VI. The maximum viable size, at which average costs exceed average benefits so that any further growth will be to the absolute disadvantage of all.

Two questions are raised by these critical sizes in Figure 10.3D. The first is: "Where are current American metropolitan areas relative to the various thresholds?" To many people they are clearly to the left of V and VI, since most continue to grow; they are probably to the left of IV, and perhaps even III. If it is accepted that decision makers, especially the economic decision makers who operate firms, make rational choices with regard to profit levels, then if factories and offices in large cities are expanding, others are being established there, and some are being moved in from smaller places, then locations in large cities must produce greater benefits than costs. Cities have yet to reach the sizes at which growth produces more disadvantages than advantages.

The counterargument to the one just posed is based on the distribution of costs and benefits between individuals and groups within the urban area. Late capitalism is characterized by price-fixing mechanisms that are oligopolistic, if not monopolistic, in form, and firms can protect their profit levels by passing on all the extra costs to the consumers. They have too few competitors in smaller places producing cheaper, comparable goods that would force them to absorb some of the greater costs of the relatively inefficient big city. Thus those who make the locational decisions that lead to city growth can reap the benefits for themselves, while at the same time they can avoid paying their full share of the costs. The costs are passed on to the general population who, although they may receive compensation for having to live in such unattractive places, are "subsidizing" the capitalists' profits.

The second question to be asked of Figure 10.3 is: "What is the optimum size for American cities?" Is it II, where costs are at a minimum and the environment is the least spoiled? Is it III, where profits are greatest? Or should cities continue to grow as long as they produce more benefits than costs? Clearly this is a decision that should be made by society as a whole. If no overt decision is made, then the size of cities will be left to the forces of late capitalism, and if, as argued in the last paragraph, firms can reap a disproportionate share of the benefits of urbanization and avoid paying their share of its costs, then unlimited city growth, at least well beyond current sizes, is likely. (One other relevant factor here is that new or expanding firms are not entirely aware of their cost/benefit contribution, since the average costs they pay are considerably lower than the marginal costs which they induce.)

Some who write about city sizes and the issue of whether policy initiatives should be taken to slow, if not halt, the growth of American metropolitan areas, believe that the dominant focus of society should be to maximize economic growth. For them, the greater the returns the better, so that urban expansion should certainly not halt to the left of III, and probably should go on to VI. In other words, there is no case at present for controls on growth (although there may be for the direction and form of that growth). City growth, it is argued, is crucial because all the major innovations that generate further economic growth are produced in big cities, where the necessary linkages abound. (Unfortunately, this claim is hard to test, since we do not know whether economic growth would be less with a different pattern of city sizes.) On the other hand, for those who see other goals as important, if not paramount, growth should be halted before it proceeds beyond III, and policies are needed that will ensure much greater decentralization. Economic activity must be encouraged to spread itself over a wider range of urban sizes and firms must be induced to consider smaller places, either by paying a greater proportion of the average and marginal costs in the larger places, or by being subsidized for their activities in the smaller. This may be possible within the current settlement distribution, or it may require new towns, on the British and European model. There are some such communities, several associated with particular projects, such as Oak Ridge, Tennessee, but many, like Reston, Virginia, and Columbia, Maryland, are really satellite communities in the orbit of major urban areas (Washington, D.C., in these two examples) and not independent entities.

COST-BENEFIT ANALYSIS OF URBAN SIZE

The progress of the debate over urban sizes in large part depends on the direction of wider social decision making—on whether economic growth is seen as the *sine qua non* for American society in the next decades or whether the quality of life (reflecting lower average costs of urban living) is to become an important criterion for social and economic policy. In the conduct of these debates and discussions, however, it will be necessary in the future to pay closer attention to the definition of costs and benefits. Conventionally, if a new job is created, and the employee is paid a wage or salary, his remuneration contributes to an increase in the national income and what is widely accepted as the major index of an economy's health, the per capita gross national product (pcGNP). Expansion of the pcGNP is seen as a benefit to society. But what if part of the expansion includes pollution control? If the work done was necessitated by the growth of a city, is it a benefit to America, or does it indicate that America is paying the cost of a particular spatial form of growth? If the expansion in city X that led to the appointment of the pollution-control engineer had occurred in city Y instead, then it might not have been necessary to create the job. It can be argued, then, that some extra jobs created by city growth in fact reflect costs rather than benefits to society, if growth elsewhere would have made that job unnecessary and the employee and the resources devoted to him could have been diverted to more directly beneficial activity.

Many other hypothetical examples could be generated to illustrate the argument that not all growth is necessarily beneficial to society. If a certain city grows, and occupies more of its land area with roads and buildings, then, as suggested above, it may well have to construct a larger storm-water drain system to cope with the potentially more rapid runoff during heavy rainfall. Does construction of this system, with the jobs it will create in the building industry and in its suppliers, produce a benefit for society? If the growth had occurred elsewhere, or at a lower density, and the hydrological problem had not been created, then clearly a cost has been produced and not a benefit. (Against this, of course, it may be that the city is to the left of III in Figure 10.3, so that the other benefits from the growth still exceed the recomputed costs. In such a situation, the society has to decide whether it wishes to reduce relative or absolute costs and whether it can easily redirect labor from costly to beneficial activities.) In other words, planning of either or both urban sizes and forms (layouts, densities) may remove the necessity for certain expenditures.

Growth in the urban system creates more growth, through multiplier processes. In exactly the same way, urban expenditures cause more urban expenditures. For example, assume that a city grows and as a consequence experiences a higher crime rate. Though the resulting injuries to people and property are properly costs to society, in fact many of them, and consequential other costs, are recorded as benefits in the national pcGNP calculations. To combat the rising crime the city authorities need more police, and probably more expensive, sophisticated equipment; more prison space and officers; more judges and lawyers; more buildings for these; and more education to provide the necessary legal and other professionals. All these mean higher taxes. In the private sector, there will be higher insurance premiums for all, which cost more to collect; perhaps more investment in burglar alarms and other anticriminal devices; and so on. All these are costs of urban growth, results of allowing the city to expand, rather than directing growth elsewhere, where the consequential increase in the crime rate may have been less. In conventional accounting these would go down as benefits, because they are payments to employees for producing goods and services, and it would appear that higher crime rates are creating a healthier economy, and thus society. And the same occurs with the increased expenditure on medical services, including the training of personnel, to cope with the health problems created by pollution.

Thus, according to the argument that many costs to society are in fact registered as benefits, American cities may already be well to the right of point VI in Figure 10.3. It then follows that more realistic planning of urban forms should be based on an improved system of social accounts that allocates costs and benefits according to whether the expenditure improves the quality of life directly, and thus can be classified as welfare, or whether it has been incurred so as to rectify costs that would not have been necessary if other policies had been pursued, in which case it can be classified as "illfare." Analysis of current settlement patterns, and simulations of what future patterns might be, could allow assessment of the ratio of welfare to illfare expenditures resulting from different settlement patterns (both inter- and intra-urban), and policies could then be based on social decisions regarding the acceptable balance between the two. The result may be a decision to allow the continued growth and sprawl of the nation's major metropolitan areas, or it may be to initiate firmer policies aimed at dispersing economic activity and the associated nonbasic functions away from the big cities.

SETTLEMENT SIZE POLICIES

If American society believes that at least some of its cities are too large (that is, above III in Figure 10.3D) and that it would be more beneficial to redistribute population and economic activity, then two types of policy may be implemented. The first type involves negative policies, those which limit growth in particular places by, for example, banning any further expansion of employment there. The other type of policy involves positive actions, aimed at attracting jobs to smaller places, both to absorb unemployed labor and other resources that might be available there and to draw both jobs and labor from the larger places.

Of these two, the first has not been applied to any extent. There are some examples, including the slow-growth planning ordinances adopted by places like Petaluma, California, and Boulder, Colorado, but these are aimed at protecting specific communities from perceived negative externalities associated with growth and not necessarily with the costs of large size. In the 1930s the state of California attempted to turn back poor immigrants from the Dust Bowl states, but this policy was ruled unconstitutional. More recently, residency requirements to prevent recent immigrants from claiming social security benefits were also ruled unconstitutional. These last two examples illustrate one of the issues surrounding negative actions, including growth controls. They may well be ruled discriminatory under federal and/or state constitutions. Further, they indicate the problem of a decentralized system of government, in which considerable autonomy is given to state and local governments whose vitality, and even viability, are related to the taxable resources available to them. A government opting to limit growth may well be committing fiscal suicide, since it will have no additional resources on which to draw.

For a variety of reasons, therefore, negative policies have not been adopted. Positive ones have, in part because the federal government can participate in these—at least indirectly—whereas it could not become involved in negative policies, which would involve infringement on states' rights. Most of the policies have been aimed at stimulating declining and depressed areas—not individual places—where unemployment is high and poverty substantial. The first, and most famous, of such policies was the Tennessee Valley Authority, inaugurated under the New Deal in the 1930s as an integrated planning exercise combining control of erosion, regulation of floods and water supply, provision of power, and the stimulation of agricultural and industrial growth. The Tennessee Valley Authority still employs some 45,000 people and spends $2.5 billion annually.

Concern for depressed regions nationally was translated into legislation in the 1960s. The Area Redevelopment Administration was established by the federal government to make loans to small businesses in prescribed areas and to make loans or grants for the provision of public infrastructure, provided that an overall economic development plan was produced by the local governments. (The federal government could not impose regional planning, only encourage it by offering grants and loans.) This agency was later reorganized as the Economic Development Administration (EDA), with a much larger budget to be spent in certain defined areas. Redevelopment areas were defined as those with median family incomes at least 40 percent below the national average (Figure 10.4); economic development districts were combinations of redevelopment areas (within particular states) containing at least one large city that could be developed as a growth center (see below), and regional development commissions were established for four interstate areas (Figure 10.4). The aim was to provide grants for businesses, through either the state and local governments or the Regional Planning Commissions, and to invest federal funds in public works in order to provide an infrastructure for development. A separate act established a fifth Regional Planning Commission for Appalachia, covering parts of thirteen states (Figure 10.4: the states are Alabama, Georgia, Kentucky, Maryland, Mississippi, New York, North Carolina, Ohio, Pennsylvania, South Carolina, Tennessee, Virginia, and West Virginia). Large sums of money ($679 million between 1965 and 1969; $13.5 million in 1976) were allocated to overcome the problems of isolation, poverty, unemployment, and industrial decline in this large region; much of the expenditure in the early years was on highways.

One aspect of the EDA's programs as they evolved was that they came to encompass more and more of the country. Figure 10.4 shows the economic development districts and the redevelopment areas in the mid-1960s; Figure 10.5 shows the designated districts and areas in 1975

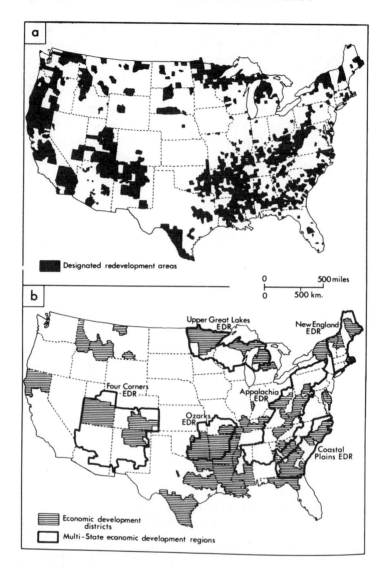

Figure 10.4. (Top) economic redevelopment areas; (bottom) economic development districts and economic development regions in the mid-1960s.

and 1976. By then, the economic development districts totaled 488 and included 1,250 of the country's 3,042 counties; the number of redevelopment areas has varied quite considerably, reaching a peak of 1,818 in 1973. (The increase was a result of a liberalization of the criteria; areas could be designated if median income was 50 percent of the national figure, instead of 40 as before.) As a result, the EDA spent $11 on every resident of a redevelopment area in 1970, but only $2.40 in 1974;

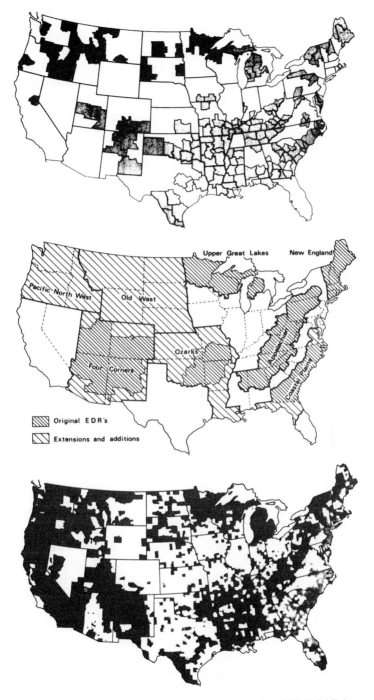

Figure 10.5.   (Top) economic development districts in 1975; (middle) economic development regions in 1975; and (bottom) redevelopment areas in 1976.

neither sum was likely to be sufficient to generate much growth. Similarly, the allocations to the Regional Planning Commissions were small—$40 million in 1970 only (excluding Appalachia). Much of the money was spent on producing regional plans, on which no action has been taken. Yet in the early 1970s, two new commissions were set up and three others were substantially expanded. The new regions were the Pacific Northwest (the entire states of Washington, Oregon, and Idaho) and the Old West (the entire states of Montana, North and South Dakota, Wyoming, and Nebraska). The Four Corners Region (Figure 10.4) was extended to cover Arizona, Utah, New Mexico, and Colorado; the Ozarks Region took in the entire states of Kansas, Oklahoma, Louisiana, Arkansas, and Missouri; and Northern Florida and Southern Virginia were added to the Coastal Plains Region. Thus by 1975, 58 million of the country's 213 million inhabitants lived in states covered by a Regional Planning Commission (this excludes Appalachia, with another 77 million); of the mainland states west of the Mississippi, only Texas, Nevada, and California are not provided for. But the expenditure in these areas has been small and spread much too thinly to have any appreciable effect. The sparse distribution of expenditures was the result of political considerations, with so many congressmen wishing to gain special status for their home districts and states, and prompted both Congress and the executive to end the programs.

A concept that has become strongly entrenched in the thinking about urban and regional development in recent years is the growth pole or growth center. The concept of a growth pole was introduced with regard to input-output matrices (Figure 4.2) and defined it as a sector in which rapid growth, through its links with other sectors, would generate considerable expansion elsewhere in the economy. This concept was translated into spatial terms as growth centers. If firms in growing sectors of the economy could be established in defined places, then this should stimulate growth there in linked sectors, provided that such links are feasible (that is, the linked industries already exist or they can be attracted there by the stimulus of the new growth pole). Over time, it is claimed, the benefits brought about by a growth pole should spread into the surrounding region, stimulating jobs in local agriculture and in towns serving the center. Thus growth centers are development foci, from which benefits diffuse outward. To be successful, it is argued, investment must be concentrated in a few places; it should not be spread widely (as in the current programs, partly for political reasons), otherwise the linkages will not be established and the self-propelling multipliers will not operate. (Others argue that concentration on a few growth poles produces more polarization than spread effects. It attracts labor and jobs from other places and further impoverishes the places not designated to receive the injections of money.)

One of the problems with the use of the growth center concept in the Economic Development Administration's programs, however, was precisely the political point referred to above. By 1975 more than 260 such centers had been nominated, with each getting only a small sum of money intended to stimulate rapid economic growth. Further, in 1970, 42 of the 171 designated centers had populations of less than 10,000 and only 30 had more than 500,000; most commentators agree that 100,000 is a minimum population for a growth center in which multiplier processes are likely to be internalized.

The level of success of growth center policies is hard to establish, in part because of their recency and in part because of the relatively small sums invested in them. But several commentators view them as ineffectual because, they point out, the market mechanism is sufficient. The basis of their case is the pattern of urban and regional population and employment change of the 1970s, discussed in Chapters 1 and 5. The biggest cities are in decline: firms are leaving them—because of the high costs of labor and of meeting taxes, for example—and are moving to the smaller centers and to the "depressed" regions. All this is happening with little or no regard to any government incentives.

This latest argument suggests that some critical size on the graphs of Figure 10.3D has been reached and that a redistribution of population and jobs is taking place in response to market forces. Several problems arise with regard to this argument, however. Many of the plants being established in small towns and rural areas are branch factories owned and operated from large cities; the jobs they bring may well be ephemeral, the wages they pay low, and their stimuli to growth via the various loops of the multiplier process few. Their distribution is widespread. That of other developments is very concentrated, and few of the rapidly growing metropolitan areas in Figure 1.4 are in formerly depressed areas. Thus it is unlikely that a move to the Sun Belt will benefit many of the areas shown in Figure 10.4. A new pattern of concentration is being created. By eliminating some of the problems of places like New York it may be creating welfare rather than helping to ameliorate illfare, but without concerted central action, the problems of the older cities may get worse. If this happens, money will be needed to revitalize them, and the inequalities in the settlement pattern will not be eliminated; only the distribution of the inequalities will be changed.

Many factors are involved in policy making with respect to the future of urban America. As shown in this chapter, most government policies are either ameliorative problem-solving efforts or attempts at allocative trend modification, although they may be phrased in terms that suggest a grand design for a better society. The sorts of policies discussed in the present section are more clearly normative and goal oriented, since they involve the initial value judgments made about the aims of a society before measures are introduced to direct its evolution to those ends. Making such judgments requires a consensus within society that the defined goals are the right ones, and that the policies are likely to produce the desired ends. To a considerable extent, some of the goals discussed here run counter to those of the capitalist ethic, since they do not give primacy to profit making and the maximization of benefits for a few over the costs to the many. Normative ends cannot be sought within the current means, unless those ends coincide with those sought by the system as it currently exists.

CONCLUSIONS

This pair of chapters has portrayed the geography of four types of problems that are found in American cities and has suggested reasons for their patterns. Some of these problems were clearly identified at the outset as problems *of* the city, having been created by the urban phenomenon itself. Those relating to the urban environment fall into this category; traffic congestion and high densities of air pollution, for example, are very much consequences of the high density concentrations of people in the metropoli. Others are just as clearly problems *in* the city, in that they reflect the failings of the capitalist economy and are not urban creations; low incomes and high unemployment rates are examples of this type. The majority of the problems identified, however, are both of and in the city. Indeed, unemployment is in the first place a problem in the city, but the concept of the cycle of poverty shows that although unemployment does not necessarily generate more unemployment, the role of unemployment is an index of who and what places are likely to suffer if job opportunities decline. In this way, a problem in the city generates problems of the city.

The distinction between problems of the city and in the city is largely an artificial one, which has analytical convenience but oversimplifies reality. The presentation here has stressed the interactions between the two sorts of problems, and also between the four types of problems identified. Basically the built environment contains some residential areas which, because of their age and their locations close to sources of various pollutants, are much less attractive than others, and so have been largely abandoned by the well-to-do. Consequently, the city's relatively poor have been excluded from the perceived pleasanter areas and have been restricted to living in the less desirable. In these less desirable areas a cycle of poverty has developed, in which the poor are left to lower standards of housing, which, in combination with their low incomes, lead to poor health status. Educational facilities are inferior as well, and the often unhealthy children of the poor are unable to take full advantage of those that are available. Thus they cannot compete in the job market as equals with those from other parts of the metropolitan area; their employment prospects are poor, as a result, especially during periods of recession, and their poverty is perpetuated.

One of the major functions of the state is to act as a protector for the relatively disadvantaged in society, by redistributing income from the rich to the poor. In the United States, the decentralized pattern of government enshrined in the Constitution entrusts much of this protective function to the states. These have delegated much of it to local governments, which raise their revenue from local sources, predominantly property taxes. By moving away from the central cities, and into their suburban municipal strongholds, however, the more affluent members of American society have been able to avoid paying for cleaning up the inner city and the care of the disadvantaged. Spatial segregation of those caught in the cycle of poverty has made them fiscally bankrupt and politically impotent, and they have been denied the power in the Congress that could enable them to get the programs and funds that might address their many problems.

Given this description of the nature of urban problems, it becomes clear that of the four types of planning identified at the beginning of Part Four, that which sets norms for the future society and then steers it in those directions is very likely to conflict with the dominant trends in the American economy. Normative designs involve planning and the abdication of certain decision making by the individual, the household, and the firm to a government that supposedly represents all equally. At present, effective planning for urban America is extremely difficult, because of the municipal balkanization and the dominance of conservative interests in Congress. There is little evidence that this situation is likely to change (and it does not seem as if it will be helped by Supreme Court rulings on issues relating to the antidiscrimination clauses of the Constitution); thus the likelihood of large-scale, metropolitan-wide planning seems remote.

This is not meant to argue that no advances have been made, that average housing standards have not improved, that air and water quality is not better than it was two decades ago, and that personal mobility is not greater. (On the other hand, there has been little or no reduction in crime rates, the rate of unemployment for inner-city youths is very high, racial discrimination continues, central cities are facing acute financial crises, and so on.) Clearly, there is much that can be done by ameliorative problem solving and allocative trend modifying in terms of improving the quality of life for urban Americans, especially the poorest and the weakest. But their relative positions in the society and economy can be altered only slightly in most cases and the cycle of poverty will not be broken while competitive capitalism continues. The rich are not prepared to share their schooling with the poor, so that the next generation of poor children can grow up to take the best jobs; the automobile and construction industries do not wish to see suburban construction rates slow down. Within the limits set by late capitalism and self-interested individualism, there is the potential for much planning with a human face, but not for wholesale social change.

While the United States remains the sort of society that it has always been, therefore, the form and fabric of its cities are likely to reflect the relative patterns of wealth and poverty, power and impotence. Changing the face of urban America will require major social change first, for norms that conflict with those that are presently being pursued will not readily be adopted by a majority that has something to lose, however little. It may be that there are major crises impending that will require that short-term aims be replaced by longer-term strategies. If this is so, urban America may well change drastically; the new urban problems will then be the problems of that new society.

SUGGESTIONS FOR FURTHER READING—PART FOUR

There is a very large literature on America's urban problems. One of the best general outlines is given in:
GORHAM, W., and N. GLAZER (eds.) *The Urban Predicament*. Washington D. C.: Urban Institute, 1976.

See also:
GORDON, M. *Sick Cities*. New York: Macmillan, 1965.

An excellent volume by geographers is:
ADAMS, J. S. (ed.) *Urban Policymaking and Metropolitan Dynamics*. Cambridge, Mass.: Ballinger, 1976.

Particular issues are considered in:
SMITH, D. M. *The Geography of Social Well-Being in the United States*. New York: McGraw-Hill, 1973.
HARRIES, K. D. *The Geography of Crime and Justice*. New York: McGraw-Hill, 1974.
SHANNON, G. W., and G. E. A. DEVER. *Health Care Delivery*. New York: McGraw-Hill, 1974.
MORRILL, R. L., and E. H. WOHLENBERG. *The Geography of Poverty in the United States*. New York: McGraw-Hill, 1971.
DE VISE, P. *Misused and Misplaced Hospitals and Doctors*. Washington, D.C.: Commission on College Geography, Association of American Geographers, 1973.
LEY, D. *The Black Inner City as Frontier Outpost*. Washington, D.C.: Association of American Geographers, 1973.
DETWYLER, T. R., and M. G. MARCUS (eds.) *Urbanization and Environment*. Belmont, Calif.: Duxbury Press, 1972.
BERRY, B. J. L. et al. *Land Use, Urban Form and Environmental Quality*. Department of Geography, Research Paper 155, University of Chicago, 1974.
BERRY, B. J. L., and F. E. HORTON (eds.) *Urban Environmental Management*. Englewood Cliffs, N.J.: Prentice-Hall, 1974.
NEWMAN, O. *Defensible Space*. New York: Macmillan, 1972.
SUTTLES, G. D. *The Social Order of the Slum*. Chicago: University of Chicago Press, 1967.
SUTTLES, G. D. *The Social Construction of Communities*. Chicago: University of Chicago Press, 1972.
HOCH, I. "Income and City Size." *Urban Studies*, 9 (1972):229–328.
GOLANT, S. *Geography of the Elderly*. New York: Halsted Press, 1980.
HERBERT, D. T., and R. J. JOHNSTON (eds.) *Geography and the Urban Environment, Vol. 3*. New York: Wiley, 1980.
LORD, J. D. *Spatial Perspectives on School Desegregation and Busing*. Washington, D.C.: Commission on College Geography, Association of American Geographers, 1977.

For a discussion of social mix, see:
SARKISSIAN, W. "A History of the Balanced Neighbourhood Concept," *Urban Studies*, 13 (1976) 231–246.
DOWNS, A. *Opening Up the Suburbs*. New Haven: Yale University Press, 1973.
MOSKOWITZ, D. H. *Exclusionary Zoning Litigation*. Cambridge, Mass.: Ballinger, 1977.

Urban size is covered in:
RICHARDSON, H. W. *The Economics of Urban Size*. Lexington, Mass.: Heath, 1974.
JOHNSTON, R. J. "Observations on Accounting Procedures and Urban-Size Policies," *Environment and Planning A*, 8 (1976), 327–340.

Urban political problems are discussed in:
O'CONNOR, J. *The Fiscal Crisis of the State*. New York: St. Martin's Press, 1973.
JUDD, D. R. *The Politics of American Cities*. Boston: Little, Brown, 1979.
MARSHALL, D. R. (ed.) *Urban Policy Making*. Beverly Hills: Sage, 1979.

Regional planning is discussed in:
ESTALL, R. C. "Regional Planning in the United States," *Town Planning Review*, 48 (1977):341–364.
CLAWSON, M., and P. HALL. *Planning and Urban Growth: An Anglo-American Comparison*. Baltimore: Resources for the Future, 1973.

INDEX

National Aeronautics and Space Administration, 149
Neighborhood, 196
balanced, 276–280
socialization and, 170–173
Neighborhood effect, 173, 259, 262, 276,
280
Nelson, H. J., 108
New England, 146
New York metropolitan area, 70, 95–96,
98, 103, 144, 150, 212
corporate headquarters in, 130, 133,
136, 140, 141
journey to work patterns in, 160, 161
New York State, 67, 145
Noise, 310–311, 313, 317
Nonbasic industries, 89, 91, 92
/basic industries ratio, 94, 95
Nonresidential land uses, 198–223
government services, 223
health facilities, 222–223
land values and location, 199–202
manufacturing industries, 202–211
office sector, 211–214
open space, 221–222
retail system, 215–221
schools, 222
suburban municipalities and, 234–235
Normative goal-oriented planning, 251,
252, 333–335

Occupation
education and, 168
social mobility and, 43–44, 45, 46, 47,
168
See also Employment
Occupational structure, changing, 27–29,
43, 44
Office parks, 213, 214
Offices, location of, 211–214
Oligopoly, 117, 325
Omaha/Council Bluffs, 73, 74
Open space, 221–222

Parks, 221
Particulates, 306–307, 313
Patents, 95–96
Pension funds, 119, 146
Petaluma, California, 300
Philadelphia, 96, 98, 105, 107, 150,
193

inter-municipality segregation in,
291–292
Pittsburgh, 87–88, 99, 136
Planning, urban, 335
Berry's classification of, 250–251
See also Spatial engineering
Political action, 302–303
municipal balkanization and, 292–293
Political conflict, intrametropolitan,
293–294
Political geography, 224–240
Political representation, 248, 284–287
Pollution, 163, 167, 312–313
air, 306–308, 313, 315–316, 317
noise, 310–311, 313, 317
removal of, 314–317
water, 308–309, 313, 316
Population
agricultural, 25, 124
characteristics, 37–40
concentration of, 51, 105, 121
See also Concentration
rank-size rule, 7–8
of Sun Belt vs. Frost Belt, 9, 10
Population density, 75, 76, 276
Population growth, 35–37, 61, 72, 92
in industrial towns, 99–101
Population potential, 101–103, 200
Ports, 82, 202–203
gateway. See Gateways—ports
Poverty (the poor), 19, 33, 42, 130, 193,
232, 233, 248, 321
balanced neighborhood and, 276–280
concentration of, 262
crime and, 275–276
cycle of, 249, 253–283, 257, 281, 302,
303, 334, 335
breaking the, 280–282
education and, 271–273
the elderly and, 282–283
employment prospects and, 273–275
fiscal disparities and, 237–239
health care and, 222, 268–270
housing and, 184–185, 263–268
inner city and, 253–262
municipal balkanization and, 288,
290–293, 298
public goods and, 270–271
race and, 261–262
Power sources
industrial location and, 82
See also Water-power-based manufacturing towns
Pred, A. R., 89, 98, 105

nonresidential land use and, 201, 202,
204, 206, 210
suburbia and, 164–165, 225–226
traffic planning and, 318–320
See also Automobiles; Freeways; Highways; Railroads; Trucks
Transport centers, 88
Transport costs, 55
Manufacturing Belt and, 102–105, 106,
107
minimizing, 5, 11, 81–86
Traveling shops, 55
Trend modifying, allocative, 250, 251,
335
Trucks, 122, 207, 225

Unemployment, 129, 249, 254, 255, 274,
321, 334
Unionization, 146, 147
Urban geography
content of, 6–7
inside the urban area, 13–17
urban pattern, 7–13
rise of, 4–6
Urbanization, 4, 7–10, 19
on a mercantile base, industrial, 89–99
under mercantile capitalism, 53–78
See also specific topics
Urban multiplier, 91–94, 96–97, 121, 124
corporate headquarters and, 139–
141
intermetropolitan, 140, 141
outside Manufacturing Belt, 145–147,
149
Urban patterns, 7–13

alternative, 322–334
See also specific topics
Urban problems, 245–252, 334–336
in vs. of the city, 246–247, 334
spatial engineering and, 249–252
types of, 247–249
See also specific topics
Urban renewal, 221, 264
Urban system, 11–13
See also specific topics

Vernon, California, 235
Vertical integration, 117
Veterans' Administration, 265

Wage rate, 313–314
Ward, D., 100
Warehouses, 55, 59, 199
Washington, D. C., 141
Wastes, solid, 309
Water pollution, 308–309, 313, 316
Water-power-based manufacturing towns,
88
Welfare programs, 33, 41, 130, 292,
301–302
West, the (western states), 144–146, 150
Wholesaling, 11–12, 199
Women in labor force, 38
Workforce. *See* Labor force
Working class, 41, 47, 48
Workshops, 199, 204

Zoning, 180, 198, 226, 288, 298–300
exclusionary, 233–235, 237, 299–300